OPERATION C3

'The Goddess of War in battle comes to commanders only once, and he who fails to seize the opportunity at such a moment will never be given a second chance.'

Hitler to Mussolini, 23 June 1942,
prefacing his decision to let Rommel
invade Egypt instead of invading Malta.

OPERATION C3
HITLER'S PLAN TO INVADE MALTA 1942

John D. Burtt

Pen & Sword
MILITARY
AN IMPRINT OF PEN & SWORD BOOKS LTD.
YORKSHIRE - PHILADELPHIA

First published in Great Britain in 2023 by
PEN AND SWORD MILITARY
An imprint of
Pen & Sword Books Ltd
Yorkshire – Philadelphia

Copyright © John D. Burtt, 2023

ISBN 978 1 39906 576 4

The right of John D. Burtt to be identified as Author of this work has been asserted by him in accordance with the Copyright, Designs and Patents Act 1988.

A CIP catalogue record for this book is available from the British Library

All rights reserved. No part of this book may be reproduced or transmitted in any form or by any means, electronic or mechanical including photocopying, recording or by any information storage and retrieval system, without permission from the Publisher in writing.

Typeset in Times New Roman 9.5/11.5 by SJmagic DESIGN SERVICES, India.
Printed and bound in the UK by CPI Group (UK) Ltd.

Pen & Sword Books Ltd incorporates the imprints of Pen & Sword Archaeology, Atlas, Aviation, Battleground, Discovery, Family History, History, Maritime, Military, Naval, Politics, Social History, Transport, True Crime, Claymore Press, Frontline Books, Praetorian Press, Seaforth Publishing and White Owl

For a complete list of Pen & Sword titles please contact

PEN & SWORD BOOKS LIMITED
47 Church Street, Barnsley, South Yorkshire, S70 2AS, England
E-mail: enquiries@pen-and-sword.co.uk
Website: www.pen-and-sword.co.uk

Or

PEN AND SWORD BOOKS
1950 Lawrence Rd, Havertown, PA 19083, USA
E-mail: Uspen-and-sword@casematepublishers.com
Website: www.penandswordbooks.com

Contents

Acknowledgements and Dedication vi
Prologue: *'Volcano!'* vii
Introduction ix
Chapter I The Bars of the Prison: The Axis, Britain and Malta, 1918–40 1
Chapter II War: June 1940 – November 1941 24
Chapter III War: December 1941 – June 1942 51
Chapter IV War: June 1942 – August 1942 70
Chapter V Malta's 1942 Defensive Plans 82
Chapter VI The Axis 1942 Invasion Plans 105
Chapter VII Saturday: 15 August 1942 134
Chapter VIII Sunday: 16 August 1942 151
Chapter IX Monday: 17 August 1942 169
Chapter X Tuesday: 18 August 1942 185
Chapter XI Battle: Aftermath – August 1942 197
Chapter XII Reality & Analysis 200

Bibliography 206
Appendix A Axis Land Order of Battle 228
Appendix B Axis Naval Order of Battle 238
Appendix C Axis Air Order of Battle 254
Appendix D British/Maltese Land Order of Battle 270
Index 275

Acknowledgements

To my friend, Lieutenant Colonel Davide Pastore, whose Italian research made this book possible.

To Mark and Natalie Vella, the late John Mizzi, Joseph Caruana and Robert Dimech – natives of Malta, our kind, gracious, generous Maltese hosts and contributors, for all their help, support and lively discussions.

To Vince O'Hara, Albert Zorge, Jack Greene, Alessandro Massignani, David Hughes, Gar Olmsted and Vance von Borries, for their knowledge, support and friendship.

Dedication

To the soldiers, sailors and airmen who didn't have to fight this particular battle, but who gave their all for their respective countries in other battles.

And to the people of Malta, who endured a literal hell on earth during the Second World War.

Prologue

'Volcano!'

As he crouched in the trench near his aircraft's blast pen at Ta'Qali airfield, Squadron Leader 'Laddie' Lucas experienced a number of different sensations. He felt hot and tired – tired of filling sandbags to protect aircraft in the intense August heat, tired of the incessant bombing and strafing, tired of feeling hungry all the time. The dust and smoke formed by the fires and bombing hung in the still air, intensifying the feelings.

He also felt angry; for the third time since he arrived on Maltan soil in February 1942, there weren't enough planes to fly. Airborne in a Spitfire's cockpit, he felt master of his environment; on the ground, he felt vulnerable and impotent. As if to underscore that feeling, a large explosion slammed him into the side of the trench. Peering out with his crew, they saw another Spitfire burning in a pen across the way. Glumly, he mentally catalogued their available aircraft now at seven. He also felt anger at the enemy. He had been scheduled to turn over 249 Squadron in July and go home, but the massive new Axis bombardment had virtually pinned everyone in place.

Lucas also found himself envious of his squadron mate, Flight Sergeant George 'Screwball' Buerling, one of the better pilots in his 249 Squadron. He knew Buerling was calmly and quietly awaiting the signal to fly, probably looking through his scrawled notebook containing his notes on successful – and failed – air-to-air engagements.

Finally, he felt nervous, especially after Flight Lieutenant Harry Coldbeck had returned from his early-morning reconnaissance flight. 'Transport aircraft', he had told them after landing; the airfield at Catania was filled with transports again, while ships off Sicily were sailing south.[1] It meant only one thing: invasion.

They had heard back in June through their various grapevines that German paratroops were massing in Sicily. Some said two full divisions' worth, along with an Italian division. Axis shipping was massing too. Every indication was there that it would be an invasion attempt in July – but the fates had other ideas. The weather turned bad in mid-July, there had been too much wind and too much sea movement. Word got around that an attack had been postponed. July had passed with no more than a renewal of the intense air attack that had been commonplace on the island. Exasperated by the gnawing hunger that everyone felt. Enemy troops had not come, but neither had more supplies.

Coldbeck's new report galvanized the military and civil authorities again into their predetermined plan of action – code name *Volcano* – to prepare for an imminent attack. Lucas knew that his main boss, Air Vice Marshal Keith Park, was holding back his remaining aircraft to have a go at any invasion attempt. He had hoped the powers in London were preparing another wave of Spitfire reinforcements like the one he had led off USS *Wasp* in May – a lifetime ago – but it looked like it was going to be too late.

---

1. *Woodhall, p.172.

As Lucas waited, Group Captain A.B. 'Woody' Woodhall, Malta's primary air controller, stood with Park on the balcony of the Air Operations room of the Lascaris War Rooms, deep beneath the Upper Barrakka Gardens in Valletta, staring down at the huge 18ft by 12ft map of Malta and southern Sicily. Maltese women moved counters around the map based on information passed from radar and ground observers. Red enemy counters dominated the board as Woodall and Park tried to decide whether to launch their remaining aircraft, of which there were pitifully few left on the chalk board beside them. Finally, they looked at each other and silently nodded. It was time.[2]

At Ta'Qali, a pair of red rockets went up from the control building and popped in the sky, followed by another pair: scramble! Lucas heard a whoop of joy as Buerling jumped up and ran for his aircraft.

Lucas also leapt up and raced for his Spitfire, followed closely by his ground crew. While he buckled and put on his leather helmet with the radio, the big Merlin engine fired off.

'Laddie, Woodie calling,' he heard Woody say. 'Big raid forming. Lots of big jobs [large aircraft] crabbing [flying low] about. More vectors when you're airborne.'

He quickly finished his cockpit overview then, as his crew chief beckoned him forward out of the pen, he instinctively patted his pocket. His 'charm' was there: a small purse with a couple of coins from friends, a St Christopher medal from his mother, an ivory elephant, and a Maltese Cross. He never flew without them.

Lucas's Spitfire Mk Vc aircraft moved quickly down the taxiway, dodging the worst bomb craters. He sensed that something was behind him and saw the second Spitfire. Then he was on the runway, and with throttle open, roared into sky, his fears falling away with the ground. Behind him, Beurling also rose. His normal wingman, Frank Jones, wasn't so lucky, having been caught just after take-off by a Messerschmitt and bursting into flames. Only seconds later, the light anti-aircraft guns ringing the field blasted the victor from the sky as well.

'Hello, Laddie,' Woody called again. 'There are 100-plus big jobs north of St Paul's Bay, course south, angels five to eight; fifty-plus little jobs [fighters] above and behind, course south, angels fifteen to twenty-one. Luqa put up four Spits. Good hunting.'

Lucas acknowledged and led Beurling skyward.

Minutes later, looking down, he saw a mass of large aircraft. 'Follow me,' he radioed Beurling, and the two Spitfires dove for the formation.

As he closed, he concentrated on the lead aircraft, a twin-engine bomber, as it filled his windshield. When close enough, he fired his cannon, watching the shells plough into the aircraft's side and tail. Part of it broke away and the aircraft tumbled. He continued to dive and pulled up near the water.

'Woody,' he called out, 'Laddie calling. Bombers, Junker eight-eights, repeat Junker eight-eights.'

But as he pulled back up into the fray, he saw different aircraft – easily identified by their three engines and corrugated sides. 'Ah, bloody hell,' he muttered, before keying his radio. 'Woody,' he yelled. 'Transports, transports – junker five-twos – a bloody great lot of them. Good luck!'

Fifteen minutes later, cannons empty, a bomber and a transport brought down and a couple damaged, his plane shaking itself apart around him – shot to pieces by the defending fighters – he bailed out over Gozo. As he drifted down, he watched helplessly as other German and Italian parachutes filled the sky over Malta.

The invasion had begun.

---

2. *Ibid., p.173.

Introduction

In June 1940, Britain had been kicked off the Continent and France was about ready to fall. Benito Mussolini, fascist leader of Italy, after nine months of neutrality, had entered the war to begin his drive for a new Mediterranean Roman Empire. New British Prime Minister Winston Churchill, refusing to knuckle under to Hitler's triumphant Germans, chose to make the Mediterranean the theatre to continue the war.

At the interception of these two decisions, lay a 95 square mile island, a "Tiny Rock" as Churchill later called it – Malta - and it's easy to see why this tiny island held such a prominent place in the War's Mediterranean theatre. Located 60 miles south of Sicily and a thousand miles from either end of the Mediterranean Sea, Malta stood directly across the transport path from Italy to its North African holdings and, more importantly after 10 June 1940, from the North African battlefields and Mussolini's legions sought to increase the new Roman Empire. It also lay on the east-west seaway the British needed to maintain easy contact with their Middle East possessions and those in the Pacific.

Despite twice being bombed nearly into submission, only to rise again, the Axis failed to take the island; many Axis commanders felt that was a major mistake. When writing his memoirs after the Second World War, German Generalfeldmarschall Albert Kesselring stated: 'Italy's missing her chance to occupy the island [of Malta] at the start of hostilities will go down in history as a fundamental blunder.'[1] As Italian Admiral Franco Maugeri, future director of the Regia Marina's (Italian Navy) Serviso Informazione Segreto, the secret intelligence service, would state later: 'Malta was the key to the entire strategic situation in the Mediterranean. In friendly hands, it was a blessing and a boon; in the hands of an enemy, a dagger aimed straight at the heart.'[2]

Malta has been both blessed and cursed with an extraordinary combination of factors that have made it desirable to various factions throughout its history: blessed because the island and its superb harbours sit in a strategic position in the middle of a highly travelled sea route; cursed because it cannot support itself. These factors have led to many changes in the island's masters – some for better, others for worse.

First the Phoenicians, then Carthage and Rome held sway, naming the island Melita (the Honeyed One). Christianity, in the form of a shipwrecked St Paul, arrived in AD 60 while it was under Byzantine rule. The Muslims took the island in 870, renaming it Malita, soon corrupted to simply Malta. In 1091, Christians regained the island, then Carlos V, King of Spain and Holy Roman Emperor, offered to lease Malta and Tripoli to the homeless Knights of St John in 1524.

---

1. Kesselring, The Memoirs of Field-Marshall Kesselring (Presidio, 1989), p.123.
2. Maugeri, From the Ashes of Disgrace, p.75.

Muslims attempted to take the island back in 1565, leading to the unsuccessful first Great Siege. The Knights held the island until 1798, when Napoleon and the French took it from them. The Maltese, incensed at the looting of their churches, rose up against the French and, with British help, kicked them out in 1800. For the next fourteen years, Malta became a bargaining chip for the European powers, with five countries laying some claim to the island: Britain, France, Sicily, Portugal and Russia. In 1813, Malta was declared a British Crown Colony, with Britain's ownership confirmed by the Treaty of Paris in 1814.

From that point, Malta became an integral part of the British Empire, with its excellent harbours providing fuel and repair facilities for the Royal Navy up to and through the First World War. With both France and Italy as allies during the conflict, Malta was spared most of the cost of war, although its hospitals overflowed with casualties from conflict around the Mediterranean.

In the 1920s, the situation began to change and the island and its 250,000 residents found themselves at the centre of a growing storm.

Chapter I

The Bars of the Prison
The Axis, Britain and Malta, 1918–40

The genesis of the Second World War lay with the outcome of the Great War and the many peace treaties that emerged from the political and diplomatic manoeuvres that followed the 1918 armistice. As historian Martin Kitchen put it, the peace treaties 'gave rise to such recriminations, resentments and misunderstandings that they contributed significantly to the outbreak of a new and more terrible war'.[1] Each of the three belligerents in the later battle for Malta took different roads to war.

Britain and Malta

Britain for the most part stayed aloof from the territorial squabbles that erupted during the Great War peace treaty negotiations, making its primary concern the protection of its empire and the avoidance of war. Its major concern in the immediate post-war years was the argument over naval parity with the United States, which some in the Admiralty predicted would ultimately lead to war between the recent allies.[2]

In 1921, Malta was given a form of self-rule with the Amery-Milner Constitution.[3] The constitution set up a thirty-two-seat Legislature and a twelve-seat Senate, with the right to vote given to men aged 21 and older – with certain literacy requirements. The new parliament was empowered to handle internal matters while the Imperial Government handled defence and foreign affairs. With the ability to vote came the creation of political parties, finally boiling down to two main contenders: the pro-British Constitutional Party and the pro-Italian Nationalist Party.

Defence and foreign issues centred around Britain's use of Malta as its key Royal Navy base in the Mediterranean. The naval presence protected trade routes to the Persian Gulf and Iraqi oilfields, as well as India and beyond. But the Great War showed the British that they couldn't just think regionally anymore; they needed to think globally. Although an ally during the Great War, Japan was beginning to flex its muscles in the Far East, something that could threaten Empire holdings in that under-defended region. In addition to the global concerns,

---
1. Kitchen, Martin, Europe between the Wars: A Political History, p.1.
2. Stern, Battleship Holiday, p.87.
3. The driving force for the constitution was L.S. Amery, British Under-Secretary of State for the Colonies. Blouet, p.181.

Britain needed to deal with the new technologies that emerged from the Great War – namely air power. Defensive problems now became three-dimensional.[4] That meant new requirements and more money at a time when defence spending had fallen by some 63 per cent.[5] Even the British squabble over naval supremacy fell victim to economics as they signed the Washington Naval Arms Limitation Treaty in February 1922, granting the US parity with the Royal Navy.[6]

In the early 1930s, the global situation worsened as Germany withdrew from the League of Nations and Japan became embroiled in China. These matters became top priorities for British defensive thinking. Although Benito Mussolini led the Fascist Party to power in Italy, Britain initially felt they posed no real threat; the British Cabinet specifically ruled out any defence expenditure aimed at Italy, and that meant Malta.

On the island, there were considerable problems too, especially over religion and language. English was the official language of the Maltese administration, but Italian was predominant in the courts, complicated by the fact that 86 per cent of the population did not speak Italian.[7] Politically, battle lines were drawn over the language issue. Matters came to a head after the elections of 1927 brought in Prime Minister Lord Gerald Strickland, 'an ardent imperialist and a vigorous opponent of all attempts to make Malta Italian'.[8] The conflict began to include the Catholic Church, which Strickland felt was disregarding the laws requiring the Church to stay out of politics. The Church retaliated with charges that Strickland was insulting the Vatican and portraying the priests as oppressors.[9]

In May 1930, the break between Church and state became irrevocable when the Archbishop of Malta and the Bishop of Gozo declared in a Pastoral letter that it was a 'grave sin' to support Strickland and any politician who supported him; the letter refused the Church sacraments to those 'sinning' in this fashion. Strickland suspended elections because of the letter, and in June, following failed negotiations, the British Government suspended the constitution, returning all matters into the hands of the Governor.[10]

Italy

Italy was a very young country, having only completed its unification in 1870,[11] a situation which came with significant problems. Despite some modernization, the unity had done little to counter the imbalances between regions, with urban and country dwellers showing the widest gaps. Widespread use of a national language was slow, while poverty forced millions to emigrate, leaving the country economically and socially weak.

When the Great War broke out in August 1914, Italy, ostensibly a member of the Triple Alliance with Germany and Austria-Hungary, chose to stay neutral. With its population

---

4. The discussion of early aircraft defence is beyond the scope of this book. Suffice it to say that early air power proponents felt strongly that fighter defence against bombers was impossible, thus the best defence against air attack was a better offensive capability.
5. Austin, Douglas, Malta and British Strategic Policy, 1925–1943, p.7.
6. Stern, p.106.
7. Foreign affairs essay, 'Malta: Church and State', October 1930.
8. Berg, p.120.
9. Foreign affairs essay, 'Malta: Church and State', October 1930.
10. Berg, p.120.
11. Trento and Trieste were added in 1918. Palla, p.9.

against the war and its army unprepared, Italy's allies had not included it in any war plans.[12] Italy's dispute with the Habsburgs compounded the issue over what it termed *Italia Irredenta* (Unredeemed Italy): the 800,000 Italians living in the Trentino, Isonzo and Trieste areas, all then under Austro-Hungarian rule.[13]

Italian Prime Minister Antonio Salandra negotiated with both the Triple Alliance and the Entente powers (Britain, France and Russia) over territorial demands as compensation for entering the war. Although Germany finally persuaded a very stubborn Habsburg Empire to offer what Italy wanted, Salandra chose to reach agreement with the Entente, concerned that Austria would back out of any agreement after the war. The Treaty of London, signed on 26 April 1915, promised Italy the Trentino and South Tyrol regions to the Brenner Pass, the Friuli-Julian area eastward to the watershed of the Julian Alps, Trieste, Istria and islands off the Dalmatian coast, plus a share of German colonies in Africa.[14]

The Great War proved less than a success for Italy, however. Italian forces suffered heavy casualties in numerous frontal assaults in the Isonzo area, although they did gain more ground than most of the Western Front offensives. They suffered a setback in the Trentino in 1916, but balanced it three months later by capturing Gorizia. In 1917, at Caporetto, German and Austrian forces struck the Italian Second and Third Armies and in three weeks drove them back 60 miles to the Piave River. The Italians lost some 40,000 dead and 280,000 capturedm and suffered 350,000 desertions.[15] That battle caused the weak government of Paolo Boselli to collapse, after which the new administration under Vittorio Emanuele Orlando requested help from the other allies. British and French troops were dispatched, but before they could arrive, the Italians, now under Generale Armando Diaz, stopped two Central Powers assaults on the Piave River in late 1917.[16] At the Battle of Vittorio Veneto in October 1918, a predominantly Italian offensive crushed the Austro-Hungarians, opening up a southern front just before the end of the war.[17]

Overall, the Great War had cost Italy some 600,000 dead and almost a million wounded.

With the exception of some territories in Dalmatia, over the next several years, Italy got all the territory it had bargained for with its sacrifices, but some in the country were still dissatisfied. Gabriele D'Annunzio, a poet and nationalist, invented the phrase *vittoria mutilate* (the mutilated victory) over what he saw as an insulting betrayal of his country, especially when French and some British writers supported Serbian demands for all of Dalmatia. D'Annunzio later led a small rebel force into the Dalmatian city of Fiume, creating a short-lived regency.

Social unrest and nationalistic resentment created internal squabbling and chaos in the country. In 1920, almost 1,900 strikes wracked the country, essentially shutting Italy down. Mobs seized factories, looted banks and vandalized libraries and post offices.[18] The government could do nothing, hampered by internal bickering and feuds. The chaos and economic recession promoted the rise of right-wing nationalists, led by Benito Mussolini.

---

12. Italy's primary reason for neutrality lay in Article VII of the Triple Alliance, which required partners to compensate each other for changes in the status quo in the region, something Austria-Hungary did not do. Burgwyn, H. James, The Legend of the Mutilated Victory, p.15.
13. Ibid., p.8.
14. Ibid., p.22.
15. Strachan, Hew, The First World War, p.257.
16. Both these battles involved naval action on the flank at Cortellazzo, respectively on 17 November and 19 December 1917, involving battleships, shore batteries, flying boats, MTBs (motor torpedo boats) and naval infantry.
17. https://encyclopedia.1914-1918-online.net/article/paive_battles_of.
18. Joseph, Mussolini's War, p.12.

Raised a socialist, and at one point the editor of the socialist newspaper *Avanti!*, Mussolini broke away from the party over Italy's initial neutrality; he saw opportunity for his country in the chaos of the war. A wounded war veteran, he formed the *fasci di combattimento* in March 1919 from returning fellow veterans. Early attempts at obtaining political power came to naught, but his fascists began to gain strength opposing some of the socialists' strikes that were paralyzing the country. He rose to power in the country's anarchy, preaching national pride. In October 1922, he gathered some 26,000 fascists outside Rome, the legendary 'March on Rome'. The Italian prime minister at the time, Luigi Facta, penned a state of emergency proclamation that would have unleashed thousands of Italian Army troops on Mussolini's marchers, but King Victor Emmanuel II refused to sign the proclamation. Instead, when Facta resigned, the king offered Mussolini the prime ministry as a compromise, recognizing that he was the only person strong enough to keep Italy from collapsing into total chaos.[19] By 1925, however, the fascist leader found he had only limited power: businesses, the state bureaucracy and, more importantly, the Church stayed outside his control.[20]

A full discussion of Mussolini and the Fascist Party in Italy is beyond the scope of this book. Indeed, the history of the period is still currently undergoing significant study and revision.[21]

For our purposes, what is important is the foreign policy that Mussolini pursued. In essence, it was a policy aimed at expansion: spreading influence in the Balkans and Danubian plain, control of the Adriatic and major influence in the Mediterranean, as well as colonial expansion in Africa.[22] Mussolini's willingness and desire to use military force to get what he wanted made his foreign policy different from previous Italian nationalists who had made the same demands of their government.[23] Sir Eric Drummond, British Ambassador to Rome in 1935, described Mussolini as follows: 'He believes in war as the means by which a country can be kept vigorous, young, powerful and progressive. He believes also that Italy is the inheritor of the ancient traditions of the Roman Empire.'[24] Mussolini had his sights set on taking French and Spanish Morocco, Algeria, Tunisia, Gibraltar, the Suez Canal and Red Sea, the Gulf of Aden and the Balkans. Such an empire would make his country self-sufficient and able to stand with the major powers.[25]

Mussolini's primary problem with his desire for expansion rested with the fact that Italy remained a poor country economically and in terms of resources, which left it reliant on outside sources for virtually everything it needed to build up its industry and military. Its coal requirements were approximately 13 million tons per year, while it produced only 2 million. Crude oil requirements, the lifeline for Italy's military, ran between 3 and 4 million tons per year – expected in wartime to rise to 8.5 million tons – but its domestic capacity was stymied at only 153,000 tons, of which 92 per cent came from Albania.[26] The rest of the country's strategic material requirements mirrored similar straits, as shown in Table 1-1.

---

19. Kertzer, pp.31–32.
20. Kershaw, Fateful Choices, p.141.
21. For further reading in English on this subject, the authors recommend Philip Morgan's Italian Fascism, 1919–1945, as well as the Burgwyn and Gooch books mentioned above.
22. Morgan, p,132.
23. Gooch, p.8.
24. Burgwyn, H. James, Italian Foreign Policy in the Interwar period, 1918–1940, p.120.
25. Ehlers, p.7.
26. Schreiber, Gerhard, Germany and the Second World War, Volume III: the Mediterranean, South-east Europe and North Africa 1939–1941, pp.25–29.

Table 1-1: Italy's Strategic Materials Requirements[27]

Material	(Thousand tons)			
	Wartime Needs	Domestic Output	Import Needs	Actual Imports
Coal	16,500	2,200	14,300	11,600
Liquid Fuel	8,500	120	8,380	1,100
Steel	4,800	2,400	2,400	800
Aluminum	65	32	33	5
Copper, Tin	160	1	159	30
Rubber	22	--	22	14

Italy's reliance on outside sources of raw materials led to conflicts within its foreign goals. For example, expansion into the Balkans and Mediterranean would be at the expense of France and Britain, yet Britain supplied some 60 per cent of Italy's raw material needs.[28] More importantly, Italy's reliance on seaborne trade left it vulnerable to blockade by those two countries at Suez and Gibraltar.[29]

Throughout the 1920s, with the exception of a quickly thwarted invasion of Corfu, Mussolini had to play a waiting game for his empire, with most of his focus on Yugoslavia and its Great Power sponsor, France. In the early 1930s, the picture changed again when Germany began to see the rise of nationalism in the form of the National Socialist Party, led by Adolf Hitler.

Germany

Anger at the terms of the Versailles Peace Treaty, economic depression and internal conflicts – the same factors that created the environment for the growth of Italian fascism – led to the rise of the German Socialist Party. Renamed in 1920 as the National-Sozialistische Deutsche Arbeiter Partei (NSDAP, the Nazi Party), or National Socialist Party of German Workers, from 1921 the NSDAP was led by Adolf Hitler, an Austrian First World War veteran. Admittedly influenced and inspired by what he later described as a 'turning point in history' – Mussolini's 1922 march on Rome[30] – Hitler tried to bully his way to power and bring down Germany's Weimar Republic with his own 'March on Berlin' in 1923.[31] However, the Germans didn't have a king who refused to face them down, as the Italians had, and the German Army put down the coup. Hitler ended up in jail.[32]

---

27. Harrison, The Economics of World War II, Ch 5, Table 5.6, p.188.
28. Gooch, p.110.
29. Mallett, Italian Navy, p.9.
30. Corvaja, p.3.
31. The Beer Hall or Munich Putsch, November 1923.
32. He was released within a year. Collotti, p.23.

Over the next eight years, the Nazi Party's popularity rose as the world economic crisis worsened. By 1932, the Nazis gained almost 40 per cent of the votes in the Reichstag elections. While Hitler and the Nazis grew in power, they continued informal contacts with Mussolini's Fascist Party, but held no formal meetings; Mussolini did not want to jeopardize relations with the Weimar Republic.

In 1933, German President Hindenburg nominated Hitler to be Chancellor. To consolidate his power, Hitler launched a purge known as the Night of the Long Knives on 30 June 1934, which removed critics from his path. Just prior to dying, Hindenburg, in August 1934, declared the offices of Chancellor and President were to be unified, putting all power in Hitler's hands.[33]

From the very start, Hitler proposed expansion by conquering 'fresh *Lebensraum* [living space] in the east',[34] but such a move initially took a back seat to regaining control of the various portions of Germany that were occupied or deemed demilitarized buffer zones, such as the Rhineland. Hitler had hoped that by not challenging them on the high seas as the Kaiser had done prior to the Great War, Britain would allow him free reign in Eastern Europe. But Britain viewed his rise with alarm, and Hitler found himself instead drawn toward Italy.

Although similar on ideological grounds, both being ultra-nationalist and anti-Bolshevik[35], major hurdles existed between the two countries' leaders. For one, the Italians saw no real purpose in German anti-Semitism. Far more important was the question of Austria. Hitler coveted the weak remnant of the Habsburg Empire – it was his birthplace after all. But Mussolini did not want a strong Germany sitting on his border, possibly looking to regain the South Tyrol and its sizeable German population. In addition, this region was the major reward Italy had received for its participation in the Great War, leaving Mussolini loath to lose it. As early as 1925, he stated without reservation: 'Italy would never tolerate the blatant breach of all the treaties that an annexation of Austria to Germany, the so-called Anschluss [Union], would represent.'[36]

The initial meeting between the two leaders, in Venice in June 1934, proved to be the start of a series of head-to-head miscommunications. Mussolini, who saw himself as the spiritual head of the Nazi–Fascist movement, came away from the meeting believing he had German encouragement for growing Italian influence in the Mediterranean. Hitler, for his part, felt he had been given acquiescence for his plans to bring German minorities together and defy the Versailles Treaty.

The July 1934 Nazi coup attempt in Austria that sprang out of the meeting resulted in the death of Austrian Chancellor Englebert Dollfuss, a close personal friend of Mussolini's.[37] Mussolini reacted strongly to the failed takeover by moving Italian troops north to the border with Austria and calling for international aid in preserving Austrian independence. However, the new Austrian Chancellor, Kurt Schuschnigg, quietly but firmly rebuffed the Italian's guarantee to the Austrians and told him that movement of Italian troops into Austria would

---

33. Ibid, p.46.
34. Hildebrand, K. The Third Reich, p.15.
35. Bolshevik, which in Russian means 'One of the Majority', was the name for members of Lenin's Russian Social-Democratic Workers' Party, which took control of Russia in 1917.
36. Corvaja, p.17.
37. In fact, Dollfuss's family was visiting Mussolini when the coup occurred. One writer, however, casts some blame on Mussolini for possibly precipitating the coup by asking Hitler during their meeting whom he wanted to replace Dollfuss. Corvaja, p.32.

be politically unacceptable. Although Hitler declared in May 1935 that he would refrain from interfering in Austria's affairs,[38] the rebuff marked the start of a change in Italian attitudes toward Austria that would culminate in 1938.

Italy

Despite concerns about his northern border, Mussolini saw possibilities in a re-emerging Germany, especially with regard to France, his primary competitor in the Balkans and Africa. He and his Foreign Minister, Count Dino Grandi, worked hard to achieve parity between France and Germany, which would allow Italy to play one off against the other.[39] Hitler's decision in 1933 to leave the League of Nations, discard the restrictions of the Versailles Treaty and start rearming, aided this endeavour. The task was made easier when the British unilaterally removed the restrictions in the Versailles Treaty by signing a naval treaty with Berlin, against the protests of French and Italian diplomats.[40]

By 1935, a worried France came calling. French Prime Minister Pierre Laval arrived, searching for support to contain Hitler, while Mussolini looked for backing for aggressive action in Africa. The accords signed in January gave both sides what they wanted – a French-Italian military agreement on Germany, and what historians refer to as a free hand for Mussolini in Africa.[41]

Italy targeted the Ethiopian Empire, also known as Abyssinia, which stretched between Italy's two East African colonies of Eritrea and Italian Somaliland. This was familiar ground for the Italians, who had unsuccessfully tried to conquer the region in 1896, being defeated at Adowa.[42] Mussolini had been seriously planning an attack on the region since a 1932 memorandum from deputy foreign minister Rafaelle Guariglia outlining an extensive plan to push the southern border of Tripolitania down to British-controlled Nigeria, then west to the Sudan, starting with taking Ethiopia.[43] Significantly, the memorandum called for the approval or acceptance of both France and Britain.

With France committed to the sidelines, Italian diplomats approached the British during a European security conference at Stresa in April 1935, held ostensibly to discuss the problems Germany created when it unilaterally instituted conscription and began openly forming the Luftwaffe, both in direct violation of the Versailles restrictions. However, Anglo-Italian discussions quickly made it clear that Britain would not step aside and let Italy have free rein in Ethiopia, despite Italy's veiled threat to back away from opposition to Germany.[44] The English

---

38. Mallett, Italian Navy, p.28.
39. Morgan, p.139.
40. The Versailles Treaty limited Germany to 100,000 men in a purely infantry army, with 15,000 men in its navy and no air force. www.wikipedia.org.
41. Mallett, Mussolini and Origins, p.27.
42. A force of about 14,000 Italians troops and askari, poorly armed and equipped, and with inadequate maps, were defeated by Ethiopian Emperor Menelik and an army of between 80,000 and 100,000 men on 1 March 1896. Approaching the horde in three widely separated columns, the Italians were soundly defeated, losing 7,000 killed and 3,000 captured. Ethiopian casualties were estimated to be 12,000–13,000. www.wikipedia.org; Hardie, Frank, The Abyssinian Crisis, p.28.
43. Gooch, p.69.
44. Mallett, Mussolini and Origins, p.32.

declarations were so blunt that Mussolini ordered his military to begin planning for military action against Britain, something they had never before considered.[45]

Comparison of military assets and capabilities between Italy and Britain left Mussolini's Naval Chief of Staff, Admiral Domenico Cavagnari, facing a horrendous problem, being outnumbered and outgunned in almost every category. Work on Italy's two modern battleships had only just begun. In mid-1935, the British had fifteen battleships to Italy's four aging ones, sixty cruisers to thirteen and a two-to-one advantage in destroyers, while Italy had no aircraft carriers at all. Only Italy's submarines were potentially on par with the British, but they were not ready for war.[46] Furthermore, all of Italy's key ports, including those in Africa, lay exposed to offshore bombardment, and the nation had fuel reserves of only three months.[47]

War planning in Italy initially focused on Malta, with the Regia Marina stating that the opening act of any war with Britain should be an invasion of the island; barring that, it should be bombed and its port raided to reduce its efficiency.[48] Italy's military leaders, however, decided Malta could not be captured since the Italians could only assume having naval supremacy for ten hours at the most before massive enemy forces arrived.[49] Cavagnari summed up his thoughts on conflict with Britain: '[T]he struggle will be extremely hard for Italy and even harder for the Navy.'[50]

The crisis did make the Italians think about how to eliminate or reduce the threat Malta posed, and they came up with a variety of possible plans:[51]

- artillery, similar to the 1918 German Paris gun, that could bombard Valletta from Cape Passero in southern Sicily;
- submarines fitted with specially designed cutters to break through anti-submarine nets protecting Valletta's port;
- saboteurs who would 'walk' into the port along the sea bottom;
- manned 'slow' torpedoes, to be driven into the port;[52]
- and from the Regia Aeronautica (Italian Air Force), winged bombs that could be released outside anti-aircraft range and flown to their target.[53]

The war plans put forth had serious limitations. First, Italy had nothing that could stop the British from closing Gibraltar and Suez, isolating the nation from outside sources, especially from its East Africa colonies. Worse, internally, there was no coordination – planning or exercises – between the Italian navy and air force during this period; a foreshadowing of the problems revealed in the future global conflict.[54]

Mussolini, angry that Britain opposed his plans for empire, remained adamant about his coming war, refusing to give in to the concerns of his military (or his king) and the British

---

45. Ibid., p.34.
46. Mallett, Italian Navy, p.23.
47. Gooch, p.288.
48. Cernuschi, p.58.
49. Mallett, Mussolini and Origins, p.73.
50. Gooch, p.289.
51. Cernuschi, pp.60–72.
52. This idea became the nucleus for the formation of the famous maiales (pigs) that the Italians used during the Second World War.
53. The Italians did little with this idea, but the Germans used the idea for their radio-controlled Fritz-X guided bombs, one of which sank the Italian battleship Roma in 1943 as the Italian fleet was sailing to Bône after Italy's surrender.
54. Mallett, Italian Navy, p.25.

rhetoric. Part of his refusal to compromise came from intelligence sources that had stolen a report from the British embassy in Rome indicating the loss of Ethiopia would not jeopardize British Imperial interests.[55]

Britain

Mussolini's intransigence over Ethiopia put Britain in an awkward spot. On the one hand, it could not afford a conflict against Italy, with Germany and Japan flexing their expansionist muscles; on the other, British public opinion supported the League of Nations' hard line against aggression. Ultimately, despite their military's assurance they could easily win any war with Italy, British politicians chose not to weaken themselves at all; when Italy did invade Ethiopia in October 1935,[56] they did little except join other League nations in voting economic sanctions against the aggressor.

Italy's African adventure, though, meant the British had to face the fact that their primary base at Malta, defended by very few aircraft and only twelve anti-aircraft guns, sat wholly vulnerable to an enemy with airbases just 60 miles away in Sicily. The Admiralty underlined that vulnerability by choosing to move the Mediterranean Fleet's base to Alexandria during the crisis. The change to the eastern port had its disadvantages: for example, Alexandria had no repair facilities and exposed fuel storage.[57]

The crisis ended without war between Britain and Italy after the Italians took Addis Ababa in May 1936, but the consequences of the near-conflict remained significant. Mussolini took British resistance as a personal rejection of Italy's dreams of empire and their inaction as a sign that his imperial designs would not be truly contested. For Malta, the crisis meant Britain began to approve funding for defence in the Mediterranean – an airfield at Ta'Qali, for example. However, the island had to stand in line with other Empire bases, eighth in priority.[58]

Neville Chamberlain, Britain's Prime Minister in 1937, compounded the military problem with his diplomatic agenda: following a policy of appeasement that led directly to the 1938 Easter Accords with Italy, formally recognizing Italy's acquisition of Abyssinia in return for a reduction in Italy's forces in Libya. There was also a failure to coordinate strategy with France, their only real ally in the Mediterranean.[59] The policy of the British Chiefs of Staff toward Italy, in line with Chamberlain's goals, remained to 'do nothing to arouse Italian suspicions or be construed as provocative'. Accommodating Italy, they reasoned, would drive a wedge between them and the Germans.[60]

---

55. The source was Francesco Costantini, a servant at the embassy recruited years earlier by the Italian military intelligence unit, the Serviso Informazione Militari, as well as by the Soviet NKVD or People's Commissariat for Internal Affairs. Ibid., p.267.
56. On 3 October 1935, Italy invaded Abyssinia with some 200,000 troops. With a tremendous superiority in armament – plus the cruel use of mustard gas – the Italians were able to take the country by May 1936.
57. Ball, Bitter Sea, p.33; Simmons, p.25.
58. Austin, Malta and British Strategic Policy, p.58.
59. First Sea Lord Sir Chatfield Ernie stated it plainly: 'It is essential that we should make friends, not enemies when we have so much valuable property to be attacked and while our defence position is still weak.' Salerno, Reynold, Vital Crossroads: Mediterranean Origins of the Second World War, p.38. Note: the effects of Mediterranean positioning pre-war on Anglo-French and Franco-Italian relationships is beyond the scope of this book. Reynold Salerno's book is highly recommended.
60. Haddendorf, p.57.

Germany and Italy

Sanctions imposed by the League of Nations did nothing to stop Mussolini's surge into Ethiopia; an oil embargo or blockade might have had an impact, but one was never put in place and the Suez Canal remained open to Italian shipping.[61] The sanctions merely pushed Mussolini closer to Hitler's Germany, especially when France joined Britain in the League sanctions and began discussing a military alliance with Britain. In January 1936, with Italian movement stalled in Africa, Mussolini stated publicly he would have no objection to an independent Austria becoming a German satellite. The announcement marked the beginning of the alliance – described as an Axis by Mussolini[62] – between Italy and Germany.

Germany played both sides during the Abyssinia crisis, professing neutrality but quietly granting material support to Italy and secretly providing arms to Ethiopia.[63] In March 1936, with his European opponents still focused on Italy, the Führer reoccupied the demilitarized zone of the Rhineland. This move eliminated the final restrictions imposed by the Versailles Treaty and initiated Hitler's own expansion plans.

The partnership between Germany and Italy became a very odd alliance, one that historians describe as 'more mistrust than trust'.[64] The Axis was more political than strategic, as neither side collaborated on war plans.[65] The two countries cemented their relationship by aiding General Francisco Franco Bahamonde's Nationalists during the Spanish Civil War in 1936. Mussolini invested some 14,000 million lire (~$1.02 billion), plus 75,000 men of the Corpo di Truppe Volontarie and 720 aircraft of la Aviazione Legionaria, into the Nationalists' cause; Germany put 540 million Reichmarks (~$217 million) into the war, plus 600 aircraft and 16,000 troops of the Condor Legion.[66] Despite this, neither did much consulting over the next few years.

Discussions in 1937 with the British – Hitler's desired alliance partner – led to an impasse over the territorial concessions that he wanted – namely Austria, Czechoslovakia and Danzig[67] – and failed to cement any kind of pact. The breakdown of talks pushed Hitler to tighten ties with Italy, especially with Mussolini having softened on the Austrian issue. Hitler and Mussolini met again in Munich in September 1937, marked as a friendship meeting, where Mussolini made his German counterpart an honorary corporal in the Italian Fascist militia and Hitler reciprocated by awarding the Iron Cross to the Italian dictator. Interestingly, while the German military display Hitler staged greatly impressed Mussolini, his chief of General Staff, Generale Pietro Badoglio only rated them as mediocre with Italy 'far ahead'.[68]

In March 1938, Hitler bullied his way into Austria, ostensibly as a 'self-defence' move. Despite last minute pleas by Chancellor Schuschnigg, Mussolini's Italy stood aside and did not interfere, paying the Austrians back for the snub in 1934, satisfied that Hitler had no designs on the South Tyrol. Despite the immediate negative effects on the country's 185,000 Jewish

---

61. Burgwyn, Italian Foreign Policy, p.126.
62. On 1 November 1936, Mussolini stated that 'the Berlin-Rome line was not a Diaphragm but an Axis'. Ibid., p.152.
63. Hildebrand, p.25.
64. Schreiber, Vol III, p.9.
65. Mallett, Italian Navy, p.49.
66. Thomas, The Spanish Civil War, Appendix 7, pp.977–78.
67. Ibid., p.28.
68. Corvaja, p.47.

residents, there was little international protest against the Anschluss: Britain declared it had no obligations toward Austria, the United States simply transferred Austria's debt to Germany, and France – in the middle of another government change – did nothing.[69]

Almost as soon as Austria was secure, Hitler began making demands on Czechoslovakia. His primary diplomatic focus was on the three million Germans of the Sudetenland that had been declared part of Czechoslovakia when the nation was created by the Versailles Treaty following the First World War. In May 1938, the war of words heightened and Hitler created a draft plan – Fall Grün (Case Green) – to take the country by military invasion. Both Germany and Czechoslovakia mobilized troops as the crisis heightened. The German Army staff, led by Chief of Staff Ludwig Beck, were appalled by the orders and actively campaigned against Hitler. Their primary concern was that both the French and the Soviet Union had guaranteed Czechoslovakia's borders in 1925 and 1935, respectively, and that an invasion could very well lead to a general European war.

Relations between Italy and Britain soured over the former's involvement with the Spanish Civil War and, as he had during the Ethiopian crisis, Mussolini again demanded his military prepare for a war with Britain. As before, Malta became the contentious part of the plan, with one version of what was known as the DG 1 plan stating flatly that only the occupation of the island would solve the threat Malta posed to sea communications between Italy and North Africa, and only a sudden unexpected invasion would be successful. But Italy's amphibious capabilities were not up to the task, a point clearly made when Spanish Nationalists tried to assault Cartegena from the sea and had their main ship – with nearly 1,500 troops aboard – sunk by shore batteries. The only concrete plan the Italians came up with was to try to block Valletta's Grand Harbour with a 470-ton river steamer, the *Porto di Roma*.[70]

Through the summer and into September, the crisis continued, with diplomats posturing and the military flexing their muscles. In mid-September, British Prime Minister Chamberlain met with Hitler in an attempt to stave off war, which the German leader had promised by 1 October. Little was accomplished during the meeting, although Chamberlain verbally backed the German position on the Sudetenland. Hitler continued to increase his demands on the Czechs, hoping to isolate them from their European supporters and allow him to move militarily. He told the British that he would have no further territorial demands after the Sudetenland.

Britain turned to Italy in a final attempt to ward off war. Despite Mussolini's basic agreement with the Germans, the Italians called for an international summit in Munich. It was Mussolini's finest hour in the international stage as he helped broker a deal that led to an appeased peace and a dismembered Czechoslovakia.[71]

The Munich agreement had several major effects on the European situation. Britain and France felt relief that war had been averted, but the Soviet Union lost respect for both countries as Stalin's representatives had not been invited to the summit. In Germany, Hitler felt angered by the summit and the need to acquiesce to other European leaders. He also lost respect for Chamberlain, and despite his protests about having no more territorial demands, almost immediately began putting pressure on Poland over the Danzig Corridor between Germany and East Prussia, another artifact of the Versailles Treaty.

An unknown effect at the time was the plan the German military had of arresting Hitler had he actually demanded an invasion of Czechoslovakia. The Führer's disgust with his military's

---

69. MacDonogh, 1938, p.64.
70. Cernuschi, pp.77–79.
71. Portions of the country went to Germany, Poland and Hungary. Ibid., p.195.

reaction to the possibility of war, which he dismissed as 'childish force calculations', led him to dismiss Beck, who had opposed virtually every move Hitler had made. He was replaced as Chief of Staff by Generalfeldmarschall Wilhelm Keitel (also not a Hitler advocate). More importantly, Hitler made the decision to upgrade the Waffen-SS to a more potent armed force, answerable only to him and separate from the German Army.[72]

Hitler followed this with immediate diplomacy aimed at Poland. When he marched into Prague in March 1939, he completed the takeover of Czechoslovakia. The move angered Mussolini as it negated the Munich Pact, his one claim to fame on the international stage; he told his Foreign Minister, Ciano: 'The Italians would laugh at me; every time Hitler occupies a country, he sends me a message.'[73] In response, Mussolini siezed Albania a month later. The Italian move forced Britain to offer the Greek government, under Prime Minister Ioannis Mataxas, a verbal agreement to guarantee its territorial integrity if attacked.[74]

When rumours of a German-backed Polish coup surfaced at the end of March, Britain responded with a guarantee of Polish independence. France followed suit several days later. Neither country was enthusiastic about having Poland as an ally nor made much effort to bolster Poland's military following the guarantee. Indeed, Britain was incapable of backing up such a guarantee; its Army was 'pathetically unprepared for a European War'.[75] When no coup occurred, both Britain and France saw it as Hitler backing down.[76] In reality, there had been no planned coup; instead of backing down, Hitler ordered the invasion of Poland to be prepared (Fall Weiss – Case White) and signed the Pact of Steel with Italy in May, ostensibly formalizing an alliance between the two nations.

In fact, both sides acted at times without informing their 'ally'. Even the vaunted and very specific Pact of Steel engendered confusion between the two countries. Pact Article 3 stated explicitly that if 'one of them were to become involved in complications of war with one or more Powers, the other Contracting Party shall immediately come to its aid as ally and shall support it with all its military forces on land, on the seas and in the air'.[77] However, Italian officials took the pact to mean war would begin in several years' time, while Hitler enjoined his negotiators to specifically not mention his impending attack on Poland.

Whatever the problems between the Nazis and Fascists, few doubted they were headed for a future war with France and Britain. Mussolini had made that very clear in his famous speech of 4 February 1939, where he described Italy as a prisoner within the Mediterranean, with Corsica, Tunisia, Malta and Cyprus as the bars of the prison and Gibraltar and Suez the gatekeepers.[78]

Britain and Malta

On Malta, the Church–State crisis abated somewhat in 1932 when Strickland sent a letter of apology to the Vatican, which responded by rescinding the Pastoral letter. Elections were held

---

72. Ibid, p.161.
73. Ciano Diaries, 15 March 1939, p.43.
74. Carr, p.14.
75. Bond, Liddel Hart, p.123.
76. Overy, 1939, pp.10–11.
77. The Pact of Steel text can be found at the website user.dickinson.edu/~rhyne/232/PactofSteel.html.
78. Burgwyn, Italian Foreign Policy, p.185; Gooch, p.451.

in 1932, which brought the Nationalist Party, led by Dr Enrici Mizzi, into power. The party was blatantly pro-Italian and, when it began distributing Fascist material – and suggesting Malta be exchanged for Italy's colony in Eritrea – the new Governor at the time, Sir David Campbell, again suspended the constitution.[79] Malta would not regain self-rule until 1947, but the political turmoil began to subside, overtaken by the warlike rhetoric internationally.

By early 1939, Imperial hopes for peace seemed doomed. Italy increased its forces in Libya, in direct violation of the Easter Accords. Britain began strategic talks with France, crippled by divergent goals in the Mediterranean – France expected war with Italy, while Britain needed peace as their whole plan for Far East security depended on free access through the Mediterranean. The Pact of Steel between Italy and Germany seemed to be the final step toward war, but even then, Chamberlain continued to work for a peace – to do otherwise would admit his foreign policy had failed.

In discussing the feasibility of defending Malta in the event of war, the British Air Ministry – still wedded to the concept that fighters could not stop bombers – reported in 1938 that even with fighter defences, Italy could still put Malta's naval base and dockyard out of commission; therefore, adding more defences to the island would simply waste resources. Leslie Hore-Belisha, Secretary of State for War, stated the quandary bluntly: 'If we were to give up the defence of Malta, it would mean giving up the challenge for supremacy in the Mediterranean. But if it's decided not to defend her, then there is no point in leaving a garrison and equipment as we already have there, just to be overrun.'[80]

The Royal Navy disputed the Air Ministry's report, and in July 1939, defence planners agreed to upgrade Malta's defences to 112 heavy and forty-eight light anti-aircraft guns, plus four fighter squadrons. The decision indicated the planners felt Malta remained important to the Empire, with them having agreed to hold the 'prestige and honour of defending a long-held part of the Empire'. However, despite the agreement, the UK and Alexandria continued to get priority for defensive equipment.[81]

Germany

By August 1939, diplomacy with the West was at a standstill, so Hitler turned east. Already in trade talks with Stalin's Soviet Union, Germany opened discussions on non-aggression. It was an odd turn for both dictators. Hitler had never hidden his ultimate goal of *Lebensraum* at the expense of the Soviet Union, including a statement in early August that 'everything I do is directed at Russia'.[82] But he wanted a free hand with Poland and knew if he moved against the Poles, Stalin would react. Stalin also expected war with Germany at some point, but wasn't ready for one. On 23 August, the two countries signed the Molotov-Ribbentrop Non-Aggression Pact, 'ensuring' peace between them for the next ten years. For Hitler, it gave him the free hand he needed and he ordered Poland's invasion to begin on 26 August; Stalin, meanwhile, got time to ready his armies for the eventual conflict – as well as his own free hand with the Baltic nations of Latvia, Estonia, Lithuania and Finland.

---

79. Blouet, p.187.
80. Attard, Britain and Malta: Story of an Era, p.138.
81. Austin, British Strategic Policy, p.62.
82. Germany and the Second World War, Vol II, p.7.

The West reacted to the Pact by guaranteeing war if Germany attacked Poland. The reaction caused Hitler to postpone the invasion for one last attempt at diplomacy. On 25 August, he met with British Ambassador Sir Neville Henderson, offering to guarantee the British Empire's existence and possible arms limitations after he had 'solved' his Polish question. The offer was rejected – the British had learned that guarantees from Hitler were meaningless.[83] The French reacted the same way, and after two days of worrying, Hitler decided the western stance was a bluff and scheduled his Polish invasion for 1 September.

Italy

On 25 August, Mussolini received a letter from Hitler explaining the Soviet Pact as well as the 'state of alarm' that existed with Poland, noting he would act immediately if there was an 'intolerable' act by that country.[84] Italian Foreign Minister (and Mussolini's son-in-law) Count Galeazzo Ciano had previously noted that Italy needed to find a way out of the situation, but that the Germans were 'implacable'.[85] Differences in outlooks between the two countries on what would happen should Poland be attacked proved part of the problem: the Germans felt the British and French would acquiesce as they had at every other aggressive German move; the Italians feared a wider war would follow.[86] Mussolini found himself torn between his sense of honour that said he should fight alongside the Germans as required by the Pact of Steel, and the reality of his country's overall readiness for a war he hadn't expected for several years.[87] In addition, as noted previously, he had limited authority to declare war. Italy's King Victor Emmanuel III, who opposed war, remained the supreme commander of the nation's armed forces, and the officer corps were generally conservative, pessimistic about their chances and against any wider conflict.[88] As General Pietro Badoglio, Chief of the Italian General Staff, would report, Mussolini 'bowed to the logic of facts'.[89]

Mussolini responded to Hitler's letter by approving the Soviet Pact, but noted:

> 'If Germany attacks and Poland's allies open a counterattack against Germany, I want to let you know in advance that it would be better if I did not take the initiative in military activities in view of the present situation of Italy's war preparations, which we have repeatedly explained to you.'[90]

The Italians had provided a list of essential materials they would need immediately to fight on Germany's side when war broke out. In Ciano's words, the list was 'enough to kill a bull –

---

83. Ibid., Vol II, p.5.
84. Hitler letter to Mussolini, https://comandosuptremo.com/hitler-letter-to-mussolini/, accessed 20 February 2020.
85. Ciano Diaries, 6–11August 1939, pp.116–19.
86. In fact, Hitler fully expected to be able to 'co-operate mutually' with Britain after the Polish question had been resolved. Hildebrand, p.37.
87. Ciano reported that Mussolini felt that a war in 1939 would have a 50 per cent probability of an Axis win, while a 1942 war would see the probability rise to 80 per cent. Ciano, 9 August 1939, p.116.
88. Kershaw, p.139.
89. Badoglio Pietro, Italy in the Second World War, p.10.
90. Mussolini letter to Hitler, https://comandosuptremo.com/lette -from-mussolini-to-Hitler/, accessed 20 February 2020.

seventeen million tons',[91] and Italy fully intended it to be an unreasonable demand. But it gave the Italians an out, and when the Germans invaded Poland on 1 September, Mussolini declared Italy a 'non-belligerent' – supporting its ally but not fighting with it. Germany did not seem too unhappy at Italy's stance. Several months later, Hitler stated to his staff that Italy would 'enter the war after great German successes', but he saw no great advantage to its entry since Germany would be burdened with the obligation of more deliveries to Italy.[92]

Britain/Malta

The German ship *Schleswig-Holstein*, anchored in the port of Danzig, opened fire on the Polish fort of Westerplatte early on 1 September, preceding full-scale invasion of Poland. Three days later, both France and Britain declared war on Germany. Italy's unexpected neutrality added to British hopes to limit the conflict. In an attempt to bolster Italy's neutrality, the British placed orders with Italian firms for military equipment such as anti-tank guns and Caproni aircraft. Although he initially allowed such contracts, Mussolini cancelled them in February 1940.[93] The two countries also initially agreed to exchange information on major military movements.[94]

Italy's neutrality continued Malta's lower defence priority for Britain. The island started the war with only twenty-four anti-aircraft guns and three airfields – Luqa with concrete runways, and Ta'Qali and Hal Far with grass fields – but still no organized fighters. It was defended by the Malta Brigade of only four battalions: 1st Battalion, Dorsetshire Regiment; 2nd Battalion, Devonshire Regiment; 2nd Battalion, Royal Irish Fusiliers; and 2nd Battalion, Queen's Own Royal West Kent Regiment – plus two battalions of King's Own Malta troops and a third battalion just forming.

On the island, some attempts to prepare for war ensued, the government establishing a Home Guard and recruiting some 3,000 men in the first three days. These men filled out an Air Raid Precautions Bureau with duties that included ascertaining damage and casualties from a raid, and providing first aid and rescue assistance that had been initially organized during the Abyssinian crisis.[95] The authorities applied lighting restrictions and enforced a curfew, requiring most people to be indoors between 7.00 pm and 6.00 am, althought the hours were modified several times to ensure workers could get to their workplaces in the morning.[96] They started building air raid shelters and obtained gas masks – memories of Italy's use of mustard gas in Abyssinia remained strong among the military and civil authorities. In May 1940, a fifth infantry battalion (8th Battalion, The Manchesters) arrived to bolster the defences.

Malta also became a part of the Royal Navy's war against Germany as a port for the Contraband Control Service in the eastern and central Mediterranean. This service intercepted neutral merchant ships for examination of their cargos, confiscating those headed for Germany. The Commercial Prize Court in Valletta made the final judgment, and if they deemed the cargo contraband, they seized and sold it at auction. The Maltese intercepted some 268 neutral

---

91. Ciano, 26 August 1939, p.129.
92. Showell, Fuehrer Conferences on Naval Affairs, 1939–1945, 26 January 1940, p.79.
93. Austin, Churchill and Malta's War, p.24.
94. Hinsley, British Intelligence in the Second World War, Vol I, p.201.
95. Zarb-Dimech, Anthony, Mobilization in Action: A History of Civil Defense in Malta, 1940–1943, pp.65–66.
96. Attard, Edward, A History of the Malta Police, 1800–1964, p.147.

freighters during this period and diverted them to the island for closer examination; ultimately, they seized fourteen cargoes.[97]

British intelligence continued to track Italian intentions, aided by the fact that almost all of Italy's codes had been broken for years.[98] After Germany's invasion of Norway in April 1940, indications of Italy's hostile intent sharpened, including the reinforcement and build-up of its Libyan forces. One significant effect of the heightened threat was that the Admiralty transferred the Mediterranean Fleet's headquarters from HMS St Angelo on Malta to Alexandria on 3 May 1940.[99] In a far more important step, they also suspended all merchant traffic in the Mediterranean, citing Italy's submarines and the narrow Straits of Sicily close to Italian air bases. The move immediately added some 20,000 miles (and two months) to round trips between Suez and Britain.[100]

Italy

Italy's non-belligerence did not sit well with Mussolini, who vacillated badly during the August crisis. He complained that 'a great nation cannot remain eternally in such a position [neutral] without losing face, and it [Italy] should prepare to intervene'.[101] The two Axis leaders met at the Brenner Pass in March 1940. Hitler wanted to explain his alliance with the Soviet Union, something Mussolini had criticized. He also wanted to negate the current attempts by the United States to negotiate a peace, as well as the efforts of anti-German advisors in Rome, namely Foreign Minister Ciano and Italy's Ambassador to Germany, Bernardo Attolico. Hitler made a push for Italian participation, pointing out that France and Britain stood in the way of all of Italy's goals, and that their two countries were linked – defeat of one would mean the defeat of the other. Communication between the 'allies' remained questionable, evidenced by Hitler choosing not to tell Mussolini of his plans to invade Denmark and Norway the following month.

At the end of the month, Mussolini finally committed himself to war. In a detailed memorandum – though far less detailed than needed for such a major decision – he outlined both his position and his plans. He used simple reasoning: '[T]o think that Italy can remain outside the conflict until the end is absurd and impossible. Italy is in the middle of nations at war, by land and by sea, and it therefore cannot avoid taking arms.' Mussolini further linked himself to Germany, writing: 'Only the alliance with Germany, a country which has not yet needed our military help and is content with our economic help and moral support, allows our current nonbelligerent status.' He made clear what he wanted out of the war: 'A parallel war to that of Germany's to reach our objectives: freedom on the seas, [a] window on the ocean.' He concluded: "Italy cannot possibly remain neutral for the entire duration of the war without abdicating its role, without disqualifying itself. Without being reduced to a Switzerland multiplied by ten.'[102]

---

97. Caruana, J., Malta's Maritime Diary, Ch 1.
98. Hinsley, British Intelligence in the Second World War, Vol I, p.199.
99. Caruana, Malta's Maritime Diary, Ch 1.
100. Page, The Royal Navy and the Mediterranean, Vol 1, p.xix.
101. Ciano, 24 September 1939, p.149.
102. Corvaja, pp.108–09.

To his military staff, he outlined his proposed strategy:[103]

- In the Alps, defence unless France collapses;
- occupation of Corsica if deemed worth the time and effort;
- observation of Yugoslavia with an eye to attack if the current regime collapsed;
- in Libya, defence;
- in East Africa, attacks toward Kassala and Kenya;
- for the Regia Marina, on offensive 'right down the line of the Mediterranean and outside of it';
- for the Regia Aeronautica, support for both the Army and Navy.

Once his service chiefs received the document, very little came of it; Badoglio promoted passivity unless France collapsed, Admiral Cavagnari worryied about enemy fleets at either end of the Mediterranean; and Air Force chief Francesco Pricolo observed that chances for Mediterranean air and naval operations remained slim.[104]

After the German invasion of Belgium and Holland in May 1940, Mussolini decided the time to intervene had arrived, declaring that 'the Allies have lost the war. We Italians are already sufficiently dishonoured. Any delay is inconceivable. We have no time to lose.'[105] He informed Hitler of his decision on 30 May, and on 10 June declared war on France and Great Britain, stating:

> 'We take the field against the plutocratic and reactionary democracies who have always blocked the march and frequently plotted against the existence of the Italian people... . There is only one order. It is categorical and obligatory for everyone. It already wins over and enflames hearts from the Alps to the Indian Ocean: Conquer!'[106]

Much has been written about Mussolini's decision to intervene, alternating between rank opportunism in hitting a beaten foe (France) and following long-term Italian goals, but it is beyond the scope of this book to discuss the issue in detail. Nevertheless, two significant points can be made. First, Mussolini's ambition of a Mediterranean empire, a goal he stood by since gaining office in 1922, could only come at the expense of France and Great Britain, so war with those countries remained inevitable. Second, the Italian view of the Pact of Steel foresaw war against the Allies in 1942, when Italy declared it would be ready, this timing very similar to the three-year preparation period used by Mussolini in his conflict with Ethiopia – planned in 1932 and launched in 1935. An early war became more a result of Italian plans being overtaken by events. One recent analysis cited it as a 'preventative step against the Third Reich's claim to European hegemony'.[107]

Regardless of why Italy entered the war when it did, it did so completely unprepared. Badoglio, in his memoirs, stated: 'It is suicide.'[108] Some 254 ships – nearly a quarter of Italy's

---

103. Knox, Mussolini Unleashed, p.89.
104. Ibid., pp.91–93.
105. Ciano, 13 May 1940, p.249.
106. Jacobsen & Smith, pp.70–71.
107. Schreiber, Vol III, p.126.
108. Badoglio, p.15.

merchant fleet – were caught in foreign ports and interned immediately after the declaration of war. That loss of 1.37 million tons of shipping could have severely impacted Italy's ability to wage war in the Mediterranean.[109]

Mussolini entered the war with no concrete plans for his parallel conflict, despite his earlier strategic memorandum. The lack of plans to capture Malta really surprised the Germans, particularly given a 1938 Italian planning memorandum that pointed to taking Malta as an 'indispensable condition for any important Italian operation in North Africa'.[110] There was also the threat the island posed against the transport routes to North Africa (see Figure 1-1). Admiral Cavagnari put it bluntly: 'The possibility thus not existing to carry out the fulfillment of important strategic objectives or to bring about the defeat of the enemy's naval forces, entering the war on our own initiative does not seem justified, given the prospect of being able to carry out only defensive operations.'[111]

Both the Axis countries began their war with unrealized expectations, and for Italy its impulsive thrust into the conflict was both unexpected and disastrous.

Britain

Following the German invasion of France and the Low Countries, efforts by the French and British to keep Mussolini out of the war intensified. At one point they invited US President Franklin D. Roosevelt to intervene, but the president's message to the Italian leader had no effect.[112]

In late May 1940, the British Cabinet held discussions about offering 'territorial concessions' to Italy in return for peace and interceding with Hitler; one of those concessions would have been the demilitarization of Malta.[113] French Prime Minister Paul Reynaud initiated the basic idea,[114] while Lord Halifax, Britain's Foreign Secretary and a member of the War Cabinet, was in favour. But Winston Churchill, who became Prime Minister on 10 May 1940, adamantly disagreed, as did most of the military staff, so the subject was dropped.[115] Britain – and the Maltese – dug in for the long term.

---

109. Schreiber, Vol III, p.91. The loss was made up by the confiscating of shipping from Yugoslavia, Greece and France, totalling almost 1.5 million tons. Cernuschi & Gazzi, 'Seapower: The Italian Way', p.145.
110. Lutton, Wayne Charles, unpublished dissertation, 'Malta and the Mediterranean', p.26. Lutton accessed a significant number of captured and foreign documents for his dissertation in 1983. However, the December 1938 plan, DG 10/A2, did not envision war until 1942 or later, by which time Italy would have a force of eight battleships to oppose the Royal Navy and support an invasion of Malta. Gabriele, pp.17–20.
111. Bragadin, Marc, The Italian Navy in World War II, p.6.
112. Austin, Churchill and Malta's War, p.34. The British later learned that Mussolini had resented the US intrusion into the matter.
113. The French proposed offering the neutralization of Gibraltar and Suez, limiting naval forces in the Mediterranean, altering Tunis's status and concessions in the Dodecanese as well as Malta in order to keep Italy out of the war. Gilbert, The Churchill War Papers, 26 May 1940, p.155.
114. Holland, Fortress Malta, p.30.
115. Exactly what Churchill's feelings were on negotiated settlements is unclear. One recent book quoted former Prime Minister Chamberlain as remembering Churchill saying he would jump at the chance to get out of the jam they were in by giving up Malta. As far as the author can determine, Churchill was in favour of negotiations from a position of strength (which they were not in during 1940) and did not want to give up anything that would undercut national resolve or territories vital to the Eempire. Reid, Churchill Under Fire, p.36.

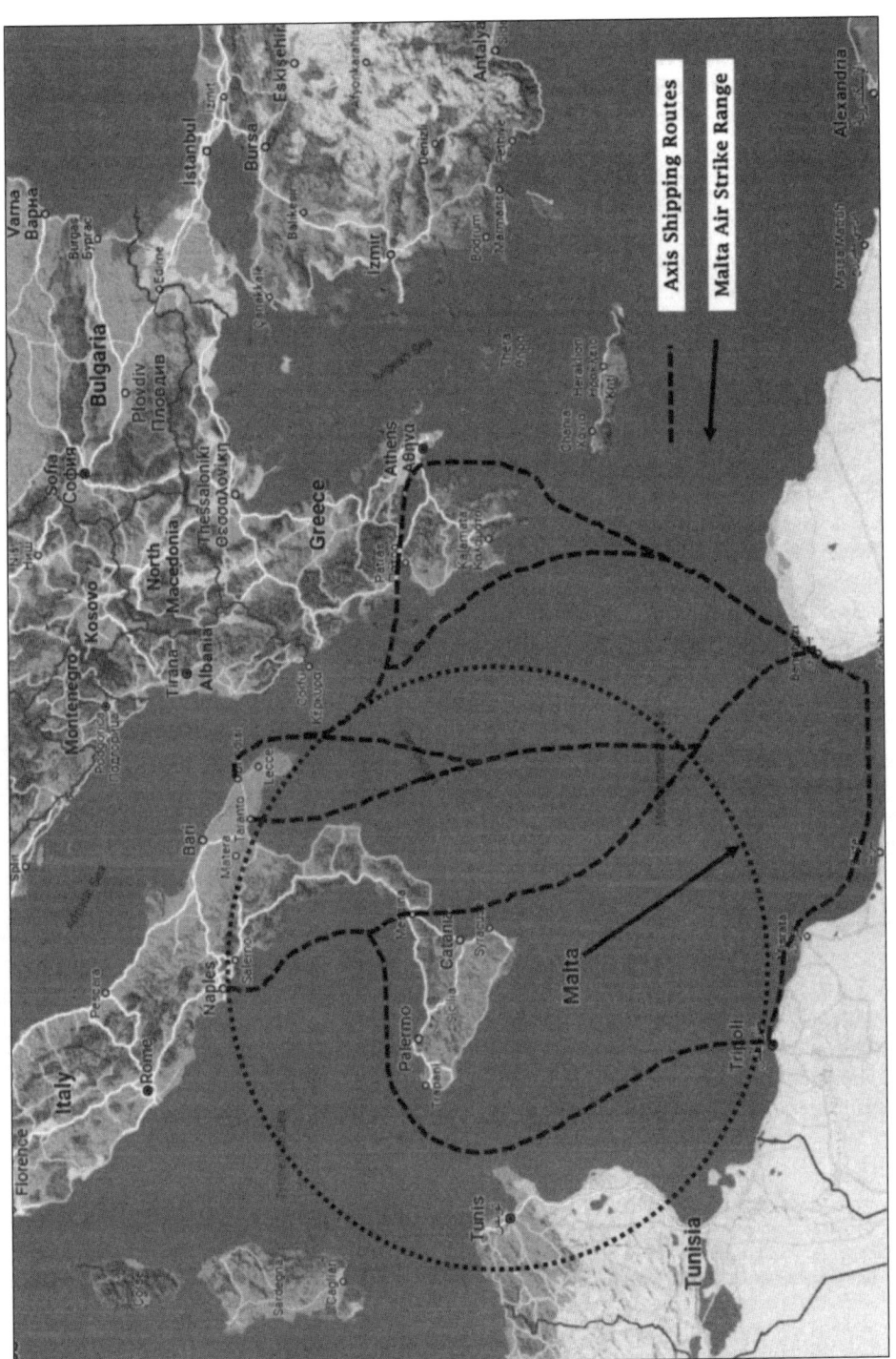

Figure 1-1: *Malta's Threat to Italy's North African Theatre.*

Churchill, when he was Chamberlain's First Lord of the Admiralty, initially felt that no offensive action against Italy would be required, since closing Gibraltar and the Suez Canal would 'inflict immense injury on Italy and it is for her to come far from her bases to retaliate or try to break this distant blockade'.[116]

However, after the German attack on the Low Countries and France, and him becoming the British Prime Minister, Churchill changed his mind about Italy. He becamed far more aggressive, stating:

> 'It is important that at the outset, collision should take place with the Italian Navy and Air Force in order that we see what their quality is and whether it has changed at all since the last war. The purely defensive strategy contemplated by the Commander-in-Chief, Mediterranean ought not to be accepted. Unless it is found that the fighting quality of the Italians is high, it will be much better that the fleet at Alexandria should sally forth and run some risks.'[117]

On 3 June 1940, Bletchley Park in Bedfordshire – location of the British Government's Code & Cypher School – intercepted and decoded an Italian Regia Aeronautica signal indicating Italy would declare war on 10 June.[118]

With war with Italy threatening, the Royal Navy had forces at either end of the Mediterranean. At Alexandria, Admiral Andrew B. Cunningham's Mediterranean Fleet consisted of four battleships: *Warspite*, *Malaya*, *Ramilles* and *Royal Sovereign*. Each were First World War-vintage ships armed with 15in guns and capable of 21–23 knots, much slower than their Italian counterparts, especially the new Littorio-class battleships. In addition, Cunningham had the carrier *Eagle*, nine light cruisers, twenty-one destroyers and six submarines. At Gibraltar, the battleship *Resolution* and carrier *Argus* were based with a single cruiser and nine destroyers.[119]

On 6 June, Cunningham signalled his war plan to occupy Crete and react to Italian moves, specifying: 'Should Malta be subjected to seaborne attack, it is intended to move with the whole Fleet to its relief.'[120]

Malta

When Italy did, in fact, declare war on 10 June, Malta's acting Governor, Major General Sir William George Shedden Dobbie, issued a prophetic statement to the island's garrison:

'It may be that hard times lie ahead of us, but I know however hard they be, the courage and determination of all ranks will not falter and, with God's help we will maintain the security of this fortress.'[121]

---

116. Gilbert, Churchill War Papers, 1 May 1940, Vol 1, p.1,181.
117. Ibid., 28 May 1940, Vol 2, p.175.
118. Caruana, Malta's Maritime Diary, Ch 1.
119. Page, Appendix F, pp.144–45.
120. Ibid., Appendix C.4, p.89. Note that the occupation of Crete was refused by the Admiralty due to Greek neutrality at that time.
121. Malta's Governor at the time was General Sir Charles Bonham-Carter, but he was seriously ill and the duties fell to his temporary replacement. Jacobs, pp.7–8; Malta at War, Vol 1, p.107.

The advent of war found Malta unprepared to fend off its belligerent northern neighbour. One historian, Charles Jellison, put it this way: 'Malta offered the strange spectacle of a naval base without a fleet, airfields without planes, a pitifully small garrison of ill-equipped troops, virtually no anti-aircraft protection and coastal guns that were few.'[122]

In total, Malta's's defences that June counted thirty-four heavy and eight light anti-aircraft guns, twenty-four searchlights and five infantry battalions (approximately 5,000 troops),[123] plus three King's Own Malta Regiment battalions, two of which had only formed at the end of 1939. They also had two radar stations – euphemistically called Air Ministry Experimental Stations, or AMES – to detect enemy aircraft, one located on the Dingli heights, some 830ft above sea level, and another at Ghar Lapsi. Both were Advanced Chain Overseas High units, capable of detecting aircraft at 10,000ft up to 70 miles away.[124] The Royal Navy was present with one destroyer – the Royal Australian Navy's *Vendetta* – six submarines, six minesweepers, one minelayer and the monitor HMS *Terror*.[125] At Hal Far, the Royal Navy's Fleet Air Arm had eleven Fairey Swordfish 'Stringbag' torpedo/reconnaissance aircraft, with a total of forty-five torpedoes available for their use.[126]

Admiral Cunningham in Alexandria authorized the use of four – later increased to six – Sea Gloster Gladiators (SS.37), crated and left behind by carrier HMS *Glorious*, for the Royal Air Force to use.[127] All metal bi-planes with four machine guns, the Gladiators' maximum speed of 250mph made them slower than their Italian opponents. The Hal Far Fighter Flight, created to fly the newly acquired aircraft, was manned solely by volunteers, none of whom was a fighter pilot.[128] Italian intelligence had estimated twenty-five fighters on the island.[129]

Acting Governor Dobbie, an engineer by training and a devout Christian, led the island into war. He had previously served as General Officer Commanding in Malaya before retiring. Recalled for the assignment to Malta as a temporary position while his ailing predecessor, Sir Charles Bonham-Carter, recovered, he became the official Governor in April 1940. The Royal Navy's Vice Admiral Sir Wilbraham Ford, RAF Air Commodore Forster Herbert Martin Maynard and the British Army's Major General Sanford John Palairet Scobell aided Dobbie in his task, along with his chief civil administrator, Sir Edward St John Jackson.

Unfortunately, an awkward chain of command existed among these leaders. Dobbie, as Governor, reported directly to the Colonial Office, while as the island's commander-in-chief, he reported to the War Office. Scobell, as the Army commander, reported to Dobbie directly, but Ford and Maynard reported to their respective superiors at Middle East Headquarters in Cairo. No individual within the command structure of Malta had overall charge of the coordinated defence of the island.[130]

---

122. Jellison, Charles, Besieged: The World War II Ordeal of Malta, 1940–1942, p.22.
123. Jacobs, Fortress Island Malta, p.5.
124. Grech, Raiders Passed, Appendix J, p.329.
125. Page, Royal Navy and the Mediterranean, Appendix F, pp.144–46.
126. Jones, Fleet Air Arm, p.18.
127. Winton, John, Cunningham, p.81. The Admiralty Stores Department sent an inquiry to Cunningham demanding to know why Fleet Air Arm spares had been given to the RAF. The Admiralty actually demanded their return, but changed their mind a day later. Poolman, Faith, Hope & Charity: The Defence of Malta, p.110.
128. Ibid., pp.39–40. Flight Lieutenant George Burges, personal assistant to Air Commodore Maynard, was one such volunteer and was selected as the flight leader. Jacobs, p.5.
129. Page, Appendix F, p.265.
130. Austin, p.155.

To defend against the possibility of invasion, Scobell's fortress scheme parcelled his infantry into concrete defence posts around the coastline. The 8th Battalion, Manchesters, provided a good example. Upon arriving on the island on 20 May 1940, the battalion found itself split into company groups: A Company to Hal Far airfield, B Company to Luqa airfield, C Company to St Paul's Bay,and D Company to Il Fawara, with the battalion headquarters located at Ghain Tuffieha. From these positions, the infantry became further scattered to coastal posts.[131]

Against this poorly defended island, some 259 Regia Aeronautica aircraft (sixty-nine fighters, 141 bombers and forty-nine assorted other aircraft)[132] operated from twenty-three airfields in Sicily. Despite their vastly superior numbers, the Italian air force suffered some serious problems. As the 'poor' (but fascist) service compared to the Italian Army and Navy, the Air Force was limited to daylight operations due to lack of training and equipment. Training was especially lacking in maritime operations; both reconnaissance and torpedo attacks had been sadly neglected in Mussolini's run-up to war, leaving the Regia Aeronautica playing catch-up. Their bombers had some severe problems, such as poor bombsights and small vertically mounted bombs that scattered upon being dropped. Fighters had radio receivers only and no self-sealing tanks, making them vulnerable in the air despite their manoeuvrability.[133]

The Regia Marina boasted over eighty modern ships. The Italians could immediately field two 12.6in battleships, the *Conte di Cavour* and the *Guilio Cesare*, First World War-vintage ships that had been extensively upgraded. Two modern 15in battleships, the *Littorio* and *Vittorio Veneto*, and two other 12.6in battleships, the *Caio Duilio* and *Andre Doria*, were almost ready for action.[134] They were supported by seven 8in heavy cruisers, twelve 6in light cruisers and almost sixty destroyers. With the French virtually out of the picture, the Italian naval and air forces enjoyed a numerical superiority in all aspects over the Royal Navy in the Mediterranean. The Regia Marina ships had excellent speed and manoeuvrability but suffered from lighter armour, little night-fighting capability and no radar or sonar.

The Italian Navy had three other far more important vulnerabilities: no dedicated air arm, a very uncertain fuel supply and a limited industrial base to back it up. The Regia Marina had started developing their own aircraft programme after the First World War, but when the Italians created the Regia Aeronautica in 1923, the airmen assumed full control over development and use of Italy's military aircraft. This contributed to the decision not to pursue the development of aircraft carriers. In addition, at the start of the war, the Italian armed forces, particularly the Navy and Air Force, had different radio systems that complicated cooperation between the services, especially at sea. An attempt to remedy this pre-war deficiency did not start until mid-1941.[135] Most of the navy's battleships and cruisers carried reconnaissance aircraft, the Ro.43, which could communicate directly with their launching ship; however, the planes could not be recovered at sea and thus had to return to a land base after completing their mission. One Italian staff member concluded: '[T]here is now an almost total absence of any clear and rational doctrine for aeronaval warfare in the Mediterranean.'[136]

---

131. Bonner, Ardwick Boys, p.11.
132. Shores, Christopher, Cull, Brian & Malizia, Nicola, Hurricane Years 1940–1941, Appendix VIII, pp.389–90.
133. Ehlers, pp.18–19.
134. The dimension listed for each ship is the diameter of its main naval armament.
135. Iachino, pp.35–36.
136. Mallett, p.147, citing Vittorio Bacigalupi's Pro-memoria sul problema della cooperazione aereo-navale of 23 June 1939.

As for fuel, the Italians started the war with 2 million tons of fuel oil stockpiled, but Mussolini earmarked 300,000 tons of that for industry. The navy expected to expend some 200,000 tons per month in active wartime duty, giving them only nine months of secure service, since they did not have a secure fuel source available. Finally, Italy's industrial base suffered in size and resources; steel output, for example, was only 23 per cent that of Britain and 10 per cent that of Germany. The country remained short of virtually every important resource, from copper to nickel and rubber.[137]

Despite the drawbacks of Italy's naval arm, the disparity in numbers between the opponents meant severe problems for Malta. The island could only produce 30 per cent of its 250,000-strong population's food supply and 5 per cent of its other needs. Most of its food imports came from Italy. Pre-war estimates suggested the island would need five ships, carrying 40,000 tons, a month to keep itself sufficiently supplied.[138] Attempting to achieve that goal would give the Royal Navy a headache for years.

Hard times indeed were ahead for Malta, but its British masters had not made a conscious choice to keep it unprepared for war. It was a result of wholly inadequate Imperial resources, a lesser priority than other strategically important locations and a blindly optimistic foreign policy.

---

137. O'Hara, On Contested Seas, p.148.
138. Cernuschi, p.9.

Chapter II

War
June 1940 – November 1941

At 6.50 am on 11 June 1940, Malta's air raid sirens sounded for the first time for real. Ten Savoia Marchetti-79 bombers from 34° Stormo Bombardamento Terrestre (BT), escorted by Macchi C.200 fighters from 6° Gruppo Autonomo Caccia Terrestre (CT),[1] attacked Hal Far and the dockyards. Military targets received little damage, with civilian properties bearing the brunt of the attack. The Second World War had arrived in Malta in deadly earnest.

A total of eight air raids struck that first day, damaging or destroying more than 200 buildings and killing twenty-eight civilians and six servicemen. The Italians did not return on 12 June, but the initial raids led to a mass exodus from Valletta and the Three Cities (Vittoriosa, Senglea and Cospicua, across Grand Harbour from the capital). Despite pre-war evacuation plans, some 100,000 people – 40 per cent of Malta's population – overwhelmed those measures as they fled the cities into the villages in the rest of the island, causing considerable hardship in housing and feeding the refugees. For example, the village of Lija – with a population of 1,800 – was flooded with 3,000 refugees.[2] Many others lived in railroad tunnels and catacombs to escape the bombing.

As well as the bombing, the first day concluded with a friendly-fire naval incident after three steam pinnaces left Grand Harbour to intercept the Italian freighter *Polinice*. Upon their return, a miscommunication caused the coastal gunners to assume the little boats were Italian and open fire, sinking all three and killing six men;[3] five others were rescued by men from the Dorsetshire Regiment who swam out to their assistance.[4] The authorities at the time blamed the deaths on the Italian bombers.

The Italians returned in strength on 13 June. Until the end of the month, a total of fifty-one raids dropped 196 tons of bombs, killing seventy civilians and destroying 137 buildings.[5] Malta's tiny air force flew just three Gladiators at a time, sparking the legend of the aircraft

---

1. Basically, three or four Sezioni of three aircraft made up a Squadriglia; two or three Squadriglia made up a Gruppo; and two Gruppo made up a Stormo. Bomber (BT) Gruppo had eighteen aircraft, while fighter (CT) Gruppo had twenty-four. Malta at War, Vol 1, # 6, p.143. See also Appendix C.
2. Micallef, Joseph, When Malta Stood Alone (1940–1943), p.15.
3. Caruana, Malta's Maritime Diary, Ch 2.
4. Jary, They Couldn't Have Done Better, p.32. The three soldiers were ultimately awarded the George Cross for their rescue.
5. Caruana correspondence.

Faith, Hope and Charity fighting off the Italian hordes.[6] They actually caused little damage to the Regia Aeronautica, but their endeavours boosted morale on the island significantly. On 22 June, a reconnaissance SM.79 became their first recorded kill; the British would not lose their first pilot until mid-July.[7] Meanwhile, the British pressed Hurricane fighters, intended for the Middle East, brought into emergency service on Malta, with five aircraft added to the island's air defences on 24 June.[8] Also in June, Malta increased its offensive bite as twelve Swordfish torpedo bombers landed at Hal Far airfield, becoming the island's 830 Squadron.

Winston Churchill himself became the single most important factor in the decision to defend Malta to the utmost, never wavering from his commitment to not only defend the island but use it offensively against the enemy. The Prime Minister had a relationship with Malta that started in 1907, when he was an undersecretary in the Colonial Office, and continued in 1912 as a member of the Admiralty. As he wrote early in the war, 'defense of Malta and Egypt are duties compulsive upon us'.[9] He sent a note to Governor Dobbie on 23 June that said (prophetically): 'I have the conviction that you will make that defense [of Malta] glorious in British military history and also in the history of Malta itself.'[10]

As early as July, Churchill began pushing for more defensive aid for the island. He also pressed for making offensive use of Malta, saying on 12 July that 'it also seems desirable the Fleet should make use of Malta more freely'.[11] Dobbie refused the request for swift offensive action, as the Italian air attacks had diminished and he did not want to provoke them into increased assaults until the island's defences had been built up.

Admiral Cunningham agreed with the Prime Minister on overall strategy. In common with the Prime Minister, the Fleet commander had a long-standing interest in the Mediterranean, having been the second-in-command of the Mediterranean Fleet in 1937. While a member of the Admiralty Staff, he – and many others – had stressed the theatre's importance. In 1938, they felt the Mediterranean had to be cleared of hostile forces, Middle East oil defended and Imperial interests were preserved before any Far East expedition could be successfully mounted.[12]

On 17 June, six days after the initial attacks on Malta, the Chief of the Naval Staff, Admiral Sir Dudley Pound, floated a proposal that, in the event of a French surrender, the Royal Navy should evacuate the Eastern Mediterranean and pull back to Gibraltar. He cited two reasons: first, Alexandria's vulnerability to air attack and limited repair facilities; and second, the need for the Fleet in the Atlantic to stave off German commerce raiders.[13]

Cunningham sent a blunt response to Pound's suggested withdrawal: 'I feel the effects of this withdrawal would involve such a landslide in territory and prestige that I earnestly hope that such a decision will never have to be made.'[14] Instead, he suggested to the Admiralty

---

6. The names were attributed to Flight Officer J.L. Waters, an original member of the Station Fighter Flight. Poolman, p.71. Mrs Queenie Lee described the planes in a broadcast: 'But our three planes worked miracles and must have frightened the Italians with their sheer impudence.' Perowne, Stewart: The Siege within the Walls: Malta, 1940–1943, p.41.
7. Shores, Hurricane Years, pp.37–38. Flight Lieutenant Peter Keeble was lost on 16 July.
8. Ibid., p.24.
9. Perowne, p.95.
10. Gilbert, Churchill War Papers, 23 June 1940, Vol 2, p.402.
11. Ibid., 12 July 1940, Vol 2, p.509.
12. Haddendorf, pp.58–59.
13. Austin, p.94.
14. Simpson, Cunningham Papers, Vol 1, p.76.

an alternate policy for the island. He noted that the defences needed to be improved significantly before the island could be used in an offensive role, agreeing with Governor Dobbie, stating:

> 'At present various deficiencies, notably lack of civilian air raid shelters, inadequate anti-aircraft defences, and lack of underground protection for certain vital services are such that if we provoke a really heavy scale retaliation the civilian morale would rapidly fall to a point when the population would become a grave menace instead of an assistance to the garrison in resisting attack. Moreover until there is greater protection Malta is of little use to us as a base and its invaluable docking and repair facilities are lost to us.'

Until the defences could be improved, Cunningham recommended the island only interdict sea targets and perform reconnaissance. He hoped to be able to use the island offensively by April 1941.[15]

Initially the only offensive punches the island had were the Swordfish torpedo bombers and the six submarines stationed there. Two of the subs – HMS *Odin* and *Orpheus* – left on patrol as soon as war was declared, with minelayers HMS *Grampus* and *Rorqual* preparing to depart. Two others O-class submarines, *Otis* and *Olympus*, were at Malta refitting.[16] Unfortunately, the initial foray proved disastrous for the service, as *Odin*, *Orpheus* and *Grampus* were all lost to Regia Marina units within the first week.[17] The O-class subs proved to be outdated and a poor fit for Mediterranean combat. On 18 June, due to Italian bombing, the Admiralty ordered the Malta-based submarines to move base to Alexandria.[18]

The same day, Italian Naval Chief of Staff Admiral Cavagnari issued a report on Italian plans for Malta. His staff had developed a tentative invasion plan, involving 20,000 troops landing at several sites around the island following an aerial bombardment and naval blockade. The lightly armed troops of the first wave would be transported to Malta in 100 Adriatic flat-bottomed trawlers and put ashore in Mellieha Bay, St Paul's Bay and Qualet Marku. This would be followed by landings at St Thomas's Bay, Marsa Scala and Marsa Scirocco, with the hope that the initial landings would have drawn the defenders northward. The attack force commander planned to hold some 7,000 troops in reserve to reinforce any area that needed extra manpower. Four tankers carrying light armoured vehicles would land at Ramla Tal-Masquqa (Golden Bay), Gnejna Bay and Fomm in-Rih Bay. The plan called for the attack to occur during the new moon period of July.[19]

However, based on Cavagnari's report, the Comando Supremo (the Italian armed forces High Command) decided the threat Malta posed against Italian communications of only 'secondary importance' because the British had abandoned its use as a main base of operations, and thus it did not need to be taken. Part of their reasoning cited the difficult conditions invaders would face against the island's defences, which according to Cavagnari's intelligence sources

---

15. Admiralty Signal 2015/2218/40, Appendix C, pp.99–100.
16. Caruana, Malta's Maritime Diary, Ch 1.
17. Jacobs, pp.21–22.
18. Page, I, section 36, p.25.
19. Gabriele, Appendix III, pp.231–34.

included 12,000 troops and '100 tanks'.[20] Aerial bombing, he decided, would be sufficient to neutralize the island.[21]

Other officers disagreed with the assessment. Admiral Franco Maugeri, future director of the Italian Navy's Serviso Informazione Segreto, the intelligence service, would state later: 'Malta was the key to the entire strategic situation in the Mediterranean. In friendly hands, it was a blessing and a boon; in the hands of an enemy, a dagger aimed straight at the heart.'[22]

Italy's decision left Malta's neutralization in the hands of the Regia Aeronautica, which, although numerically superior to the defence forces they faced, was simply not ready or designed for the task required. Their primary bomber was the Savoia-Marchetti SM.79, a medium bomber capable of carrying 2,756lb of bombs, but of the almost 600 SM.79s available, only 400 were operational initially, and those were spread out over the whole of the Italian empire. Tactically, the bombers suffered from a pre-war manual bombsight, the Jazzo U.2/U.3, that had no gyroscopic stabilization, and from vertical bomb loading that significantly scattered bombs after dropping, lowering their accuracy significantly. Furthermore, the Italians started the war with only a six-month supply of aviation fuel and a munitions supply in which just 2 per cent were bombs heavier than 100kg (220lb).[23]

With Malta's threat assessment low – and despite the selected neutralization programme – Italian air attacks tapered off in July as their attention turned elsewhere. They would revisit Malta only 153 times from July until the end of 1940. By August, refugees were returning to their homes. By the end of the year, many people ignored air raid warnings and treated aerial battles as entertainment – so long as the planes weren't flying directly toward them.[24]

Italy did not limit its entry into the war to attacks on Malta. It had sent troops into the French Alps following the declaration of war, but their assaults had not gone well. The Italians attacked with little support and less planning directly against the French Alpine defences, suffering almost 3,900 casualties against French losses of about 230.[25] Achille Starace, Chief of Staff of the Fascist militia, later said that the Alpine fighting 'showed a total lack of army preparation, a total lack of offensive means, and a complete lack of capacity in the higher officers'.[26] The fighting there ended on 17 June.

Italian hopes for the 'spoils of war' following the German victory in France were expansive, including the French fleet, its colonies and even the Mona Lisa.[27] However, those Italian hopes ran into a German leader who did not want to further humiliate France – Hitler hoped that reasonable peace terms for France would convince Britain to also come to the negotiation table.

---

20. At the time there were no 'tanks' on Malta – there were about 100 Bren carriers, however. The Italians considered these to be 'tankettes' which could conceivably allow a rapid response to any landings. In addition, these carriers were invulnerable to Italian L3 tankettes' 8mm machine-gun fire. Cernuschi correspondence.
21. The thought that aerial bombing could neutralize the island and potentially cause Malta to sue for peace derived from the work of Italian general Giulio Douhet, an advocate of strategic bombing in aerial warfare. In his 1921 work Il dominio dell'aria (Command of the Air), he predicted that 'people bombed today and bombed yesterday will know they'll be bombed tomorrow and will see no end to their martyrdom and will call for peace'.
22. Maugeri, From the Ashes of Disgrace, p.75. At the time of the decision not to invade, Maugari had no influence on it.
23. Noppen, Malta 1940–42, pp.21, 35.
24. Caruana correspondence.
25. Boog, Horst, Germany and the Second World War, Vol III, p.247.
26. Ciano, 25 June 1940, p.269.
27. Corvaja, p.118.

Thus, most Italian demands were discarded. With the French Armistice signed on 24 June, Italy gained a little territory and the demilitarization of French territories around its African holdings – far less than Mussolini had been hoping its dead and wounded would gain him.

Cunningham decided in July to run merchant ships through to Egypt in conjunction with a fleet-sized sweep through the region. With three battleships, a carrier and escorting cruisers, he confronted a numerically larger Italian fleet, commanded by Admiral Inigo Campioni,[28] returning from running their convoy to Africa, off Calabria on 9 July. Despite being outgunned by three battleships to two, and outclassed as the 15in British battleships outranged and out-armoured Campioni's two capital ships, the Italian commander engaged aggressively. The quick Italian response meant Cunningham was unable to get all three of his battleships engaged. The brief battle saw little damage caused on either side, apart from a 15in hit scored against the Italian battleship *Giulio Cesare*, Italian cruiser *Bolzano* being hit and the British suffering splinter damage to multiple ships.[29]

More significantly, however, Italian aircraft dropped nearly 900 bombs during the battle – on both navies – but scored only a single hit. The actions by the Regia Aeronautica in bombing both fleets showed a significant weakness in Italian communications, as the bombers were following outdated orders which had indicated only British ships in their area of operation, ignorant of current Italian naval manoeuvres.[30] Abysmal communication between the Regia Aeronautica and Regia Marina caused Campioni to have no idea where the British were, despite the fact the Italian aircraft were attacking them.[31]

Six months after the battle, Cunningham wrote:

> 'The meagre material results derived from this brief meeting with the Italian Fleet were naturally disappointing to me and all under my command, but the action was not without value. It must have shown the Italians that their Air Force and submarines cannot stop our Fleet penetrating into the Central Mediterranean and that only their main fleet can seriously interfere with our operating there. It established, I think, a certain degree of moral ascendency, since although superior in battleships, our Fleet was heavily outnumbered in cruisers and destroyers, and the Italians had strong shore-based air forces within easy range, compared to our few carrier-borne aircraft.'[32]

However, despite the 'moral ascendency' mentioned, it would be three years before a major British battle fleet entered the central Mediterranean.

The battle initially left the Italians happy: Campioni because they had received little damage to their ships and had completed their mission of convoy escort, and the Regia

---

28. The Italians engaged with two battleships, six heavy cruisers, eight light cruisers and sixteen destroyers. Cunningham's Mediterranean Fleet had three battleships, four light cruisers and fourteen destroyers. The British carrier Eagle and light cruiser Gloucester were also in the area. O'Hara, Struggle for the Middle Sea, p.37.
29. ADM 234/444. Recent Italian analyses of the battle indicate they might also have scored 8in and 6in hits on the British ships. Cernuschi & Michele Maria Gaetani, 'La corazzata di vetro: La cinematica segreta di Punta Stilo, 9 Lugio 1940', Rivista Marittima (September 2018).
30. Greene & Massignani, p.77.
31. Simmons, p.36.
32. Grehan, John & Mace, Martin, War Despatches, p.3.

Aeronautica because they believed they had 'annihilated' half of the British naval power in the Mediterranean.[33] However, they soon learned differently. In response to the air force's poor anti-ship performance, Air Force Chief Francesco Pricolo formed an experimental torpedo bomber unit, the Reparto Sperimentale Aerosiluranti, at Gorizia-Merna airfield on 25 July. The unit of seven S.79 Sparvieros was trained and became operational at Tobruk's El Adem airfield in mid-August.[34]

On 2 August, a flight of twelve Hurricane reinforcements arrived on the island, delivered from the aircraft carrier HMS *Argus* in Operation *Hurry*, and Malta's first real fighter unit, 261 Squadron, was formed. Cunningham, noting the decrease in Italian bombing, sent a memorandum to the Chiefs of Staff, stating he wanted to start using Malta as a fuelling stop and to station better submarines there.[35] He recommended once again that the anti-aircraft defences on the island be bolstered. At the end of the month, the Chiefs approved his plan and added that they intended to ship an eight-month stock of provisions by April 1941 and maintain a consistent six-month reserve.[36]

Mussolini continued to push for more aggressive action, both to keep pace with the Germans and to advance his own imperial agenda. Consequently, in East Africa, Prince Amedeo of Savoy, Duke of Aosta, led an invasion of British Somaliland in early August and took the colony by the middle of the month at a cost of 2,000 casualties and most of his supplies.

But North Africa remained foremost on Mussolini's mind. The Italians had fourteen full regular divisions there, all with two regiments. The three Camicie Nere (CCNN) or Blackshirt divisions, plus two native divisions, each contributed 7,000 and 5,500 troops respectively. In total there were 221,000 troops in Libya in June 1940, increasing to 235,000 by November. Initially under the command of Maresciallo dell'Aria Italo Balbo, the plan was to take Mersa Matruh, a port 150 miles west of Alexandria, with two divisions, using 5,000 trucks escorted by a small armoured column. Balbo would wait there for his air force to compel the Royal Navy to evacuate its base at Alexandria. When friendly anti-aircraft fire near Tobruk killed Balbo on 28 June, Italian plans for a quick attack into Egypt came to an abrupt halt. Mussolini nominated Maresciallo Rodolfo Graziani, then the Army Chief of Staff, to replace Balbo. The elderly Graziani did not receive the posting well and created a significant delay in putting together an advance.[37]

Facing them initially were three incomplete Allied divisions: the 7th Armoured Division, with its 7 Brigade only partially equipped; the Fourth Indian Division, missing its entire 3 Brigade; and the New Zealand Division, with only three infantry battalions. There were also fourteen independent British battalions, creating a total of some 36,000 troops.[38] The intelligence arm of the Italian military, the Serviso Informazione Militari, provided pre-war assessments offering inaccurate estimates of 100,000 troops[39] opposing any Italian advance into Egypt, although they correctly identified the divisions directly facing them.

---

33. Simmons, p.40.
34. Mattioli, S.79 Sparviero Torpedo Bomber Units, p.7.
35. Four T-class submarines were returned to being based on Malta from 1 September 1940. Page, I, p.62.
36. Caruana, Malta's Maritime Diary, Ch 2.
37. Faldella, Guerre in Marmarica: Storia Illustrata, December 1970.
38. Prasad, Bisheshwar, North African Campaign, pp.44–45.
39. The number included troops stationed in Palestine and Sudan, as well as the 10,000 troops who arrived in July.

In early September the British Chiefs of Staff provided Churchill and his War Cabinet with an assessment of future strategy. They concluded that Germany's primary vulnerability was oil, adding that 'the wearing down of Germany by ever-increasing force of economic pressure should be the foundation of our strategy'. Their document predicted that Italy would attack Egypt from Libya and attempt to drive the British out to 'ensure tranquil trade for the transport of oil from the Black Sea'. Finally, they stated that 'the elimination of Italy and the consequent removal of the threat to our control of the Eastern Mediterranean would be a strategic success of the first order.... It will therefore be of great importance to turn to the offensive against Italy as soon as our resources permit.'[40]

On 13 September, Graziani led the Italian Tenth Army – the Cirene and Marinarica Divisions, the 23rd Marzo CCNN Division and two Libyan divisions, supported by 336 aircraft – into Egypt from Libya.[41] The Italians advanced 70 miles to Sidi Barrani and then stopped. Other than losing an airfield that cramped their air support, the British lost little in the invasion. Mussolini and the Germans immediately began pushing for a continued advance to Mersa Matruh.

Italy's incursion into Egypt gave the British the incentive to seriously upgrade the status of Malta. Churchill remained adamant about reinforcing the island, especially after a signal from Dobbie indicating that each of the island's battalions had been tasked with holding 15 miles of coastline, with no reserves 'worth speaking of'. Churchill's note to the War Cabinet stated the danger was 'extreme' and the island 'at the mercy of a landing force', which he later characterized as a 20,000–30,000-strong expeditionary force from Italy.[42] He wanted four more battalions sent, but would settle for two 'good' ones. While the Prime Minister pushed for more troops, the infantry on Malta spent their days 'dodging bombs, repairing bomb damage, filling in holes in runways and roads, rescuing people and salvaging food and equipment from bombed buildings, manning observation posts and trying to maintain their training for when they might be called upon for operations elsewhere'.[43] They also continued to prepare for the worst, stringing barbed wire along potential landing sites, sowing mines and building pillboxes and tank traps.[44]

In September, the convoy running under Operation *Hats* reinforced Cunningham's forces with the carrier HMS *Illustrious* and battleship HMS *Valiant*, plus several cruisers. It also delivered 7,800 tons of supplies to Malta, plus more anti-aircraft guns and ammunition.[45] The Italians failed to interdict the *Hats* convoy, despite the British being within the Regia Aeronautica's range for forty-eight hours. Their poor bombing accuracy, inadequate reconnaissance and slow command decision time proved a handicap in stopping the convoy.[46] The new S.79 torpedo bombers in North Africa were still working up; renamed the 278th

---

40. CAB 66/11/42, 'Future Strategy', paragraphs 5, 11 and 18.
41. Boog, Vol III, pp.271–72.
42. Gilbert, Churchill War Papers, 21–24 September 1940, pp.848, 865.
43. Jary, They Couldn't have Done Better, p.33.
44. Boffa, Second Great Siege, p.31.
45. At least one source stated that Hats delivered 40,000 tons of supplies (Thomas, Malta Convoys, p.28); however, the two cargo ships Volo (1,587 tons) and Cornwall (11,288 tons) couldn't have carried that much. Caruana correspondence.
46. O'Hara, Passage Perilous, p.16.

Squadriglia Autonoma Aerosiluranti, they finally achieved a success by torpedoing the British heavy cruiser HMS *Kent* off Bardia on 17 September.[47]

Convoy MF3 arrived on 11 October with four ships carrying another 30,000 tons.

As the Italians settled in at Sidi Barrani, German and Italian officials met to chart future events. The continuing conflict with Britain remained foremost on Hitler's mind, so he did not want distractions, urging the Italians to press their assault on Egypt. Furthermore, Hitler wanted the Balkans, a key Italian interest, to stay quiet. However, miscommunication between the two sides left a huge gap in what each took from the meeting. The Italians came away feeling they had been given carte blanche in the Balkans, while the Germans felt they had persuaded Italy to agree not to start anything there.[48] When German troops arrived in the Romanian capital of Bucharest in mid-October, without prior notification to Italy,[49] Mussolini felt insulted.

In response to the perceived affront, Mussolini decided to pay the Germans 'back in their own coin'[50] and at the same time settle accounts with Greece by invading from Albania. His decision was a direct challenge to his ally – Germany's Foreign Minister, Joachim von Ribbentrop, had twice warned the Italians not to attack Yugoslavia or Greece, and Mussolini had promised no action without discussing it first with Germany.[51]

The timing for Mussolini's payback proved awkward as the Italians had just started a major demobilization of nearly 600,000 troops affecting all of their units – a move needed to bolster the country's economy and agriculture; some 54 per cent of its military expected to be sent home.[52] However, Sebastiano Visconti Prasca, commander-in-chief of Italy's forces in Albania, assured Mussolini that they held a two-to-one superiority in troops against what he termed as 'depressed' Greek soldiers who probably wouldn't fight, and that he could finish the campaign in ten to fifteen days.[53] One historian described the discussion to invade Greece by Mussolini and his generals as 'one of the most superficial and dilettantish discussions of high risk strategy ever recorded'.[54]

On 28 October 1940, the Italians invaded Greece with six divisions, led by their elite Julia Alpine Division's 10,800 men, along a 150-mile front. Mussolini's orders to Prasca were to 'attack with maximum decisiveness and violence; success of this action depends above all on speed'.[55]

The Italian leader proudly announced the invasion to a surprised Hitler at Florence the same day; the Germans had noted the build-up of Italian troops on the Albanian border, but had been told it was precautionary in nature in case Britain decided to violate Greece's neutrality. Mussolini ended his announcement with the prediction: 'Don't worry; in two weeks, it will be all over.'[56]

---

47. Mattioli, p.9.
48. Boog, Vol III, p.403.
49. This point is controversial. German historians claim that Italy was informed by Foreign Minister Joachim von Ribbentrop at the 19 September meeting (Boog, Vol III, p.402), but others claim there was no prior warning (Cervi, The Hollow Legions, p.59). The German history does make the stipulation that Mussolini himself might not have known, since the aforementioned notification went to Italy's Foreign Minister, Ciano.
50. Ciano, 12 October 1940, p.300.
51. Cruikshank, Charles, Greece 1940–1941, p.31.
52. Carr, p.23.
53. Boog, Vol III, p.411.
54. Kershaw, p.171.
55. Carr, p.28.
56. Corvaja, p.142.

Hitler's reacted to the Greek invasion with anger and disgust. He opined to his commanders that the Italians had blundered seriously with inadequate forces and should have attacked Malta.[57] Worse, it improved the British strategic picture with moves into Crete which brought the invaluable Romanian oil fields within range of British bombers based in Greece.[58]

The reinforced Greek 8th Division initially opposed the Italians, defending from trenches and falling back slowly, planning to delay the Italians for at least three weeks while the rest of the country mobilized.[59] Despite Mussolini's call for speed, poor weather and unexpectedly heavy resistance kept the Italian advance to a crawl, gaining only 20 miles in three days.

Churchill almost immediately began demanding support for the Greeks, stating that 'the collapse of Greece without any effort from us would have a deadly effect on Turkey and the future of the war'.[60] British bombers were dispatched to Greece and Crete, with additional bombers sent to Malta to increase pressure on Italy.

In November, the Greek cavalry counter-attacked, surrounding and virtually destroying the Julia Division and driving the Italians back into Albania. Hitler began to make plans to intervene in Greece, with both a lecture on strategy and a promise of support for the flagging Italians. Despite relief at the rescue by his Axis partner, the moves deeply embarrassed Mussolini, who complained: 'Hitler rapped me on the knuckles like a school boy.'[61]

On the same day the Italians invaded Greece, twelve Wellington heavy bombers were sent to Luqa on Malta specifically to bomb Naples' oil tanks. However, they remained on the island, forming 148 Squadron, much to the satisfaction of Malta's leaders – both air commander Maynard and Governor Dobbie witnessed the initial send-off on 31 October.[62] However, the next mission on 3 November ended badly with two of four bombers crashing upon take-off, one into nearby Qormi, killing most of the crew plus civilians on the ground.[63]

There were other events in November that affected Malta. The Royal Navy launched MB8, a complex series of eight separate smaller-scale operations. Among them was convoy MW3 (*Coat*), which delivered 26,000 tons of supplies and the Royal East Kent Regiment's 4th Battalion (The Buffs) to Malta on 9 November.[64]

More significantly, the British also launched Operation *Judgment*, an attack on the Italian anchorage at Taranto. Such an attack had been discussed since the mid-1930s when the possibility of war with Italy loomed. On 11 November, Swordfish torpedo bombers of 813, 185 and 824 squadrons led by Lieutenant Commander K. Williamson, flying off the carrier HMS *Illustrious*, attacked the southern Italian anchorage in two separate waves.[65] Reconnaissance flights out of Malta had shown virtually the entire Regia Marina's battle force at anchor at Taranto: all six battleships, including the modern *Littorio* and *Vittorio Veneto*, and six heavy cruisers. At the cost of two aircraft and one crew, three Italian battleships were severely damaged. The *Littorio* would not return to the Italian Fleet until March 1941, the *Caio*

---

57. Ibid., p.144.
58. Showell, Naval Affairs, 4 November 1940, pp.146–47.
59. Boog, Vol III, p.433.
60. Gilbert, Vol 2, p.1,033.
61. Corvaja, p.147.
62. Jacobs, p.46.
63. Malta at War, Vol 1, pp.319–20.
64. Kostam, Taranto, p.42.
65. Simmons, p.51. Such a raid had been discussed from the time of the Abyssinian crisis in 1935.

Duilio in May 1941, while the *Conti di Cavour* never saw action again.[66] The naval situation had changed so dramatically that Churchill actually suggested using Malta-based troops to invade the small Italian-controlled island of Pantelleria between Sicily and Tunisia.[67]

The second operation to reinforce Malta's Hurricane force, code name *White*, ended in disaster on 17 November. Launched from HMS *Argus* too far away from the island, eight of the twelve aircraft failed to make it to Malta, losing their way and running out of fuel. Seven of the eight pilots were lost.[68]

Following the Taranto success, the *Collar* convoy delivered 20,000 tons of supplies, troops, an artillery unit and a troop of tanks – four Matilda Mk II infantry tanks and two Mk VI light tanks – on 26 November to bolster Malta's ground defences. The incoming convoy sparked another brief clash between the two fleets off Cape Teulada the following day.

The British, under the Gibraltar-based Force H's Admiral James Somerville, had the battlecruiser *Renown* and battleship *Ramilles*, along with one heavy and four light cruisers; also supporting him was the carrier *Ark Royal*. The Italians were led by Admiral Campioni, who had two battleships, including the newer *Vittorio Veneto*, and six heavy cruisers, but he operated under amazingly contradictory orders: 'Avoid action with the enemy if he enjoys an evident superiority ... [but] be animated by a highly aggressive spirit at all times.'[69]

Both sides were perplexed by inaccurate reconnaissance reports, garbled communications and mechanical difficulties. After an hour of gunfire at extreme ranges and air attacks from the British carrier, Campioni withdraw, suffering damage to a single destroyer, while the British cruiser HMS *Berwick* took two hits.[70] The British chose not to pursue the faster Italians, returning instead to their primary duty of convoy protection. Churchill and some Admiralty officials were incensed at Somerville's lack of 'offensive spirit' and almost fired him for it, but an inquiry cleared him and he stayed in his position.[71]

Most Italians were happy with the battle's outcome, but the Navy was not. Mussolini replaced Cavagnari, the Naval Chief of Staff, with Ammiraglio Arturo Riccardi, and Campioni, the Fleet commander, with Ammiraglio Angelo Iachino.[72]

If events in Greece and at Taranto embarrassed Mussolini, matters became even worse in North Africa. There, Graziani had deployed his army into nine fortified positions while he developed better logistics to continue his assault eastward into Egypt. General Sir Archibald Wavell, the British commander-in-chief in the Middle East, took advantage of the fact that the Italian positions did not mutually support each other, sending the

---

66. Mawdsley, p.120.
67. Operation Workshop, the capture of Pantelleria, was one of Churchill's pet projects. He felt its seizure would 'give good Air command of the most used line of enemy communication with the Libyan Army as well as increase Air protection for British convoys'. Cunningham disapproved of the venture, as did the Defence Planning Council and the War Cabinet, and the project was dropped from consideration. Gilbert, Churchill War Papers, pp.1033, 1174, 1205–07.
68. Shores & Cull, Hurricane Years, pp.87–88.
69. O'Hara, Struggle, p.66.
70. Simmons, p.93.
71. Churchill was still unhappy about Somerville's critical views on the British action at Mers-el-Kebir in July 1940, when, after France signed an armistice with Germany, Force H bombarded the French Navy at Churchill's orders to avoid it being delivered into Hitler's hands. First Lord of the Admiralty A.V. Alexander and First Sea Lord Admiral Sir Dudley Pound supported Churchill's suggestion that Somerville be replaced. Roskill, Churchill and the Admirals, pp.169–70.
72. Mawdsley, pp.121–22.

4th Indian Division and 7th Royal Tank Regiment, under General Richard O'Connor, to infiltrate the Italian front line in early December. On 9 December, they attacked the Italians from the rear and in just three days drove the Italians out of Egypt, capturing 38,000 prisoners along with 237 guns and over 1,000 vehicles.[73] Four days later, the pass at Sollum on the Egyptian border fell.

With the Italians in retreat throughout the Mediterranean region, Hitler felt he had no choice but to intervene and help shore up the ally holding his southern flank. In late November he offered German bombers to Mussolini, who readily agreed. On 10 December, the Führer formally ordered Operation *Mittelmeer*, assigning the Luftwaffe the objectives of protecting the convoy routes to Africa, shutting the Royal Navy out of the central Mediterranean and neutralizing Malta. His initial orders did not envision sending any ground forces to Africa.[74] As a result, Fliegerkorps X's General Hans Ferdinand Geisler, acknowledged as one of the foremost anti-shipping experts in the Luftwaffe,[75] was ordered to the Mediterranean from Norway. On 29 December, his aircraft started landing at five Sicilian airfields – 102 Me109s, thirty-six Me110s, eighty-four Ju88s, 144 Ju87 Stukas and thirty-six He111 torpedo bombers – along with a trainload of ground crews.[76]

Malta ended 1940 in considerably better shape that it had been at the start of its war in June. Despite some 153 air raids,[77] it boasted increased troop strength, increased anti-aircraft weaponry and increased offensive aircraft – sixteen Wellingtons and twelve Swordfish torpedo bombers. Some 178,000 tons of supplies had been delivered safely to Valletta but, although consumptive reserves now stood at a seven-month level,[78] the deliveries actually represented only 75 per cent of what Cunningham had felt the island needed. Plus, Malta's defensive fighter strength still amounted to only sixteen Hurricanes and four Gladiators, a marginal strength level against the Italians even in their current state of inactivity – the island had suffered less than eighteen raids from mid-October to mid-November, with two full weeks without a raid.[79]

In addition to being infrequent, Italian bombing also proved less than effective. One resident described the Italian bombing style as half-hearted and uncommon.[80] The wife of a battalion officer recalled:

> 'Italian bombing, such as it was, began quite soon, but it was all their air force could do to hit the island, let alone any specific targets, and we were much amused to hear Italian radio bulletins claiming they had destroyed "the main railway station of Malta" (there was no rail system on the island) or "had sunk HMS St Angelo in Valletta Harbour" (HMS St Angelo being the naval headquarters, a medieval stone fortress).'[81]

---

73. Playfair, Vol I, p.273; Boog, Vol III, p.654.
74. Ibid., p.315.
75. Probert, The Rise and Fall of the German Air Force, p.129.
76. Grech, p.46.
77. Jary, They Couldn't have Done Better, p.39.
78. Austin, Churchill and Malta's War, p.73.
79. Jellison, p.55.
80. Agius, Maurice, Recollections of a Malta HAA Gunner, p.16.
81. Suzanne Parlby, wife of Captain John Parlby, 2nd Devonshires. Jary, Yells, Bells & Smells, p.20.

The original leader of the Hal Far Fighter Flight, Lieutenant George Burges, recalled that only 'half the bombs went off and those that did went pop instead of bang'.[82]

During December, Italy had sent 136 freighters to Africa, carrying over 29,000 men and 297,000 tons of supplies with minimal losses. In supplying Malta, the British had sent twenty-five ships, only one of which was damaged. Neither side was interdicting the other's supply lines in a significant way.[83]

In January 1941, Captain George 'Shrimp' Simpson[84] arrived on Malta to assume command of the submarines that had been operating out of Manoel Island inside Marsamxett harbour, with their headquarters in Lazzaretto, an abandoned leper hospital. Up to that point, Malta-based submarines had sunk nine ships and an Italian U-boat totalling about 37,000 tons, but had also lost nine boats. The Admiralty had concluded that the modern T-class submarines (1,290 tons with ten torpedo tubes, four of them external) were too large for the Mediterranean and were thus sending Simpson the smaller U-class boats (540 tons, four torpedo tubes and four reloads). Initially, Simpson commanded four U-class boats: N89 (*Upright*), N19 (*Utmost*), N95 (*Unique*) and P37 (*Upholder*). His orders were 'to deprive the Italian Army in Libya of supplies by sinking southbound shipping'.[85]

In Africa, O'Connor continued his advance in early January, reinforcing the attacking troops with the 6th Australian Division. On 5 January, the Italian fortress of Bardia fell, netting the Allies another 40,000 Italian troops killed or captured, along with 400 guns and 130 tanks.[86] Twenty-five thousand more were taken prisoner three weeks later during the Australians' successful assault on Tobruk.[87] In a single month, Graziani had lost the equivalent of eight divisions.

Italy's African disaster compelled more action on the part of the Germans. Hitler told his commanders that while he didn't care whether Libya fell to the British or not, he felt its fall would affect Italian public opinion and possibly knock Italy out of the war, and he could not afford to let Italy collapse.[88] Consequently, he decided to dispatch an anti-tank blocking force to Africa to bolster the Italians and, as part of his 11 January Directive 22, ordered Operation *Sonnenblume* – the dispatch of the 5th Light Motorized Division,[89] under General Erwin Rommel, to Tripoli. Even as the Germans arrived, the Italian retreat continued. By mid-February, they had been driven completely out of Cyrenaica, with the Italian Tenth Army virtually destroyed, suffering the loss of 130,000 prisoners. Almost as a sideline, Hitler ordered his operations staffs to work up invasion plans against Malta.[90]

---

82. Poolman, Faith, Hope & Charity, p.83.
83. O'Hara, Six Victories, tables 1.1 and 1.2.
84. 'Shrimp' was Simpson's nickname due to his 'small and stocky' nature. Jacobs, p.43.
85. Simpson, p.101. At the end of 1942, Churchill ordered submarines to receive names rather than just pennant numbers. Most U-class submarines, with the exception of Una (N87) and Utmost (N19), were known only by their pennant number; names such as Unbroken (P42) and United (P44) were assigned in late 1942 and early 1943. Caruana correspondence.
86. Playfair, Vol I, p.287.
87. Ibid., p.293.
88. Boog, Vol III, p.654.
89. The 5th Light Division as dispatched had a strong reconnaissance unit, two machine-gun battalions and two anti-tank battalions, plus a two-battalion panzer regiment with seventy light and eighty medium tanks. Playfair, Vol II, p.14. Some 25,000 men and 8,500 vehicles were safely delivered to Tripoli.
90. Caruana, Malta's Maritime Diary, Ch 3.

Meanwhile, once operational, Geisler's aircraft in Sicily had an immediate impact, surprising the Mediterranean Fleet, which had not been warned of the German presence on Sicily.[91] The carrier HMS *Illustrious* was participating in Operation *Excess*, a complex four-convoy passage, escorting the merchant ship *Excess*, carrying ammunition, seed potatoes and crated Hurricane fighters to Malta, when German and Italian Ju87 Stuka dive bombers[92] struck. Within minutes they had slammed six bombs into the carrier, which barely made it to Malta with damaged steering and able to make only 15 knots; 126 of its crew had been killed and ninety-one more injured in the attack and subsequent fires. The battleships *Warspite* and *Valiant* were also hit and damaged; one of their escorts, the cruiser *Southampton*, wasn't so lucky, being sunk by the aerial onslaught.

At Malta, the damaged *Illustrious* limped into Grand Harbour, still ablaze, and berthed at Parlatorio Wharf in French Creek for emergency repairs. Three days later, after several reconnaissance flights, a small group of Stuka dive bombers tried to hit the damaged carrier using 2,000lb bombs.[93] They missed, but the bombs gave a portent of what was coming.

London sent Malta a warning on the morning of 16 January about impending raids, intercepted through Ultra.[94] To protect the carrier, the authorities put together a plan for a box barrage system,[95] a carefully coordinated anti-aircraft gun orchestration to keep a continuous cloud of flak that aircraft would have to fly through, disrupting their attack. At 2.00 pm, the Luftwaffe launched what the Maltese called the '*Illustrious* Blitz', as forty-four Stukas and seventeen Ju88 bombers, heavily escorted by fighters, hammered the Grand Harbour area trying to finish off the carrier. In the two-hour attack, they only succeeded in hitting the carrier once, but the surrounding cities, Cottonera and Senglea especially, took the brunt of the collateral damage[96] – records say over 301 homes were destroyed, with dozens of civilians trapped in the rubble for days after. One eyewitness thought 'it was the end of the world'.[97] The bombers also hit the freighter *Excess* while it was unloading, killing fifteen of the crew and seven Maltese stevedores.[98] Fortunately, the fires that started were extinguished before the ship's cargo of 4,000 tons of ammunition exploded.

---

91. The lack of warning was either because the Air Ministry didn't inform the Admiralty, or the Ministry assumed no warning was needed because of the current threat from the Italian Regia Aeronautica. Whatever the case, neither Cunningham nor Force H at sea had much warning prior to the initial attack. Hinsley, Vol I, p.385.
92. The Italians received and were trained in Ju87s starting in July 1940, operating them through 96 and 97 Gruppo Bombardamento a Tuffo (BaT). Dunning, Courage Alone, pp.119–21. The Ju87s which were part of the attack on Illustrious were part of 236a Squadriglia. Noppen, p.50.
93. The three-day respite was due to the lack of German ordnance in Sicily; Geisler's pilots had used virtually all heavy bombs available during the attack at sea. Ibid., p.51.
94. Boffa, Illustrious, p.20. Ultra was the code name given to German Enigma machine intercepts during the war. These intercepts had a tightly controlled distribution to avoid revealing the breakthrough to the Axis.
95. A box barrage is defined as each anti-aircraft gun directing its fire at certain segments of the sky, rather than specific enemy aircraft. Jellison, p.90. Credit for organizing the barrage was given to Colonel N.V. Sandler, commander of 7 Anti-aircraft Brigade and Anti-aircraft Defence Commander at the time. Rollo, Guns and Gunners of Malta, p.211. Credit for actually devising the box barrage concept went to Professor Mark Appleby, a Royal Engineer who taught mathematics at the Royal University of Malta. Malta at War, Vol 2, p.470.
96. Boffa, Illustrious, p.27.
97. Wingate, p.25.
98. Caruana, Malta's Maritime Diary, Ch 3.

needed.[118] While they planned and positioned troops, they requested Italian naval action against the influx of British troops to Greece.

On 16 March, the German Liaison Office gave a memorandum to the Regia Marina stating that Luftwaffe attacks three days previously had damaged two British battleships, leaving only a single enemy battleship available, thus making the situation in the eastern Mediterranean 'favourable' for the Italians. The Italian Fleet therefore had the opportunity to seriously disrupt British shipping and troop transport into Greece.[119]

As the Italians and Germans negotiated their interdiction operation, Cunningham ran a supply convoy (MW6) of four ships into Malta, surprisingly with no opposition, delivering some 35,000 tons of supplies on 23 March.[120] At sea, his entire battle force – including the battleships the Germans had reported 'damaged' – provided distant escort and returned to Alexandria the following day.

As Ammiraglio Riccardi had noted at Merano, the Regia Marina continued having difficulty with its fuel supply – it had used about 55 per cent of its stockpile and had only another four months' worth left for full service. The Germans offered 50,000 tons a month, but this proved a stop-gap and only provided a quarter of monthly usage.[121] Nevertheless, for political reasons, the Italians agreed to send their ships out. Promised strong air support from the Germans, Ammiraglio Angelo Iachino, Campioni's replacement as the Italian Fleet commander, launched Operation *Guado*. This took a strong force of cruisers and his flagship, the battleship Vittorio Veneto, to perform offensive sweeps north and south of Crete, sailing on the evening of 26 March.

Before the Italians left port, Cunningham, through what he called 'various indications', knew the Italians were planning a major operation. He assessed it as an attack on the ongoing Greek troop convoys, although he did not rule out an attack on Malta.[122] He therefore cancelled the Greek convoys as a precaution and prepared to react when the Italian fleet was spotted at sea.

Although the Luftwaffe reconnaissance sighted a major Royal Navy force at sea, this report failed to be passed on to Iachino.[123] On 28 March, a running gun battle between cruisers, air attacks from the British carrier *Formidable* – which had arrived that month as a replacement for *Illustrious* – and no air support from the Germans led Iachino to retire. The aerial attacks succeeded in hitting the *Vittorio Veneto* with a torpedo that afternoon, which initially stopped the ship. Repairs allowed it to get under way in short order. At dusk, the final air attack hit the heavy cruiser *Pola*, forcing it out of formation.

That night, off Cape Matapan, Iachino dispatched Ammiraglio Carlo Cattaneo's 1st Cruiser Division (heavy cruisers *Zara* and *Fiume*) back to find the crippled *Pola* and escort

---

118. Showell, Naval Affairs, p.185.
119. Simmons, pp.77–78. According to Thiele in Luftwaffe Aerial Torpedo Aircraft, the 13 March attack was made by two He111s from II/KG26. He also states: "It was thought that two British battleships may have been hit and despite some doubts on the part of the Germans, the Italian Navy considered the presumed hits as an accomplished fact." This is a different view of who thought what. Thiele, pp.28–29.
120. Thomas, Malta Convoys, Appendix II, p.197.
121. Simmons, p.76.
122. Simpson, Cunningham Papers, pp.313–14; the 'various indications' were Ultra/Enigma decryptions. Hinsley, Vol I, p.404.
123. Boog, Vol III, p.669. The non-notification was odd, since Iachino had two Luftwaffe officers, Captain Withus and Lieutenant Moser, aboard his flagship specifically to provide Luftwaffe communications. Iachino, Gaudo & Matapan, p.60.

it to safety. The unprepared Italians blundered into point-blank range of the radar-equipped British battleships *Warspite*, *Valiant* and *Barham*. The *Fiume* was hit by the first five of six 15in rounds that *Warspite* fired from a range of only 2,900–3,000 yards.[124] Both cruisers were sunk. The British also found the immobilized *Pola* and sank it too. Cunningham wrote in his report: 'The Italians were quite unprepared. Their guns were trained fore and aft. They were helplessly shattered before they could put up any resistance.'[125] In Britain, Churchill exulted in the destruction of 'the paper fleet of the Italians'.[126]

The disaster led to recriminations between the Axis allies, with the Italians blaming the lack of promised air support and the Germans the inadequate tactical execution and training of the Italian Navy.[127] Mussolini himself blamed the lack of air cover and quickly authorized the conversion of the passenger liner *Roma* to be the aircraft carrier *Aquila*. Other Italians pointed the finger at Mussolini: 'Matapan was the result of the mistake of 1923. We were like a well-trained powerful boxer who had lost his eyesight.'[128]

In Africa, however, the Axis supply situation improved significantly, with 80,000 tons of supplies delivered in February and 93,000 tons in March, plus nearly 40,000 troops.[129] Rommel, against the orders of his purported superior, Generale Italo Gariboldi – who took over after Graziani resigned – launched a 'tactical reconnaissance' at the end of March.[130] Striking the weak forces Wavell had left on the western frontier of Cyrenaica,[131] Rommel's mixed force of German and Italian armoured units made spectacular progress eastward, rivalling Wavell's progress west two months previously. Two weeks later, he was throwing his troops against the British enclave at Tobruk.

In late March, a coup in Yugoslavia overturned the national government's signature into the Axis Tripartite Agreement. Then on 6 April, the Germans launched their anticipated attack into Yugoslavia and Greece. The German Twelfth Army sent some 230,000 troops into southern Yugoslavia and Greece, while the Second Army, with 125,000 troops, poured into northern Yugoslavia. Overwhelmed, the country surrendered on 17 April.[132] A day later, Greek Prime Minister Alexandros Koryzis committed suicide and the Greeks surrendered the following week. After Greece's surrender, the British spent the following week evacuating as many troops as possible. Ultimately, over 50,000 were rescued, with 60 per cent of them transported to Crete – with very little of their equipment. The Greek intervention had cost the British some 16,000 casualties, including almost 14,000 captured.[133]

---

124. Simmons, p.122; Pack, p.85.
125. Winton, Cunningham, pp.162–63.
126. Gilbert, Vol 3, p.424.
127. Both sides had valid reason for their arguments, but the key factors were the British radar and Italian lack of night-time combat-readiness. Boog, Vol III, p.670; Sadkovich, p.132.
128. In 1923, Mussolini created the Regia Aeronautica, giving the new organization total control of aircraft assets in Italy. Naval requests for an aircraft carrier – with aircraft under their control – were refused on the grounds that Italy itself was an unsinkable flattop. Maugeri, pp.18, 28.
129. O'Hara, Six Victories, Table 1.4.
130. Kitchen, Rommel, p.73.
131. Covering forces included 3 Armoured Brigade, with one regiment made up of captured Italian tanks, 3 Indian Motorized Brigade and the newly arrived 9th Australian Division. Bharucha, p.137. Against them, Rommel ultimately had his 5th Light Division and 15th Panzer Division, plus the Italian Ariete Armoured Division and the Brescia Division. Boog, Vol III, p.679.
132. Boog, Vol III, p.522.
133. Playfair, Vol II, p.105; Higham, Diary, p.259, n.272.

By mid-April, Rommel had invested Tobruk and reached the Egyptian border at Sollum.

Coinciding with the German blitz into the Balkans and North Africa, Fliegerkorps X increased their attacks on Malta throughout April and May. Some 2,000 homes were damaged or destroyed and more than 11,000 people made homeless.[134] One of the more devastating weapons used at this time was the parachute mine. Ostensibly aimed at making Malta's harbours unsafe for ships, these mines caused massive damage to land structures when they drifted inland.[135] The Germans achieved almost full air superiority despite the reinforcement of thirty-six Hurricanes flown in from the carrier *Ark Royal* with operations *Winch* (3 April) and *Dunlop* (27 April.)[136] Air Vice Marshal Maynard outlined the weaknesses in Malta's air defences: too little ground support, inferior aircraft and tired, overworked and inexperienced pilots.[137] The Maltese government continued putting a major effort into digging shelters in the island's limestone.

In April, rationing started for sugar, matches, soap and coffee. The Governor requested voluntary rationing of kerosene, which unfortunately caused the monthly purchases of the fluid to immediately double, so in May he was forced to add it to the rationing list.[138]

Rationing didn't initially cause too much discomfort. Maltese meals at the time typically consisted of bread, tomatoes and onions in olive oil, so flour and edible oils were essential. The island had these in good supply. In addition, potatoes were abundant. Malta usually exported some 10,000 tons of potatoes a year, but now these were available for the population.[139]

The ground troops stayed very busy supporting the RAF on the island. In two months, they laid 27 miles of dispersal runways and built fourteen large bomber pens, 170 fighter pens, seventy reconnaissance aircraft pens and thirty-one naval air pens – all this on top of patrolling Malta's 95 miles of coastline.[140]

In early April, Churchill made it clear that he thought it 'vitally important to attack German transports by surface, submarine and air forces with the utmost vigour'.[141] Cunningham concurred, but warned: '[T]hese destroyers run considerable risk of damage from air attacks at Malta, but in view of the situation, I consider this risk must be taken.'[142] On 10 April, the 14th Destroyer Flotilla – *Nubian*, *Jervis*, *Mohawk* and *Janus*, commanded by Captain Philip John Mack – arrived at the island to begin that risky work.

Mack's flotilla, constrained by the Luftwaffe to operating only at night, missed their first two interception attempts, something Churchill declared as 'a serious Naval failure'.[143] The Prime Minister, faced with a deteriorating situation in the Mediterranean, issued two directives in April, the first on the 12th stating: 'A heavy risk should be run by the Royal Navy to break up Tripoli and cut the communications. Not only should destroyers and light cruisers from Malta prey on the convoys, aided by our submarines, but a strong assault should be made by capital

---

134. Micallef, p.77.
135. Boffa, Second Great Siege, p.36.
136. Vella, Philip, Malta: Blitzed but not Beaten, p.239.
137. Austin, Churchill and Malta's War, p.88.
138. Malta at War, Vol 1, #12, p.318.
139. Jellison, pp.131–32.
140. Originally, the pens were made up of sandbags, but the troops were soon using empty petrol cans and oil drums, plus stones from ruined buildings. Air Battle for Malta, Ch VI. Full text is located at ww2airfronts.org/theaters/mto/hmso-malta/hmso).html.
141. Austin, Churchill and Malta's War, p.99.
142. Ibid., p.100.
143. Ibid., 102.

ships.'[144] He followed this on the following day with: 'It becomes the prime duty of the British Mediterranean Fleet ... to stop all sea-borne traffic between Italy and Africa by the fullest use of surface craft, aided so far as possible by aircraft and submarines. For this all-important objective, heavy losses in battleships, cruisers and destroyers must if necessary be accepted.'[145]

Mack's flotilla finally scored on 16 April. For the loss of the *Mohawk*, they sank five merchant ships and two escort destroyers of a convoy ferrying Germans troops, vehicles and stores to Africa. The attack, directed by Ultra intercepts,[146] resulted in the loss of over half the troops being transported, along with 300 vehicles and 3,500 tons of supplies.[147] The disaster caused the Luftwaffe, at its commander Hermann Göring's personal insistence, to concentrate their efforts on the ships at Malta rather than the harbour installations or warehouses. The change put more emphasis on Großadmiral Raeder's recommendation (made at Merano in February) to capture the island.

Mack's success was not the only blow suffered by Italy. Early on the morning of 21 April, Cunningham led his fleet's three battleships and carrier *Formidable* to bombard and bomb Tripoli, the only large-capacity Axis port in North Africa. However, other than 400 casualties on the ground, the attack had minimal effect – Tripoli closed for a single day in its aftermath despite being hit with over 500 tons of naval ordnance. The worst part of the attack was the fact that it came as a complete surprise to the Axis.[148]

The Italians also failed to interdict the passage of the *Tiger* convoy – five ships carrying nearly 300 tanks and fifty crated aircraft from Gibraltar to Alexandria right through the central Mediterranean. A single ship was lost to a mine and one destroyer was hit with a torpedo, but 238 tanks were landed in Egypt, altering the balance of power. The Italian services pointed fingers at each other for the interdiction failure – the mariners for the Air Force not doing much despite grandiose claims, and the airmen for the Navy's total absence in the battle.[149]

Simpson's submarines, operating out of Malta since January, had been having a slow start to their campaign against Axis shipping, sinking only six freighters and one light cruiser until March.[150] One of his captains, Lieutenant Commander Malcolm Wanklyn in P37, had carried out four patrols and fired twenty torpedoes with nothing to show for it, which had Simpson seriously doubting his ability.[151] Wanklyn finally scored on his fifth patrol at the end of April, then made up for it with three successes in May, including the 18,000-ton liner *Conte Rosso*, carrying some 2,700 troops to Africa – half of whom were lost. That particular sinking earned him the Victoria Cross.[152] By the end of May, Simpson's flotilla had sunk over 64,000 tons of shipping, but at the cost of the loss of N65 (*Usk*) and N55 (*Undaunted*).

The increase in naval activity created its own problems; the Luftwaffe's dominance in the air, the mining of the harbour and its approaches and the scarcity of fuel oil all impacting

---

144. Gilbert, Vol 3, p.483.
145. Ibid., p.496.
146. Hinsley, Vol I, pp.394–400. In order to protect Ultra decryption, any Ultra-directed interception at sea had to be 'covered' by an air or submarines reconnaissance report.
147. Smith, Peter & Walker, Edwin, The Battles of the Malta Striking Forces, p.26.
148. Playfair, Vol II, p.112.
149. The Regia Aeronautica claimed two battleships, two aircraft carriers, four cruisers and three of the five merchantmen hit by their attacks. Malta at War, Vol 3, p.818.
150. Caruana, Malta's Maritime Diary, Ch 3, Appendix 16. The Italian cruiser Armando Diaz was sunk by HMS Upright on 25 February1941.
151. Wingate, pp.34–35; Simpson, p.126.
152. Austin, Churchill and Malta's War, p.100.

operations. These problems came to a head when, on 2 May, the destroyer HMS *Jersey* hit a mine while entering the harbour, breaking the ship in two. The wreck closed the harbour for three days before divers could place enough explosives to sink it enough to allow other shipping to pass it.[153]

Meanwhile, as the Greek campaign came to a close, German leaders meeting in Monichkirchen, Austria, faced a difficult choice for a follow-on assault: Malta or Crete. An attack on Malta would open the shipping lanes from Italy, interdict the central Mediterranean and provide a blocking position against any future Allied move on Southern Europe.[154] But the capture of Crete from the British would allow Luftwaffe bases to interdict shipping through the Suez Canal as well as push the British back from threatening the Romanian oil fields.[155] Hitler's decision the previous December to invade the Soviet Union complicated the issue,[156] something the Italians did not know about. With that stupendous effort in the wings, only one of the islands could be assaulted. The Wehrmacht operations staff supported an attack on Malta as an 'essential prerequisite for a successful war against Britain in the Mediterranean'.[157]

Yet, however much strategic sense it made for the Axis to take Malta, Hitler's concern for his oil supply took precedence. Prior to the war, much of Germany's oil came from the United States, Venezuela and Iran. Once the war began, those import sources were blockaded, only partially being made up for from Romania and the Soviet Union. Since the Führer planned to invade Russia, the Romanian oil fields became his only certain source of oil prior to the expected capture of the Soviet Caucasus fields. Thus, he felt that 'the very life of the Axis depends on those [Romanian] fields'[158] and he chose to attack Crete to protect that supply from British bombers. Hitler's Directive 28 specified Operation *Merkur* against Crete, but also mentioned that after occupying Crete, the airborne forces would be prepared for new tasks, implying Malta would be next.[159]

While the Germans prepared for *Merkur*, the Italians began rethinking their June 1940 assessment of Malta. Then, they had dismissed Malta as a non-decisive target; now, with the threat confirmed against their supply line to North Africa and the increased escort costs needed to protect those convoys – especially after the convoy slaughter of 16 April – they revisited and revised their invasion plans. The initial revision, labelled N.103, called for the use of 40,000 troops, with 4,000 of them landed in the vanguard. However, the Italians realized they needed specialized equipment – the invasion plan called for motor barges of about 8 tons, equipped with silent motors, a drop ramp, machine guns and space for forty troops. Construction started, with aid also requested from Germany, but the Italians realized it would be months before they could execute the attack.[160]

On 20 May, German paratroops dropped on Crete, where 32,000 defenders awaited them, partially warned ahead of time by Ultra intercepts. Yet despite the forewarning, the attack succeeded, but only at a heavy cost to the elite Fallschirmjäger troops. Of the island's defenders, some 18,000 were eventually evacuated to Egypt, leaving over 15,000 as prisoners

---

153. Caruana, Malta's Maritime Diary, Ch 3.
154. Boog, Vol III, p.528.
155. Ibid., p.529.
156. Directive 21, 18 December 1940: Operation Barbarossa; Showell, Naval Affairs, p.159.
157. Boog, Vol III, p.530.
158. Quoted in Hayward, Stopped at Stalingrad, p.4.
159. Trevor-Roper, Hitler's War Directives, p.118.
160. Gabrielle, Operation C3, Appendix IV, p.235.

or casualties.[161] However, a third of the attacking paratroops were casualties, and the Luftwaffe suffered over 300 aircraft destroyed or damaged, leading Hitler to shy away from further airborne operations.[162]

The Royal Navy's role in defending Crete initially focused on stopping seaborne enemy reinforcements from arriving on the island, since at the time it was reasoned that airborne troops alone could not take the island. The effort became, as Cunningham would signal the Admiralty, 'nothing short of a trial of strength between the Mediterranean Fleet and the German Luftwaffe, which had air supremacy over the area'. Britain's naval forces succeeded in stopping seaborne reinforcements, but at high cost – a cost which increased after the decision to evacuate the island. Cunningham's report after the battle was blunt:

> 'There is no hiding the fact that in our battles with the German Air Force we have been badly battered. We have brought down perhaps 30 enemy aircraft and damaged a like number, but there is no question but they have had much the best of it.
>
> 'Our losses are very heavy [with battleships] *Warspite*, *Barham* and [carrier] *Formidable* out of action for some months, [cruisers] *Orion* and *Dido* in a terrible mess, and I just heard that [cruiser] *Perth* has been hit today. Eight destroyers lost outright and several badly damaged. All this not counting [cruisers] *Gloucester* and *Fiji* [sunk early in the battle]. I fear the casualties are over 2,000.'[163]

The fall of Crete to paratroops, and the horrific losses suffered by the Royal Navy during the operations around the island, led Cunningham to report that supplying Malta had become impractical for the moment.[164] The news made Malta's Governor Dobbie understandably concerned about the fate of his island, and his assessment of the situation to London stressed the need for additional defenders and more aircraft.

But the Luftwaffe's Mediterranean presence was already decreasing as aircraft transferred east toward Germany's next priority target. The movement basically left the neutralization of Malta up to the Italian Regia Aeronautica as the Luftwaffe's Fliegerkorps X had its sphere of influence extended to cover all of the Mediterranean, including North Africa, with only 390 aircraft.[165]

The Regia Aeronautica could not keep Malta neutralized, and the island's fortunes began to revive. Three new radar stations were set up – 501 AMES at Fort Tas-Silg, 502 AMES at Fort Madliena and 504 AMES at Dingli, all Chain Overseas Low units, capable of tracking low-flying aircraft.[166] Five additional reinforcement flights in May and June brought in

---

161. Playfair, Vol II, p.146.
162. Boog, Vol III, p.552. The paratroops lost 3,250 killed and 3,400 wounded in the battle.
163. Simpson, Cunningham Papers, Vol 1 (30 May 1942), p.416. The actual tally was three cruisers (Gloucester, Fiji and Calcutta) and six destroyers sunk, plus damage to three battleships, a carrier, six light cruisers and seven other destroyers, killing some 1800 sailors during the battle. Pack, S.W.C, Battle for Crete, Appendix H, p.126.
164. O'Hara, Passage Perilous, p.26.
165. Probert, Rise and Fall, p.130.
166. Grech, Raiders Passed, Appendix J, p.329.

180 Hurricanes, with about half that number staying on the island.[167] Convoy MW7 reached Malta in May with 24,000 tons of supplies and 14,000 tons of fuel. The tankers *Hoegh Hood* (9,351 tons) and *Svenor* (7,616 tons) arrived, but events would prove them to be the last to do so until August 1942.

On 22 June, Germany invaded the Soviet Union with 101 infantry divisions, seventeen panzer divisions and some 2,000 aircraft. In Britain, most felt the German attack would be successful.[168] With limited strategic choices, the Admiralty tasked the Royal Navy with supporting the ground forces in the Western Desert, maintaining Tobruk as a base and attacking Italian sea routes to Libya.[169]

Malta received a new RAF commander in June, Air Vice Marshal Hugh Pughe Lloyd arriving to relieve Maynard.[170] Lloyd had been given the priority task of organizing an air offensive against the Axis supply lines to 'sink Axis shipping sailing from Europe to Africa'.[171] The new emphasis became felt almost immediately, with new Swordfish aircrews arriving for 830 Squadron. One significant aid for Lloyd was that the Code & Cypher School at Bletchley Park began sending information gleaned from their decryptions of the German Enigma code, the Regia Aeronautica's C35 code and the Regia Marina's C38M administrative codes, bundled together as Ultra, which provided some access to Axis shipping plans. This was partially offset by the fact that the Italians had broken the Royal Navy's administrative and cypher codes in the mid-to-late 1930s, and were thus able to decrypt British sighting reports quickly and order evasive action by the sighted ships.[172]

In the year to July, the Axis had sent 404 ships to North Africa and had lost only nineteen, delivering 90 per cent of supplies sent and 95 per cent of the troops.[173] Although only about 10 per cent of materiel sent had been lost, the propaganda created by the loss of an entire convoy in April pushed the Germans to continue to demand maximum Regia Marina protection, which further depleted Italian fuel stocks and limited other naval activities. Cunningham was only able to deliver 107,000 tons of supplies to Malta in the first six months of 1941 – half of his targeted goal.[174]

In early July, General Scobell ran a three-day infantry anti-invasion exercise that showed that penny-packeting troops in small posts around the coast was not a good defensive scheme. It also revealed that the participating troops were sadly out of training and condition for forced marches or uphill assaults.[175] Scobell decided to initiate six-week anti-parachute training courses for individual battalions on the island of Gozo . Unfortunately, each battalion had charge of its own training, so there was little consistency. The 8/Mancs, for example, simply

---

167. Shores, Hurricane Years, p.388.
168. Austin, Churchill and Malta's War, p.117.
169. O'Hara, Passage Perilous, p.28.
170. Douglas Austin cites Maynard as one of Malta's unsung heroes, 'who had the misfortune to be sent into battle against a well prepared foe with inadequate resources'. Austin, Churchill and Malta's War, p.91.
171. Lloyd, Hugh, Briefed to Attack: Malta's part in African Victory, p.13. These were the specific orders give to Lloyd by Air Chief Marshal Sir Charles Portal, Chief of the Air Staff, in May 1941.
172. The whole story of code breaking in the Second World War has yet to be written; Hinsley's British Intelligence in the Second World War has many errors, especially about Italian codes. Cernuschi, 'Breaking Ultra: The Cryptologic and Intelligence War between Britain and Italy', Warship (2018).
173. O'Hara, Six Victories, Tables 1.2 and 1.4.
174. Caruana, Malta's Maritime Diary, Ch 3.
175. Bonner, p.64.

trained with orders from their battalion commander such as 'A and B Company will attack C and D'.[176]

In June, the submarines HMS *Cachalot*, *Rorqual* and others commenced supply runs into Malta in an operation dubbed *Magic Carpet*, carrying petrol, kerosene, ammunition and mail. Although *Cachalot* was sunk at the end of July, *Magic Carpet* had delivered 283,000 gallons of petrol and 133,400 gallons of kerosene to the island by the end of the month, plus additional stores like ammunition, mail and passengers.[177]

Operation *Substance*, a convoy of six ships, made it through to the island in late July, carrying some 65,000 tons of badly needed supplies, guns and ammunition. The cruiser *Edinburgh* also dropped off the 11th Battalion, Lancashire Fusiliers, to reinforce the garrison. The 8th Battalion, King's Own Royal Regiment, scheduled to arrive with the Fusiliers, landed later after a delayed voyage that included a transport running aground and a cruiser being torpedoed. Their arrival brought the garrison strength to 22,300 troops and supplies, both military and civilian, to an eight-month level.[178]

After the arrival of the *Substance* convoy, the Italians launched a daring attack on Malta. It had been planned and authorized in April, but previous attempts in May (lack of targets) and June (equipment failure) had been cancelled.[179] On 26 July, the Italian corvette *Diana* ferried nine *barchini* (Motoscafo Turismo motorboats with a 300kg warhead in their bow) and two two-man guided Siluro a Lenta Corsa (submersible torpedoes with a detachable warhead – also known as a *maiale*, or pig, because of their penchant for broaching and steering difficulties) to the vicinity of Grand Harbour and launched them. Their goal was to blow through the barriers across the harbour and attack the merchant ships with the *barchini*, ably manned by the X^a Flottiglia Motoscafo Anti Sommergibili (MAS).[180] Unfortunately for the Italians, the radar station at Fort Madliena spotted the *Diana* as it approached and alerted the harbour defences. The plan had been to have one of the *maiales* blow a hole in the protective steel netting across the harbour entrance, through which the *barchini* would rush to attack the unloading ships. For unknown reasons, the *maiale* failed and the Italian tried to break in using two of the *barchini*, but they had bad luck as the resulting explosion also brought down the viaduct that spanned the side entrance to the harbour, completely blocking it. The harbour defence artillery and Hurricane fighters made short work of the rest of the Italian force.[181]

Toward the end of July, with Axis shipping losses mounting, mostly due to Maltese submarines and aircraft (20 per cent were lost in that month),[182] Raeder began raising the issue with the Führer. Hitler's initial thought was to send German submarines into the Mediterranean, a decision Raeder disagreed with since it would not affect Allied anti-shipping efforts there but would hurt German Atlantic operations.[183]

---

176. Ibid., p.66.
177. Dimech, Robert, 'Submarine supply trips to Malta' (Dimech correspondence).
178. Austin, Churchill and Malta's War, p.115.
179. Borghese, Sea Devils, pp.97–99.
180. Malta at War, Vol 3, p.996. The Xa Flottiglia MAS was created on 15 March 1941 to handle special weapons activity, both underwater (manned torpedoes) and surface (explosive motorboats.) It was based at La Spezia on the Tyrrhenian Sea. Zapotoczny, pp.70–71.
181. Zapotoczny, p.82.
182. O'Hara, Six Victories, Table 1.4. Interestingly, the Italians thought at the time the losses were double what they actually were. Iachino, le due Sirte, p.41.
183. Paterson, U-Boats, pp.26–27.

In August, responding to an exaggerated report of Axis shipping to North Africa, Churchill suggested to Chief of the Naval Staff Pound and the Admiralty that they send a 'cruiser or two' to Malta to strengthen the island's anti-shipping forces, pointing out both that Malta had been significantly strengthened and that the Luftwaffe had been drawn to the Eastern Front. Neither Pound nor Cunningham were enthusiastic about the idea.[184]

In September, Operation *Halberd* brought nine ships to Malta with 75,000 tons of supplies and reinforcements, bringing the garrison's anti-aircraft complement to its requested 112 heavy and 118 light anti-aircraft guns.[185] The convoy's only loss, the merchant ship *Imperial Star*, eventually turned out to be a major one as it had been carrying 4,000 tons of seed potatoes for planting on the island.[186]

Rationing was still in effect, but concerns grew about when the next convoy would be received, which led government officials to discuss further rationing. The potato glut was ending and the loss of seed potatoes (needed because of Malta's climate) from the convoy had hurt. One thing the government agreed upon was that bread was the most important article of consumption, stating in a memo that 'it was undesirable that any rationing of bread be attempted'.[187] In addition, water was becoming scarce due to a very dry summer.[188]

Malta's garrison itself now consisted of ten regular infantry battalions and three Maltese battalions. The RAF counted seventy-five Hurricanes in its defensive force, formed into three main squadrons (Nos 185, 249 and 126), plus 800X Squadron of Fulmers and the Malta Night Fighter Unit.[189] Two squadrons of Blenheim bombers (Nos 105 and 107), a squadron of Wellingtons (No 38) and the Swordfish torpedo bombers of 830 Squadron out of Hal Far supplied the island's offensive punch.[190] Finally, in October, a detachment of Wellington Mk II bombers from 104 Squadron arrived at Luqa for additional punch.

Malta also received a significant upgrade in September for its anti-shipping campaign in the form of three Wellingtons mounted with Air to Surface Vessel (ASV) radar. These planes, part of Malta's Special Duties Flight, enhanced the island's night-time search and interception capability, especially when paired with Swordfish torpedo bombers.[191]

In addition, the Admiralty officially named Simpson's U-class submarines the 10th Submarine Flotilla. The smaller submarines, after their slow start, were proving effective. In September, Ultra directed the flotilla to a convoy, resulting in the sinking of Italian transports *Neptunia* and *Oceania*, carrying some 6,000 Axis troops to Africa, by Wanklyn's P37.[192] The Italians lost 28 per cent of the supplies they sent across to Africa during September due to submarines, ships and aircraft based on Malta, 21 per cent in October and a staggering 62 per

---

184. Gilbert, Vol 3, (22 August 1941), p.1,092.
185. Vella, p.49.
186. Cernuschi, p.131.
187. Bradford, Siege Malta, p.147.
188. Jary, They Couldn't have Done Better, p.39.
189. The Malta Night Fighter Unit was created at the end of July to combat Italian night attacks. The all-black Hurricanes would circle and target bombers located by searchlight. Shores, Hurricane Years, p.270.
190. Ibid., Appendix I and II, pp.365–68.
191. Caruana, Victory, pp.66–69.
192. Jacobs, p.92. Simpson states that 5,000 enemy troops were drowned (p.152), but the reality was less than 400 were lost as the Italian escorts concentrated on saving troops rather than prosecuting the submarine. Caruana, Malta's Maritime Diary, Ch 4.

cent in November.[193] Surprisingly, the November losses at sea had little effect on the situation in North Africa as the Axis purchased replacement supplies from the French.[194]

In mid-September, with ship losses increasing, Hitler stepped in, ordering the Luftwaffe to concentrate solely on protecting Axis transports. Luftwaffe commander Göring became angry that he had not been consulted about the order and perversely limited Luftwaffe operations solely to German convoy escort.[195] Less than a week later, the Kriegsmarine Operations Staff sent a report to the OKW (Oberkommando der Wehrmacht, the armed forces high command), citing that the aircraft and submarines on Malta posed the greatest threat to Axis transportation and that 'a further deterioration in the Mediterranean transport situation … may result in major military reverses with corresponding effect on the entire situation in the Mediterranean and on Italy's situation as an ally'. They recommended full neutralization of Malta and more Luftwaffe units for the region.[196] However, once again, Hitler did not act on the recommendation.

Instead, the Führer ordered U-boats into the Mediterranean with specific orders to interdict seaborne supplies between Alexandria and Tobruk. The first U-boat passed Gibraltar on 21 September, and by 5 October Raeder had six U-boats in the area, ported at Salamis in Greece, where he created the 23rd U-Boat Flotilla.[197] Between 21 September and the end of the year, twenty-seven U-boats arrived in the Med, with sixteen others failing to get past Gibraltar.[198]

Churchill increased the pressure on Admiral Pound to station cruisers on Malta to interdict African supply lines, growing angrier and more sarcastic in his notes; at one point he 'reminded' Pound and Cunningham: 'We are still at war.'[199] Pound was against the proposal, saying he was extremely doubtful 'a weak force … would be able to achieve anything commensurate with their loss'. Cunningham concurred, noting that 'they might have heavy losses from air attacks'.[200] But in late October, Pound bowed to the pressure and changed his mind, signalling Cunningham:

> 'It is with great reluctance that we are sending [light cruisers] *Aurora* and *Penelope* to Malta… . I have no exaggerated hopes as to what these two ships will be able to achieve, and I think it quite likely that at the least we shall get both ships badly damaged.'[201]

Thus, Force K – light cruisers *Aurora* and *Penelope*, plus destroyers *Lance* and *Lively* – were added to the Maltese interdiction forces. Their initial sorties were fruitless, despite direction from Ultra intercepts. Although Vice Admiral Ford on Malta had been added to the Ultra reception list in September, all decryption was still taking place in London. Consequently,

---

193. Sadkovich, James J., The Italian Navy in World War II, p.344.
194. Rainero, Mussolini e Petain: Storia dei Rapport tra Italia e la Francis di Vichy.
195. Macintyre, Battle of the Mediterranean, p.110.
196. Lutton, p.131, quoted from captured Kriegsmarine files.
197. Paterson, p.27.
198. Ibid., pp.186–88.
199. Austin, Churchill and Malta's War, p.135.
200. Simpson, Cunningham Papers Vol 1, pp.506–08.
201. Ibid., p.514.

all C38 intercepts had to first be decrypted and then sent to Malta before being turned into operational orders. The delays involved made interception at sea more difficult.²⁰²

However, on the night of 9 November, again directed by Ultra, Force K proved Churchill correct by intercepting the Beta (*Duisberg*) convoy, composed of seven merchantmen carrying 389 vehicles and 17,281 tons of fuel. The convoy had a close escort of seven destroyers and a more distant escort of two heavy cruisers, *Trento* and *Trieste*, with their own escort of four destroyers.²⁰³ The British were able to manoeuvre close enough to open fire at 5,700 yards, and within fifteen minutes all seven merchant ships were hit and on fire. Some of them assumed they were being attacked from the air and added to the general confusion by firing their anti-aircraft weapons. The Italian cruisers, out of position trailing the convoy, engaged with their 8in primary guns. But in the confusion of smoke laid by the close escort and from the burning ships themselves, the response was ineffective; of the 207 8in rounds fired, HMS *Lively* was the only British ship hit, and that by splinters only.²⁰⁴

The convoy's slaughter stunned the Italian government. Ciano, Italy's Foreign Minister, recorded in his diary:

> 'An engagement occurred, the results of which are inexplicable. All, I mean all our ships were sunk and one or two destroyers. Naturally today our various headquarters are pulling out their usual inevitable and imaginary sinking of a British cruiser by a torpedo plane; nobody believes it.'²⁰⁵

Cunningham himself was surprised by the success. He had opined earlier: 'Force K may not achieve much, but their presence should result in the Italians putting [in] much greater escort effort.' After the attack he wrote: '[T]he sinking of the convoy in the Central Med was nice work. I personally thought they were wasted at Malta and the Italians would not … give them a chance, but they did and Agnew leaped at it.'²⁰⁶

The disaster led Raeder to complain: 'The enemy has complete naval and air supremacy in the area of German transport routes. The Italians are not able to bring about major improvements in the situation due to … their own operational and tactical impotence.'²⁰⁷ Raeder's own forces helped where they could, with the recently arrived U-81 (Kapitanleutnant Friedrich Guggenberger) sinking the carrier HMS *Ark Royal* off Gibraltar on 13 November. The carrier had just completed Operation *Perpetual*, delivering Hurricane fighters to Malta.

The destruction of the Italian convoy came at a good time for the British – and a bad one for the Axis – as both sides were ramping up their forces for offensives in North Africa: the Axis to take Tobruk and the British to relieve the port. The British were able to strike first, opening their Operation *Crusader* offensive on 18 November, sending 477 tanks in five divisions against Rommel's three German and five Italian divisions and their 390 tanks – more than half

---

202. Hinsley, Vol II, p.319. The Admiralty suggested all C38 decryptions be performed on Malta to decrease the delay, but this was turned down by Bletchley Park.
203. Sadkovich, p.196; O'Hara, Struggle, p.144, Table 9.1.
204. Iachino, le Due Sirte, pp.48–49.
205. Ciano, 9 November 1941, p.404.
206. Simpson, Cunningham Papers, pp.520, 533. Commodore William Agnew on Aurora was the commander of Force K.
207. Fuehrer Naval Conferences, p.240.

of the latter being inferior Panzer II and Italian M13/40 types.[208] The British had high hopes for their attack, expecting not only to relieve Tobruk but to demoralize the Italians enough to open the way to invade Sicily in December while continuing to move on Tripoli.[209]

The only bleak spot for the British was the supply situation in Malta. During November, they tried sending two single ships to slip through the Axis blockade, but both – the *Empire Defender* and *Empire Pelican* – were sunk by S.79 torpedo bombers, guided to their targets by Regia Marina spy ships.[210]

The Italians reacted to the British attack by increasing efforts to resupply North Africa in a variety of ways, but it was coming at a bad time as by the end of September, Italy had used some 94 per cent of its initial fuel stock of 1.67 million tons. They had less that 150,000 tons remaining and a monthly consumption of between 80,000 and 95,000 tons.[211] On 20 November, they launched multiple small convoys, hoping some would get through, but Malta-based submarines and aircraft stymied the move; HMS *Utmost* (N19) torpedoed the heavy cruiser *Trieste* and an 830 Squadron Swordfish torpedoed light cruiser *Abruzzi*, forcing the Supermarina, the headquarters of the Regia Marina, to recall the convoys.[212] Another attempt to send multiple small convoys across four days later was again thwarted as Force K caught one of the groups and sank the freighters *Maritza* and *Procida*.

The success of Force K – and the apparent inability of the Axis to counter the surface ships at Malta – led the Admiralty to order Cunningham to send another cruiser force to the island. They hoped to be able to always keep one at sea to cut off the Axis convoys. On 29 November, Force B (cruisers *Ajax* and *Neptune*, plus destroyers *Kingston* and *Kimberley*) arrived in Grand Harbour.[213]

The Axis shipping losses were partially paid back when the German U-331 (Oberleutnant zur See Hans-Dietrich von Tiesenhausen) torpedoed and sank the battleship HMS *Barham* off Alexandria on 25 November. Tiesenhausen reported that he had hit a battleship and this was communicated to the Comando Supremo, but fortunately for the British its sinking was not confirmed by the Italians for two months.[214]

On 29 November, another set of five small convoys with six merchantmen was sent out. However, Force K and Maltese strike aircraft sank three and damaged and repulsed two others, leaving a single ship to make it through to North Africa with its cargo.[215]

---

208. Playfair, Vol III, p.30.
209. Simpson, Cunningham Papers, p.519.
210. Mattioli, p.26.
211. DatiStatistici, pp.245, 277.
212. Barnett, Engage the Enemy, p.371.
213. Caruana, Malta's Wartime Diary, Ch 4.
214. Iachino stated that Tiesenhausen thought he had hit a cruiser (Iachino, le Due Sirte, p.58), but this was incorrect.
215. Ibid., p.60.

Chapter III

War
December 1941 – June 1942

The destruction of the *Duisberg* convoy and repulse of the other Italian convoys became the high-water mark for the British anti-shipping offensive around Malta in 1941, as it again aroused the wrath and attention of the German High Command and the Italian Comando Supremo. Chief of the Italian Supreme Command Generale Ugo Cavallero instructed his army chief of staff, Generale Mario Roatta, to start drafting a plan, entitled *C3*, to take the island.

In early December, Hitler issued Directive 38, which read in part:

> 'Secure mastery in the air and sea in the area between Southern Italy and North Africa in order to secure communications with Libya and Cyrenaica and, in particular, keep Malta in subjection.
>
> 'Paralyze enemy traffic through the Mediterranean and British supplies to Malta and Tobruk, in close cooperation with the German and Italian forces available for this task.'[1]

To get the Mediterranean back under control, he sent Generalfeldmarschall Albert Kesselring, naming him Oberbefehlshaber Süd (Commander-in-chief, South), plus the veteran Fliegerkorps II, directly from the Eastern Front. Despite the grandiose title, Kesselring only had direct command of the Luftwaffe; naval and land affairs remained under Italian supreme command, but that did not stop him from asserting himself into the other areas.[2]

Upon his arrival in Rome, Kesselring immediately recommended invading Malta, but the resources were not available. Instead, his priorities became:

- destroy all British aircraft in the air or on the ground;
- destroy Malta's radar and anti-aircraft defences;
- block all supplies from reaching the island;
- attack all warships and harbour installations; and
- mine the approaches to isolate the island.[3]

---

1. Hitler's Directive 38 (2 December 1941); Trevor-Roper, Hitler's War Directives, pp.163–65.
2. Boog, Vol III, p.713.
3. Shores, Christopher, Cull, Brian & Malizia, Nicola, Malta: the Spitfire Year, 1942, p.23.

On 7 December 1941, the global strategic picture changed completely as the Imperial Japanese Navy attacked the US naval base at Pearl Harbor, Hawaii, bringing the United States officially into the Second World War. Churchill reacted to the news with joy, writing later that 'at our side stood two mighty allies… . [Russia and the United States …] irrevocably engaged to fight to the death in closest concert with the British Empire. This combination made final victory certain.'[4] However, victory stood a long way off; the Japanese also invaded Malaya and, in the process, sank the British battleship *Prince of Wales* and battlecruiser *Repulse*. Mussolini greeted the news with the view that Russia would be liquidated and the United States would be preoccupied with Japan, as would British strength. He felt conditions were 'ripe' for victory in the Mediterranean.[5]

Malta began feeling the effects of Hitler's Directive 38 as General Bruno Loerzer's Fliegerkorps II pilots and aircraft arrived, with the number of raids jumping from seventy-six in November to 169 in December.[6] But with losses mounting and supplies running low in North Africa, Rommel ordered his forces to pull back from Tobruk on 7 December, allowing Eighth Army to relieve the fortress several days later. Five days after that, Rommel began pulling out of Cyrenaica completely.

At sea, initiative and strength began to shift. The Supermarina tried sending supplies using capital ships; on 12 December, light cruisers *Alberico da Barbiano* and *Alberto da Giussano* were each loaded with 950 tons of fuel in Palermo and sailed for Tripoli. The two cruisers ran into the 4th Destroyer Flotilla (British destroyers HMS *Sikh*, *Maori* and *Legion* and the Dutch destroyer *Isaac Sweers*) off Cape Bon and succumbed to gunfire and torpedoes, with decks ablaze from ruptured fuel drums.[7]

The loss of the cruisers and failure of the small convoys forced the Supermarina to bulk up their convoy process, putting together larger convoys with more powerful escorts. The first attempt, M41, on 14 December failed immediately due to Ultra intercepts and Malta's submarines: N89 (*Upright*) sank two of the merchantmen and caused two others to collide, while N17 (*Urge*) sent a torpedo into the battleship *Vittorio Veneto*, putting it out of action for the next four months.[8]

The Italians tried again several days later, sending four freighters (M42) with 17,000 tons, including forty-four tanks, 3,100 tons of fuel and nearly 1,200 tons of ammunition, toward Tripoli and Benghazi. There were seven destroyers with the ships as close escort, while virtually the entire Italian capital fleet provided distant escort: three battleships, including Ammiraglio Iachino on *Littorio*, and the heavy cruisers *Gorizia* and *Trento*. At the same time, Rear Admiral Philip Vian's 15th Cruiser Squadron (light cruisers *Naiad* and *Euryalus*) was at sea escorting the *Breconshire* with 5,000 tons of crucial aviation fuel for Malta. Vian was joined enroute by Force K (cruisers *Aurora* and *Penelope*, plus six destroyers) from Malta.

Late on 17 December, Italian reconnaissance aircraft spotted the British, and Iachino moved to intercept and block any British approach to his convoy. However, his reconnaissance pilot reported the enemy course incorrectly and compounded the problem by misidentifying *Breconshire* as a battleship.[9] The misinformation led to the two forces only tangling with

---

4. Churchill, The Hinge of Fate, p.3.
5. O'Hara, Passage Perilous, p.39.
6. Shores, Hurricane Years, Appendix XI, p.399.
7. O'Hara, Struggle, p.153.
8. Greene & Massignani, p.200.
9. Breconshire had possibly been mistaken as a capital ship due to the camouflage used. Caruana correspondence.

long-range fire for a few minutes as evening fell. The action was not pressed by either side as their primary missions were to protect their respective convoys.

The battle, known as First Sirte, was a non-event but left both sides feeling victorious. The British felt they had driven off a superior force and succeeded in getting their charge to Malta. Vian would recall: '[W]ithin range of my cruiser guns, the enemy turned away, to be lost in the gathering darkness.'[10] The Italians, however, were ecstatic at getting a full convoy intact to North Africa and at having beaten off a British attack, especially since their initial reports indicated they had sunk two British destroyers.[11] As Iachino later wrote:

> 'The arrival of the convoy, with a change of strength, despite the presence of the enemy was the first and foremost task of the operation. It had an immediate material importance because it bore to our troops in North Africa the necessary supplies for the continuation of fighting in defence of Cyrenaica, but had especially a great moral importance because the arrival of the convoy was intended to show the country and the world that the control of the Mediterranean has not escaped from our hands.'[12]

Disaster for the British followed First Sirte's brief clash. On the night of 18 December, chasing the convoy from the First Sirte engagement, the Malta cruisers ran into a deep-water minefield: *Neptune* and the destroyer *Kandahar* sank, with cruiser *Aurora* damaged. In one night, Force K had been reduced to light cruiser HMS *Penelope* and three destroyers. Worse was to follow the next night, when three Italian *maiale* from X^a MAS, transported by the submarine *Scire*, penetrated Alexandria harbour, placed charges and sank the battleships *Queen Elizabeth* and *Valiant*, and damaged the Norwegian tanker *Sagona*.[13]

The loss of Force K, and the Mediterranean Fleet's battleships, on top of the increased aerial pressure on Malta, completely altered the strategic picture in the Mediterranean. However, the Italians did not realize the extent of British naval weakness, and continued to massively escort convoys, to the detriment of their critical fuel oil supplies.[14] Despite the year's losses – a battleship, eight cruisers, twenty-one destroyers and thirty-eight submarines[15] – the Regia Marina held the upper hand at the moment.

At the beginning of 1942, Malta's supply situation was still relatively good. Warehouses held enough flour to last until May, coal to the end of March, benzene and kerosene until the end of April and aviation fuel to last the summer. Fuel oil and ammunition were in the shortest supply and required replenishment if the island was to continue offensive operations. Churchill insisted on keeping the island offensively active, and on 5 January, the Admiralty endorsed his proposal to send a minimum of 45,000 tons a month to the island.[16] The first such convoy (MW8) brought in three supply ships (of the four sent) with 21,000 tons of supplies, along with

---

10. Vian, p.80.
11. Both the cruiser Gorizia and destroyer Maestrale reported 'seeing' enemy vessels sunk. Iachino, le Due Sirte, p.119.
12. Ibid., p.162.
13. O'Hara, Struggle, p.160.
14. Iachino, le Due Sirte, p.156.
15. Mawdsley, p.292.
16. Playfair, Mediterranean and the Middle East, Vol III, p.156. CAB 79/17/4.

most of the 1st Battalion, Durham Light Infantry, and eight Cruiser tanks.[17] However, raids on Malta continued to increase during January, rising to 263 throughout the month. Pressure on the overworked fighters continued, with losses mounting, including eight in one day on 25 January.[18]

Two of the three service commanders on Malta rotated during the month, with Vice Admiral Sir Ralph Leatham taking over the Royal Navy position from Ford and General D.M.W. Beak, VC,[19] replacing General Scobell.

Beak's motto, 'work hard, train hard, play hard', earned him the nickname 'The Terrible Beak' among his half-starved troops.[20] Beak had been assigned to Malta because of rumours that the aerial bombardment had demoralized the troops. However, he brought an intensity to inspections and drills that seemed out of place with the island's conditions, telling officers in a lecture: "You will do PT [Physical Training] every morning before breakfast; you will cycle in full equipment for twenty miles; you will walk and run alternately for fifteen miles.'[21] One of the island's brigadiers remembered Beak as 'a difficult man but a terrific fire-eater'.[22] Aside from his attitude being at odds with his troops' actual situation, his arrival compounded the already complicated command structure on Malta because he took his orders directly from Middle East Headquarters in Cairo, not Dobbie, further eroding the Governor's authority.[23]

Also arriving in January was Brigadier General Pearce Smith, who assumed command of Southern Brigade. Both Beak and Smith were 'shocked' at the defensive preparations they found. Smith noted:

> 'The ground defence policy was purely static. Around the coast and aerodromes in some depth were situated concrete pillboxes, about 300–400 yards apart, supplemented by a continuous belt of wire and landmines. Each pillbox was garrisoned by a section of eight or so men with Bren guns and other weapons. Undoubtedly, they would have presented considerable opposition and inflicted many casualties, but smoke and modern weapons would have defeated them.'[24]

The minimal infantry training that the battalions received during their summer sojourns on Gozo became quickly overwhelmed by the work needed to keep the airfields active. As one memoir noted, the jobs for the infantry were 'many and varied and besides filling craters,

---

17. Caruana, Malta's Maritime Diary, Ch 5, Appendix 32.
18. Shores & Cull, Spitfire Year, p.58.
19. Daniel Marcus William Beak earned his Victoria Cross in the First World War as temporary Commander Royal Naval Volunteer Reserve (Drake Battalion, Royal Naval Division). During the period 21–25 August and on 4 September 1918, at Logeast Wood, France, Commander Beak led his men and captured four enemy positions under heavy fire. Four days later, although dazed by a shell fragment, in the absence of the brigade commander, he reorganised the whole brigade under extremely heavy gunfire and led his men to their objective. When an attack was held up, accompanied by only one runner he succeeded in breaking up a nest of machine guns, personally bringing in nine or ten prisoners. www.victoriacross.co.uk.
20. Malta at War, Vol 4, #9, p.1,309.
21. Hampshires Regimental History, 1st Bn, p.51.
22. Jary, They Couldn't have Done Better, p.44.
23. Jellison, pp.191–92.
24. Jary, p.89.

included parties for refuelling, servicing, armourer's assistance, ammunition belt fillers, motor and steam roller drivers, dispatch riders, liaison officers and even personnel for control duties'.[25] At one point the entire 1st Battalion, Hampshires, found themselves employed filling craters.[26]

Despite the siege and the garrison's weakness, the British Joint Intelligence Committee (JIC) opined in early January that 'a combined operation against Malta would be of such difficulty that it is improbable that the enemy would attempt it'.[27]

However, with Malta under significant aerial pressure, Axis *C3* planning moved ahead in early January with a group of twenty-five officers from all three services under the supervision of Cavallero's chief operations officer, Generale Antonio Gandin.[28]

Also in early January, the Italians launched a larger supply convoy, M43, carrying some 15,000 tons of fuel and lubricants, 2,400 tons of ammunition and 144 tanks. Once again, virtually the entire Italian Navy escorted the convoy. Despite Ultra warnings, the British were unable to intercede against this convoy. Cunningham later wrote: '[T]he enemy had a striking success in running a large convoy into Tripoli which was not attacked on passage.... . this was a dismal story ... inadequate air reconnaissance ... [meant] our surface forces were powerless to intervene.'[29]

On 21 January, a reinforced and resupplied Rommel attacked the British near El Agheila and, as he had a year earlier, smashed through the covering forces. By the end of the month, he had once again driven them across the hump of Cyrenaica to positions west of Tobruk near Gazala. As Rommel moved west, the Italians sent another large convoy, T18, into Tripoli. Ultra once again warned the British and this time their response was better, torpedoing and sinking the liner *Victoria*, carrying some 1,400 crew and troops, of whom 400 were lost. The rest of the convoy, with 13,000 tons of supplies and ninety-seven tanks, arrived safely.[30]

Overall, despite the change in the naval situation, both sides were able to continue running supply convoys with little opposition during January; the British were able to get five of six ships into Malta, while the Italians managed nine of ten ships to Tripoli.

Kesselring met with Cavallero and the Chief of the Italian Naval Staff, Ammiraglio Riccardi, in early February to discuss the seizure of Malta, with a target date of July or August. At a meeting a week later, an impatient Hitler agreed to take the island, telling Kesselring: 'Keep your shirt on, Field Marshal, I am going to do it.'[31] Joint planning for the invasion started a week later, the first time the two Axis allies had tried organizing something together.[32]

While in the Far East the Japanese invaded Burma and invested Singapore, the noose around Malta tightened in February. Three ships left Alexandria in convoy MW9, but the *Clan Chattan* (7262 GRT) was sunk, *Rowellan Castle* (7798 GRT) was damaged enough to have to be scuttled, and the third, *Clan Campbell* (7255 GRT) was damaged and barely made Tobruk.[33] It was the first Malta supply convoy completely blocked by the Axis. Failure of the convoy

---

25. Bonner, p.10.
26. Hampshire Regimental History, p.52.
27. O'Hara, Passage Perilous, p.40.
28. Boog, Vol VI, p.656.
29. Simpson, Cunningham Papers, p.564.
30. Cocchia, Difesa del traffico, VII, p.235.
31. Kesselring, Memoirs, p.109.
32. Lutton, p.162.
33. Malta at War, Vol 4, pp.1,377–81.

made Governor Dobbie put the island on 'siege-level' rations.[34] The black market thrived on the island, despite government attempts to control it. Food was available – if you could afford it. A dozen eggs, for example, fetched 30 shillings, which at the time was a week's wages for a dock worker.[35]

While supplies into Malta had been stopped, the Italians continued to send their own merchantmen across to Libya and Tunisia: K7 (six ships with 15,000 tons of fuel, 13,000 tons of other materiel and 133 tanks) made safe passage to North Africa. Ultra again provided good information, allowing aerial and submarine forces to converge, but weather and much better air–sea cooperation between the Italian Navy and German airmen blocked their attempts.[36]

The news continued to be bad for the British, with Singapore surrendering on 14 February and the Japanese onslaught continuing into the Dutch East Indies. Meanwhile, at the end of the month, the first attempt to fly Spitfires onto Malta, Operation *Spotter*, failed when a defect was discovered in the aircrafts' auxiliary fuel tanks, forcing postponement of the effort.[37]

Kesselring called a high-level meeting at Catania airfield on 12 March to detail his plans for Malta's neutralization. Along with General Loerzer, commander of Fliegerkorps II, and Generale Silvio Scaroni, Commandante dell'Aeronautica in Sicily, the meeting included all Stormi and Gruppe leaders. Kesselring opened the conference by citing the need to destroy the offensive and defensive capabilities on the island as a preparation for invasion, and to ensure that no supplies reached the island. Loerzer then laid out the plan of operation: first, eliminate the anti-aircraft defences; second, destroy the airfields with massed bombings; and finally, destroy the port facilities and ships. Tactically, the Axis would send three waves of 100 bombers each day until they completed the neutralization.[38]

While Kesselring discussed the island's neutralization, General der Fallschirmtruppe Bernhard Ramcke inspected the Italian Folgore Parachute Division at their Tarquinia training site as part of the preparation for its use in the *C3* invasion plan. Ramcke's assessment of the division was positive, although he felt that the Italians' armament, especially their hand grenades and anti-tank guns, were too light to be of use against the concrete fortifications they expected to find on Malta. He made a formal request for better arms – rifles, mortars and anti-tank rifles – for the division, to be delivered prior to the invasion.[39]

During February and March, a major argument brewed up between Middle East Command and London, with Malta at its centre. Churchill demanded the Eighth Army attack to regain airfields in Cyrenaica in order to protect supply convoys to Malta: 'Our view is that Malta is of such importance, both as a staging area and as an impediment to enemy reinforcement route that the most drastic steps are justifiable to sustain it.' The Commander-in-Chief Middle East, General Claude Auchinleck, disagreed, writing: 'Critical nature of Malta maintenance situation thoroughly understood. We cannot have reasonable superiority before 1 June and to launch major offensive before that would be to risk defeat in detail and possibly endanger safety of Egypt.'[40] The argument continued for several months.

---

34. Jellison, p.161.
35. Ibid., pp.134–35.
36. Cocchia, Difesa del traffico, VII, p.747.
37. Jacobs, p.117. Shores & Cull, Spitfire Year, p.98.
38. Malta at War, Vol 5, #1, p.1,438.
39. Morisi, p.28.
40. Austin, Churchill and Malta's War, pp.151–52.

The Axis air blitz had whittled Malta's fighters down to about twenty-one Hurricanes when they finally received some welcome reinforcements in the form of superior Spitfire fighters. Fifteen of them arrived on 7 March in Operation *Spotter II*, with sixteen more toward the end of the month (Operation *Picket*). Their arrival coincided with a massive bombing campaign organized by Kesselring and a change in Axis tactics. Losses had been high when small formations attacked the island, so he decided to switch to large concentrated raids, using carpet bombing tactics: four daylight raids, composed of between seventy and 100 aircraft, hit the island every day, with additional night-time bombing.

The first such concentrated attacks hit Ta'Qali on 20 and 21 March, with 114 tons dropped on the airfield and surrounding villages in the first attack and 182 tons the following day.[41] One eyewitness to the assault, a member of the Royal Irish Fusiliers 2nd Battalion, described the 'main runway straddled by dozens of large craters, grounded planes on fire, and the whole area an utter shambles'.[42] High explosive, anti-personnel, incendiary and delayed-action bombs, as well as parachute mines, were all used.

Even as the Axis air blitz heated up, the British attempted another supply run to the island. Convoy MW10, with four merchant ships carrying over 37,000 tons, left Alexandria on 20 March with an escort of one light cruiser and seven Hunt-class destroyers. Admiral Vian and his 15th Cruiser Squadron (HMS *Cleopatra*, *Dido* and *Euryalus*), along with the 22nd and 14th Destroyer Flotillas, provided cover for them, joined by the light cruiser *Penelope* and destroyer *Legion* from Force K on Malta.

The convoy was sighted by Italian submarines and was soon under attack by German and Italian aircraft. The Supermarina ordered Cruiser Division III (heavy cruisers *Gorizia* and *Trento* and light cruiser *Bande Nere*) to sail from Messina, and the battleship *Littorio*, with Fleet commander Iachino, from Taranto, to intercept.[43] The Italian cruisers found the convoy mid-afternoon on 22 March in the midst of a growing storm. In increasingly heavy seas and winds that blew directly into the Italians' faces, Vian managed to hold off the cruisers with smokescreens and radar-directed gunfire in a battle dubbed Second Sirte. An hour after the initial interception, *Littorio* joined the fight, opening fire at 4.41 pm from 16,000 yards.[44] Refusing to try to circumvent the smokescreens and wind by sailing east, Iachino chose to keep his force between the convoy and its destination as long as possible, forcing it to sail south.

A torpedo attack by the 22nd Destroyer Flotilla and nightfall caused Iachino to break off the action and retire north.[45] In the two-hour battle, in the midst of horrific sea conditions that mitigated accurate firing, the British suffered only a single hit on *Cleopatra*, which took a 6in shell on its bridge, a hit on the destroyer *Kingston* (either a 15in or 8in shell), minor damage to *Euryalus* – straddled by *Littorio*'s 15in shells and shredded with splinters – and splinter damage to three destroyers, from the 1,490 shells fired by the Italians.[46] The Italians suffered a

---

41. Shores & Cull, Spitfire Year, pp.130–31.
42. Williams, Defenders, p.74.
43. Iachino, le Due Sirte, p.198.
44. Ibid., p.235.
45. Italian tactical guidelines required their admirals to retire at night if engaged by radar-equipped enemy forces.
46. O'Hara, Passage Perilous, p.50. Iachino, p.316.

single hit (out of 2,800 shells fired at them) during the battle,⁴⁷ but had two destroyers, *Lanciere* and *Scirocco*, founder in the storm on the way home. While a week later, N17 (*Urge*) sank the storm-damaged *Bande Nere*.

Admiral Cunningham would call the Battle of Second Sirte 'the most brilliant action of the war'. Churchill echoed the view:

> '[Second Sirte was] a resolute and brilliant action by which the Malta Convoy was saved. That one of the most powerful battleships afloat attended by two heavy cruisers and four light cruisers and a flotilla should have been routed and put to flight with severe torpedo and gunfire injury in broad daylight … constitutes a naval episode of the highest distinction.'⁴⁸

The Italian view of the battle was one of disappointment, as Iachino reported:

> 'We returned convinced that, if the weather conditions had been better, not only would our air strikes not have failed, but also the naval shooting results would have been more positive… . [W]e had the consciousness of having done everything possible in these difficult circumstances.'⁴⁹

The battle can only be considered a draw or an Italian tactical victory, since it had forced the convoy south, leaving it vulnerable to more air attacks before making port in Valletta. Indeed, Axis aircraft caught the ships outside the harbour, sinking one merchantman and damaging the *Breconshire*. After the remaining two ships – the *Talabot* and *Pampas* – moored, the Axis air blitz, which had primarily been targeting the airfields, switched to the harbour area in an effort to finish what they had started. Air attacks continued, finally sinking both merchant ships, as well as the *Breconshire* off Marsaxlokk harbour to the south-east. One eyewitness recalled: 'Tongues of fire, as high as the Floriana bastions were leaping from the *Talabot*.'⁵⁰ Of the 16,000 tons each the two ships carried, the Maltese only salvaged about 5,000 tons.⁵¹ In addition, three destroyers, four submarines, a tanker and five trawlers were sunk in the harbour blitz.⁵²

Despite the public hyperbole about the battle, Cunningham recognized what the Italians had achieved: the weather had played the key role in defending the convoy, which had ultimately essentially failed. He stated it baldly in his memoir, writing: 'And so, to a great extent, the enemy had achieved his purpose.'⁵³ He sent a signal to the Admiralty stating that 'before any further attempt [to resupply Malta] could be made it was necessary for destroyers

---

47. Initial reports had the British claiming a torpedo hit on the Littorio and significant other damage. However, the 'torpedo hit' observed by the attacking destroyers was in reality the burning Ro.43 observation aircraft on the Littorio that caught fire after the battleship's aft 15in turret fired at the attacking destroyers. Iachino, p.264.
48. ADM 223/548 (Sirte Signal 241).
49. Iachino, le Due Sirte, p.309.
50. Grech, p.179.
51. O'Hara, Six Victories, Table 11.1, p.244.
52. Ibid., p.248.
53. Cunningham, A Sailor's Odyssey, p.458.

to be reinforced; to strengthen Malta fighters very substantially; to plan some form of diversion to disperse the enemy air and surface forces'.[54]

Shortly after this signal was sent, Cunningham was reassigned, becoming the head of the British Naval Mission in Washington DC and Admiral Pound's representative to the Combined Chiefs of Staff Committee.[55] He left Cairo on 3 April 1942.

The dismal result of the convoy created additional controversy on the island almost immediately. Initially, Vice Admiral Leatham had chosen to rely on civilian labour to unload the ships.[56] Due to the weather and air raids, the *Talabot* and *Pampas* lay moored for almost twelve hours before serious unloading began, resulting in charges of cowardice levelled at the civilian stevedores for staying in shelters during air raids.[57] Air Vice Marshal Lloyd became one of the most vocal critics of the unloading and of Governor Dobbie's leadership, stating: 'Too many old and worn out men, some far too bomb shy. Civilian stevedores did practically no work. They must be conscripted and worked under guard. People want a leader and someone with energy. Excuses are given for failure to take off cargo, but I accept none.'[58] However, since eight civilians died in the holds of the *Pampas* due to the bombing, the charges overstated the problem. Ultimately, servicemen from the Cheshire Battalion joined the stevedores in salvaging what they could.

In London, the JIC began to seriously worry about the potential for invasion, rethinking their January position. In March, additional intelligence indicated invasion was now probable and they warned Malta to expect it in April. Once again, lack of Axis troop movements later made them downgrade the threat.[59]

The weight of bombing had been increasing during this new blitz: in February some 995 tons were dropped, in March 2,174 tons.[60] The amount tripled in April, when the Axis flew 5,715 sorties and dropped 6,728 tons of bombs,[61] killing over 300 civilians and 200 servicemen – 150 troops from Southern Brigade alone[62] – creating horrific damage described as 'a wilderness of craters, the docks a shambles, Valletta, a mass of broken limestone'.[63] By the end of April, 15,500 buildings had been destroyed on Malta, including seventy churches and eighteen convents and monasteries. [64] The heavy anti-aircraft guns

---

54. Simpson, Cunningham Papers, p.592.
55. Roskill, The War at Sea, Vol II, p.56.
56. O'Hara, Six Victories, p.240.
57. Jellison, p.162. The story of the 'cowardly' stevedores is more complex than Lloyd indicated. On 16 January 1941, stevedores died on the merchant ship Excess when bombs struck the ship. Their wives asked for the same pension as the wives of dockyard workers or soldiers killed in action. Their request was denied, because as civilians, no one had ordered them to stay on board; if they stayed, they did so 'voluntarily'. After that denial, the stevedores abandoned ship when air raid warnings sounded. Caruana correspondence.
58. Tedder, p.263.
59. Ibid., p.344.
60. Jary, Yells, Bells & Smells, p.99.
61. Perowne, pp.117–19; attacks averaged over 170 bombers per day. Attackers dropped 3,156 tons of bombs on the dockyards, 805 tons on Luqa, 841 tons on Ta'Qali, 750 tons on Hal Far and 196 tons on Kalafrana, with 980 tons elsewhere on the island. Air Battle for Malta, Ch VIII. Note: the number of sorties tends to vary in different sources; Grech, for instance, notes 9,600 Axis sorties in April, but only a single ton of bombs more. Grech, p.168.
62. Jary, They Couldn't have Done Better, p.46.
63. O'Hara, Passage Perilous, p.54.
64. Attard, Joseph, The Battle of Malta, p.170.

fired more than 72,000 shells and the light anti-aircraft guns over 88,000 rounds.[65] During the month the gunners of Malta claimed 102 aircraft destroyed and another sixty-nine damaged, while the fighters claimed only fifty-three shot down, twenty-nine probables and 118 damaged.[66] Even accounting for claim inflation, the month took a heavy toll on the Axis air forces.

The effect of the raids on the Maltese people was as horrific as to their island. The combination of a cold, damp winter and shelters with only primitive sanitation facilities – if any at all – little heat and no electricity meant disease became rampant. The shelters, described as 'crowded, steaming, stinking noisy dungeons',[67] led to typhoid, tuberculosis and dysentery reaching epidemic proportions.

The scarcity of food contributed to the problem. The seed potatoes sent from Egypt to replace those lost on the *Imperial Star* on 28 September 1941 proved sterile, leading to a failed March harvest.[68] The new daily ration on the island provided just 12oz of meat, 4oz of fish and 5oz of rice, doled out bi-weekly. People got two quarts of kerosene per week.[69] The Maltese had to subsist on a daily intake of between 1,000 and 1,500 calories, about half that needed for just a sedentary life; the servicemen got only slightly more. One resident recalled: 'Starvation, exhaustion from lack of sleep and many diseases related to malnutrition were now taking their toll... . Everyone smelt of mold and dampness from the long nights under cover in wet shelters.'[70] Despite the slightly larger ration, the effects of the food shortage on the soldiers was still heavy; orders to 'cease running and vigorous exercise' and observe a compulsory rest period in the afternoon were passed to the garrison.[71] Brigadier Smith recalled: '[E]ach soldier's ration was reduced ... to 1,250 [calories], we had all lost a stone [14lb] or more in weight.'[72]

The government established Victory Kitchens to mitigate the lack of food. They set up communal kitchens and people registered to get a single meal a day in exchange for part of their ration, which provided an economy of both food and fuel. Described by one participant as 'vegetable soup, goat meat stew, tinned sardines and herring, beans and macaroni',[73] others remembered it less enthusiastically – for three people, 'three thin sausages and fifteen peas, plus half a potato twice a week'.[74]

On 15 April, King George VI sent the following message to the island:

> 'To honour her brave people, I award the George Cross to the island fortress of Malta, to bear witness to a heroism and devotion that will long be famous in history.'[75]

---

65. Vella, p.102.
66. Shore & Cull, Spitfire Year, p.228.
67. Jellison, p.177.
68. Cernuschi, p.131.
69. Ibid., p.174.
70. Grech, Raiders Passed, p.203.
71. Williams, Defender, p.90.
72. Jary, They Couldn't have Done Better, p.46.
73. Grech, p.136.
74. Perowne, p.123.
75. Attard, p.175.

Established in 1940 and generally awarded to individuals and organizations for valour, Malta's George Cross became unique as the first time the medal had been awarded to a group. Italian propaganda denigrated the award, calling it 'a preposterous deception by the British Government'.[76]

In mid-April, the Admiralty recognized the need for another convoy attempt to Malta, planning to run two converging convoys in May, from Gibraltar and Alexandria, to ensure enough supplies got through. However, they cancelled the Gibraltar convoy due to the lack of capital ships for escort duty, and ultimately chose not to try any convoy that month.[77] Admiral Sir Henry Harwood, who was preparing to take over as Commander-in-Chief Mediterranean, agreed with the decision not to send a May convoy, saying that March's 'winds of Force 6 made conditions for smoke laying entirely favourable to our forces; weather also prevented enemy destroyers from remaining in company with his main force at speed requisite to intercept the convoy before dark.... [It] would be quite exceptional for such favourable conditions to occur in May.'[78]

Governor Dobbie's response was blunt:

> 'The decision not to run a convoy from the west for present is based on general considerations outside my sphere. I can only speak for Malta itself and our situation is so grave that it is my duty to restate it in the clearest possible terms.
>
> 'This decision materially reduces our chances of survival, not because of any failure of morale or fighting efficiency but because it is impossible to carry on without food or ammunition.'[79]

The Admiralty moved the two-convoy plan into June; one, Operation *Harpoon*, would sail from Gibraltar in the west, and another larger convoy, Operation *Vigorous*, from the eastern Mediterranean. The two convoys would carry some 125,000 tons. To aid the convoys, the admirals and Churchill pressed for a ground offensive that would regain the Cyrenaica hump's airfields to provide air support.

Malta's forces continued to diminish. By March, the Blenheim and Wellington bomber squadrons had been withdrawn. Initial discussions over withdrawing the 10th Submarine Flotilla led to vehement opposition by its commander. Simpson pointed to his flotilla's submarines as the only force left capable of 'preventing the enemy bombarding Malta with heavy surface forces and … the bad effect on local morale' that would ensue with their removal.[80] However, submarine losses reached catastrophic proportions as April continued – the flotilla's remaining subs spent the daylight hours submerged trying to escape the bombing. The loss of Wanklyn's P37 (*Upholder*) in mid-April was a heavy blow to the beleaguered unit; it had survived twenty-four patrols and sunk 119,000 tons of Axis shipping before being sunk.[81] At the end of the

---

76. The Italians added that 'had not our Maltese brethren been under the heel of British domination which is being forced on them under threat of gun and bayonet, we have no doubt as to how the Maltese would behave'. Air Battle for Malta, Ch VIII.
77. Austin, Churchill and Malta's War, p.166.
78. ADM signal 223/548, 17 April 1942.
79. Austin, Churchill and Malta's War, p.166.
80. Simpson, Up Periscope, Appendix 3, p.297.
81. Jacobs, p.136; Wingate, p.176.

month, 'conditions had not improved, enemy mine-laying was expected and personnel were showing signs of fatigue', so Simpson agreed that the remaining submarines be withdrawn to Alexandria. Four of the five remaining submarines made it safely there.[82]

Lloyd reported he had some 600 aircraft pens built but few aircraft to fill them. On 20 April, he almost filled some of them. Through arrangement with the United States, the large carrier USS *Wasp* entered the Mediterranean and launched forty-seven Spitfires toward Malta in Operation *Calendar*. However, they came under attack from nearly 300 bombers almost from the minute they landed on Malta. Dobbie reported:

> '47 Spitfires arrived and in two and a half days 357 tons and 122 tons of bombs have hit the aerodromes where they are accommodated. 17 destroyed, 29 damaged, we can only put six in the air.
>
> 'If Malta is to be held, it must be revictualled and to do so we must (repeat must) gain a good measure of air superiority.
>
> 'We can deal with invasion but the enemy need not attempt that if he can maintain the air blockade as at present.'[83]

The fact that the newly arrived Spitfires were not combat-ready – the guns dirty and unsynchronised, many without radios – compounded the problem. That meant they could not be used immediately.[84] Worse, the pilots were not prepared for the level of combat over the island. In a scathing signal, the Air Ministry was told:

> 'Seven pilots out of 23 have had no operational experience and a further four have less than 25 hours flying on Spitfires. 12 of the 23 have never fired their guns in action. Only fully experienced operational pilots must come here. It is no place for beginners.'[85]

Acrimony and accusation at the losses again reared their head on the island, adding to the bad blood from the March convoy disaster. Dissension reached its peak when Churchill received a telegram from the Middle East Defence Committee requesting that Governor Dobbie be replaced. The message complained that Dobbie had lost his grip on the situation and was not capable of directing the island.

Churchill immediately dispatched a personal representative to Malta. Robert Casey, the Minister of State in the Middle East, reported back a 'bad state of affairs, with cross currents of distrust'.[86] The top secret *aide memoire* from the Middle East Defence Committee stated baldly: 'The three Service Commanders in Malta and the Lieut. Governor all expressed the view that the Governor was a tired old man who had lost his grip of the situation and is no longer capable of affording the higher direction and control.' The signal recommended replacing Dobbie with 'a young, vigorous personality' from outside the island 'to remove the possibility of internal jealousy and friction'.[87] Dobbie also did not have the backing of Mabel

---

82. N17(Urge) was lost enroute; HMS Una, P31, P34 and P35 made it safely. Simpson, pp.298–99.
83. Dobbie telegram, HE/747 23 April 1942.
84. Lloyd, p.183.
85. Caruana, Victory in the Air, p.39.
86. Austin, p.157.
87. Malta at War, Vol 6, #1, p.1,792.

Strickland, owner of the *Times of Malta* newspaper, who conspired against him, convinced he would surrender the island.[88]

At the end of April, Hitler and Mussolini met at Castle Klessheim near Salzburg to discuss the world situation. When the topic of the Mediterranean came up, they agreed that Malta needed to be taken, and were supported by Rommel, busy planning his own offensive. The primary problem was the strength of the Luftwaffe in the region, being too weak to both support Rommel in North Africa and continue to wage the campaign against Malta. Out of that meeting came a commitment to launch the *C3* invasion after Rommel had attacked the Gazala Line and taken Tobruk. Once the crucial port had been taken, the bulk of the Axis aerial forces would be transferred back to Sicily, while PanzerArmee Afrika would dig in near Sollum on the Egyptian border. The two leaders expected both objectives to be achieved by June.[89] Hitler made a point, though, of telling Mussolini that the land war would be decided in the East – only victory over the Soviets would force Britain to discuss peace terms. While victory in North Africa and Malta would significantly contribute to that end, in themselves they would not be decisive.[90]

In London, while the Axis leaders debated their Mediterranean plans, Churchill acted quickly to dampen the dissension disrupting Malta, naming as Dobbie's replacement the current Governor of Gibraltar former Chief of the Imperial General Staff and commander of the British Expeditionary Force in France from 1939–40, John Standish Surtees Prendergast Vereker, the 6th Viscount Gort. The island's new Governor arrived on 6 May, symbolically in the middle of an air raid.[91] In addition to his title as Governor, Churchill also designated General Gort the Supreme Commander of Fighting Services and of Civil Administration.[92] The military and civilian leaders on Malta did not receive the new position and its powers well, but the designation finally put a single individual in charge of everything needed to defend the island. Almost immediately, Gort began reaching out to the population, sharing their rations and danger and using a bicycle to travel around.[93]

Even as Gort arrived, changes were being made. Ultra picked up orders assigning some of Fliegerkorps II – one fighter Gruppe and two Ju88 bomber Gruppes – away from Sicily to Cyrenaica in late April.[94] Other Gruppes were sent to Russia and France. The effects of the transfers were quickly apparent; on 29 April there were 220 Axis sorties over the island, the next day there were sixty-eight.[95]

USS *Wasp* returned to the Mediterranean and, in company with HMS *Eagle*, sent sixty-four Spitfires to Malta on 9 May. Lloyd and his troops had learned their lesson from April, and this time they planned appropriately. The plan – to have all the aircraft serviced and launched within minutes of their arrival – worked perfectly and paid off immediately.

---

88. Strickland apparently disliked Dobbie from the beginning, based on the number of vitriolic letters recently found in the Maltese Archives she wrote against him during that period. Caruana correspondence.
89. Cavallero, Comando Supremo, p.251.
90. Magenheimer, Hitler's War, p.141.
91. Gort's arrival initiated some additional controversy, as departing Governor Dobbie asked the new arrival to see the George Cross which, by Royal Command, Gort was supposed to be carrying. However, a mixup in transportation orders left Gort without the award to show Dobbie. The medal arrived two days later, wrapped in the pyjamas of a courier. Betty, Malta Cross and Controversy.
92. Colville, J.R., Man of Valour, p.248.
93. In November, Gort was severely burned while helping pull petrol tins out of a blazing dump. Colville, p.253.
94. Shores, Spitfire Year, p.221.
95. Bradford, p.221.

On 10 May, the remaining Luftwaffe and Regia Aeronautica pilots who attacked the island ran into a heavily reinforced air defence. Pilots reported sixteen Axis aircraft shot down, with twenty probable kills and twenty-one more damaged.[96] Anti-aircraft gunners claimed an additional seven aircraft shot down. The ecstatic Maltese increased the rumours to claim sixty-three Axis aircraft downed.[97] The *Times of Malta* reported:

> 'After two days of the fiercest aerial combat that has ever taken place over the island, the Luftwaffe, with its Italian Lackeys, have taken the most formidable beating that has been known since the Battle of Britain.'[98]

The reality proved much less than reported – fifteen aircraft were lost and the only plane shot down by anti-aircraft fire was in fact a Spitfire[99] – but it still marked Malta's return to the skies. Ironically, Kesselring reported to Berlin the same day that Malta was completely neutralized as a base. His opinion counted, as more Luftwaffe units left Sicily – four Gruppes to North Africa and one to Crete – and the tonnage of bombs dropped on the beleaguered island fell by more than 90 per cent.[100]

But despite the change in fortune in the air, the problems on the ground still existed. Just before he left, Dobbie had reported that the island's wheat would be used up in early June, other foodstuffs by the end of June, coal in May and kerosene in July.[101] The scarcity of oil made

---

96. Shores, Spitfire Year, p.259.
97. Galea, Michael, Malta: Diary of War, 1940–1945, p.142.
98. Jacobs, p.147.
99. Shores & Cull, Spitfire Year, p.255.
100. Ibid., p.299.
101. War Cabinet, Chiefs of Staff Committee memorandum COS(42) 91.

the water well pumps unusable.[102] Surrender due to starvation remained a looming prospect. Gort ordered the bread ration, the staple of Maltese life, lowered in early May to 10½oz per person per day.[103] Cargo submarines and minelayers such as HMS *Welshman* tried to help, but their small capacity could not offset more than a fraction of the problem. Dobbie's signal had ended: 'If Malta is to be held, drastic action is needed now; it is a question of survival.'[104] They needed a convoy.

In Africa, the stand-off between Rommel and the Eighth Army at Gazala continued, with both sides building up for the inevitable clash. Eighth Army Commander Major General Neil Ritchie and his superior in the Middle East, General Auchinleck, prepared a mid-June attack. Churchill continued his verbal demands for an earlier assault, citing in May that Malta's loss 'would be a disaster of the first magnitude to the British Empire and probably fatal in the long run to the defense of the Nile Valley'. Auchinleck responded that Malta's fall would not necessarily be fatal to Egypt.[105]

On Malta, the defence council finalized a plan in the event of an invasion that all concerned felt was simply a matter of time, even with the apparent decrease in air attacks. The creation of a Western Brigade to be concentrated on the high ground of the Dingli Plateau became a key provision of the new defence plan. The brigade's three battalions – 8th King's Own, 4th the Buffs and 1st Durham Light Infantry – were to act as the fortress reserve, along with the Malta Tank Regiment, and respond in force to any incursion.[106]

Adding to the invasion worries in May, enemy action around Malta's coast picked up. Italian frogmen reconnoitred possible landing areas; they were caught once, losing one man to beach sentries. Island authorities also apprehended two spies. Italian Sottotenente Giuseppe Guglielmo was caught in an abandoned tram car near St Thomas's Bay after being dropped off to study the defences around the bay.[107] The other spy, Maltese exile Carmelo Borg Pisani, had been dropped off at Ras id-Dawwara, ostensibly to get a feel for local sentiment toward an Italian invasion. Pisani failed to negotiate the sheer cliffs in the area, however, and troops rescued him two days after landing. Recognized at the hospital, officials arrested him; he was later tried and executed for treason.[108]

In addition to the British capturing the spies, photo-reconnaissance flights discovered three satellite airfields being built in the vale of Catania on Sicily. Analysts labelled them suitable for glider operations, adding to the worries of airborne attack.[109]

On 26 May, Rommel finally unleashed Operation *Theseus*, attacking the Eighth Army at Gazala. He had a straightforward plan: the Italian infantry would assault the British line to pin and distract the defenders, while his mobile forces – 15th Panzer, 21st Panzer, 90th Light and the Italian Trieste and Ariete divisions – swept around the southern flank. All except the 90th Light would then attack north to cut the British off; the 90th would move toward Tobruk,

---

102. Bradford, p.236.
103. Vella, p.74.
104. Malta at War, Vol 6, #1, p.1,810.
105. Austin, Churchill and Malta's War, pp.190–91.
106. Malta Defence Scheme, May 1942, Part 17, p.8.
107. Operazione 110; Caruana, Battle for Grand Harbour, p.101.
108. Operazione 111; ibid., p.102.
109. Air Battle for Malta, Ch VIII.

acting like a larger force to deter any British reaction.[110] Rommel expected to take Tobruk in four days.[111]

However, the British expected the attack thanks to both Ultra intercepts and local reconnaissance.[112] Rommel, instead of the swift success he envisioned, found himself embroiled in an attritional dogfight. He would later say he failed because he underestimated the British armoured divisions and their new American Grant tanks.[113]

While Rommel attacked, Kesselring presented Cavallero with a plan for taking Malta, developed by German and Italian staff over the past several months. He anticipated a month for the return of Luftwaffe units sent to Africa and their deployment to regain air supremacy. Assuming Rommel being successful in his battles and Operation *Theseus* completed by 17 June, the invasion could take place between 14 and 18 July, the period of the dark moon for the month.[114] General Kurt Student, commander of the German Fallschirmjäger paratroops, inspected the Italian Folgore Parachute Division in June. He declared the division ready for its task in the *C3* plan, but also noted the same problem General Ramcke had months earlier – their weaponry was still too light for the expected fortifications on the island.[115]

The basic *C3* plan involved a landing on Malta's nearly unprotected but rugged south-western coast. The Italians put significant effort into collecting and modifying the boats to be used, outfitting them with wooden bumpers to protect against rocks and with ladders for the infantry to climb the rocky shore – 5–25ft high in places. They also identified a key requirement – fuel oil for their navy. Fuel remained critical for the Regia Marina, which was already idling some ships to provide fuel for others. At Taranto, they siphoned some 500 tons of fuel out of the battleship *Cesare* to fuel destroyers. On 1 June, planners estimated that they would need some 43,000 tons of fuel for the first ten days of the operation. Four days later, Cavallero sent an urgent request to Berlin for 40,000 tons needed in Sicily and southern Italy at least twenty days prior to *C3* to allow rail transport to support troop and equipment transfer.[116]

With the Axis focusing on Rommel's battle in Norfth Africa, Malta slowly recovered from the beating it had endured. The Wellingtons of 104 Squadron returned to the island on 23 May and began flying night-time bombing missions over Sicily and Italy.[117] New Spitfires flew in on three separate occasions to refill Lloyd's depleted squadrons, giving him about ninety-seven aircraft to defend the island.[118]

By 8 June, it became apparent that Rommel could not capture Tobruk in time to launch *C3* in July. A meeting between Kesselring and Cavallero officially postponed the invasion, to allow Rommel to complete his operation. Cavallero noted that the long battle being waged had allowed Malta to start offensive operations again, writing in his diary that re-neutralization of the island would be necessary.[119]

---

110. Pimlot, Rommel in his Own Words, p.95.
111. Boog, Vol VI, 'Global War', p.672.
112. Ibid., p.667.
113. Pimlott, p.97.
114. Lutton, from captured German documents, p.183.
115. Morisi, p.44.
116. Gabriele, p.200, n.11.
117. Shores, Spitfire Year, p.290.
118. Seventeen aircraft in Operation LB on 18 May; thirty-one in Operation Style on 3 June – although five were lost when the flight from HMS Eagle was intercepted by Me109s of II/JG53 from Pantelleria; and thirty-two in Operation Salient on 9 June. Ibid., pp.283, 302, 310.
119. Cavallero, Comando Supremo, p.272.

In Berlin, Hitler had second thoughts about *C3* and, when informed of the fuel oil requirement, initially turned down the request, telling Raeder that regardless of Malta's importance, his upcoming Eastern Front offensive had priority.

By the time the *Harpoon* and *Vigorous* convoys prepared to launch in mid-June, Rommel had broken out and forced the British into retreat. Despite the ongoing battle and the lack of airfields to cover the eastern passage, the Admiralty launched the twin convoy operations.

Operation *Vigorous* came under Admiral Harwood, who formally became Commander-in-Chief Mediterranean on 20 May. It would be his first major command operation since his engagement with and the subsequent scuttling of the German raider *Graf Spee* in the South Atlantic in December 1939.[120] Under his plan, *Vigorous* would launch eleven ships from three different ports toward Malta – five from Haifa (totalling 37,114 tons), two from Alexandria (13,481 tons) and four from Suez (28,072 tons). Supporting them would be a force of eight light cruisers under Admiral Vian, half of which came on loan from Admiral Somerville's Eastern Fleet.[121]

Harwood's basic plan was to set up a picket line of submarines to detect and ambush any Italian incursion against the convoy and to use the Desert Air Force and Malta's renewed air strength against anything the Italians threw at it. His decision to personally command the operation from Alexandria, along with the Air Officer Commanding Middle East, Sir Arthur Tedder – purportedly to improve coordination between the Navy and Tedder's Desert Air Force defenders – became a cornerstone of the plan. With heavy Wellingtons, Beaufort torpedo bombers and American B-24s at their disposal, Tedder felt confident he could repulse any surface threat. Vian, however, had little confidence in either Harwood or his plan.[122]

Between 11 and 13 June, the three sections of the convoy sailed, losing one merchantman that could not keep up. The next day, the Italians sailed from Taranto to intercept with Iachino's two modern battleships, plus two heavy and two light cruisers.

On 15 June, communications problems overwhelmed Vigorous. Signals between Alexandria and Vian took almost two hours for delivery. The assessments of bombing results also took just as long to be delivered, but when they were reported spectacular results:

> 'The attack was made by the two forces [Malta-based aircraft and Desert Air Force units] simultaneously. A number of hits were scored and there was no doubt both the bomb and torpedo attacks were well executed. One of our submarines observed numbers of hits on the battleship *Littorio*, while one "Trento" class cruiser was set on fire by bombs and another sunk by a torpedo. Naval observers in the Liberators [B-24 bombers] saw a cruiser and a destroyer hit by torpedoes.'[123]

The trouble was, the assessments were completely inaccurate: the air attacks actually achieved only a single non-effective bomb hit.[124] The attack on the Italian fleet by Beaufort torpedo

---

120. Harwood had been acting as Assistant Chief of Staff (Foreign) in the Admiralty up to his appointment. Churchill hoped he would instill an offensive spirit in the depleted Mediterranean Fleet, although others in the Admiralty were not as thrilled by the appointment. O'Hara, Passage Perilous, p.54.
121. Churchill had also requested a battleship and carriers from Somerville, but the admiral reportedly demurred, stating that 120 of his carrier aircraft against 1,000 Axis aircraft was an unacceptable risk. Ibid., p.92.
122. O'Hara, In Passage Perilous, p.93. Vian's comments were made ten years after the operation.
123. Tedder, p.297.
124. O'Hara, Passage Perilous, p.113.

bombers had similar results – of the twelve aircraft sent out, seven were lost to defending Axis fighters and the remaining five failed to score any hits, although they claimed two.[125]

Harwood sent six 'reverse course' messages to Vian during the day, having the convoy and escorts move back and forth, based on late and erroneous bombing reports. The various changes in direction spoiled the convoy formation, allowing Axis air attacks and S-boats to score hits. Ultimately, low on fuel and anti-aircraft ammunition, Vian simply continued back to Alexandria. Three destroyers and two merchant ships were lost during the operation, but the final blow came as the convoy was returning, when German U-boat 205 (Kapitänleutnant Franz-Georg Reschke) torpedoed and sank the cruiser HMS *Hermoine*. The Italians suffered torpedo hits (from Malta-based Wellingtons) on the battleship *Littorio* and cruiser *Trento*.

Harwood later reported: '[O]ur air striking force had nothing like the weight to stop a fast and powerful enemy force, and in no way compensated for our lack of heavy ships.'[126]

Meanwhile, to the west, Operation *Harpoon* got under way, with the main convoy – six ships carrying 46,874 tons – passing through the Straits of Gibraltar. The battleship *Malaya*, two small carriers and three light cruisers composed the main escort. The battleship and carriers would turn back south of Sardinia, while a smaller escort of the light anti-aircraft cruiser *Cairo* and nine destroyers would take the convoy through the Straits of Sicily and on to Malta.

Harpoon suffered both submarine and air attacks on its way to the separation point, but lost only one merchant to those attacks. However, after the *Cairo* and convoy split off from the main escort, they were intercepted by the Italian 7th Cruiser Division under Ammiraglio Alberto Da Zara – two light cruisers and five accompanying destroyers – off Pantelleria. On the morning of 15 June, Da Zara sighted the British and, in a nine-hour battle, sank one British destroyer and damaged two others, as well as hitting the outranged and outgunned *Cairo*.[127] While the British fended off the Italian cruisers, air attacks destroyed three of the remaining five merchant ships.

Worse followed off Malta when the convoy remnants sailed into the wrong channel due to miscommunications with the island and hit a minefield, sinking one destroyer and damaging a destroyer and a merchantman. But the two surviving merchant vessels, *Orari* and *Troilus*, did manage to deliver some 15,000 tons of badly needed supply to Malta – little more than 10 per cent of what had been sent in the two convoys. Maltese stevedores and combat troops unloaded the ships in 108 hours.[128]

The exhaustion of Italy's precious fuel oil reserves – four battleships being literally left empty – proved another crucial outcome of the twin operations.[129]

The poor results of the two convoys led Gort to broadcast to the island:

> 'I must break to you what the arrival of only two ships means to us. For some time past we have been short of supplies and further privations lie ahead of us…
> . we must stand on our own resources and everyone of us must do something in

---

125. Gibbs, pp.74–81.
126. Roskill, Vol II, p.72.
127. HMS Cairo was armed only with 4in naval guns, with a theoretical range of 19,000 yards, while the Italians sported 6in guns with a range of 22,600 yards. Ibid., pp.145–46.
128. Hampshires Regimental History, p.54.
129. Gabriele, p.199.

his or her power to conserve our stocks and to ensure the best use is made of all the available resources that remain to us.'[130]

Three days after Gort's broadcast, Lieutenant Governor St John Jackson was more specific, announcing further ration cuts. Bread was not one of them, but Jackson added:

> 'We first calculated the time for which our bread could be made to last. That calculation gave us a certain date … called the "Target Date". Our next task is to make our vital necessities last to the Target Date.'[131]

One key 'vital necessity' – fodder for the island's animals – became so scarce that the goat population began to be consigned to the Victory Kitchens at a rate of 1,000 goats a week, which also began to limit the availability of fresh goats' milk to the island's children and cheese for everyone else.[132]

On 20 June, with Rommel finally closing in on Tobruk, Mussolini stepped in with a personal letter to Hitler, specifying that 'the centre of our strategic framework is the problem of Malta… . [T]he action against Malta is required more than ever … to keep the results achieved in Marmarica [North Africa] and ensure future needs.'[133] The Italian leader also stressed that fuel oil remained vital to the operation.

Rommel's assault on Tobruk quickly broke through its weakened defences. The fortress that had withstood 242 days of siege in 1941 fell in just a day on 21 June. Churchill, in Washington at the time, returned to London to face a vote of 'no confidence' in Parliament. Despite the stunning defeat in North Africa, he easily won that vote by 475–25, but came under increasing political pressure. He later admitted his political weakness, stating that 'it is indeed remarkable that I was not in this bleak lull dismissed from power, or confronted with demands for changes in my methods, which it was known I should never accept'.[134]

Cavallero wrote in his diary on 22 June: 'And now it is essential to carry out *C3*. Otherwise, we cannot have the freedom of manoeuvre.'[135] He sent orders to Generale Ettore Bastico, Commander-in-Chief North Africa and Rommel's superior, to order the German to halt his forces at the Halfaya–Sollum area to begin the build-up for *C3*.

---

130. Galea, Diary, p.142.
131. Perowne, p.153.
132. Jellison, p.230.
133. Galea, Diary, pp.201–02.
134. Reid, Churchill under Friendly Fire, p.219.
135. Cavallero, p.276.

Chapter IV

War
June 1942 – August 1942

However, the easy victory at Tobruk gave Rommel other ideas.[1] Following the capture of the vital port – and its massive fuel and supply depot[2] – Rommel, through direct contact with Hitler, demanded he be allowed to continue his attack into Egypt. He stated: '[T]he condition and morale of the troops, together with the current supply situation resulting from the captured stocks and the enemy's current weakness warrant pursuing him deep into Egyptian territory.'[3] Rommel also stressed the intelligence from what he termed a 'Good Source' that indicated British military weakness and apparent panic in the rear areas around Cairo.[4]

Although the OKW and its head, General Alfred Jodl, concurred with Rommel's thoughts, Kesselring did not. While he agreed that pursuing a beaten enemy and not giving him time to recover was a sound military strategy, Kesselring feared that the breakdown of armour from a deep push into Egypt would be high and replacements could not be expected for a long time. Worse, his airmen would be exhausted and at the end of a long and tenuous supply line, attacking toward intact enemy air bases. He pointed out that British reserves from the Near East would already be on their way.[5] He added that Malta again posed a growing threat, citing as an example the loss of the German freighter *Reichenfels*, a 7,744-ton ship loaded with ammunition, fuel and equipment sunk the previous day by Malta-based Beaufort torpedo bombers.[6] Noting the need for his Luftwaffe pilots to redeploy and rest before undertaking another major operation, he said: 'British sea and air activity against Axis convoys is increasing

---

1. Clarification: At this point, my story of the Second World War takes an alternate direction. Had the alternate events actually occurred, they would have generated sources as did the historical events, and these 'alternate' sources are listed here. All fictional sources are marked with an * to differentiate them from actual historical sources.
2. Along with 33,000 prisoners, Rommel's forces captured 2,000 vehicles, 5,000 tons of food and 2,000 tons of fuel. Greene & Massignani, Rommel's North African Campaign, p.166.
3. Boog, Vol VI, 'Global War', p.709.
4. The 'Good Source' cited by Rommel was intercepted and decrypted signals from the US Military Attaché in Cairo, Colonel Bonner F. Fellers. Italian intelligence agents had succeeded in obtaining the American Black Code keys in August 1941 and were thus able to read all of Fellers's very detailed reports on Britain's North African situation, including orders of battle, tank strength and losses, etc. This wealth of information persisted until July 1942. Behrendt, Rommel's Intelligence in the Desert Campaign, pp.145–46.
5. Kesselring, Memoirs, p.123.
6. The large Bristol Beaufort torpedo bombers that had been stationed on Malta during Operation Vigorous/Harpoon were kept to provide a stronger daylight torpedo bombing capability for the island's anti-shipping operations. Caruana, Victory, pp.90–91.

and with the restrengthening of Malta's air force, Axis supremacy in the Mediterranean is again in danger of crumbling away. Malta must be taken. I must adamantly reject any advance with the objective Cairo at this time.'[7]

Cavallero agreed with his German counterpart, repeating on 26 June that 'the air base in Malta has resumed offensive operations, thus the Tripoli route must be temporarily abandoned. Malta also endangers the routes to the Cyrenaica harbors. It *must* be neutralized again and taken.'[8]

Mussolini wanted to continue the advance into Egypt, and initially Hitler agreed. In a blunt discussion with his paratroop commander, Student, the Führer stated his concerns:

> 'The establishment of the bridgeheads with the airborne forces had been assured. But I guarantee you the following. When the attack starts, the British ships at Alexandria will sail out and also those from the British fleet at Gibraltar. Then see what the Italians do. When the first radio messages arrive about the approach of the British naval forces, the Italian Fleet will run back to its harbours. The warships and the transporters with the forces to be landed will both head back. And then you'll be sitting alone with your paratroops on the island.'

Student responded quickly:

> 'Generalfeldmarschall Kesselring has taken that eventuality into consideration. Then the English will experience what happened to them a year before at Crete when Richthofen came in and sank a portion of the Alexandria squadron. It will be worse for the English, since Malta is within effective range of the Luftwaffe. Malta, *mein* Führer, can thus become the grave of the British Mediterranean Fleet.'[9]

The response mollified the German leader and he finally sided with his Luftwaffe commander on site, wanting to get this thorn in the Mediterranean removed and out of his Eastern Front focus.[10] Rommel received orders to stop at the Egyptian border and regroup while the Malta operation took place. Hitler also finally authorized the transfer of the requested fuel oil for the Regia Marina, as well as the weapons for the Folgore that General Ramcke had requested.[11]

Kesselring issued orders for the Luftwaffe to reconcentrate in Sicily. He argued vehemently that the invasion should take place as soon as air superiority was established and named 27 July as a possible date for the attack. He noted the full moon then would make it easier to go ashore on the selected coastline, as well as aid the defending escorts should the Royal Navy intervene.[12] The Comando Supremo, however, argued against launching the attack then, maintaining that

---

7. *Ibid., p.123.
8. *High Level Reports and Directives dealing with North Africa Campaign, 1942. British Air Ministry Historical Branch, VII/80, pp.11–12.
9. *Kurowski, Jump into Hell, p.215.
10. *Fuehrer Conferences on Naval Affairs, 1939–1945, 26 June 1942, p.290.
11. Morisi, p.28. The weapons included rifles, machine pistols and 225 mortars.
12. *Macksey, Kesselring, p.119.

they needed new moon conditions for surprise. Kesselring acquiesced, but told his superiors that the invasion would now have to occur in August as they did not have enough time before the dark moon period on 13 July to achieve air superiority.[13]

At the end of June, a major landing exercise took place on Italy's rocky coast south of Livorno, between Antignano and Querciannella. Some 4,500 troops swarmed ashore, with King Victor Emmanuel watching and expressing his delight. Other exercises took place between Marina di Pisa and Cecina, all of them being handled well.[14]

The Luftwaffe, following Kesselring's orders, began their redeployment back to Sicily. To back up the bombers, another experienced Jagdgruppe of Bf109F fighters, I/JG77, was ordered from the Eastern Front to support the II/JG53 fighters already there. The new unit was commanded by Hauptmann Heinz Bar, a veteran with 113 victories to his credit.[15]

While the Luftwaffe redeployed, Italy's newly reinforced Regia Aeronautica units in Sicily opened the hoped-for final assault on Malta at the start of July. Colonnello Giuseppe Gaeta, the commander of Comando Bombardmento della Sicilia, had eight bomber groups along with a reinforced fighter contingent. The increased activity – and the Ultra intercepts indicating the return of the Luftwaffe – caught the British Middle East Command at an awkward time. With less activity over the island in June, the British had thought it safe to transfer a full squadron from Malta to Egypt to shore up their defences there, so 601 Squadron had left just prior to the new Italian surge.[16] Within two weeks, the new assaults destroyed thirty-six of Lloyd's fighters and damaged many more. In addition, thirteen pilots had been lost.[17]

In the middle of the air offensive, Lloyd's replacement as RAF commander on Malta arrived; Air Vice Marshal Keith Park, a New Zealander, had commanded the famous 11 Group during the Battle of Britain.[18] In addition to the aircraft reinforcements, Middle East Command also sent a new commanding general for the Malta garrison, General Sir Ronald Mackenzie Scobie, relieving General Beak. A combat veteran of North Africa, having commanded the British 70th Division and the Tobruk fortress in 1941, Scobie had led the breakout during Operation *Crusader*.[19]

Rommel, frustrated at the inactivity he was forced into, invaded Egypt on 7 July in what he termed a reconnaissance in force and hit the Eighth Army's new positions at Mersa Matruh two days later with three German divisions.[20] He hoped to panic the British into a flight he could exploit. But the Eighth Army, now commanded by Auchinleck himself – having sacked former commander General Ritchie after Tobruk fell – refused to conform to Rommel's wishes, holding the line for a day-and-a-half before starting a disciplined fighting withdrawal toward new defensive positions near El Alamein.

---

13. *Kesselring, Memoirs, p.124.
14. Gabriele, p.198.
15. Shores, Spitfire Year, p.380.
16. Ibid., p.371.
17. Cull, Spitfires over Malta, p.212.
18. 11 Group was part of the RAF's Fighter Command that defended England's southern coast and the southeast, as well as the city of London itself. www.battleofbritain.net.
19. One source, the commanding officer of the 8th King's Own Battalion, asserted that both Lloyd and Beak were replaced because they didn't acknowledge Gort's supreme command on the island. Jary, p.127.
20. *Pimlott, p.102.

Despite the determined defence of Auchinleck's troops, Rommel's attack caught the British by surprise as it contradicted what their intercepts had been telling them – that the Axis were going to dig in on the Egyptian border and Luftwaffe units were being recalled to Sicily.[21] With the Germans again moving forward, and facing the threat of escorted air attacks and potential capture, the Royal Navy hurriedly revived the plans it had made in late June to evacuate Alexandria and move eastward to Haifa. The Mediterranean Fleet's commander-in-chief, Admiral Sir Henry Harwood, not wanting to recreate another Singapore disaster,[22] initiated the evacuation.

Although Rommel's panzers pushed the British back, the lack of Luftwaffe support due to their redeployment hurt as the Desert Air Force ruled the skies over him. Indeed, a strafing attack slightly injured the German general and Hitler recalled him to Italy for treatment, leaving the Deutsches Afrikakorps in the hands of General Walther Nehring. The new commander, under strict orders from both the Comando Supremo and Kesselring, withdrew to the Egyptian frontier and dug in at Sollum.[23] When army and air reconnaissance showed the Axis pulling back to the Egyptian frontier, Harwood rescinded his evacuation order and Alexandria returned to normal.[24]

On 15 July, HMS *Eagle* sailed south of Sardinia to transfer thirty-two more Spitfires in Operation *Pinpoint*, bringing Malta's fighter strength back up to where it was before the initial July air offensive. However, the reinforcements received a rough welcome as the newly redeployed Luftwaffe bomber groups began their operations against the island.[25] Kesselring reinstituted the tactics he felt had been successful in March, with large-scale carpet bombing in conjunction with massive fighter sweeps.

Informed of a possible aerial reinforcement for the defenders on Malta, 15 July started with a large raid by the Italians, five Z.1007 bombers being escorted by forty Mc.202 and Re.2002 fighters. Malta responded with twenty-four Spitfires which tangled inconclusively with the escorts. Another raid by some thirty-six German BF109s struck while the defenders were attempting to land to refuel and rearm. As the *Pinpoint* reinforcements began to arrive in the midst of the melee, the Luftwaffe struck with a massive force of sixty-five Ju88 bombers that blanketed Ta'Qali, Kirkop and Safi with 150 tons of bombs and incendiaries; more than twenty of the arriving Spitfires were destroyed or damaged in the initial attack, adding to the day's already heavy losses of seven defending aircraft shot down and three pilots killed. Park, who had wanted his pilots to fly north and hit the attackers aggressively before they got to the island, found his tactics unusable given the scale of the Axis assault. The following day saw more massive raids, with Luqa and Hal Far receiving damage as well.[26]

On 19 July, the Ultra codebreakers at Bletchley intercepted orders to the 1st and 3rd Fallschirmjäger regiments, rebuilding and retraining in Germany and France after their

---

21. *Hinsley, British Intelligence in the Second World War, Vol II, p.392.
22. Harwood felt the withdrawal from Singapore had been left too late. Barnett, Engage the Enemy More Closely, p.516.
23. *Greene & Massignani, p.187.
24. *Playfair, Vol III, p.315.
25. *Greene & Massignani, p.415.
26. *Cull, Spitfires over Malta, pp.225–26.

Eastern Front ordeals, to move to Sicily for 'Operation *Malta*'.[27] The intercept caused a major stir in both London and Valletta as it indicated the Axis finally planned to do what Malta had been expecting since April. The intercept perplexed Churchill. The island's supply situation continued to be poor, and the revived air blitz posed serious problems – mounting losses had dwindled the RAF on the island down to thirty fully functional Spitfires. The Prime Minister doubted the Axis would invade with even that level of air defence awaiting them. Gort agreed with that assessment, but he reminded Churchill of signals sent from the island several months previously indicating the scarcity of small-arms ammunition reserves in the event the threat was genuine.[28] The Admiralty made plans to use HMS *Welshman* to send more ammunition, while they again revisited the possibility of sending a convoy.

When Churchill requested anti-invasion action plans from the Admiralty, he ran into surprisingly stiff opposition. Sir Henry Harwood, still angry over the abject failure of Operation *Vigorous* in June, became the vocal leader of those resisting further naval support for Malta. He had been reluctant then to send that convoy through 'Bomb Alley' – the stretch of sea between Africa and Crete. As he had feared, *Vigorous* failed to deliver any cargo to Malta but cost the light cruiser *Hermoine* and two destroyers, with three other cruisers damaged.

Harwood's arguments were blunt and to the point: under heavy air assault, Malta could not support surface ships, thus any naval invasion reaction would have to come from Gibraltar and Alexandria, each nearly 1,000 miles away. At best speeds, leaving as soon as an invasion started, Royal Navy ships needed a minimum of thirty-six hours to reach Malta from Alexandria, and longer from Gibraltar. With Tobruk in enemy hands, refuelling of the destroyers could only be performed at sea from capital ships. To get to the island with any dispatch would leave the destroyers low on fuel with nowhere to refuel. Their time in the Malta area would be very limited before having to run back to base. With Sicilian bases only sixty miles away, any Axis shipping off Malta would have ample time to retreat to those sanctuaries. Thus, Harwood summarized:

> 'Quite frankly, I do not see how, under the present conditions envisaged, serious loss to the ships can be avoided with no possibility of an acceptable effect on any invasion effort. Any Royal Navy intervention could do too little, be too late and accomplish nothing but sacrifice ships. May I remind the Admiralty of the loss of HMS *Prince of Wales* and HMS *Repulse* off Malaya six months ago.'[29]

Harwood's reservations echoed throughout the Admiralty, especially from First Sea Lord Sir Dudley Pound, who earlier in the war had advocated abandoning Malta. Pound stated:

> Personally, I am extremely doubtful whether any force would be able to achieve anything useful in the face of total enemy supremacy.'[30]

---
27. *Hinsley, British Intelligence, Vol II, p.389. REALITY: On 26 April 1941, Ultra intercepted orders for the Luftwaffe to select air bases for 'Operation Crete' as well as photographs of the island. Hinsley, Vol I, p.416.
28. Dobbie telegram, HE/340 31 March 1942.
29. *Hore, Harwood, p.172.
30. *Roskill, Churchilll and the Admirals, p.325.

Even former Mediterranean Fleet chief Cunningham noted that although he had written earlier in the war that he would have sent every ship he had in the event of an invasion, the situation was different now, with the fleet at such low strength.[31]

Despite the dissension, an angry Churchill ordered the Admiralty to prepare a response; he reminded Pound and the rest of the Admiralty of his statements from April 1941, about accepting losses for important objectives.[32] Frustration abounded in London, the Admiralty's Director of Naval Operations, Captain J.A.S. Eccles, writing in his diary: 'If only the honorable gentleman were to confine himself to statesmanship and politics, and leave naval strategy to those properly concerned, the chances of winning the war would be greatly enhanced. He is without a doubt one of history's worst strategists.'[33]

Substantial naval resources had been focused on convoys to Murmansk in June and July, but the Admiralty was working on preparations for a massive convoy, code-named *Pedestal*, to push through to Malta. However, the plans for *Pedestal* – fourteen fast merchantmen with 100,000 tons of supplies – required air superiority over the island to give the Maltese a chance to unload the ships, and the new Axis blitz now threatened that superiority. Estimates provided by Vice Admiral Leatham on the island stated a maximum of four ships could be unloaded at a time, given the damage to barges, unloading equipment and the wharves themselves, and that the unloading process could take as long as ten to fourteen days.[34] Additional Spitfires were scheduled to accompany the August convoy, set for the mid-month new moon period, aboard the carrier HMS *Furious*, but until then Park would have to handle the new attack with what he had. If the island stayed under significant attack, sending merchant ships would be untenable. On the brighter side, they would have a strong concentration of naval power, a heavy escort of three carriers, two battleships and several cruisers having been designated to take part in *Pedestal* from Gibraltar.

However, the heavy escort was never meant to win through to the island; the Admiralty now needed ships to get to the island to do something against an invasion – cruisers alone might not have a chance against the Italian Navy, especially in good weather. As an additional resource, Churchill suggested adding the battlecruiser HMS *Renown*, having gone through a recent refit and currently idle with the Home Fleet, to the escort, now designated Force X. The big ship would have the speed to keep up with the cruisers and its 15in guns would help balance the enemy superiority. The Admiralty quietly shelved the suggestion after the planners pointedly reminded the Prime Minister of HMS *Repulse*'s fate.[35]

The Admiralty had fewer ships available at Alexandria to provide a threat from the eastern Mediterranean. A large portion of Somerville's Far East fleet remained committed to take part in Operation *Stab*, a feint against the Japanese-held Andeman Islands in support of US operations against Guadalcanal in the Solomon Islands.[36] That left the Mediterranean Fleet with the light

---

31. *Cunningham, p.224.
32. Austin, Churchill and Malta's War, p.88. His quote, speaking about stopping seaborne traffic from Italy to Africa, was: 'For this important objective, heavy losses in battleships, cruisers and destroyers must if necessary be accepted.'
33. *Eccles diary, 19 July 1942. REALITY: this quote was made by the former Director of Operations, Captain Ralph Edwards, in August 1941. Hastings, Winston's War, p.175.
34. Serial T.681/2, 4 May 1942. Most Secret cipher from Vice Admiral Malta to Admiralty.
35. *Pack, S. W. C., August Battle for Malta, p.18.
36. Rohwer, Chronology of the War at Sea, 1939-1945, 184.

cruiser *Arethusa* (6in guns) and three other cruisers (*Cleopatra*, *Dido* and *Euryalus*, each with 5.25in guns) available. As a partial fix, the Admiralty returned the light cruiser *Birmingham* (6in guns) and its escort of three Royal Australian Navy destroyers (*Napier*, *Nizam* and *Norman*) to reinforce the Alexandria force.[37]

While the ships congregated, the Admiralty staff continued their brainstorming discussions on what, if anything, their post-invasion sortie could accomplish. Among the discussed options were the following:

- Resupplying the garrison: but this was improbable if the Axis held full air superiority over Malta. In addition, regular supply ships would slow any combat response. Ammunition resupply by fast minelayers like the *Welshman*, which could carry some 500 tons, and submarines such as HMS *Porpoise* and *Clyde* (configured to carry 70–110 tons) would be included in any response.
- Reinforcing the garrison: this was rejected if not combined with a resupply effort. More mouths on the island would mean quicker exhaustion of the remaining food supply, even if they repulsed the invasion.
- Reinforcing the RAF squadrons: this was possible and attractive as it would impact any battle ashore if the aircraft could arrive, be serviced and get into action without being destroyed enroute or on the ground.
- Distracting or disrupting the Axis: naval intervention would pull Axis air and naval power away from the defenders on Malta. Brainstormed ideas included attacking a target somewhere else, such as Genoa in northern Italy or Tobruk. One additional suggestion was to have Eighth Army, currently holding the line at Sollum, attack westward against the Axis; however, the Admiralty remembered the last failed attempt at coordination between the Eighth Army and the Royal Navy prior to Operations *Harpoon* and *Vigorous*, and felt the plan was unrealistic.
- Night air attack on Sicilian ports by aircraft and/or bombardment.
- Bombardment of any beachhead the Axis had captured: this would pay some dividends and announce to the Maltese that the Royal Navy was trying to help them, as well as disrupt any ongoing supply activities.

The final organization of the naval forces is shown in Table IV-1. Ultimately, the planners realized they couldn't come up with a good idea, so decided to give the on-site commanders the widest latitude possible regarding their orders since they would only know the situation after arriving: they could either sink enemy shipping, disrupt enemy landing areas or support Maltese ground forces as needed. The orders simply read: stop the invasion.

---

37. HMS Birmingham And the Royal Australian destroyers -7th Destroyer Flotilla – had taken part in Operation VIGOROUS in June where a sister ship, RAN Nestor, was sunk. O'Hara, In Passage Perilous, 118.

Table IV-1: Royal Navy Reaction Force Composition*

Force Z – Gibraltar Escort Force	Force X – Malta Reaction Force
Vice Admiral E. Neville Syfret	**Rear Admiral H.M. Burrough**
Battleships	
Nelson (flag), Captain H.B. Jacomb	
Rodney, Captain J.W. Rivett-Carnac, DSC	
Aircraft Carriers	**Light Cruisers**
Rear Admiral A.L. Lyster	*Manchester*, Captain H. Drew
Victorious, Captain H.C. Bovell	*Kenya*, Captain A.S. Russell
809 Squadron, 884 Squadron – 16 Fulmers	*Nigeria* (flag), Captain H.S. Paton
885 Squadron – 6 Sea Hurricanes	*Cairo*, Captain C.C. Hardy
817 Squadron, 832 Squadron – 14 Albacores	**Destroyers**
Indomitable, Captain T.H. Troubridge	*Ashanti* (6 DF), Captain (D) Cmdr R. Oslo
806 Squadron – 10 Martlets	*Tartar*, Cmdr St.J.R.J. Tyrwhitt, DSC
800 Squadron, 880 Squadron – 24 Sea Hurricanes	*Eskimo*, Cmdr E.G. Le Geyt, DSC
827 Squadron, 831 Squadron – 14 Albacores	*Laforey* (19 DF), Captain (D) R.J. Hutton
Eagle, Captain L.D. Mackintosh, DSC	*Lightning*, Cmdr H.G. Waters, DSC
801 Squadron, 813 Squadron – 16 Sea Hurricanes	*Lookout*, Lt Cmdr C.P.F. Brown
Furious, Captain T.O. Bulteel	
804 Squadron, 807 Squadron – 24 Sea Hurricanes	
823 Squadron – 14 Albacores	
Light Cruisers	**Force V – Alexandria Force**
Phoebe, Captain C.P. Frend	**Rear Admiral Sir P.L. Vian**
Sirius, Captain P.W.B. Brooking	
Charybdis, Captain G.A.W. Voelcker	**Light Cruisers**
Destroyers	*Arethusa*, Captain A.C. Chapman
Ithuriel, Lt Cmdr D.H. Maitland-Makgill-Crichton	*Birmingham*, Captain H.B. Crane
Iscarus, Lt Cmdr C.D. Maud, DSC	*Euryalus*, Captain E.W. Bushall
Intrepid, Cmdr E.A. de W. Kitcat	*Cleopatra* (flag), Captain G. Grantham
Foresight, Lt Cmdr R.A. Fell	*Dido*, Captain H.W.U. McCall
Fury, Lt Cmdr C.H. Campbell, DSC	**Destroyers**
Pathfinder, Cmdr E.A. Gibbs, DSO	*Napier* (RAN 7 DF), Captain (D) S. H. Arliss

Penn, Lt Cmdr J.H. Swain	*Nizam* (RAN), Cmdr M.J. Clark
Quentin, Lt Cmdr A.H.P. Noble, DSC	*Norman* (RAN), Cmdr H.M. Burrell
Antelope, Lt Cmdr E.N. Sinclair	*Sikh* (22 DF), Captain (D) St.J Macklethwait
Wishart, Cmdr H.G. Scott	*Zulu*, Cmdr R.T. White
Vansittart, Lt Cmdr T. Johnston, DSC	*Hero*, Lieutenant W. Scott
Westcott, Cmdr I.H. Bockett-Pugh, DSO	*Jervis* (14 DF), Captain (D) A.L. Poland
Wrestler, Lt Cmdr R.W.B. Lacon, DSC	*Javelin*, Lt Cmdr H.C. Simms
Destroyer Escorts	*Kelvin*, Cmdr M.S. Townsend
Derwent, Cmdr R.H. Wright, DSC	*Pakenham* (12 DF), Captain (D) E. Stevens
Bramham, Lieutenant E.F. Baines	*Paladin*, Cmdr A.F. Pugsley
Bicester, Lt Cmdr S.W.F. Bennets	
Ledbury, Lt Cmdr R.P. Hill	
Zetland, Lieutenant J.V. Wilkenson	Sources: Smith, Peter, *PEDESTAL*
Wilton, Lt. A.P. Northey, DSC	website: www.unithistories.comin

Despite the vague mission statement, both Vian and Burrough immediately recognized their primary goal would be the disruption/destruction of the enemy transports, and signalled that intention to the Admiralty.

The Royal Navy's operational staff immediately discarded the suggestion that the Alexandria squadron leave as soon as possible to intervene on the second night after an invasion started, as Vian's cruisers would then face the bulk of the Italian Fleet on their own.[38] Planners then used as an initial guide the convergence of the two forces off Malta at midnight on the third night after the invasion, despite Harwood's immediate and strenuous objection that this would be far too late to be meaningful. The admiral sent a personal and very blunt signal to the Prime Minister: 'We are here trying to face realities and to present to you the situation as it appears to us, not as you would like it to be.'[39]

The planners then discarded the midnight convergence plan itself when Burrough, designated commander of Force X, noted that his ships would have to navigate the Cape Bon area's extensive minefields in broad daylight well within range of Axis airfields. He brusquely stated that having to manoeuvre ships in that restricted area under attack would be sacrificial at best, lunacy at worst.[40] Accordingly they altered the plan to put Force X off Malta near dawn.

Harwood continued his objections to the whole intervention plan, especially for his small Mediterranean Fleet's use and their vulnerability to the Axis air gauntlet they would run. However, Churchill gained some support from Air Chief Marshal Tedder. Despite the lack of success his bombers had achieved against the Italian fleet during the failed Vigorous convoy

---

38. *Pack, August Battle for Malta, p.24.
39. *Reid, p.108. REALITY: this was a signal that General Auchinleck sent to Churchill when the Prime Minister demanded offensive action from the Eighth Army.
40. *Pack, August Battle, p.26.

attempt in June,[41] Tedder pointed out that his air forces were strong and still growing. He had five full squadrons of Wellington bombers at his disposal, as well as B-24 and B-25 bomber squadrons newly arrived from the United States.[42]

Furthermore, while his strength grew, the Axis air strength opposing his in the desert was being significantly weakened by the diversion of aircraft to Sicily for the continued blitz against Malta, giving what intelligence estimated was a two-to-one advantage in the air. He argued that a strong assault by his bombers could disrupt enemy air reaction to Vian's cruisers, giving them a chance to break through Bomb Alley relatively intact.[43]

Ultimately, the Royal Navy's staff arrived at a hodge-podge plan putting Vian's Alexandria force off Malta at midnight and Burrough's Force X off the island the following dawn to do what they could to stop the invasion's success, while Force Z made a feint north after separating. The only major change the planners made discarded the intent to fly Spitfires into Malta during the operation; Malta HQ informed them that all the airfields on the island would be blocked and mined in the event of an invasion and loss of their own aircraft. The Admiralty ordered the nominal squadron pilots from HMS *Furious* to return from the UK to Gibraltar and rearm the carrier with Sea Hurricanes and Albacores, adding their strength to the air defences of Force Z. Home Fleet officers protested this change, concerned about potential Kriegsmarine activity when most of the carriers were involved in the Med.[44]

While the Admiralty staff struggled with orders and goals for its surface forces, another discussion took place at Northways in Swiss Cottage, north London, headquarters of Vice Admiral Sir Max Horton, Flag Officer, Submarines. Plans had been in the works to transfer Captain George Simpson's 10th Submarine Flotilla back to Malta before the current air blitz got under way. Horton hesitated about recommitting Simpson's boats back to the island because of the potential for heavy losses; those sustained by the submarines during the April–May blitz had been the reason Horton had ordered their withdrawal then.[45]

However, Simpson and his immediate supervisor in the Middle East, Captain (S)1 Philip Ruck-Keene, stressed to their flag officer that submarines would be the only immediate Royal Navy response to an invasion. They could potentially interdict bombardment and transport forces as well as provide reconnaissance and early warning. Simpson had made the same arguments against withdrawal back in April.[46] The two men noted the recent signal from Vice Admiral Leatham in Malta, citing the work of minesweepers clearing the approach channels.[47]

---

41. During Operation Vigorous, very little damage had been done. The Italians reversed course back to Italy when they realized they could not catch the retreating convoy. Tedder and the Americans took credit for the repulse, explaining the lack of success on poor reconnaissance and bombs that were too small. Tedder, p.297.
42. The United States had begun sending military aircraft to the Middle East in June 1942. The first unit, designated Halpro, consisted of thirteen B-24 Liberator bombers, which bombed the Ploesti oil refineries in Romania on 11 June. As noted above, the Liberators took part in attacks on the Italian Fleet that same month, claiming hits on the battleship Littorio and cruiser Trento. By mid-August, the US Army Air Force had the 57th Fighter Group, 12th Bombardment Group (Medium) and 98th Bombardment Group (Heavy), as well as the 1st Provisional Bombardment Group, as the Halpro aircraft were redesignated. Craven, Army Air Forces in World War II, Vol III, pp.8–27.
43. *Tedder, pp.344–46.
44. *Pack, August Battle, p.28.
45. Wingate, The Fighting Tenth, p.179.
46. Ibid., p.172.
47. Ibid., p.197. Signals from Leatham sent 5 July 1942.

80   Operation C3: Hitler's Plan to Invade Malta 1942

Given Churchill's adamant demands for action, Horton reluctantly issued orders for Simpson to redeploy his flotilla back to the beleaguered island for use against the invasion.

The 10th Flotilla's complement initially included only four submarines: P31, P34, P35 and *Una* (N87). Knowing more coverage would be needed, Horton provided P42, P44, *Utmost*, P43, P46 and the promise of an S-class submarine, P222, if it arrived in time. Given the paucity of fuel and torpedoes on the island, the submarines would only be able to deploy nominally against the invasion, not in a true war patrol function. Simpson and Ruck-Keene began puzzling over how best to deploy this limited resource in the time they had.

On Malta, Governor Gort and his staff studied their own options. They had a defence scheme in place, developed in May when the last invasion scare occurred. That scheme spread the infantry into battalion sectors that covered the island and its airfields. They had now also set aside three battalions and their tanks into a separate brigade – the recently renamed 4 Brigade – that would act as their reserve reaction force.

More problematical were the local air and naval resources that could conceivably challenge the invasion. Gort and Park had to assume they would have minimal aircraft available, given the level of bombardment they were experiencing. They also had pitifully few naval options. Only the destroyer escort *Badsworth* with six 4in guns and no torpedoes, minesweepers *Speedy*, *Rye* and *Hythe* – sporting either a single 3in or 4in gun – plus the trawler *Beryl* remained afloat at Valletta. The destroyer HMS *Matchless*, the only ship with torpedoes, had been under repair after mine damage in Operation *Harpoon*, but had been sunk at the dock days earlier. Its wreck in #1 Dock also kept the minesweeper HMS *Hebe* out of the action, as its underwater damage could not be repaired.

The seven Fairmile motor launches of the 3rd Motor Launch Flotilla (Lieutenant Commmander E.J. Strowlger commanding) represented the only other naval asset they had. These sleek 112ft craft could make 21 knots, but they only carried First World War-vintage 3-pdr guns and twin Lewis machine guns. Several of the launches, including the flotilla's lead boat, ML-126 (Lieutenant G.W. Stead, second–in–command of the flotilla), had been upgraded with 20mm Oerlikon cannons to provide some additional firepower.

Realistically, Gort and Leatham had little hope that these naval assets could have a decisive impact on an invasion. Discussion with the commanding officers of the ships and motor launches brought up an additional coordination problem, namely their speeds. Lieutenant Gordon Gray, commander of the *Badsworth*, noted that while his ship had a maximum speed of 27 knots, the minesweepers could only make at most 16 knots and the motor launches 21. Pinning the destroyer escort to either or both groups, he noted, would not allow him to use his ship to the best of its ability.

Knowing that these small ships could not make a significant difference, Gort suggested using them to block the harbour if needed and forming their crews into a naval battalion. But both Strowlger and Stead were adamant to try something, suggesting to split the flotilla into two packs to better react to enemy moves.[48] Lieutenant Gray was even more vociferous about 'fighting his ship'.[49] Gort granted them their attempt. Thus, once an invasion became imminent – and word of naval moves were received – three motor launches, led by Strowlger, would be relocated to St Thomas's Bay in the south, and four, led by Stead, to St Paul's

---

48. *Stead, A Leaf upon the Sea, p.92.
49. *Colville, p.212.

Bay in the north. Gray on *Badsworth* would act independently, but initially accompany the minesweepers out of the harbour to make use of his radar.

Axis air attacks continued ramping up in size and began once again to seriously wear down the defending forces. By the end of July, Malta had lost its offensive punch again and operational Spitfires, while taking their toll on attackers, were dwindling. By mid-August, bombing totals were reaching April levels. Fliegerkorps II commander Generalleutnant Loerzer reported to Kesselring:

> '[I]n the period July 15 to August 13, 1942, Malta has once again been destroyed as a base. Total sorties flown: 5,622 bomber, 5,435 fighter and 322 reconnaissance; 2,320 tons of bombs dropped on the airfields of Ta'Qali, Luqa and Hal Far: another 1,940 tons on the harbour and shipyards.'[50]

The renewed German air blitz, building off the earlier Italian offensive, reduced Park's assets to eight serviceable fighters,[51] forcing him to hold his remaining platforms for a last-ditch effort against the enemy paratroop transports.

Special Intelligence[52] from London reported Italian naval signals calling for a significant concentration of shipping in the Sicilian ports of Reggio Calabria, Milazzo, Riposto, Termini Imerese, Palermo, Mazara del Vallo, Marsala, Augusta, Syracuse, Licata and Porto Empedocle.[53] Photo-reconnaissance flights spotted gliders and increased shipping in Sicilian harbours, while decryptions picked up large numbers of sailing orders for 14 August. Simpson began deploying his submarines, sending three to patrol off the Sicilian ports of Augusta, Licata and Porto Empedocle. In addition, he sent one boat south-east to the Medina Banks and another north-west toward Pantelleria. He retained three for deployment to cover Malta's northern shoreline, and kept the P43 boat at Manoel Island as a last reserve. From his headquarters in Cairo, Air Marshal Tedder suggested flying eight Wellingtons to Malta with extra crews, to fly several sorties at night against the Sicilian ports to attack the shipping there; Park turned down the request because night-bombing accuracy had been dismal, except in full moon conditions, and aviation fuel was scarce.[54]

General Scobie issued orders for his troops to increase their ration intake to prepare for the inevitable. On 14 August, Gort and Scobie initiated the procedures for an imminent invasion, code word *Volcano*, to put the entire island on heightened alert.

---

50. *Cull, Spitfire, p.241.
51. *Vella, p.119; Cull, Spitfire, p.242.
52. Ultra and C38m intercepts.
53. *Hinsley, British Intelligence, Vol II, p.395.
54. *Tedder, p.268.

Chapter V

Malta's 1942 Defensive Plans

Infantry

When Britain entered the First World War, the British Army had a very human-centred battle doctrine; basically, victory would go to the side with the higher morale and greater determination to prevail.[1] Under that doctrine, the British Army suffered almost 2,000,000 casualties, a slaughter that greatly affected the country's preparations for another conflict. For most of the inter-war period, as noted earlier, Britain's focus was on Empire preservation and avoidance of another major war.[2] With an eye toward deterring potential opponents, spending priorities put the Army last behind the Royal Navy and Royal Air Force.

Following the Great War, the British Army reverted to its pre-war organization of a 200,000-man Regular Army, backed up by its Territorial Army reserves. Its objectives were to defend the home country, police the Empire and secure the naval bases abroad.[3] It wasn't until March 1939 that the Army began a belated gearing-up for a potential role in another war on the continent. However, the government made two basic assumptions that governed the Army's re-tooling: first, that British society would never allow another slaughter of men as occurred in the First World War; and second, that the soldiers themselves would not sacrifice at the same level.[4]

With those assumptions in mind, the war planners created a battle doctrine that stressed firepower over manpower and mobile operations. However, government priorities and an autocratic command structure failed to provide the equipment or the training needed to make such a doctrine work.

The basic building block of British infantry units was the section, which included a light machine gun and seven to ten riflemen. Three such sections combined with a small headquarters group and a 2in mortar team to create a platoon, while three such rifle platoons created a company. Four companies and a variety of additional support platoons – engineers and 3in mortars – made up a rifle battalion. Figure V-1 shows this organization.

The Bren light machine gun, a derivative of a Czech-designed machine gun retooled to take the British .303cal round, formed the primary firepower of the section. A magazine-fed machine gun, it used thirty-round magazines inserted at the top. Unfortunately, the magazine

---
1. French, Raising Churchill's Army, p.17.
2. Williamson & Millett, Military Effectiveness, Vol 2: Inter War Period, Ch 4, 'The British Armed Forces, 1918–1939', p.99.
3. Bidwell & Graham, Fire-Power, p.150. Policing included counter-insurgency tasks in Palestine, Iraq and India, plus riot control.
4. French, p.275.

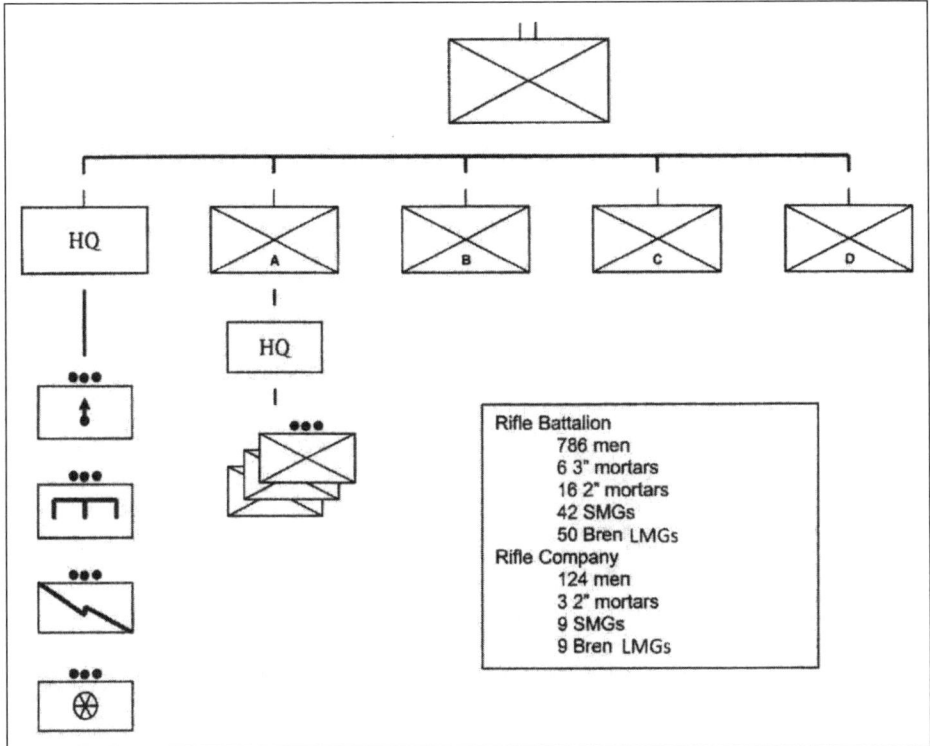

Figure V-1: *Typical British Rifle Battalion Organization.*

kept it from providing the sustained fire that the German belt-fed MG34 light machine gun could; the Bren could achieve 120 rounds per minute in rapid fire, but normally saw just half that rate,[5] while the MG34 fired nearly 900 rounds per minute. The remaining troops in the section carried the Short Magazine Lee Enfield (SMLE) No1 rifle, a bolt-action rifle fed by a ten-round magazine which had an effective range out to 550 yards.

Mortar support for British infantry came from a 2in mortar assigned to each platoon and from 3in mortars that could be assigned from the battalion. The 2in mortars had a very limited range of 500 yards and were generally best used to provide smoke to cover an assault. The 3in mortars, though, had a range of 1,600 yards and proved to be effective support pieces.

The First World War-vintage Vickers water-cooled machine gun remained the only heavy machine gun in the British arsenal. Grouped into specifically developed machine-gun battalions, these belt-fed guns could provide sustained fire at a maximum of 500–600 rounds per minute out to 2,000 yards.[6] The 1st Battalion, the Cheshire Regiment, stationed on Malta, was organized as a machine-gun battalion with its four companies armed with forty-eight Vickers machine guns to augment 566 rifles among its 711 troops.

---

5. TM 30-410, p.132.
6. Ibid., p.138.

Several battalions that started the war on Malta created an exception to the above organization by establishing a fifth company, E Company, to provide more coverage of the island early in the war before reinforcement battalions arrived. The King's Own Malta Regiment battalions organized the same way, with five companies. Comparing them their potential opponents, a full-strength German Fallschirmjäger company fielded 162 men supported by forty MP40 submachine guns, eleven MG34 machine guns and three 50mm leGrW36 mortars that had an effective range of 600 yards. The Italian Folgore parachute companies fielded three platoons and a weapons platoon, totalling about the same size as a basic British company, supported by eighteen light machine guns, a like number of submachine guns plus four heavier machine guns and 45mm mortars. On a full-strength company basis, the British had a disadvantage against the Germans but were on a par with the Italians.

The brigade organization on Malta focused solely on administrative duties. Prior to August 1942, no brigade-level training plan existed on the island; most of the infantry trained sporadically at the platoon, company and battalion level, interspersed with the required war effort work done by the infantry in maintaining and repairing airfields and unloading ships when necessary. This war effort work took priority over all else. As noted in the war diary of 1 (Southern) Brigade, 'anything in the nature of an uninterrupted training programme has been impossible'.[7]

1 (Southern) Brigade

Malta's 1 Brigade, as it was designated on 13 July 1942, consisted of the 2nd Battalion Devonshire Regiment; 1st Battalion, Dorsetshire Regiment; 1st Battalion, Hampshire Regiment; and 3rd Battalion, King's Own Malta Regiment. The brigade, commanded by Brigadier Kenneth Pearce Smith from its headquarters located at Bubakra, had as its primary responsibilities the defense of the southern coastline, Marsa Scirocco Bay, Hal Far airfield, Kalafrana seaplane base and the incomplete Qrendi airfield that was under construction.

2nd Battalion, Devonshire Regiment
The 2nd Battalion of the Devons landed on Malta in July 1938 aboard the troopship *Lancashire* to become part of the pre-war Malta Brigade. Their primary responsibility consisted of defending Hal Far airfield and the Kalafrana seaplane base. In the early days of the war, prior to substantial reinforcement, the Devons established an E Company to their basic organization to allow them to provide coverage of a greater area. Lieutenant Colonel A.W. Valentine commanded the battalion, with his battle headquarters outside Ghaxaq.

1st Battalion, Dorsetshire Regiment
The 1st Battalion landed in Malta in June 1939, again aboard the *Lancashire*, to join the Malta Brigade after three years in India.[8] Originally tasked with protecting the south-eastern section of the island, they covered St Thomas's Bay to Marsascala from their headquarters near Zejtun. They also included an E Company in their tactical organization. Lieutenant Colonel A. Grimley commanded the battalion following Ivan de la Bere's promotion to brigadier and assignment to command Central (3) Brigade in August 1941. On 31 July 1942, they fielded a force of 846 officers and men.[9]

---
7. WO 169/7396, 1 Brigade war diary, May 1942.
8. Malta at War, Vol 1, #5, p.123.
9. WO 169/7427, 1st Dorsetshire war diaries, July 1942.

1st Battalion, Hampshire Regiment

The 1st Battalion arrived in Malta from Alexandria in February 1941 aboard the cruisers *Orion*, *Gloucester* and *Ajax* after a tour of duty in the desert at Mersa Matruh, along with the 1st Battalion, Cheshire Regiment. Lieutenant Colonel J.L. Spencer commanded the battalion, with headquarters at Ix Xlejli Tower. Their reported strength at the end of June was 766 officers and men.[10]

Its experience on the island typified that of all the infantry battalions: war effort parties for aircraft pen building, bomb crater filling and a very little infantry training. They also defended Hal Far and the Safi dispersal strip with small-arms fire – they expended 1,222 rounds of machine-gun fire during the first week of May, for example.[11] In 1942, the battalion became the mobile reserve for the Southern Brigade.[12]

3rd Battalion, King's Own Malta Regiment

The King's Own Malta Regiment had its beginnings back in 1801, when the British formed the Cacciatori Maltesi from Maltese natives to help them blockade the French in Valletta. They took various forms until 1923 before being disbanded, with only a cadre left in place. At the outbreak of the Second World War, the British re-formed the regiment, which ultimately included four battalions and some 5,000 officers and men.[13]

The 3rd Battalion formed in early 1940, with Lieutenant Colonel Mario Apap Bologna as its commander. It included an E Company in its basic tactical organization, intended to supply replacements for casualties among the regular companies. In 1941, the battalion moved to the south-east corner of the island, placing its headquarters at Qrendi village. Its area of responsibility included defending Hal Far and Luqa airfields, as well as the Qrendi and Safi landing sites. They also had responsibility for the Zurrieq cliff area, one of the few areas on the southern coast with a relatively easy landing area (Wied iz-Zurrieq creek).[14] The battalion had 725 officers and men on its rolls at the end of July 1942.[15]

2 (Northern) Brigade

Consisting of the 8th Battalion of the Manchester Regiment, 2nd Battalion of the Royal Irish Fusiliers and 1st and 2nd Battalions, King's Own Malta Regiment, 2 Brigade was commanded by Brigadier Frederic Adrian Joseph Evans Marshall from his headquarters at Castello Tas Sultan. It had the defence of everything north of the Victoria Defence Lines, plus Ta'Qali aerodrome, as its primary responsibility.

8th Battalion, Manchester Regiment

The 8th (Ardwick) Battalion landed on Malta in May 1940 aboard the troopship *Oronsay*, only three weeks before Italy declared war. Initially penny-packeted all over the island, they covered airfields and coastline. By 1942, their responsibility had changed to include the area east of the

---

10. WO 169/7429, 1st Hampshire war diaries, June 1942.
11. Ibid., May 1942.
12. Malta at War, Vol 2, p.570.
13. Ibid., Vol 1, #3, p.58.
14. Wismayer, J.M., The History of the King's Own Malta Regiment and the Armed Forces of the Order of St John, p.201.
15. WO 169/7422, 3rd KOMR war diary, July 1942.

Victoria Lines up to Ta'Qali airfield and from the northern coast to Rabat. Lieutenant Colonel G.A. French (from the 2/Royal Irish Fusiliers) commanded the battalion following General Brittorous's promotion to command 4 (Western) Infantry Brigade. They had their headquarters at San Pawl tat-Targa. They initially followed the habit of creating an E Company to help cover their assigned territory early in the conflict, but amalgamated the unit into A Company in July 1942.[16]

2nd Battalion, Royal Irish Fusiliers

The 2nd Battalion landed on the island in September 1939 aboard the troopship *Dunera*. Much of their early duties included fortifying the northern coastline with wire and mines to forestall landing attempts there, as well as providing the initial security for Ta'Qali airfield.[17] Once the island infantry split into four brigades, the Irish became the mobile reserve of 2 Brigade, ready to move against any incursion. Led by Lieutenant Colonel A.A.J. Allen from headquarters near the Tas-Salib crossroads on Wardija Ridge, his troops practiced 'fighting patrols' and company manoeuvees when not providing work parties at Ta'Qali.[18]

1st and 2nd Battalions, King's Own Malta Regiment

The 1st Battalion of the King's Own Malta Regiment initially formed from the cadre of its previous incarnations and numbered some 1,400 troops among its five line companies and headquarters company. As with the 3rd Battalion, E Company was intended as a replacement unit. Lieutenant Colonel E.J. Newell commanded the unit in 1942, which posted in the north covering the island from the Comino Channel to the Bajda Ridge from its headquarters in Mellieha.

The 2nd Battalion formed, with 900 troops, in September 1939, initially under Lieutenant Colonel A.V. Mallia. After training, the battalion spent time in the Marsaxlokk area, then Rabat, and finally further north to cover St Paul's Bay from its headquarters at Casa Torregiani on Wardija Hill. Lieutenant Colonel R. Strickland commanded the 675 troops at its wartime strength in July 1942.[19]

3 (Central) Brigade

The island's 3 Brigade consisted of the 11th Battalion, Lancashire Fusiliers; 1st Battalion, Cheshire Regiment (machine-gun battalion); and 2nd Battalion, Queen's Own Royal West Kents. Commanded by Brigadier General Sir Ivan de la Bere (formerly of the Dorsetshire Regiment) from a battle headquarters at the Government Technical School at Mriehel (between Attard and Birkirkara), the brigade defended Valletta Keep, Luqa airfield and the coast between Madliena Tower and Sliema as its primary responsibilities.

11th Battalion, Lancashire Fusiliers

Most of the 11th Battalion reached Malta in July 1941 aboard the light cruiser *Edinburgh* as part of the larger Operation *Substance* resupply convoy. The battalion's C Company arrived

---

16. WO 169/7433, 8th Manchester war diary, July 1942.
17. Malta at War, Vol 1 #5, p.126.
18. WO 169/7430, 2nd Royal Irish Fusiliers war diary, July 1942.
19. WO 169/7421, 2 KOMR war diary, July 1942.

on the fast minelayer *Manxman* a month later. Attached to the Central Brigade, they had responsibility for defence on the northern coast and for supporting Luqa airfield in any capacity needed. Work parties of 200-plus at Luqa became the usual order of the day.[20] They also took part in the detailed plans to unload any ships that arrived in June 1942 from Operations *Harpoon* and *Vigorous*. The battalion was put in charge of the temporary dumps set up to take the unloaded supplies prior to their distribution around the island.[21] Lieutenant Colonel G.F. Page commanded the Fusiliers from his headquarters in Birkirkara.

1st Battalion, Cheshire Regiment

The 1st Battalion arrived in Malta from Alexandria in February 1941 aboard the cruisers *Orion*, *Gloucester* and *Ajax*, along with the 1st Battalion, Hampshire Regiment. Engineering turned out to be their initial assignment, preparing Luqa airfield for more aircraft. Their primary responsibility soon included the defence of Valletta and the dockyard area. In this capacity, they aided in repulsing the MAS attack on Grand Harbour in July 1941, being officially (but erroneously) credited with the sinking of an Italian E-boat.[22] Lieutenant Colonel D.E.F. Waight commanded the battalion from their headquarters in Floriana, which was destroyed four times by bombs.[23]

Their war effort tasks took up a significant amount of their time, with work parties of 100-plus filling bomb craters and building aircraft pens at Luqa.[24] They also spent time unloading ships on the docks. For example, they received citations for courageously helping unload the merchant ship *Pampas* in March 1942 after it had been sunk at its moorings. Seventy-two soldiers of the Cheshires actually attended 'skilled labour' training at the dockyard to learn how to handle dock winches, among other skills.[25]

2nd Battalion, Queen's Own Royal West Kents

The 2nd Battalion landed in Malta from Palestine on the troopship *Dunera* in August 1939, just prior to the outbreak of the war, and received responsibility for defence of the south-east coast, including Marsa Scirocco Bay, Wied Zurrieq and Ghar Lapsi, where their first duty became creating the beach posts they needed.[26]

In May 1940, the battalion began preparing Hal Far and Ta'Qali airfields for defence, but soon moved to Luqa airfield.[27] Because of the prime target status of Luqa, the battalion's headquarters relocated underground near the civil abattoir.[28] Their tactical organization included an E Company. Lieutenant Colonel R.O. Pulverman commanded the battalion.

---

20. WO 169/7432, 11th Lancashire Fusiliers war diary, May 1942.
21. Ibid., June 1942.
22. Malta at War, Vol 2, pp.569–70. The Cheshires opened fire on the enemy boat while it was going away from them. When they stopped firing, the boat was gone, so they claimed the sinking. The boat they were firing at was actually sunk by gunfire from St Elmo Fort twenty minutes later. Caruana correspondence.
23. Ibid., p.570.
24. WO 169/7425, 1st Cheshire war diary May 1942.
25. Ibid., June 1942.
26. Chaplin, The Queen's Own Royal West Kent Regiment, 1920–1950, p.113.
27. Ibid., p.84.
28. Malta at War, Vol 1, pp.124–25.

4 (Western) Brigade

Malta Headquarters formally established Western Brigade on 12 May 1942 and posted it on the high ground in the Dingli–Rabat area to act as the Fortress Reserve tasked, along with Malta's tank squadron, with being the island mobile reserve to strike any enemy penetration. The brigade consisted of the 4th Battalion of the Buffs, 8th Battalion of the King's Own Royal Regiment and the 1st Battalion, Durham Light Infantry. Commanded by Major General Francis Gerrard Russell Brittorous (formerly of the Manchester Regiment,) it had its brigade headquarters at Annunziata Church outside Rabat. As with the other brigades, its designation was changed, to 4 Brigade, in July 1942.

4th Battalion, the Buffs

The 4th Battalion sailed for France in November 1938, and when the German armies swept through Belgium in May 1940, it became part of a brigade sent to help the French stem the breakthrough. They fought hard but suffered from a lack of artillery and air support, losing the best part of two companies before the remainder managed to withdraw through Cherbourg to England.

The battalion landed in Malta on 10 November 1940, transported from Gibraltar on the battleship HMS *Barham* and cruisers HMS *Berwick* and *Glasgow* as part of Operation *Coat*. Initially commanded by Lieutenant Colonel F.A.J.E. Marshall, the unit was posted near Ta'Qali to provide security and work parties. In May 1942, the Buffs received an assignment to 4 Infantry Brigade for service in the event of an invasion. With headquarters near Nadur Tower, their commander became Lieutenant Colonel David P. Iggulden when Marshall received command of 2 Brigade.

8th Battalion, King's Own Royal Regiment

The 8th Battalion's journey to Malta proved to be an adventure in itself. First, the troopship they embarked on for Operation *Substance* ran aground, then the cruiser they reembarked upon, HMS *Manchester*, was torpedoed enroute and had to turn back to Gibraltar. Finally, on 2 August 1941, the battalion arrived in Malta aboard cruisers *Hermoine* and *Arethusa* and the minelayer *Manxman* as part of Operation *Style*. Their initial assignment on the island was defence of Luqa airfield and anti-parachute patrolling.[29]

In May 1942, Lieutenant Colonel L.H. Westropp and his battalion became part of 4 Brigade and relocated with headquarters near the Palace at Girganti located on high ground overlooking most of the island. Their work party requirements continued, but the battalion also instituted training programmes focusing on anti-parachute action against both disorganized and organized paratroop resistance, and 'night attack over walled country'.[30]

1st Battalion, Durham Light Infantry (DLI)

The 1st Battalion became the last infantry reinforcement to reach the island, arriving in two parts in January and March 1942. One of the few infantry units that had combat experience, the battalion had taken part in Operation *Brevity* in North Africa, in which they suffered some

---

29. Malta at War, Vol 3, p.1,033.
30. WO 169/7434, 8th King's Own war diary, July 1942.

160 casualties. They served in Egypt with 23 Infantry Brigade, 70th Infantry Division. In January 1942, C and D Companies and the headquarters loaded onto the transport *Breconshire*, with B Company on accompanying destroyers, as part of supply convoy MF4 to Malta. They arrived on 27 January 1942 to be stationed near Verdala.

The Durhams' A Company tried to make the journey in February as part of convoy MF5, but that attempt ended with two of the three merchant ships sunk and the damaged survivor rerouted to Tobruk. They tried again aboard the *Breconshire* as part of the ill-fated MW10 convoy that ran afoul of the Italian Navy in the Gulf of Sirte (see Chapter III). Although Admiral Vian's force of light cruisers held off the Regia Marina, Axis aircraft caught the remaining merchantmen short of Malta. The disabled *Breconshire* had to be beached at Marsaxlokk, allowing A Company to finally join its battalion.[31]

After its assignment to 4 Brigade, the battalion split its time, with two companies providing work parties for Luqa, one company performing night patrols along the southern coast from Ta Zuta to Il Kaws, and the final company training at the platoon and section level. The battalion, with Lieutenant Colonel E.A. Arderne commanding from their headquarters at Boschetto Gardens, had a strength of 648 officers and men at the end of July 1942.[32]

Armour

The Maltese received their first tanks in November 1940 with the arrival of a detachment from the Royal Tank Regiment. Christened No 1 Independent Troop, Royal Tank Regiment, the unit consisted of two Light Tank Mk VICs and four Matilda Mk IIIs (A12, Infantry Tank Mk IIA), the latter being detached from the 7th Royal Tank Regiment. Acting Major R.E.H. Drury commanded a total complement of sixty-eight officers and men.

In early 1942, A Squadron, 6th Royal Tank Regiment, reinforced the troop with four A9s (Cruiser Tank Mk I), three A13 Mk IIs (Cruiser Tank Mk IVA) and one Light Tank Mk VI.[33] Five more tanks of unknown type did not make it to the island from Alexandria. Acting Major S.D.G. Longworth took over command of the combined force[34].

The new Malta Tank Squadron,[35] (or simply 'Malta Tank') reorganized as follows:[36]

- 1 Troop: one Light Tank Mk VI plus two Light Tank Mk VICs.
- 2 Troop: three A9s (Cruiser Tank Mk I).
- 3 Troop: three A13 Mk IIs (Cruiser Tank Mk IVA).
- 4 Troop: three Matilda Mk IIIs (A12, Infantry Tank Mk IIA).[37]
- Reserve: one A9 plus one Matilda Mk III.

---

31. Rissik, The D.L.I. at War, p.71.
32. WO 169/7428, 1st Durham Light Infantry war diary, July 1942.
33. According to some sources, these eight new tanks were all Cruisers. If true, this means one Cruiser was soon lost, and one light tank arrived at some unspecified time.
34. Vella, pp.85–86.
35. David Fletcher, Matilda Infantry Tank 1938–45 (Osprey Publishing, 1994), p.44.
36. Malta Command Military Defence Scheme, Appendix C.X.
37. Fletcher, p.44.

On the island, the Matildas' rugged build and armour allowed them to be used on airfields as well-protected tractors, to move aircraft around or to remove wreckage. The Cruiser tanks also acted as tractors for a while, but used too much fuel in that capacity.[38] The unit spent time at the Ghajn Tuffieha range for field firing and battle practice.[39]

The older-model tanks provided to Malta were already obsolete, as shown by the 1940 battles in North Africa. All except the Mark VIs had been armed with the 40mm 2-pdr gun, which had been selected in the 1930s under the assumption that the maximum thickness of armour they needed to penetrate was 2in (50mm).[40] Furthermore, the 2-pdr had nothing but solid shot for anti-tank usage; it had no high explosive rounds available, making the tank's main armament minimally effective against infantry.

In the event of invasion, if confronted by Italian tanks, the 2-pdr guns would have been effective, but the more heavily protected German Panzer IV and captured Russian tanks projected to be landed would have been almost impervious to their fire. Moreover, the presence of four different tank types, each with its peculiar mobility characteristics, guaranteed a source of trouble in case of combined action.

Artillery

At the start of the war, as noted previously, Malta had minimal artillery defences. Fortunately, Italian overseas adventures in Africa and Greece gave them the chance to reinforce before any invasion of the island. The artillery defences of Malta took four forms: field artillery, anti-tank guns, anti-aircraft artillery and coastal artillery.

Field Artillery
In the summer of 1942, the four infantry brigades on the island had two field artillery regiments to back them up: the 26th Defence Regiment and the 12th Field Artillery Regiment.

In 1942, the 26th Defence Regiment reorganized as follows, including pre-arranged missions and deployment in case of battle:[41]

- 15th/40th Defence Battery, Royal Artillery
  troop: 4 x 6in howitzers
  (attached to Northern Artillery Group, deployed at Gebel Ghawzara);
  troop: 4 x 6in howitzers
  (attached to Southern Artillery Group, deployed at Ghaxaq);
  troop: 4 x 3.7in howitzers
  (attached to Reserve Artillery Group, deployed at Xaghra tal Isqof).

---

38. WO 169/7395, Malta Tanks war diary, May 1942.
39. Ibid., July 1942.
40. This assumption was made by Major General Sir Percy Cleghorn Stanley Hobart, Deputy Director Staff Duties with responsibility for tank doctrine. Bidwell & Graham, p.179.
41. Malta Command Military Defence Scheme, Appendix C.III, C.VIII and D. However according to Denis Rollo, pp.232–33, the 1942 structure was instead as follow: 15th/40th Battery with a troop of four 3.7in, one of four 6in and one of six 18-pdr; 48th/71st Battery with one troop of four 6in and two troops of six 18-pdr; 13th Defence Battery with three troops of 18-pdr.

- 48th/71st Defence Battery, Royal Artillery
  troop: 4 x 18-pdr
  (attached to Southern Artillery Group, deployed at Ta Buleben);
  dispersed in independent defence positions: 14 x 18-pdr.
- 13th Defence Battery, Royal Malta Artillery
  dispersed in independent defence positions: 24 x 18-pdr.[42]

The 12th Field Artillery Regiment arrived aboard the battleship HMS *Barham* and cruisers *Berwick* and *Glasgow* on 10 November 1940, along with the 1st Independent Troop, Royal Tank Regiment. At the time, the 12th Regiment consisted of 632 officers and men under Lieutenant Colonel W E. Vaudrey, with two batteries (6th/23rd and 49th/91st) of twelve 18/25-pdrs each.

In 1942, the 12th had acquired two more guns and was organized as follows:[43]

- 6th Field Battery, Royal Artillery
  troop: 4 x 18/25-pdr guns
  (part of Central Artillery Group, deployed at Tal Handaq);
  troop: 4 x 18/25-pdr guns
  (attached to Central Artillery Group, deployed near Addolorata cemetery);
  section: 2 x 18/25-pdr guns
  (attached to Central Artillery Group, deployed at L'Imsierah).
- 23rd Field Battery, Royal Artillery
  troop: 4 x 18/25-pdr guns
  (attached to Southern Artillery Group, deployed at Gebel Ciantar);
  troop: 4 x 18/25-pdr guns
  (attached to Reserve Artillery Group, deployed at Ta'Dekotzu).
- 49th/91st Field Battery, Royal Artillery
  troop: 4 x 18/25-pdr guns
  (attached to Northern Artillery Group, deployed at Iz-Zebbieh);
  troop: 4 x 18/25-pdr guns
  (attached to Northern Artillery Group, deployed at Mosta).

The northern, central and southern artillery groups reported directly to their respective infantry brigades; the reserve artillery group reported to 4 Infantry Brigade. Command and control group functions devolved respectively to the 26th Regiment, 12th Regiment, 6th Battery and 23rd Battery commanders.[44]

In case of battle, when they didn't have direct observation of the target and employed blind fire, the troops trained to deliver three minutes of 'rapid fire' (18/25-pdr) or 'intense fire' (3.7in and 6in) against each target,[45] a rate of fire of five rounds per minute. In theory (ideal conditions, well-trained crew, stationary target, no concern for barrel wear), the artillery could fire very fast: up to thirty rounds per minute for the 18-pdr. However, the different conditions of a real battle drastically reduced this figure.

---

42. Two guns manned by 1st Coast Regiment RMA.
43. Malta Command Military Defence Scheme, Appendix C.III, C.VIII and D.
44. Ibid.
45. Ibid.

The independently deployed 18-pdr guns expected to deliver up to twenty rounds against each target, and only where they could see the target.[46] This possibly means there was an acute shortage of ammunition of that calibre, or was a realistic assessment of how long a direct-fire gun site could fire before retaliation.

For the deployment of British field artillery on Malta, see Figure V-2.

Anti-tank Artillery

Malta's anti-tank capabilities constituted a significant weakness in the defences on the island. Given the emphasis on building up their anti-aircraft capabilities, which addressed their greatest threat, this is no surprise.

Historian Denis Rollo listed only three different types of anti-tank weapons on the island.[47] First, there was the 6-pdr. This 57mm gun began as a coastal defence gun and was used as a sub-calibre training tool for crews of the 6in and 9.2in coastal guns. However, as war threatened, Governor Dobbie had some of the guns mounted on locally made carriages for infantry anti-tank use. The gun actually had a slightly higher muzzle velocity than the British Army's 6-pdr gun (2,356ft/sec verses 2,150ft/sec) and a slightly heavier projectile, so its anti-tank capabilities would have been quite good. There were seven of these guns on Malta, all in static (immobile) positions: four in 2 Brigade's area and three in 1 Brigade's area.

Malta also had a small number of 3-pdr (47mm) Hotchkiss guns, designed in 1886 (incidentally also used for sub-calibre shooting). While this gun had a theoretical range of 6,000 yards, the muzzle velocity was only 1,873ft/sec; the Army 2-pdr (40mm) anti-tank gun had a velocity of 2,650ft/sec. This weapon would have had only marginal capabilities against armour. The island also had the even older 3-pdr Nordenfelt guns, which were even less capable against armour than the Hotchkiss. Malta's 1 Brigade had two 3-pdr static positions and two other mobile guns, while 2 Brigade had three static positions.

The Malta Defence Scheme also listed ten Breda 47mm anti-tank guns as part of its weaponry.[48] Rollo did not include these at all; they were, in all probability, captured Italian guns from North Africa. The 1 Brigade area had four static Breda positions, with two mobile guns, the north had three static positions and 3 Brigade also had one static Breda position.

Sited to cover possible landing areas, the guns necessarily ended up scattered. In the north, there was a static Breda covering Mellieha Bay, with two 6-pdr guns covering the road over Mellieha Ridge. Another 6-pdr covered St Paul's Bay and the final gun overlooked Ghain Truffieha Bay. There was a 3-pdr that covered the Wardia crossroads and two more on the eastern side of the Victoria Lines covering the main gap in that fortification. To the south, two 3-pdrs and a 6-pdr covered St Thomas's Bay and the rest of the static positions covered Marsa Scirocco Bay. The mobile Bredas were to be situated near Gudia and Imbakka.[49]

Anti-aircraft Artillery

As noted above, the anti-aircraft defences on Malta when Italy entered the war were wholly inadequate, despite the 1939 decision to upgrade the defences to 112 heavy anti-aircraft (HAA) guns and sixty light anti-aircraft (LAA) guns. By June 1940, the actual strength numbered only thirty-four heavy guns and eighteen light guns, an increase of just twenty guns

---

46. Ibid.
47. Rollo, p.427.
48. Malta Defence Scheme, Appendix C.I.
49. Ibid., Appendix F.II.

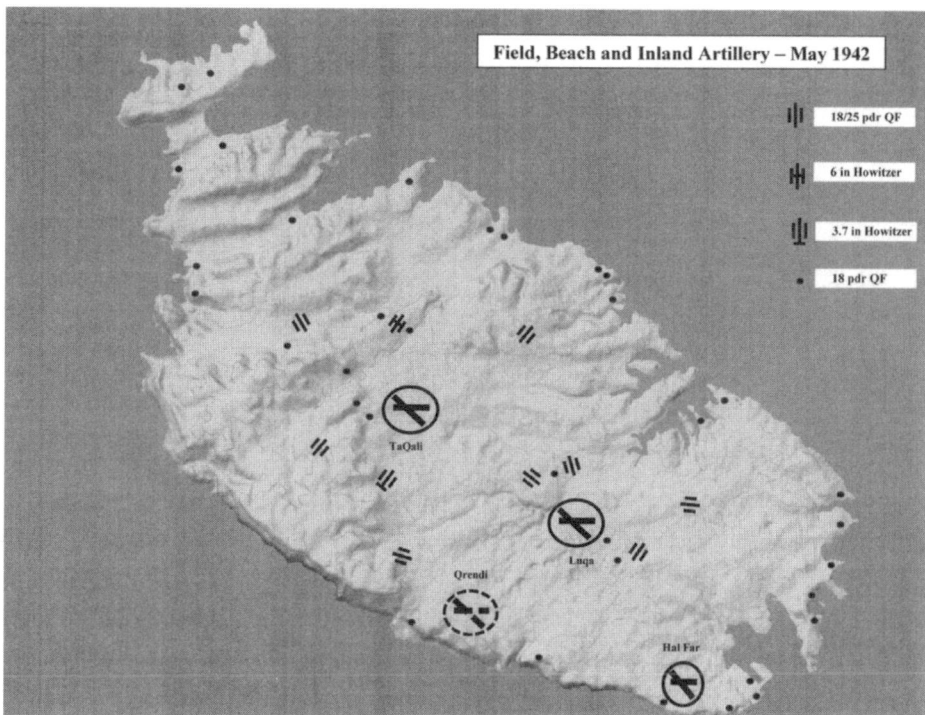

Figure V-2: *Artillery deployment, 1942.*

overall from the previous September.[50] By January 1941, the number of guns had increased to seventy heavies and thirty-four light guns,[51] and that same month saw the merchant ship *Essex* arrive with a cargo of twenty-four HAA guns and eighteen LAA guns – all underneath the equally welcome cargo of seed potatoes. In mid-1941, the number of heavy guns had reached its goal of 112, while the number of light 40mm Bofors exceeded the initial goal by almost 50 per cent.

The shift in defensive priorities on the island created the reason for the increase in anti-aircraft artillery strength. In 1939, when the British made the initial decision to place 112 HAA and sixty LAA guns on the island, protecting Grand and Marsamuscetto harbours for use as a naval base remained the priority. Initial plans had 100 of the heavy guns and forty-eight of the light guns designated for the harbour areas, leaving the remainder for the rest of the island.[52] In 1941 and 1942, it became apparent that, as important as the two harbours were to the defence (and wellbeing) of the island, its airfields and their aerial complement had become the first line of Malta's defense and were equally important. By mid-1942, Maltese airfields and taxi-ways covered almost 19 square miles – some 20 per cent of the island's surface. Despite the doubling

---

50. Rollo, p.386.
51. Ibid., p.212.
52. Ibid., p.183.

of the light anti-aircraft guns, Valletta ended up being covered by only thirty-six of them; the rest protected the airfields.[53]

The main anti-aircraft guns used on Malta were as follows:[54]

- 4.5in Mk II heavy AA gun: eight rounds per minute, effective ceiling 34,000ft, 90ft burst radius.
- 3.7in Mk I–III heavy AA gun: twelve to fifteen rounds per minute, effective ceiling 25,000ft, 60ft burst radius.
- 3in Mk I heavy AA gun: twelve to fifteen rounds per minute, effective ceiling 16,000ft.
- 40mm Bofors light AA gun: 120 rounds per minute, maximum range 15,000ft, effective range 10,200ft; these could also be used in an anti-ground capacity.

The deployment of the anti-aircraft units is shown in Figures V-3 and V-4.

Coastal Artillery
The primary responsibility for naval defence of Malta lay with two Coastal Defence Regiments, armed with anti-ship weapons that hadn't changed much from the pre-war period. The guns and their locations were as follows:[55]

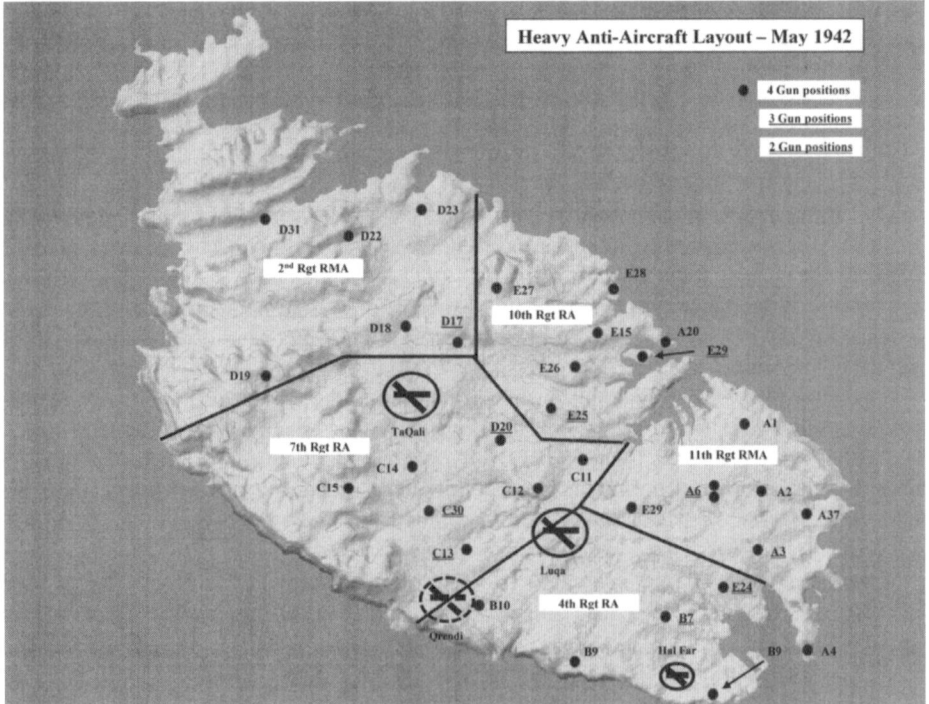

Figure V-3: *Heavy Anti-aircraft artillery deployment. Source: Rollo:* Guns and Gunners.

---

53. Ibid., p.247.
54. Ibid., p.428.
55. Ibid., pp.421–22.

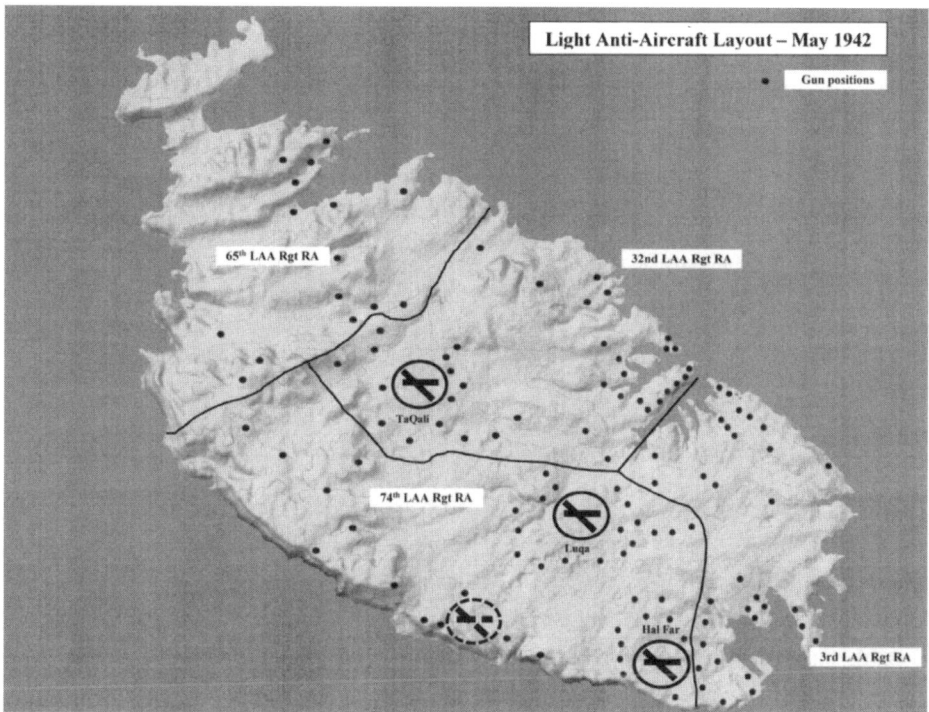

Figure V-4: *Light Anti-aircraft artillery deployment. Source: Rollo,* Guns and Gunners.

- 9.2in Breech Load Mk X: the guns had a range of 21,000 yards for their 380lb shells, which could be fired once every three minutes. Malta had seven of the guns, located at Forts St Leonardo (two), Madliena (two), Bingemma (one) and Benghajsa (two).
- 6in Breech Load Mk VII: located at Forts Campbell (two, increased to three in 1942), Tigne (three), St Rocco (three) and Delimara (two), the guns had a range of 14,000 yards for their 100lb shells and could be fired once every ninety seconds.
- Twin 6-pdrs: located at Forts Ricasoli (three) and St Elmo (six), these guns fired a 6¼lb shell 5,500 yards at a rate of seventy-two rounds per minute.
- In addition to the primary guns listed above, they had two 12-pdr guns mounted at Fort Delimara, plus seven 4in naval guns mounted at Grand Harbour as an anti-motor torpedo boat defence in the event any penetrated into the harbour.

The Royal Air Force

By June 1942, Malta had survived the blitzes of 1941 and early 1942 and, while the Axis concentrated on Russia and North Africa, the RAF on the island had been reinforced to ninety-seven Spitfire fighters by June 1942. However, given the prerequisite of air supremacy for the *C3* invasion, RAF participation in the defence of the islands would ultimately consist mostly of ground personnel acting as infantry helping to defend the airfields.

The Royal Navy

Any Royal Navy response to the invasion would come from both Gibraltar and Alexandria – both nearly three days' sail from the island. The fleet concentration at Gibraltar, ostensibly for the August convoy code-named Operation *Pedestal*, consisted of no less than three fleet carriers (*Eagle*, *Victorious* and *Indomitable*) and the battleships HMS *Nelson* and *Rodney*, along with anti-aircraft cruisers HMS *Phoebe*, *Sirius* and *Charybdis*, to escort twelve merchantmen and an American tanker. Most of this force would have to remain west of the Sicilian Straits due to Axis minefields, submarines and MAS torpedo boats. To push through all the way to Malta, the cruisers HMS *Manchester*, *Nigeria*, *Kenya* and *Cairo*, plus their destroyer escorts, would provide the muscle.[56]

From Alexandria, only a smaller force of light cruisers and destroyers was available to intercede.

The Royal Navy's global deployment as of August 1942 is listed in Table V-1.

Table V-1: Royal Navy Force Deployment – August 1942

Home Fleet – Scapa Flow	Alexandria
2 Escort Carriers (CVE) (*Biter*, *Dasher*)	4 CL
3 Battleships (BB) (*King George V*, *Duke of York*, *Anson*)	9 DD
1 Battlecruiser (BC) (*Renown*)	5 DE
6 Light Cruisers (CL)	
7 Destroyers (DD)	**Kilindini (Kenya)**
1 Destroyer Escort (DE)	3 BB (*Resolution*, *Royal Sovereign*, *Valiant*)
	1 CA
Arctic	6 CL
6 Heavy Cruisers (CA)	8 DD
8 DD	5 DE
3 DE	
	Colombo (Operation *Stab*)
Operation *Pedestal*	2 CV (*Illustrious*, *Formidable*)
4 Carriers (CV) (*Eagle*, *Indomitable*, *Furious*, *Victorious*)	1 BB (*Warspite*)
2 BB (*Nelson*, *Rodney*)	2 CL
7 CL	6 DD
18 DD	
7 DE	

---

56. Smith, Pedestal, pp.41–43.

Malta's Defensive Plan

Defensive plans for the island were developed by the Malta General Staff and documented in the Malta Defence Scheme, dated 8 May 1942. The only true defensive scheme developed on the island, it represented the near certainty they felt about an impending invasion.

The first thing to be noticed about the scheme is its realistic view of the situation. Specifically, the scheme states that the sister island of Gozo could not be defended adequately and would not be. To do so would split the defence, with little chance any Gozo force could be recalled in the event it was needed to defend the main island.

They also assumed enemy air superiority, and did not expect immediate help or reinforcement from the Royal Navy fleet units at Alexandria and Gibraltar due to distance.

One area of disinformation existed in the plan – the writers assessed the warnings of invasion based solely on aircraft reconnaissance and Radio Direction Finding (RDF), and expected at most two days' warning 'unless intelligence is received from outside sources'.[57] Since the Special Liaison Unit in the Lascaris War Rooms was routinely sent Ultra intercepts of Italian naval and Luftwaffe radio messages, additional warning of impending invasion could have been received.

The Defence Scheme did an excellent job of assessing important aspects of the island; not only the obvious, like the harbours and airfields, but dominant positions such as the high ground from around Laferla Cross to Rabat that 'could provide observation over the area in which the aerodromes were situated and land and sea approaches to VALLETTA'.[58] They also assessed key roads needed for rapid concentrations of troops and resupply, and especially vulnerable points, such as the ordnance and ammunition depots. To help in this regard, they expected the Malta Volunteer Defence Force – 3,000 volunteers partially trained and armed with shotguns and some service rifles – to keep the civilian population out of the way and off the roads to facilitate any troop movements needed to respond to threats.[59]

The General Staff anticipated an intense bombardment of both coastal defences and anti-aircraft positions prior to any invasion. They planned for both sea and air landings, given the experience gained from the loss of Crete in May 1941.

Seaborne landings would be met by an outpost line on any part of the 60 miles of potential coastal landing sites, followed by a concentration of force against the landing. The scheme identified eight specific landing sites in its Appendix A. All 250-yard sections of the coastal beaches had been mapped and identified with a unique alphanumeric identification, allowing artillery to target any threatened section with the two field artillery regiments. They protected probable and significant landing areas with the use of electrically controlled mines and/or concrete pyramids with spikes laid in rows to deny immediate access to certain areas, such as St Thomas's Bay or St Paul's Bay. Concrete defensive bunkers had been constructed in the areas expected to see potential landings. Not intended to be a major hindrance, the bunkers were expected to merely disrupt enemy landings and provide targeting information to the War Rooms. Most had little protection against any attack from the rear of the bunker.

The planners felt that attacks by paratroops would be the most dangerous assault form, requiring the defenders to spread out in order to strike the airborne attackers as soon as

---

57. Defence Scheme, paragraph 7 (b) (ii), MDS-3.
58. Ibid., paragraph 3, MDS-2.
59. Ibid., paragraph 18 (b) (ii), MDS-9.

98   Operation C3: Hitler's Plan to Invade Malta 1942

possible. The scheme admits they could land anywhere, although the staff identified only four areas suitable for gliders other than the existing aerodromes. They anticipated a primary target of any airdrop would be an airfield, reasoning that a captured field would allow the enemy to concentrate airborne troops, land heavy equipment and support weapons and bring in other supplies.

To combat such a diffuse attack potential, Malta's four brigades and their battalions were each assigned a specific part of the island as their primary responsibility, 'to defeat and utterly destroy any enemy'.[60] Any airfield within their area would be heavily defended and denied to the enemy for as long as possible. Battalion and brigade deployment for the invasion is shown in Figure V-5. Each of the four brigades expected to be able to provide a mobile reserve to help neighbouring units if the need arose.

Battalion infantry planned to 'deal instantly' with any enemy paratroops dropped in their area, with the defenders expected to 'run up to a mile' to deal with the drop, using 'rifle and bayonet' as their most effective weapons.[61] Speed was considered essential. General Beak had come to the island with the draft study on anti-parachutist tactics gleaned from the 1941 invasion of Crete.[62] The study emphasized that paratroops were most vulnerable immediately after a drop and before they retrieved their weapons from their containers and got themselves organized. Thus, a quick attack against them aimed to:[63]

- kill/capture as many as possible;
- confine the remainder into a small area, isolated from other paratroops;
- capture supplies and weapon containers for defensive use;
- finalize action against one drop in order to be ready for follow-up drops.

This requirement, motivated by General Beak and trained for with his mobility marches prior to his departure, did not consider the near-starved condition of the defenders.

Single infantry companies had responsibility for airfield defence, with their parent battalions backing them up with mobile reserves. As with the beaches, field artillery covered each airfield. Of equal importance, the defending troops had to be aware of where their mobile reinforcements were coming from to keep the lines of approach open and avoid friendly-fire incidents. They planned to prepare the airfields for destruction (using explosive mines and scaffolding barriers) after friendly aircraft were no longer able to use the facility, so as to deny their use for additional time in the event of its capture.

The key to the mobile defence of the island was 4 Brigade, located on the high ground – identified in the scheme as vital to the defence. Its three battalions, with support from dedicated artillery and the Malta Tank Squadron, had no airfields in their immediate area so they would be able to respond quickly in any direction. The 1 and 2 Brigades had identified specific battalions to act as their mobile reserves (1st Hampshires and 2nd Royal Irish Fusiliers, respectively) to support 4 Brigade in any counter-attack.

Finally, the Defence Scheme called for the creation of a final redoubt called the Valletta Keep, which 'will be defended by its commander and troops with the greatest determination

---

60. Ibid., paragraph 12 (a) (i), MDS-5.
61. Ibid., paragraph 14 (d), MDS-6.
62. The study – Tactical and Technical Trends #8: Lessons from Crete in Anti-Parachutist Tactics – was formally published in September 1942. Carruthers, p.112.
63. Ibid., p.116.

Malta's 1942 Defensive Plans 99

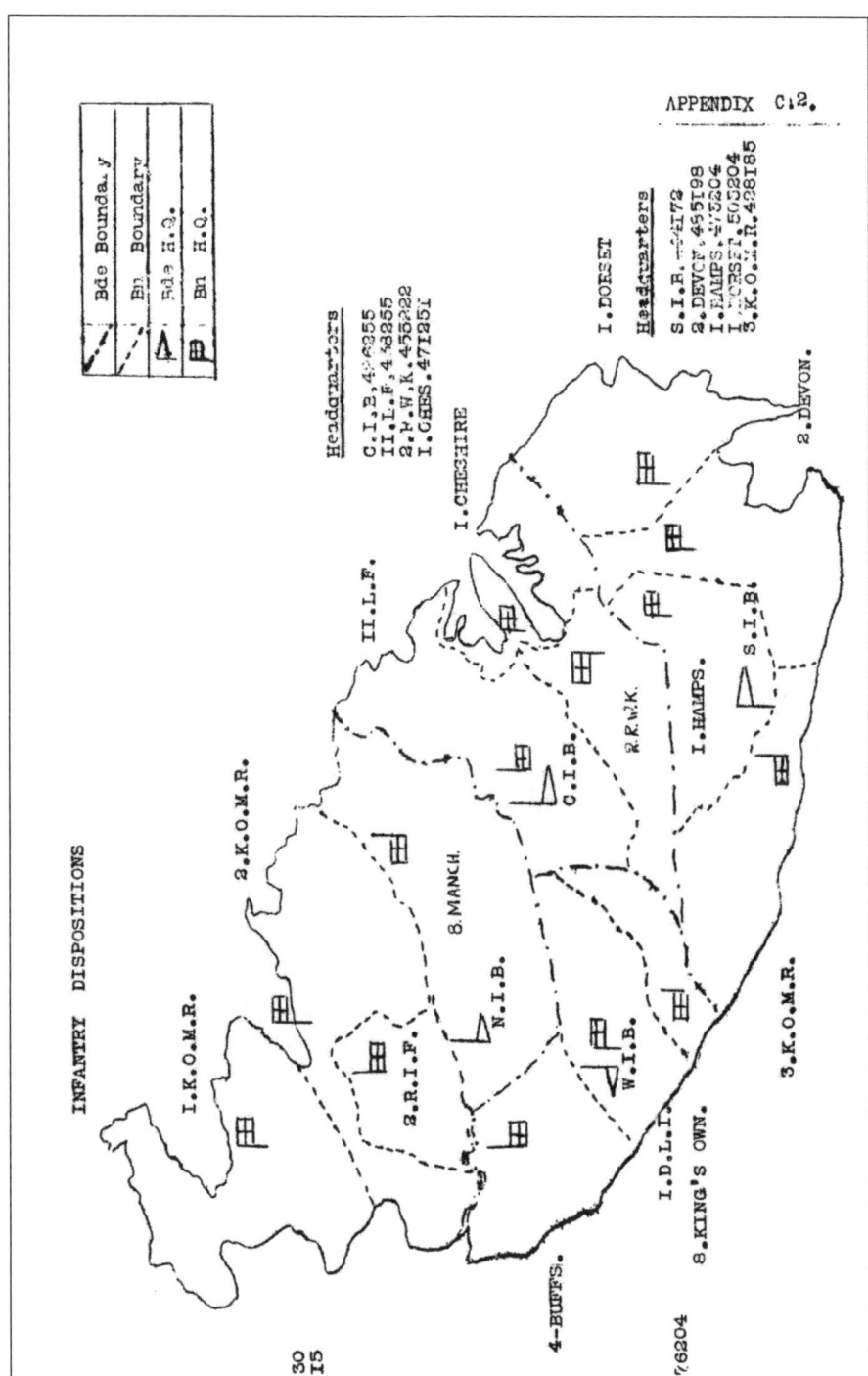

Figure V-5: *Battalion and Brigade Invasion assignments.*

to the last man, the last round and the last bayonet'.[64] The short-term objective of the Keep was to deny Grand and Marsamuscetto harbours to enemy use. A morale-boosting exercise seemed to be the longer-term goal, to bring back the memory of the First Great Siege in 1565, when the keeps defeated the Saracen invader. How effective the Valletta Keep would be in this case if the rest of the island was under Axis control was not mentioned in the scheme.

Factors favouring the defenders

Terrain

Malta's terrain affected the potential invasion in many ways. First, it is a small island – 95 square miles, more than fifty times smaller than Crete. The island had no place that paratroops could quietly regroup and recover unit cohesion, as they had been able to do on Crete. They would have been under attack in small groups immediately after the initial disruption of landing. General Student, commander of German Fallschirmjäger forces, used Malta's small size and its walls in his 1941 arguments promoting the alternative air assault on Crete.[65]

The next obstacle the Axis invaders would have faced were the man-made terrain features of Malta – each and every agricultural field being lined with stone walls. Furthermore, at many points, even along main roads, strongly defended pillboxes dotted the entire island. This would have made cross-country manoeuvre very slow and costly. Tanks might have helped by simply knocking down the walls, but the armour planned for *C3* might not have stood up to that kind of punishment. The walls would have fragmented the paratroops dropping in, unless they dropped directly onto the island's airfields. Gliders missing their landing zones in clear areas also stood a good chance of being wrecked against these walls. The ability of the Axis to mass superior numbers against the defenders would have been hampered significantly. Luftwaffe studies on the possibility of invading Malta in 1941 used the walls as a reason NOT to invade – they felt it would aid defence and foil attack assembly.[66]

This terrain became a double-edged advantage, though, as the initial British attacks on the paratroops would be equally hindered by the same terrain.

Intelligence

The British government's Code and Cypher School (GC&CS) at Bletchley Park had been able to decrypt German codes since early 1940, based on a captured German Enigma coding machine. In addition, the British had broken the Italian C38m naval code in May 1941, which gave them access to Supermarina plans.[67] The GC&CS also decrypted German Luftwaffe and railway Enigma messages, and the Regia Aeronautica's C35 codes. Historically, these decryptions have been lumped together as Ultra messages. Decrypted messages averaged

---

64. Ibid., Appendix C.XII.
65. Beevor, Antony, Crete, the Battle and the Resistance, p.75.
66. Ansel, Walter, Hitler and the Middle Sea, p.192.
67. The Germans insisted the Italians use a version of the Swedish C38 cipher machine because they felt the Italian codes were vulnerable to interception. Hinsley, British Intelligence in the Second World War, Vol II, p.22.

nearly thirty a day between November 1941 and July 1942; since September 1941, Malta had been the recipient of Ultra decryptions.[68]

Ultra decryptions could be very effective: a C38m decrypted intercept led to Force K's slaughter of the *Duisberg* convoy in November 1941. In addition, decryptions from this source picked up the details of twenty-six separate shipping movements between Sicily and the Cyrenaica front in April and May 1942. Given the enormous role that the Italian Navy was going to play in *C*3, most of the plans, routes and times of the convoys and supporting ships would have been intercepted – at least as far as Sicily, the final assembly and embarkation point for the invasion. Once the transports assembled at their Sicilian ports, it is probable that the final 'go' order would have been handled through (non-interceptable) Sicilian landlines. However, a single convoy of supply ships scheduled for the invasion planned to depart from the island of Lampedusa, so the orders for this convoy might have been intercepted and the actual date for the invasion revealed.

As noted above, British intelligence also had decryption capability for the Luftwaffe's Enigma messages. This source told the British that a supply base for Fleigerkorps XI (the air landing command) had been set up in Reggio Calabria in February and that a 'senior' Fallschirmjäger general (Student) arrived in Rome in April 1942. The Luftwaffe decryptions also picked up the transfer of Fleigerkorps II aircraft out of Sicily to Cyrenaica in May.

British intelligence on the Axis plans for Malta through Ultra intercepts became limited early in the planning process, since most of the discussions and planning by the Germans went through land telephone lines and thus were not intercepted. Only a single reference to *C*3 had been picked up – the Italian Chief of Staff's request for two train ferries for exercises in connection with the operation. The codebreakers had no idea what the named operation was at that point. However, any concentration of paratroops, transport planes and Italian shipping for an invasion would have been intercepted. From these sources, there is little chance that the Germans and Italians could have surprised the British on Malta.

Consequently, the British should have had an edge in intelligence through the codebreaking. However, up to that point, the effect of Ultra was a mixed bag. A post-war study indicated that while Ultra informed the British of 82 per cent of Italian convoys or sailings during the period November 1941 to March 1942, only 26 per cent of these were intercepted and attacked. Some of the problem was the intercepts themselves, which might miss vital information (such as port of departure or timings); others were cluttered with GC&CS interpretations and conjecture which clouded the information.[69]

On the other side of the intelligence issue, the Axis were quite good at attacking Allied codes. The German naval interception and cypher unit, Beobachtungsdienst (B-Dienst), as well as the Italian Serviso Informazione Segrete (SIS) had cracked most of the Allies naval and air force codes, providing a lot of good information. Although Axis rivalry tended to mar the effective cooperation between the two services, any plans to respond to an Axis invasion of Malta would have been clear to both Axis partners.

---

68. O'Hara, Six Victories, p.28.
69. Ibid., p.257.

Factors hindering defenders

Island conditions

Conditions on Malta were horrific at this point. Rationing had been in force since April 1941 and had grown more stringent as time went on. The daily rations for servicemen included:

- 11oz of bread;
- 4oz of tinned meat;
- 1oz of tinned milk;
- ½oz of sugar;
- 1oz of tinned potatoes;
- 2oz of onions;
- 2oz of fresh vegetables (when available);
- 1½oz of tea.[70]

Major General Beckett, the commander of Malta's artillery, noted: '[W]e were fighting exhaustion on a ration of three thin slices of bully, [and] three thin slices of bread twice a day and a cabbage-stalk once a week!'[71] The extra rations occasionally doled out when expecting exceptionally strenuous duty proved to be the only caveat to this starvation diet, for example when ships needed to be unloaded.[72]

The water storage tanks near Ta'Qali had been destroyed in March 1942, flooding store rooms and gardens and making water very scarce for more than four months. Air Vice Marshal Hugh Lloyd, the island's air commander, recalled that with both reservoirs destroyed and very little oil to run water pumps, Malta had little water for drinking or sanitation.[73]

In addition to the effects of the rations, disease also took its toll among the weakened population: polio, typhoid fever, tuberculosis, pneumonia, dysentery and a nasty stomach flu nicknamed the Malta Dog struck hard at everyone. Parasites like scabies affected the whole population.

The effects suffered by the military from this near-starvation made their strenuous duties more difficult. Military leaders tried to keep the battalions at their peak, but the demands by the 'Terrible Beak' – intended to promote hardiness, agility and pride in his soldiers – only left the troops more exhausted than ever. Other officers established compulsory rest periods each afternoon to limit the exertion of their men and the effects of starvation.[74] Air Vice Marshal Lloyd opined before he left in July that 'after two days of stiff fighting on our siege ration, I doubt if anyone would have been able to walk a mile in half an hour, let alone fight'.[75]

As noted previously, the lack of real infantry training for the troops on the island compounded these effects. In short, Malta's infantry defenders found themselves ill-prepared, militarily and physically, to face the rigours of an active defence of the island. Combat exertion would have sapped the staying power of the troops.

---

70. Vella, Appendix H, p.230.
71. Beckett, C.T., The Siege of Malta, p.164.
72. WO 1269/7424, 4th Buffs war diary, June 1942, for the Operation Harpoon ships.
73. Lloyd, Hugh, Briefed to Attack, p.170.
74. The Royal Irish Fusiliers was one such battalion. Williams, The Defenders of Malta, p.90.
75. Ibid., p.199.

Ammunition supply

Another potentially serious concern was the ammunition supply on Malta. Unless the Royal Navy could break through to the island, the ammunition stocks on Malta would be all they had to repel an invasion. Fast minelayers like HMS *Welshman* could (and did) run the gauntlet to deliver small quantities of vital supplies, as did several supply submarines. But as the Defence Scheme points out, the Royal Navy could not be counted on for immediate assistance.

An anti-invasion reserve of 1,000 rounds for all guns was rigorously held on the island by General Beckett, as noted by former Royal Artillery officer H.E.C. Weldon. However, Weldon also wrote: 'But even these reserves of ammunition would not last forever, and if the enemy could have kept up the pressure for an indefinite period, the time would have come when the resistance of the garrison would be overwhelmed for want of shells and bullets.'[76]

Organization and training

The overall infantry training and tactical organization of a British company proved a major factor working against the defenders on Malta, compared to their potential counterparts in battle. Their training gave them a disadvantage in two aspects, one very specific to Malta.

The specific disadvantage lay with the war effort and the conditions on the island already discussed. The infantry spent much of its time at the airfields providing support in building aircraft pens, filling bomb craters and doing everything else the RAF needed to keep their aircraft flying. That left little time for training. Some training did occur, most of which took place at platoon and company levels. Some battalion-level training also took place. For example, the Southern Brigade held an exercise that pitted the 1st Dorsetshires and a troop of the 12th Field Artillery Regiment against a company from the 8th King's Own Royal Regiment and two companies of the 3rd King's Own Malta Regiment. The exercise practiced concentrating from the Dorsets' scattered battle positions and attacking after a forced march.[77] But significantly, there was no training with supporting armour, no training at the brigade/multiple battalion-strength level, and no training in coordination with the anti-aircraft gunners on the island.[78]

The other training disadvantage lay with the British regimental system itself. Although the system promoted strong unit loyalty and cohesion, it also stressed social skills and conformity over tactical capability and junior officer initiative.[79] With no centralized direction for training, regiments had very little realistic training. They trained their junior officers at the regimental (i.e. battalion) level in whatever way the regiment's commander saw fit – and most of that training appeared to be conformity to superior orders.

British training had two other distinct disadvantages when compared to German training.[80] First, the Germans trained both their commissioned and non-commissioned officers to command higher-level formations,[81] while the British limited this to commissioned officers. Second, British regiments trained in isolation, not encouraging cooperation with other services,

---

76. Weldon, Drama on Malta: A Personal Flashback, p.114.
77. WO 169/7396, 1 Brigade war diary, April 1942.
78. Agius, Maurice, Recollections of a Malta HAA Gunner, p.106.
79. Bond & Murray, 'British Armed Forces, 1919–1939', from Millett & Murray (eds), Military Effectiveness, Vol II: The Interwar Years, p.122.
80. Italian training is discussed in Chapter VI.
81. French, David, Raising Churchill's Army: The British Army and the War against Germany, 1919–1945, pp.58–59.

like armour and the air force, or even other battalions; the Germans trained for and demanded total cooperation. On Malta, battalion-level training shared these weaknesses.

As noted earlier, central tactical doctrine emphasized consolidation rather than rapid exploitation. The end result of this and the other disadvantages mentioned created a force that could defend itself well, especially from prepared positions, but was considerably weaker and more cautious on attack. Combined operations – either with armour or another battalion – became problematical because it had not been practiced. Going up against a disorganized force of just-arrived paratroops, the British would give a good account of themselves; attacking a more organized force of paratroops would have been more difficult, especially in Malta's defensively favourable terrain.

Chapter VI

The Axis 1942 Invasion Plans

The Italian Royal Army (Regio Esercito)

In June 1940, when Italy entered the war, the Italian Army mobilized 56,500 commissioned and 41,200 non-commissioned officers in service, along with about 1,500,000 enlisted men.[1] By 1942, the number of men under arms had risen to well over 2.5 million; eventually about 4 million served during the war.[2]

The leadership of the Regio Esercito rigidly and stubbornly set itself in a virtual caste system, maintaining distinctions between officers, non-commissioned officers and enlisted men (particularly between officers and the others). Pay, living conditions, rations and even uniforms remained significantly different at various levels, isolating officers from the men they led. This system eliminated trust, compromised communication and lowered flexibility to deal with tactical events.[3]

In 1936, Italian Ministro della Guerra (Secretary of War) Generale Alberto Pariani created the Divisione Binara in Ordinamento Pariani (1938.) He removed one infantry regiment (and its related light Gruppo) from each division and paired it with another one to create new infantry divisions. The division's inner structure experienced many changes and is fully described later.

Countless authors have criticized the resulting division as too weak and an obvious step in the wrong direction.[4] However, the Regia Esercito's official doctrine identified the corps (with three divisions) as the main manoeuvre element. This meant they employed the Divisione Binara as if they were brigades, and the Corps as if a very large division. Unfortunately, as noted, training in the new organization was poor and more often than not the divisions faced the same number of full-size enemy divisions, hence their string of failures.

The Divisione Binara Table of Organization and Equipment supported its infantry better than the type it replaced, as the ratio of mortars, guns and howitzers divided among infantry battalions more than doubled (from 18.1 to 37.8), including the re-equipping of the regimental gun company with eight modern 47/32mm pieces. Only the number of heavy machine guns went down, reduced from 17.3 to just eight per infantry battalion, because such weapons were seen as at odds with the new mobile kind of warfare that Pariani had in mind.

---

1. Unless stated, strengths are from Montanari, L'Esercito, pp.209–30.
2. Rochat, Le Guerre, p.312.
3. Murray, Military Effectiveness, Vol II, p.200.
4. The same authors are not usually found criticizing Wehrmacht motorized and Jäger divisions that had the same structure (although with much superior equipment).

The standard Italian infantry division[5]

The smallest unit was a large rifle squad of eighteen men, divided into a machine-gun group (squad leader and eight privates, manning two light machine guns) and a rifle group (assistant squad leader and eight privates). Two rifle squads made a rifle platoon under a lieutenant.

The rank-and-file troops were armed with the Carcano mod. 91 bolt-action rifle (actually most weapons were of the shorter-muzzle musket variant, but generally called 'rifle' nevertheless) with a clip holding six 6.5x52mm cartridges. The mod. 91 has been much maligned, but it was not seriously inferior to similar bolt-action rifles used by other armies. Its effective range was 220 yards (although sighted up to 2,200 yards), with a sustained rate of fire of twelve rounds per minute. Each rifleman carried twelve clips, with six more in the regimental train.

During the inter-war era, Italy planned to rebuild all its rifles into mod. 91/38 (7.35x51mm cartridges, with a flatter trajectory and simple fixed sight). Effective range would have been 440 yards. Only few weapons were converted before war started, then the project was quickly shelved.

The standard squad automatic weapon was the Breda mod. 30 light machine gun, firing the same cartridge as the mod. 91 rifle (and intended for a similar conversion into mod. 30/38). Another much-maligned piece of equipment, the inner lubricating mechanism remained over-sensitive to sand, dirt, mud and frost, and jammed frequently. The side-mounted magazine (twenty rounds) was delicate and exposed. Each normal infantry squad included a machine-gun group with two mod. 30s, each manned by four men. The squad leader (sergeant) acted as group commander. The mod. 30 had an effective range of 440 yards (sighted up to 1,650 yards), with a sustained rate of fire of 150 rounds per minute. Ammunition came stored in boxes containing fifteen magazines.

This two-squad version of the 'fire and movement' organization was tactically unwieldy. Motorized units used a ternary type platoon – using three smaller squads; why foot infantry maintained the binary platoon is a mystery.

Three rifle platoons plus a command platoon made a rifle company under a captain. Three rifle companies plus a heavy weapons company and a command company made an infantry battalion under a major or lieutenant colonel.

The heavy weapons company (Compagnia armi di accompagnamento) had a command platoon, two machine-gun platoons (each had two squads with two heavy machine guns each) and two mortar platoons (each had three squads with three mortars each).

The battalion-level automatic weapon was the Breda mod. 37 (8x59RB M35 cartridge) heavy machine gun. With an effective range of 1,100 yards (on paper, up to 4,400 yards against area targets), and sustained rate of fire of 300 rounds per minute, it was a satisfactory weapon, sturdy, reliable and well-liked. The Breda 37 was fed through box magazines of twenty rounds, inserted from the left side and ejected from the right side; in a curious quirk, the spent cases were automatically reinserted into the magazine, which slowed its rate of fire. The machine-gun squad included two mod. 37s, each manned by three men. Ammunition was stored in boxes containing fifteen magazines.

The 45mm Brixia light mortar was the standard light support weapon. Complicated and expensive, the Brixia was breech-loaded through translation of the barrel, with a separate cartridge box holding ten propulsion rounds; it was also capable of direct firing. Its effective range was 550 yards, with a sustained rate of fire of ten rounds per minute (up to twenty-five to

---

5. The most common source about Italian organization is probably George F. Nafziger's Italian Order of Battle, that unfortunately has a number of errors.

thirty if sight was not readjusted). Troops fighting in open terrain generally discarded it quickly as not worth the trouble, but in hill and mountain country the Brixia kept its usefulness. Each squad included a firing group of three mortars, each manned by three men. The squad's three weapons and twelve ready boxes were normally carried by five of the train's mules; in action, half the boxes were shouldered by the ammunition carriers. One more box (plus 110 unboxed rounds) per weapon were in the regimental train.

Three infantry battalions plus a regimental headquarters, a gun company and a mortar company composed an infantry regiment under a colonel. When initially created (1934), the regimental gun company received four old 65/17 mountain guns (two platoons with two pieces each). According to Pariani's reforms they were to be replaced by more modern weapons but the change was very slow; in August 1942, the Friuli Division still carried the older weapons. The regimental mortar company originally had two platoons with three larger mortars each, but a third platoon was later added.

The larger 81mm mortar (virtually identical to foreign similar types, all variants of the original Stokes-Brandt type) was a much better and useful weapon with effective range of 1,100 yards and an effective rate of fire of eighteen rounds per minute (up to thirty if sight was not readjusted); eventually the light mortar units were re-equipped with it. Each squad included one mortar and fifteen men.

The standard infantry gun was the Austrian Böhler Infanterie-geschütze M.35, built under license by Breda and adopted in Italy in 1935 as the Cannone da 47/32. Employed both for infantry fire support and against tanks, the gun proved superior to the British 2-pdr. However, the inability to be towed faster than walking pace, the lack of a shield and the requirement of separate aimer and firer (making hits on a fast target difficult) proved serious defects in the weapon. The 3lb armour-piercing grenade carried an explosive warhead (that the 2-pdr lacked) and was able to penetrate 40mm, at 30 degrees angle, at 700 yards; the 5½lb high explosive shell had an effective range of 1,100 yards, with a sustained rate of fire of eight to ten rounds per minute. Ammunition was stored in shoulder boxes containing four rounds. Each squad included one gun and twenty men.

Two infantry regiments plus a mortar battalion made an infantry brigade-level command[6] under a Generale di Brigata. Infantry regiments had consecutive numbers and bore a name as well, often the same as the division (with some exceptions). The mortar battalion, usually numbered as the division, originally had two 81mm companies (two platoons as above) plus one 45mm company (three platoons as above) for a total of twelve plus twenty-seven weapons; it was later upgraded to three 81mm companies of three platoons (total of twenty-seven mortars). Friuli's battalion had a fourth company as well. Figure VI-1 shows the Divisione Binera.

The planned *C3* divisions were:
- **20ª Divisione di Fanteria 'Friuli':**
    - 87° Reggimento Fanteria 'Friuli'
    - 88° Reggimento Fanteria 'Friuli'
    - XX Battaglione Mortai (four companies, thirty-six 81mm mortars)
- **26ª Divisione di Fanteria 'Assietta':**
    - 29° Reggimento Fanteria 'Pisa'
    - 30° Reggimento Fanteria 'Pisa'
    - CXXVI Battaglione Mortai (three companies, twenty-seven 81mm mortars)

---

6. This largely superfluous command layer has often escaped detection in many Italian Army studies. Unnamed and unnumbered, it was no longer officially named 'brigade', its general being identified in orders of battles as 'Commander of the infantry'. Lacking any useful command and control asset, his precise role in action was nebulous.

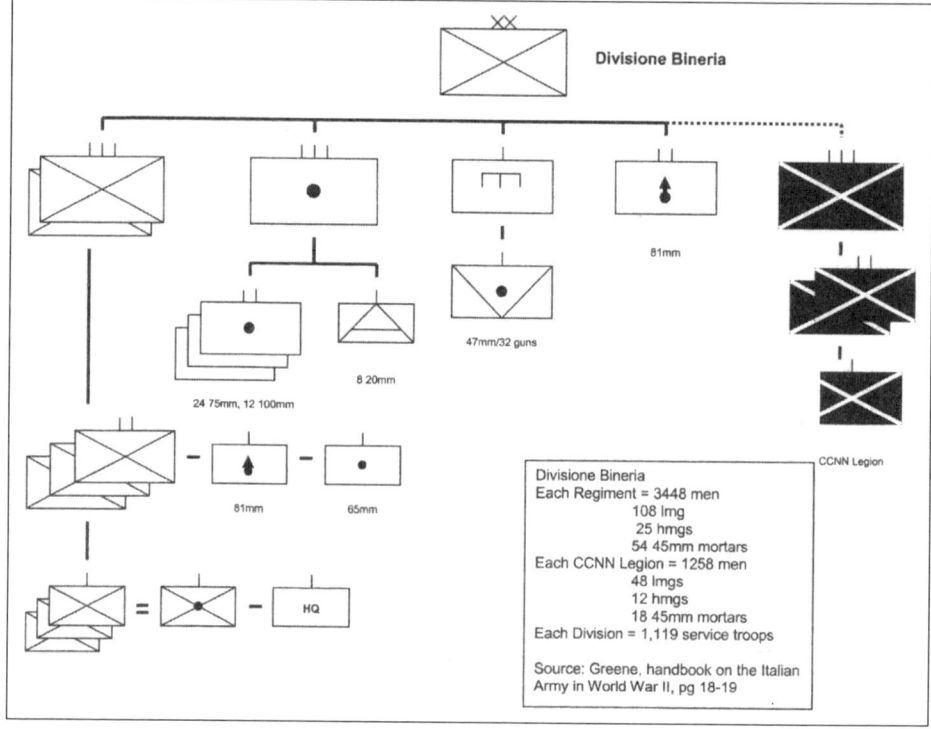

Figure VI-1: *Italy's Divisione Binera.*

54ª Divisione di Fanteria 'Napoli':
    75° Reggimento Fanteria 'Napoli'
    76° Reggimento Fanteria 'Napoli'
    LIV Battaglione Mortai (three companies, twenty-seven 81mm mortars)

The Friuli division had been selected for upgrading to an assault division as described below; however, the upgrade did not occur in time for the *C3* operation.

The 1935–36 war against Ethiopia saw the introduction of the Milizia Volontaria per la Sicurezza Nazionale (MVSN) into the military with the creation of seven infantry divisions under Army control. The MVSN had its origins following the First World War when, as Squadre d'Azione, they supported Mussolini's rise to power with violence and intimidation. On 1 February 1923, Mussolini officially incorporated the MVSN into the Fascist state, both to keep order and to combat opposition to Fascist policies.[7] In Ethiopia, Blackshirts composed 58 per cent of the invading Italian forces.

MVSN legions augmented the strength in some of the Italian divisions. Legions attached to infantry divisions consisted of two infantry battalions, supplemented by a single machine-gun company. At full strength, a legion fielded 1,230 officers and men, armed with twelve mod. 37 heavy machine guns and eighteen 45mm mortars.

---
7. Crociani & Battistelli, Italian Blackshirt 1935–1945, pp.4–5.

Legions attached to the *C3* divisions were:

'Friuli': 88ª Legione 'Cappellini'
   LXXXVIII Battaglione
   XCVI Battaglione
   96ª Compagnia Armi di Accompagnamento
'Assietta': 17ª Legione 'Cremona'
   XVII Battaglione
   XVIII Battaglione
   259ª Compagnia Armi di Accompagnamento
'Napoli': 173ª Legione 'Salso'
   CLXIX Battaglione
   CLXXIII Battaglione
   174ª Compagnia Armi di Accompagnamento

A brigade-level command plus an artillery regiment, a MVSN Legione and various assorted support units made an infantry division under a Generale di Divisione. The artillery on paper had three Gruppi (one armed with 100mm/17 howitzers, the others with one of the various 75mm guns or howitzers in service), each with three batteries of four pieces, plus an anti-aircraft battery of eight 20mm/65 (four platoons); but there were countless variations. *C3* divisions had:

'Friuli': 35° Reggimento Artiglieria 'Friuli'
   I/35° Gruppo Artiglieria (12x 100mm/17 mod. 14 T.M. howitzers)
   II/35° Gruppo Artiglieria (12x 75mm/27 mod. 11 T.M. guns)
   III/35° Gruppo Artiglieria (12x 75mm/18 mod. 35 T.M. howitzers)
   320ª Batteria Antiaerea (8x 20mm/65)
   356ª Batteria Antiaerea (8x 20mm/65)
'Assietta': 25° Reggimento Artiglieria 'Assietta'
   III/25° Gruppo Artiglieria (12x 75mm/18 mod. 35 T.M. howitzers)
   IV/25° Gruppo Artiglieria (12x 75mm/13 mountain howitzers)
   326ª Batteria Antiaerea (8x 20mm/65)
'Napoli': 54° Reggimento Artiglieria 'Napoli'
   III/54° Gruppo Artiglieria (12x 75mm/18 mod. 34 howitzers)
   IV/54° Gruppo Artiglieria (8x 75mm/18 mod. 35 T.M. howitzers; two batteries)
   354ª Batteria Antiaerea (8x 20mm/65)

The four Gruppi towed by horses (I/25°, II/25°, I/54°, II/54°) would have been left behind for *C3*.

Regio Escercito also planned to augment two infantry divisions into what they called Divisione di Fanteria d'Assalto, or assault divisions. One key change between assault divisions and normal infantry divisions was how the divisions distributed infantry guns. In normal infantry divisions, the 47/32mm guns operated at the regimental level. In the assault divisions, each battalion had control of four of the guns, with three-wheeled motorcycles to tow the guns. In addition, six flamethrowers were assigned to each battalion, making them more of a combined-arms battalion than normal infantry.

In addition, the assault divisions – and the Folgore Parachute Division – had battalions of Guastatori (assault engineers) attached. The Italian Army had entered the war without units trained specifically to assault fortified positions, so in July 1940 they created the Scola Guastatori del Genio at Civitavecchia, creating a six-week training course for 1,000 men at a time, to remedy that lack.[8]

As organized, a Guastatori battalion had three companies each with 343 men, divided into a headquarters platoon, four engineering platoons, plus communications and logistics squads. Each engineering platoon comprised two large squads, each representing the main tactical unit of the Guastatori. The squads were split into a demolition group – armed with demolition charges, Bangalore torpedoes and flamethrowers – and a support group with light machine guns and 45mm mortars.[9]

Adding to the power of these assault divisions, each also had two battalions of L40 semoventi (mobile assault guns) assigned to them. The armour provided both mobility and striking power. The two fully upgraded assault divisions assigned to *C3* were:

1ª Divisione di Fanteria (d'Assalto) 'Superga'
    91° Reggimento Fanteria 'Basilicata'
    92° Reggimento Fanteria 'Basilicata'
    I Battaglione Mortai
    5° Reggimento Artiglieria 'Superga'
        I/5° Gruppo Artiglieria (4x 75/18 howitzer)
        II/5° Gruppo Artiglieria (4x 75/18 howitzer)
    CXXXIII Battaglione Semoventi (18x L40 du 47)
        I Battaglione Controcarro Semovente (18x L40 du 47)
    I Battaglione Guastatori

4ª Divisione di Fanteria (d'Assalto) 'Livorno'
    33° Reggimento Fanteria 'Livorno'
    34° Reggimento Fanteria 'Livorno'
    IV Battaglione Mortai
    28° Reggimento Artiglieria 'Monviso'
        I/28° Gruppo Artiglieria (4x 75/18 howitzer)
        II/28° Gruppo Artiglieria (4x 75/18 howitzer)
    CXXXII Battaglione Semoventi (18x L40 du 47)
        IV Battaglione Controcarro Semovente (18x L40 du 47)
    XI Battaglione Guastatori

The best large Italian unit assigned to the Malta invasion was its only parachute division, the 1ª Divisione Paracadutiste, more commonly known as the Folgore (Thunderbolt) Division. Parachute troops had a rocky start in Italy, despite glowing recommendations stemming from Soviet airborne exercises in 1935. The Comando Supremo authorized the creation of a paratroop battalion in 1936, but the rivalry among Army and Air Force officers delayed any movement toward such training for years.[10] The Regia Aeronautica finally established the Regia Scula Paracadutisti dell'Aeronautica at Tarquinia in October 1939, with training to commence in January 1940.

Actual training finally started in July 1940[11] – a full month after Italy entered the war and the German Fallschirmjäger operations proved so effective – using outdated Caproni CA

---
8. Crociani & Battistelli, Italian Army Elite Units, p.29.
9. Ibid., p.31.
10. Morisi, p.25.
11. Ibid., p.26.

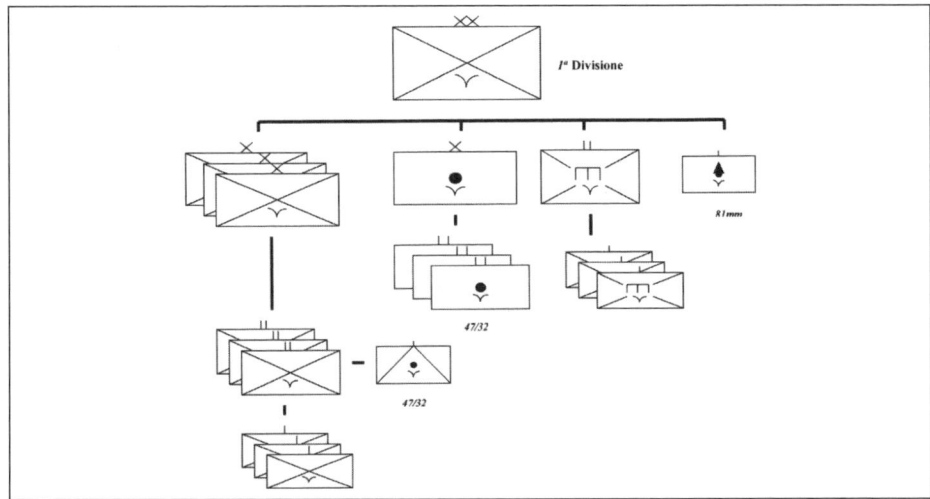

Figure VI-2: *Organization of 1a Divisione Paracadutiste.*

311 aircraft as their transport. Initially, the paratroops had been expected to be used in small units for infiltration and sabotage, but the German experience showed the need for a large unit deployment and, thus, the need for a full division.

By April 1941, a full regiment (three battalions) had been created. In the same month, the Italians performed their first (almost) combat drop when the 5ª Company/2ª Battalion dropped on the island of Kefalonia, the largest Ionian island in western Greece, in support of a Camicie Nere amphibious assault. The island fell with no fighting.[12]

By September 1941, a full parachute division had been created, including three regiments, a regiment of anti-tank guns and an attached Guastatori battalion, as shown in Figure VI-2. The whole division, commanded by Generale Enrico Frattini, was originally expected to drop on Malta; however, the lack of transport cut the Italian participation to two regiments, the artillery and Guastatori.

The divisional organization prior to the drop was:[13]

1ª Divisione Paracadutiste
    1º Reggimento Paracadutisti
    2º Reggimento Paracadutisti
    1º Reggimento Artigliera Paracadutista
    VIII Battaglione Guastatori

At the regimental level, the paratroop division remained organized similar to nominal infantry divisions; each regiment of 1,500 troops consisted of three battalions each with three infantry companies and a heavy weapons company. At the platoon level, however, the Folgore paratroops differed from the nominal Italian infantry organization. Platoons organized themselves around three ten-man squads rather than two, with a single mod. 30 light machine gun in the platoon;

---

12. Crociani & Battistelli, Italian Army Elite Units, pp.26–27.
13. The Folgore Division was renamed the 185th Division in July 1942, after C3 was postponed and the division sent to North Africa.

the other two squads probably had MAB 38 submachine guns instead.[14] The artillery regiment consisted of three groups, each with eight 47/32mm anti-tank guns and twelve 81mm mortars.[15]

In addition to the Folgore Division, earmarked for the initial invasion, the Italians also assigned their 80ª Divisione di Fanteria Aerotrasportabile (Spezia) as the final large unit held in reserve for Operation *C3*. Structured similar to the Friuli Division, the Spezia (Generale Pizzolato) expected to be flown into a captured field on Malta if required. The availability of air transport remained a key decision point for the use of the division, since transporting its six infantry battalions, plus equipment, would have required over 100 SM.82 aircraft and multiple sorties. As noted below in the discussion of supply, the transports were a vital supply link to Sicily until a port on the island, such as Birzubbujia, could be captured. The division as organized for the invasion consisted of:

80ª Divisione di Fanteria Aerotrasportabile (Spezia)
    125° Battaglione Fanteria
    126° Battaglione Fanteria
  80° Reggimento Artigliera
    I/80°
    II/80°
    III/80°
  LXXX Battaglione Anticarro
  XXXIX Battaglione Esplorante (motorcycle infantry)

Aside from the Folgore paratroops, each branch of the Italian military contributed special forces to their assault on the Maltese islands.

The Regia Escercito contributed the Battaglione Speciale Arditi, special forces that the Italians began forming in May 1942, inspired by the British Long-Range Desert Group. Initially the battalion consisted of three small companies – the 101ª Arditi paracadutisti (paratroops), 102ª Arditi Nuotatori (swimmers) and 103ª Arditi Camionettisti (jeep-mounted)[16] – with only the first two assigned to *C3*. The companies trained in weapons and demolitions with the intended purpose of operating in ten-man teams, raiding behind enemy lines. It is not clear how the companies would have been utilized on Malta; however, raids away from the intended drop zone could have kept the island's defenders distracted.

For the Regia Marina, the San Marcos Marine Regiment would lead the amphibious assault. In June 1940, only a single San Marcos battalion, Bafile, existed. Another formed with plans to land behind French lines, but the French armistice stopped that plan. The two battalions, Grado and Bafile, saw service in Greece and Yugoslavia before being brought home for *C3* training.

Each San Marcos battalion was made up of four line companies, supported by an 81mm mortar company and one of 47/32mm infantry guns.

In addition to these two battalions, two other specialist battalions were created by the Italians. A parachute unit was formed in March 1941, entitled P Battalion. Composed of 300 men, they trained in day or night parachute drops, long-distance swimming and demolitions, with

---

14. The tactical organization of the Folgore prior to C3 and its assignment to Africa after C3 was abandoned is problematic. One source, Nina Arena's Paracadutisti references a battalion strength of 650 men, but his numbers are in question; a better source, Sisto Bodriti's I Grifi della 6a Compagnia del II Battaglione Paracadutiste, had a battalion strength of less than 400 men.
15. Morisi, p.43.
16. The Arditi's (The Daring Ones) title stemmed from First World War Italian assault troops, formed in 1917, Crociani & Battistelli, p.45.

a primary purpose to be dropped behind enemy lines or to lead an amphibious assault. In addition, they created the Battaglione Nuotatori-Guastatori (assault swimmers) in June 1941, from 200 San Marcos Marines and 200 volunteers from the Milizia Marittima (MILMART).[17]

The Regia Aeronautica also contributed special forces to Operation *C3*. In May 1942, the air force created the Iª Reparto Paracadutisti della Regia Aeronautica,[18] with a strength of 300 troops. Organized as a headquarters and ten teams, the unit's goal was occupying enemy airfields, defending them and getting them back into operation. A second unit, the Loreto Battalion, fully 850 men, formed in June 1942 to organize and administer captured airfields.[19]

Finally, the MVSN contributed specially trained amphibious troops in addition to the Legions already mentioned. The Gruppo Battaglioni da Sbarco (Group of Sea-Landing Battalions) formed in February 1941 and first saw action in capturing the Greek Ionian islands. Composed of four battalions – XLII (Vicenza), XLIII (Belluno), L (Treviso) and LX (Pola) – totalling 3,100 troops, their organization was similar to that of the Legions, only more highly trained and motivated.[20]

Italian armour

The Italians assigned a lot of armoured support to the invasion of Malta in the form of assault guns.

The 10° Raggruppamento Corazzato, attached to Comando Tattico Superiore headquarters, had the DLV Gruppo Artiglieria Semovente, with eight Semovente M41 da 75/18 assault guns. These 16ft wide, 15-ton armoured vehicles sported a 75mm/18 gun and an 8mm machine gun. The main gun fired both high explosive and armour-piercing rounds capable of penetrating up to 59mm of armour.[21] The M41s would have had a difficult time negotiating the narrow roads and rock walls on Malta.

The smaller L40 da 47/32 assault guns had been assigned to the Superga and Livorno Assault Divisions. Narrower (12½ft rather than 16ft) and lighter (7 tons versus 15 tons) than the M41s, the L40s came armed with an Ansaldo 47/32mm gun and an 8mm machine gun. The gun again fired both high explosive and armour-piercing rounds and could penetrate 50mm of armour at 437 yards.[22] Seventy-two assault guns would land on Malta and Gozo.

Italian naval forces

With the expected transfer of some 40,000 tons of fuel oil from the Germans, Italy's naval forces were ready for their part in *C3*, which included interdiction of the island, bombardment of key coastal fortifications and escort for the invasion forces. Since the primary threat to the *C3* invasion lay with Britain's Royal Navy, stationed at Alexandria and Gibraltar, Supermarina assigned two strong squadrons of surface ships to blocking/interdiction duties.

---

17. MILMART was the Regia Marina version of the fascist MVSN Blackshirts.
18. This was the original title; the battalion was later designated I Battaglione d'Assalto Paracadutisti dell'Aeronautica; Lundari, p.91.
19. Ibid., p.92.
20. Crociani & Battistelli, Italian Army Elite Units, p.57.
21. Pignato, pp.44–45.
22. Ibid., pp.26, 39.

The First *Squadra*, based in Napoli, commanded by Ammiraglio di Squadra designate d'Armata Angelo Iachino, centred around the 9ª Division's battleship *Vittorio Veneto*. Italy's two other 15in modern battleships, the *Littorio* and *Roma*, were part of 9ª Division, but unavailable for duty in August: *Littorio* was repairing torpedo damage sustained during the June interception attempt of Operation *Vigorous*, while *Roma* had just finishing its post-construction work-up at Trieste. To add some weight to 9ª Division, the 12.6in battleship *Giulio Cesare* transferred in from 5ª Division. Ammiraglio di Squadra Alberto da Zara's 7ª Division of light cruisers, operating out of Cagliari in Sardinia, also came under Iachino's operational control. Ten destroyers accompanied the capital ships.

First *Squadra* planned to block access to Malta from the west, where the British had massed a significant naval force. Italian intelligence reported a strong force of carriers, battleships and cruisers at Gibraltar. The Supermarina did not expect the British carriers and battleships to try to sail through the Sicilian Narrows, but the cruisers could. The disaster at Matapan made an already cautious Iachino more so, and First *Squadra* would not be expected to take on the British heavy ships; the Regia Aeronautica had that responsibility, along with a swarm of submarines. Iachino's primary responsibility would be to engage and block any forces that came through the Narrows. The Italians entrusted the actual defence of the Narrows to the motoscafo armato silurante (armed torpedo boats) of 1ª Flottiglia Vedette MS and 2ª Flottiglia MAS.

Second *Squadra*, based along the coast in Sicily and Reggio Calabria and commanded by Ammiraglio di Squadra Carlo Bergamini, included his flagship, 5ª Division battleship *Caio Duilio*. With the *Conte di Cavour* still repairing damage taken during November 1941's Taranto raid and *Cesare* transferred to Naples, Bergamini's only other battleship was the *Andrea Doria*. However, his squadron also included three heavy cruisers of 3ª Division (Ammiraglio di Divisione Angelo Parona) and three light cruisers from 8ª Division (Ammiraglio di Divisione Raffaele De Courten), with fourteen destroyers providing support.

Second *Squadra's* role in *C3* had two parts.[23] First, accompanying the invasion convoys, Bergamini's main task for the invasion was to provide fire support against identified ground targets of opportunity; attacking reserve movements and pockets of resistance in identified villages was expected. Their main targets were to be Forts Bingemma and Delimara, the reduction of which would eliminate potential gunfire against the invasion beaches. Fort Benghajsa's guns could also impact the invasion beaches; German pioneers were expected to take Benghajsa while Bergamini's battleships reduced Delimara to open the way into Marsaxlokk Bay. The Regia Marina had allocated a total of 200 12.6in armour-piercing common rounds (1,157lb or 525kg each) for use against ground targets.[24]

Bergamini's second task was to block any Royal Navy incursion from Alexandria. There, the considerably understrength British had only a force of light cruisers to be used in an offensive capacity. Second Squadra's force of two battleships, three heavy cruisers and three light cruisers outweighed their opponents by a wide margin.

The composition of First and Second *Squadra* are shown in Table VI-1 and detailed in Appendix B.

Several key factors hampered the main forces of the Regia Marina:

- Air cover – without aircraft carriers, Italy's surface fleet depended upon air cover from the Regia Aeronautica or possibly the Luftwaffe. Communications for such cover had to be routed through higher headquarters and, thus, had a very slow reaction time.

---

23. Letter DG 8-ter, Gabriele, Appendix XIX, p.299.
24. Bagnasco, Le Armi della Navi Italiane nella seconda guerra Mondiale (The weapons of the Italian ships in the Second World War), p.17.

Table VI-1: Regia Marina Force Composition

1ª **Squadron** (A.S.d.A. Angelo Iachino), at Napoli	2ª **Squadron** (A.S. Carlo Bergamini) Aa Messina
9ª Division at Napoli	**5ª Division** at Messina
BB *Vittorio Veneto* [F] (C.V. Corso Pecori Girardi)	BB *Caio Duilio* [F] (C.V. Giorgio Conti*)*
BB *Giulio Cesare* (C.V. Sesto Sestini)	BB *Andrea Doria* (C.V. Mario Bussola)
10ª Destroyer Squadron at Napoli	**15ª Destroyer Squadron** at Reggio Calabria
Maestrale [F] (C.V. Riccardo Pontremoli)	*Pigafetta* [F] (C.V. Enrico Valle)
Legionario (C.F. Corrado Tagliamonte)	*Da Verazzano* (C.F. Angelo Lo Schiavo)
Oriani (C.F. Paolo Pesci)	
Gioberti (C.F. Vittorio Prato)	**16ª Destroyer Squadron** at Reggio Calabria
Grecale (C.F. Luigi Gasparrini)	*Da Recco* [F] (C.V. Aldo Cocchia)
Premuda (C.F. Alessandro Mirone)	*Malocello* (C.F. Mario Leoni)
7ª Division at Cagliari	
CL *Eugenio di Savoia* [F] (C.V. Franco Zannoni)	**3ª Division** at Messina
CL *Montecuccoli* (C.V. Arturo Solari)	CA *Gorizia* [F] (C.V. Paolo Melodia)
CL *Attendolo* (C.V. Mario Schiavuta)	CA *Bolzano* (C.V. Mario Mezzadra)
	CA *Trieste* (C.V. Umberto Rouselle)
11ª Destroyer Squadron at Cagliari	
Aviere [F] (C.V. Gastone Minotti)	**7ª Destroyer Squadron** at Augusta
Corsaro (C.F. Lionello Sagamoso)	*Freccia* [F] (C.F. Alvaro Minio Paluello)
Ascari (C.F. Teodorico Capone*)*	*Folgore* (C.C. Renato D'Elia)
Geniere (C.F. Marco Notarbartolo)	*Lampo* (C.C. Antonio Cuzzaniti)
Camicia Nera (C.F. Adriano Foscari)	*Saetta* (C.C. Enea Picchio)
8ª Division at Augusta	
CL *Garibaldi* [F] (C.V. Vittorio De Pace)	
CL *Duca d'Aosta* (C.V. Luciano Bigi)	
CL *Abruzzi* (C.V. Giovanni Viansino)	
13ª Destroyer Squadron at Augusta	
Alpino [F] (C.V. Ferrante Capponi)	
Fuciliere (C.F. Umberto Del Grande)	
Mitragliere (C.F. Silvio Garino)	
Bersagliere (C.F. Anselmo Lazzarini)	
Corazziere (C.F. Antonio Monaco di Longano)	

* [F] = Flagship

- Radar – basically, the Italians did not have any. One small surface search unit had been installed on the destroyer *Legionario* in May 1942.
- Ground support – the Regia Marina had never practiced close-support bombardment and their centralized command structure made requests for the same very slow.
- Night time combat – at the tactical level, the Italians did not prepare for night combat, partly due to training and partly due to a lack of radar. Thus naval leaders were ordered not to engage their main units (light cruisers and above) at night.
- Industrial base – Italy's weak industrial base could not effectively support both construction of capital ships and repair of damaged units. Thus, the Regia Marina wanted to avoid the loss of a major fleet unit. This left the Supermarina's primary strategic choice to remain a 'fleet in being' rather than be an offensive tool.
- Fuel – without the requested transfer of fuel oil specifically for *C3* by the Germans, much of the Regia Marina would have been unable to sail.

There are a number of books claiming Italian admirals (and sailors) were cowards and/or idiots (for example, the American historian Samuel Morison coined the term 'Dago Navy'[25]). However, as noted above, Italian admirals were ordered not to risk large ships because the top brass considered the balance of force to favour Britain over Italy in the strategic sense as the Royal Navy would always be the stronger navy, even if the Regia Marina held a momentary numerical superiority. Simply stated, the British could send reinforcements from other theatres and the Italians could not. A battle where both navies sank the same number of ships would be an Italian defeat in the strategic sense, since after the battle, the balance of world-wide force would be worse than before.

Take, for example, the instructions that the Supermarina gave to Admiral Inigo Campioni prior to the action off Cape Spartivento on 27 November 1940:

> 'Avoid action with the enemy if he enjoys an evident superiority; favour any opportunity for naval guerrilla actions; try to fight near base; be animated by a highly aggressive spirit at all times and remember that the material difficulty of replacing our warship losses during the war dictates that we must coolly examine of the convenience of any action.'[26]

As per Supermarina doctrine, MAS and the like were expendable, torpedo boats were nearly expendable, destroyers a bit less expendable, light cruisers a bit more precious, heavy cruisers quite precious, old battleships very precious and new battleships as precious as life itself.

The Regia Marina fleet tactical doctrine called for a cautious approach to the enemy (the larger the Italian ships, the more cautious the approach), to open fire at maximum distance, close with the enemy only if the enemy was clearly inferior, and otherwise to maintain distance. Given the geographical distances and limitations and the Royal Navy's numerical inferiority in the Mediterranean in August 1942, it remained unlikely the Italians could stop a determined Royal Navy attempt to reach Malta, but they could make it costly.

---

25. Morison, Samuel, History of United States Naval Operations in World War II, Vol II: Operations in North African Waters, 'the Dago Navy had long been regarded by British tars as a huge joke', p.189. More modern studies (Sadkovich, Greene and O'Hara to name three) are less biased.
26. Quoted from Azione Navali, Vol 4, in O'Hara, Struggle for the Middle Sea, pp.66–67.

The Regia Marina's invasion convoys and escort fell under the auspices of Forza Navale Speciale (FNS), commanded by Ammeriglio di Squadra Vittorio Tur, including all landing ships and escorts. Tur commanded the landings on Malta himself, while Ammeriglio di Divisione Luigi Biancheri commanded the forces landing on Gozo. The escorts included two destroyers, three destroyer escorts, twelve torpedo boats and thirteen VAS (anti-submarine) vessels. The torpedo boats and VAS carried 17.7in torpedoes, packing less than half the power of the larger 21in torpedoes the main Italian ships carried, with half the range as well.[27] Regardless of the tactical doctrine mentioned above for the main fleet units, light units such as MAS and the torpedo boats escorting the convoys would fight against any level of enemy opposition, because it was their mission and they were expendable.

Finally, Italy's submarines force would try to block the approaches to Malta, particularly from the west, where VII Gruppo Sommergibili at Cagliari numbered ten boats.

Italian air forces[28]

At the time of *C3*, the Regia Aeronautica had over 2,400 aircraft in its arsenal, with nearly 25 per cent assigned some part in the reduction and invasion of Malta.

Prior to the invasion, the Italian fliers had shared responsibility with their German counterparts for regaining air supremacy over the island by destroying British aircraft and interdicting the many airfields on Malta.

At the time of the invasion and throughout the battle, the Italian air force had two key roles. The first and most important consisted of delivering the Folgore paratroops, delivering supplies and possibly delivering the Spezia air landing division onto a captured airfield if needed. For this, they had seventy-two SM.82 aircraft at Castelvetrano airfield on Sicily, organized into three groups. These large aircraft had been specifically modified to carry forty personnel or 10,000lb of cargo; seventeen aircraft could deliver a single infantry battalion, while four additional aircraft could deliver 81mm mortar and 47/32mm gun units. Elsewhere on Sicily, another seventy-seven transport aircraft were available to provide service.

Once the invasion started, the role of the Italians would be interdicting the island from the Royal Navy. They stationed a large portion of their anti-shipping strength on Sardinia with 36° Stormo AeroSiluranti (A.S.) and 46° Stormo A.S. The two Stormos combined for twenty-four SM.79 torpedo bombers and nineteen SM.84 bombers modified to take torpedoes. Two other detachments provided eight more SM.79s, with escort provided by 24° Gruppo Caccia Terrestre, composed of fourteen G.50bis and twenty Cr.42 fighters. To provide additional support, twenty Mc.202 and almost thirty Re.2001 fighters were on the island. They also had an additional twenty-nine SM.79 torpedo bombers stationed on Pantelleria.

In addition to the basic bombers, the Italians also prepared two special assault forces. One was a radio-controlled SM.79, loaded with explosives that would be directed in flight from a nearby Cz.1007bis aircraft. The other special force consisted of two modified Re.2001/GV

---

27. Fraccaroli, Italian Warships, p.190.
28. Author's note: assessing actual air strength for all combatants during this period is difficult, given the vagaries of weather, maintenance and enemy action. The numbers here represent the best estimates of the author and his Italian researchers.

aircraft configured to look like Royal Navy Sea Hurricanes, which would hopefully be able to get close to a British carrier without undergoing anti-aircraft fire to deliver their bombs.[29]

Against the Royal Navy out of Alexandria, the Italians had aircraft spread out over the Eastern Mediterranean. They had the fourteen SM.79s of 41° Gruppo based at Gadurra on the island of Rhodes, with escort available by twelve G.50bis and sixteen Cr.42s based at Maritza. In Africa, the 131° Gruppo A.S. had fourteen SM.79s at Derna and another fourteen with 133° at Benghazi. This latter group had questionable value as it had never operated in anti-ship mode before. The Italians had twenty-five Mc.200 fighters at Benghazi to escort any bombing missions. Finally, they had three groups stationed in Calabria at Crotone and Reggio Calabria, with thirty-four SM.84s and twenty-four SM.79s.

The one thing the Regia Aeronautica would not do on Malta was provide close air support for the troops on the ground. Italian fliers never trained to support troops in this manner; they would leave that task to the Germans, who were trained in such tactics.

Appendix C has details of the Axis air order of battle.

German paratroops (Fallschirmjäger)[30]

German interest in parachute troops, like the Italians, spawned watching Soviet experiments in the 1930s, especially impressed by the 1,000-troop drop in 1935 and the 6,000-troop drop the following year.[31] When the Luftwaffe was created in 1935, its commander-in-chief, Hermann Göring, with a major push from his Chief of Staff, General Walther Wever, ordered a German parachute unit to be developed. The first unit designated for parachute training became his own Regiment General Göring of the Prussian State Police, a paramilitary police unit Göring had assembled to combat communist cells while he was the Prussian Minister of Police.[32]

At the start of the war in September 1939, they had four trained battalions. Small groups took part in attacks on Norway and Denmark. When *Fall Gelb* (Case Yellow) launched against France and the Low Countries, all five battalions dropped to capture bridges and airfields in the Netherlands. One group, Sturmabteilung Koch, eliminated the Belgium fortress of Eben Emael in a classic glider-borne raid.

The only time the 7th Flieger Division dropped as a full unit was on Crete, where its three regiments, along with LuftLande-Sturm Regiment's four battalions, spearheaded the attack. The attack plan spread the regiments out, though, and basically, they fought separate battles. Nearly a third of their force was killed or wounded in the battle.[33] This disastrous battle ended Hitler's interest in large-scale parachute operations, with him using the highly trained paratroops as elite infantry, particularly on the Eastern Front, until the plan for taking Malta emerged.

---

29. Smith, Pedestal, pp.106–07.
30. The German Fallschirmjäger were one of the elite forces in the Second World War and have been the subject of many popular histories. For example, James Lucas' Storming Eagles, Volkmar Kuhn's German Paratroops in World War II, Roger Edwards' German Airborne Troops and Ben Christensen's two-volume The 1st Fallschirmjager Division in World War II.
31. The Soviet experiment came to a halt in 1937 due to the purges Stalin waged against his generals. Ellis, pp.6–7.
32. McGuirl & Feist, p.9.
33. 3,162 dead, 1,528 wounded, totalling almost 33 per cent of the force dropped. Christensen, Vol I, p.239.

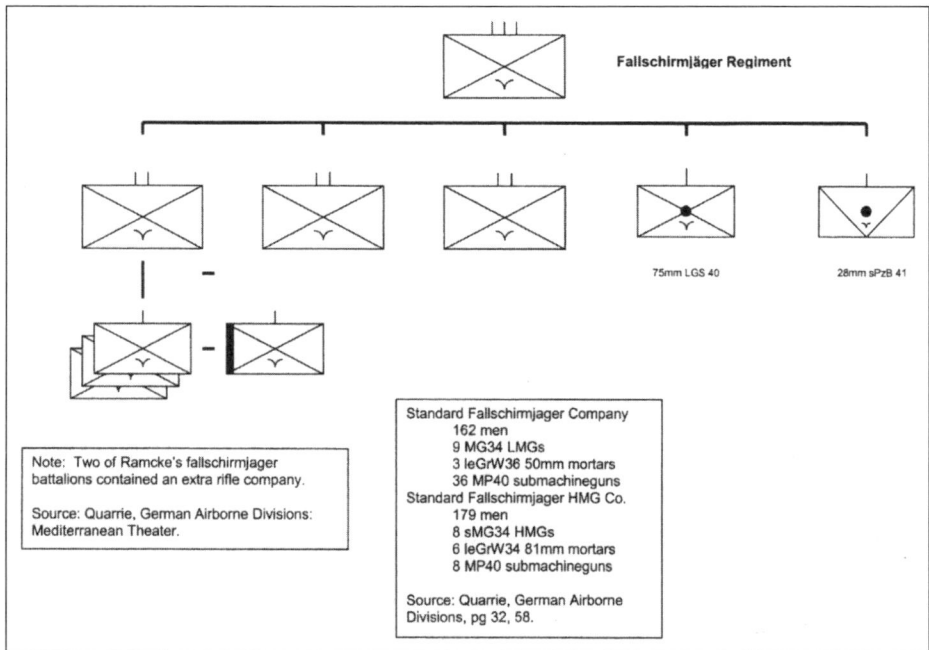

Figure VI-3: *Organization of a Fallschirmjäger Regiment.*

As previously noted, the basic administrative unit for the *fallschirmtruppe* was their regiment. The regiment consisted of three battalions, plus a company of infantry guns and anti-tank guns. Each battalion had three rifle companies and one heavy weapons company. Rifle companies were composed of three platoons (zug) of three twelve-man squads (trup). Figure VI-3 shows the basic composition of a Fallschirmjäger regiment.

Kesselring's original plan for Malta called for the full 1. Fallschirmjäger Division – three regiments, plus a detachment from the fourth regiment being formed – to be used in the invasion.

The First and Third Regiment had rebuilt and retrained in France and Germany after service on the Eastern Front near Leningrad, where they suffered another 3,000 casualties;[34] the Second Regiment, however, had been recalled to Ukraine to meet a Soviet offensive there and did not return to Germany until June 1942, and thus lacked time to recondition its exhausted troops to take part in a new operation. In its place, a scratch brigade was formed in April under General Bernard Ramcke, who had been in Italy since March, working with the Italian Folgore paratroops.[35] Ramcke's brigade included four rifle battalions, with two battalions (the former I/FJR3 under Major Freidrich Freiherr von der Heydte and the II/FJR5 under Major Freidrich Hübner) reinforced with an extra rifle company.[36]

The Fallschirmjäger order of battle is detailed in Appendix A.

---

34. Bohmler, German Paratroops, p.108.
35. Quarrie, German Airborne Divisions: Mediterranean, p.26.
36. Ibid., Table 3, p.27.

The primary personal weapon of the paratroops was the Karabiner 98K rifle, which shot a 7.92mm round from a five-round magazine.[37] NCOs (and lucky paras) were equipped with the 9mm Maschinenpistole MP40 submachine gun, which had a rate of fire of 500 rounds per minute and used a thirty-two-round magazine. It had proved invaluable on the Russian Front, where engagements began at ranges under 800 yards. The standard machine gun support came from the excellent Leichtes Maschinengewehr 34 (MG34), which fired a 7.92mm round from fifty-round drums or 300-round belts. A heavy version of the MG34, with tripod for use with a three-man crew, was available at the battalion and company level for extra support.

For fire support, the paratroops used both the 5cm Granatwerfer (GrW) 36 mortar and a version of the standard 8cm GrW 42; the Fallschirmjäger version, called a Stummelwerfer (Stump mortar), had a shorten barrel and lighter carriage for ease of dropping with the troops.

As straight infantry, the Fallschirmjäger used the standard 75mm and 105mm howitzers for support both in the artillery regiment and the infantry gun companies (Company 13) of each regiment; however, when being paradropped, these weapons were difficult to disassemble and load, drop and reassemble for use. To provide gun support, the Germans therefore developed the 7.5cm Leichtgeschutz (LG or light gun) 40, a recoilless rifle firing a nonstandard 75mm round. Although the weapon had a range of 6,500 yards and could be elevated to 65° for indirect fire, its best usage was in direct fire mode. The main drawback was the backflash from the weapon that revealed its location. The LG40 dropped in several pieces by parachute or was delivered by Go242 glider complete with ammunition and Sd.Kfz.2 Kleines Keltenkraftrad, a hybrid tracked motorcycle, for transport. A heavier version, the 10.5cm LG40, also dropped with paratroops.[38]

Initially, anti-tank support from the regiment's Company 14 used a 2.8cm schwere Panzerbuchse (sPzB) 41 specifically designed for the paratroops. The weapon had a tapered barrel that squeezed the 2.8cm round down to 2cm with increasing velocity that allowed the tungsten shot to penetrate significant armour thickness.

German armour

As well as the Fallschirmjäger regiments, the Germans planned to support the *C3* operation with a special armoured company. The planned 66. *Panzer Abteilung zur besonderen Verwendungs* (66. abV) had two companies of armour, the first one with twelve Panzer IVGs, five Panzer IPs and five Panzer IIJs, and the second made up of captured Russian tanks – at least ten KV-Is and probably one KV-II, along with between two and twelve T-34s. Created on 28 April 1942 at Wunsdorf under the auspices of the Panzer Lehr Regiment, the detachment would be commanded by Hans Bethke.

The tanks, apart from the obsolete Panzer Is and IIs, were more heavily armoured than anything the Maltese defenders had. However, they first had to land on the island to be useful. The Germans planned to land them at the seaplane base of Kalafrana, inside Marsaxlokk Bay, so they would have had to negotiate the bay's defences first, especially Fort Delimara.

---

37. There are a variety of sources for the equipment of the German paratroops; one good one is McGuirl & Feist, pp.94–131.
38. Lucas, Storming Eagles, p.186.

German naval forces

Germany had limited naval forces in the Mediterranean, but would put them to use during *C3*.

The Deutsches MarineKommando Italien (DMI) provided the headquarters and administrative requirements. Fifty-year-old Vizeadmiral Eberhard Weichold, DMI's commander, had been assigned to the Italian staff since June 1940. He headed up the German Liaison staff with the Regia Marina, as well as the DMI. Technically, he controlled all Kriesgmarine forces in Italy and North Africa, but remained operationally subordinate to the Supermarina. A strong proponent of taking Malta, he had commented as early as September 1940 that 'Malta is the stumbling block to Italy's conduct of the war at sea … .[F]rom a purely military standpoint, [the Italian Navy] must take action immediately and forestall the British by eliminating Malta.'[39]

The 3. Schnellbootflotille, based in Licata, Sicily, would be his primary force to be used in *C3*. These ten S-boats would be used off Malta at night to screen the invasion convoy area. Weichold also had the 6. Räumbootflotille, with eight small anti-submarine/minesweepers to provide additional coverage. Finally, he had twenty-one marinefahrprahm (MFP) vessels – naval ferries similar to US landing craft. These vessels would be used to transport invasion troops and materiel to Malta, especially the 66. Panzer abV and its many medium tanks.

German U-boats, commanded out of Fuhrer der Unterseeboote Italien headquarters in Rome, acted as another force for the interdiction campaign against the Royal Navy. The 29. U-flotille at La Spezia had five submarines operational to be used again western British forces, and four submarines based at Salamis in Greece to be used against naval forces out of Alexandria.

More details can be found in Appendix B.

German air forces

As noted previously, air group strength at the time of the invasion fluctuated radically. This proved most true for the Luftwaffe units, as they bore the brunt of the air assault against Malta prior to the invasion.

The 2. LuftFlotte, with Generalfeldmarschall Kesselring in command, controlled all Luftwaffe units in the Mediterranean area. He had three fliegerkorps under his headquarters.

II Fleigerkorps, based in Sicily and commanded by General Bruno Loerzer, had the main responsibility to reduce Malta's air capability and support the invasion forces. For this he had several groups:

- Jagdgeschwader 27, nominally 104 Bf109F fighters;
- Sturzkampfgeschwader 3, nominally ninety-two Ju-87D dive bombers;
- Kampfgeschwader 54, nominally 156 Ju88A level bombers, plus a group of Ju88C night fighters;
- Jagdgeschwader53, nominally 118 Bf109F fighters with a group of Me110 twin-engine fighters.

---

39. Weichold, Eberhard, *Axis Naval Policy and Operations in the Mediterranean 1939 to May 1943* (German Naval Historical Series, US Navy Department, Washington DC, 1951), pp.10–12.

X Fliegerkorps was based in Greece and Crete and commanded by General Hans Geisler. These 100-plus aircraft, mostly Ju88s and Bf109s, had the responsibility of interdicting the eastern Mediterranean.

Fliegerfuhrer Afrika was based in North Africa and various airfields and commanded by General Otto Hoffman von Waldau. Its 150-plus aircraft probably would not have seen much action in a *C3* invasion scenario. With PanzerArmee Afrika dug in at the Egyptian border, under threat of the British Desert Air Force and the growing United States bomber force, von Waldau's aircraft would have been hard pressed to protect the Axis forces there.

XI FliegerKorps, the transport command for the Germans, would provide about seven groups of Ju52 transports (nominally about fifty-three aircraft per group) for the paradrop of the Fallschirmjäger and subsequent supply drops. In addition, they had two groups of DF230 gliders and two of the larger Go242 gliders and their tugs.

A detachment of Kampfgeschwader 26 comprised twelve He-111H-6LT aircraft undergoing anti-ship training in Sardinia at the time of the invasion. These aircraft, each carrying two torpedoes at one time, would be available against the western Mediterranean British forces.

More details can be found in Appendix C.

Axis *C3* plans – the airborne landings

C3 planners scheduled the initial drop of the Folgore and Fallschirmjäger to begin at 1.00 pm on X-day. Luftwaffe and Regia Aeronautica aircraft would be over Malta early, starting at dawn (4.00–5.00 am), specifically targeting defensive installations in the landing area, airfields, anti-aircraft positions and coastal forts. They planned a final mission to drop smoke bombs to screen the incoming transports.

The initial drop included a total of six German and three Italian battalions. Their aircraft would swing south of the island and fly straight north, dropping their human cargo as soon as they crossed the Maltese coast. Figure VI-4 shows the initial landing targets of the nine first-wave battalions, with two German battalions landing on the left flank, the Italians in the centrer and four German battalions on the right. Gliders carrying heavy weapons and artillery followed on the heels of this initial drop, as well as a load carrying supplies.

Two more waves of German paratroops, dropping the remaining three Fallschirmjäger battalions, would take place around 5.00–6.00 pm, with the Italian wave containing the I Battaglione d'Assalto Paracadutisti dell'Aeronautica and Battaglione Riattatori 'Loreto' to be dropped on the Qrendi airfield site, with the primary task of holding and preparing the field for use.

Overall, the task of the paratroops was to establish a defensive perimeter, as shown in Figure VI-4, with specific anti-vehicle sites to be established to control road access to the area.

The Axis expected a quick counter-attack coming from the Luqa/Hal Far direction, with another smaller riposte from Zebbug. They did not expect much of a response from the Mdina area on the Dingli Plateau.

A final assault force of German pioneers in Go242 gliders planned a direct assault landing on Fort Benghajsa just before dusk, with the goal of removing the fort's coastal guns from threatening the sea invasion force due that night.

The plan encompassed two complications. First, although the southern coast of Malta did not sport the same intensity of anti-aircraft capability as Valletta or the areas around the airfields,

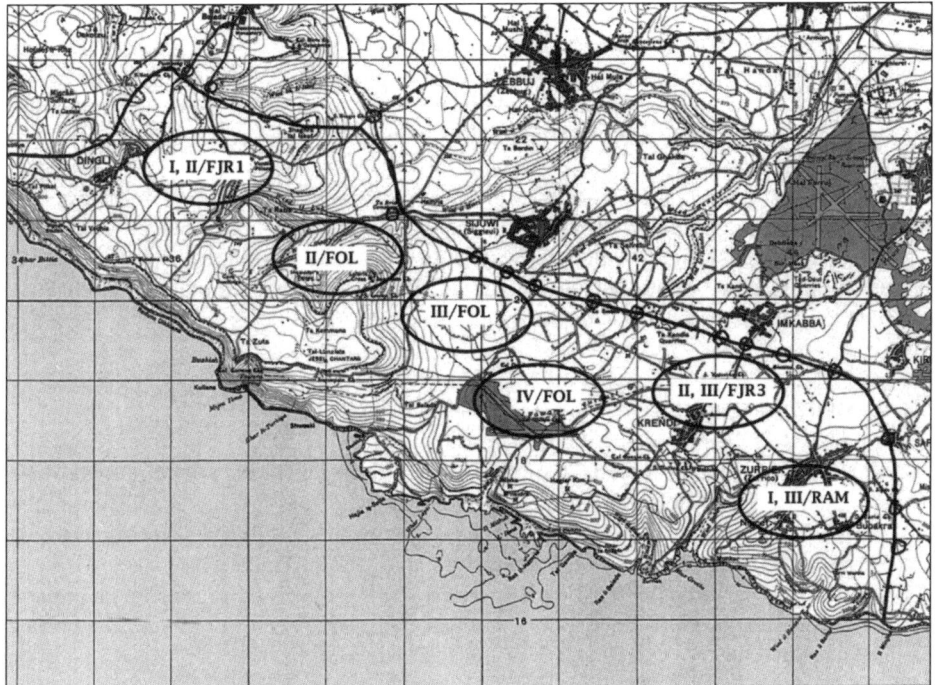

Figure VI-4: *Battalion Drop Zones and Perimeter to be established by the paratroopers. Circles are anti-tank blocking positions.*

the south-to-north flight path for the transports would have them flying through that intense flak after they unloaded. Aircraft losses would be substantial. Axis plans for subsequent aircraft transport waves reflected this concern, as losses of 50 per cent were used for reinforcement and resupply predictions.

The second significant complication was the Axis assumption of where the British counter-attack would come from. Given the strength they were assigning to their right flank and the paucity of same on their left, Axis intelligence had not discovered the formation or location of the island's 4 Brigade reserve on the Dingli Plateau.

Axis *C3* plans – the seaborne landings

The Axis plans for their *C3* seaborne contingent predicated their landings on arriving where the Maltese and British did not expect them – namely, the inhospitable southern coastline. That rugged shoreline had only Fort Benghajsa's coastal defence artillery to cover the area.

The primary landing zone, code-named Famagosta, stretched from Hagra S-Sewda in the west to Wied-il-Bassasa in the east, a stretch of some 5,900 yards. Onto these rocks, the Italians planned to land some 14,000 troops of the Friuli Division and San Marcos Marines, forty-five armoured Semoventes and fifty-six 75mm guns, with the 8,600 troops of the Livorno Division right behind them. To make matters even more difficult than the terrain, the initial landings were to commence before dawn, at ten separate locations.

The secondary landing zone, code-named Larnaca, centred around Marsa Scirocco Bay, with commando landings on the far more hospitable shorelines near Forts Benghaisa and Delimara at seven locations and the landing of German armour inside the bay at the British seaplane base of Kalafrana.

The final part of the *C3* landings were to be at Gozo, where the landing of the Superga Division would take place, code-named Cipro. A total of nine landing sites around the island had been selected to put the 10,000-plus troops ashore. Given that the entire island held approximately the same number of adult males, with no organized defence, the Italians expected this portion of the invasion plan to succeed easily.[40]

Famagosta (Figure VI-5)[41]

Landing Zone A1–A3: Two battalions of the Fruili's 87th Regiment and two companies of the Grado Battalion, San Marcos Marines, targeted this landing zone at Hajia-is-Soda on the far left flank of the invasion. In addition, the command teams from the 87th and San Marcos would come ashore here. The landings would be solely infantry, as the landing boats would have to put ladders up the 27ft-high cliffs along the ashore; shallow water would require the boats to position themselves bow-on. Once ashore, troops could move to their right toward a narrow road leading up to the top of the plateau.

Landing Zone B1-B2: The landings on this promontory near Ghar Lapsi would again require ladders to get off the boats up the 20ft cliffs. Grado's third company and two platoons of Guastatori would make the landing here to begin securing the area.

Landing Zone C: The small cove at Ghar Lapsi, a very narrow and shallow body of water leading to the fishing pier there, was the 87th's third battalion target, along with a battery of 65mm/17 guns. A stone blockhouse covered the entrance to this little cove, with firing ports facing directly into the cove. A road, steep at times, led toward the plateau above.

Landing Zone D1–D2: The Italians planned for the cove and promontory just east of Ghar Lapsi to be a major landing site for their armour. Here the coast dipped to just 6ft above sea level, close enough for ramps to extend and allow the Semoventes to drive off their transports. Thirty-two 75mm guns of the 28° and 35° artillery regiments, two batteries of 20mm anti-aircraft guns and forty-five armoured vehicles were to be landed here. Once ashore, with the command group of XXX Corpo d'Armata, the armour could move to their left toward Ghar Lapsi and up the road there.

Landing Zone E: This area at Wied Maghluq was to be the landing site for the 88th CCNN Legion's LXXXVIII Battalion and command group, two other companies of CCNN troops plus two platoons of Guastatori. An isolated landing site, it had only a 2ft-wide path leading to

---
40. Caruana correspondence, 12 June 2009.
41. In the following discussion, only the primary combat units being landed will be discussed.

the landing sites to the west and high ground slopes to the east. The 1,500 troops here would be forced to struggle through difficult terrain to reach the top of the plateau before making contact on either side.

Landing Zone F1–F2: The rocky promontories at L'Ilsna, with their 33ft cliff face, were targeted by three companies of CCNN troops from XCVI Battalion/88th Legion and L Battalion/M da Sbarco, plus more Guastatori and mortars. These troops faced the same problem as their fellows at landing site E to their west – a hard climb up to the plateau.

Landing Zone G1-G3: The landings on both sides of Ghar ix-Xaghra would constitute the second major infantry landing of the pre-dawn hours, with the Friuli's Generale Carboni and his headquarters group, plus I Battalion/88th Regiment, half of II Battalion and two batteries of 65mm/17 infantry guns. These troops would move eastward to get to a narrow country road leading north.

Landing Zone H: The other half of II/88th Regiment and the command group of the 88th would land on the western edge of the Wied Zurrieq fiord. They would have to overcome a stone bunker before moving up the rocky slope toward the Qrendi road on the plateau.

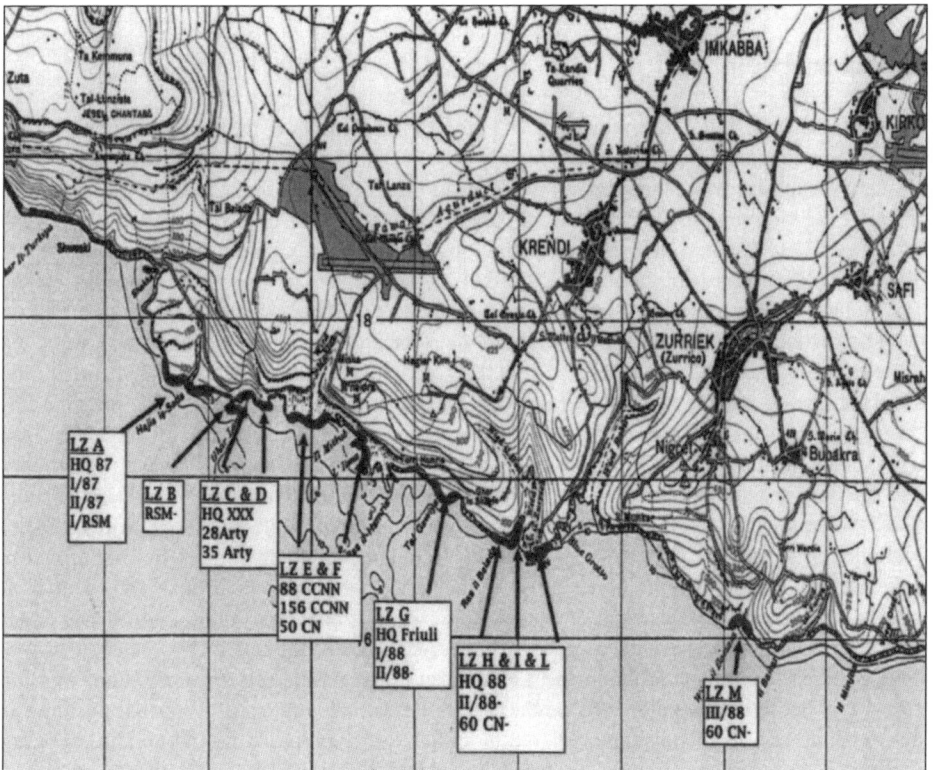

Figure VI-5: *Famagosta Landing Area.*

Landing Zone I: Guastatori, supported by flamethrowers, planned to penetrate the Wied Zurrieq fiord to land at the small fishing pier there. The stone bunker mentioned above covered the pier and the boats would have had to deal with the heavy cable that closed the fiord except for a few hours each day.

Landing Zone L: Two companies of LX Battalion/M da Sbarco would be landed by ladder on the eastern edge of the Wied Zurrieq fiord to support the Guastatori above. One platoon with two 47/32mm guns was also supposed to land with these troops, the guns probably being dismantled so they could be hauled up the 27ft-high ledge.

Landing Zone M: The III Battalion/88th Regiment was scheduled to land at Wied il Bassasa, over a mile to the west of the Wied Zurrieq landings. The region had a very narrow fault gorge in the high cliffs surrounding the area and no communication with the other landing sites until the top of the gorge was reached. This was the furthest western landing zone of Famagosta.

The Livorno Division was to follow the Friuli ashore, but the exact landing site locations were left open. Their deployment and its timing would depend on how well the initial troops were faring.

Larnaca (Figure VI-6)

The eight landing sites chosen for the 5,780 men and equipment of the Larnaca landings were split into three main grouping.

One group planned to land around Benghajsa Point, following the neutralization of the fort there by the German pioneers who were supposed to land on it in Go242 gliders on the eve of X-day. These landings at Points N, O and P by Guastatori assault engineers and the CCNN XLII Battalion troops, totalling some 1,800 men, would provide secondary pressure on the British base at Kalafrana and a threat against the Hal Far airfield.

The second group, including the German 66. Panzer abV and its pioneers, was supposed to land inside Marsa Scirocco Bay against the base at Kalafrana (Point Q and R), where the seaplane landing jetty would allow the tanks to be unloaded easily. The primary problem this group faced was the defences of the bay itself – mines that could be electrically detonated from a command position in Fort Delimara.

The third group – possibly the most daring and under-strength attempt – consisted of some 200 saboteurs who would land in small assault boats at three locations around Fort Delimara and attempt to take the fort by *coup de main*, following its bombardment by 2nd *Squadra*. The group at Point S had the hardest task as they had to negotiate their boats into the bay to land below the fort, then face a near-vertical 80ft cliff. The boats for Points T and U had easier beaches to land at, but more defences to infiltrate just to get to the fort.

The most significant problem the Larnaca landings faced was the alert status of both forts. The paratroops would have landed hours before the sea assault started, putting the entire island on alert. The chance of finding either fort unprepared was slim, and any guns that survived the bombardment would be manned and in action against any ship approaching the coast.

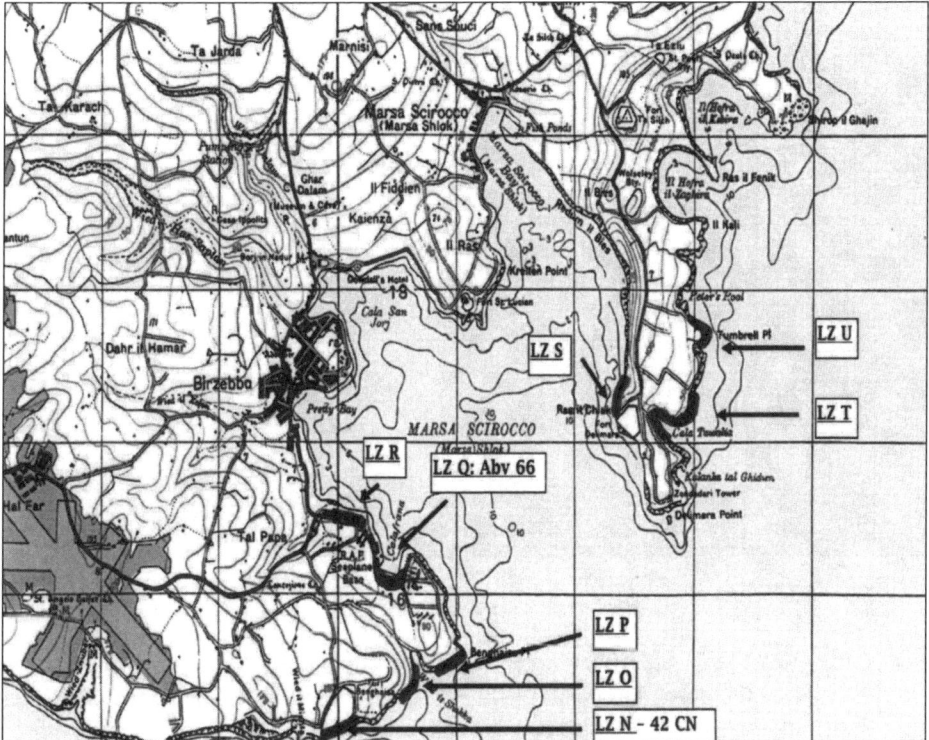

Figure VI-6: *Larnaca Landing Areas.*

Cipro (Figure VI-7)

The third and easiest landing areas for the Italian seaborne forces was expected to be on the smaller islands of Gozo and Comino, north-west of Malta. Gozo, a quarter the size of Malta (26 square miles versus 95 square miles) with only a tenth of its population, had food production as its primary function during the war years. Comino was an even smaller island (1.9 square miles) between Malta and Gozo. With no real military presence on either island, except for a small unit on Gozo whose function was to operate the RDF station at San Dmitri Point, the Malta Defence Scheme ceded them to the enemy.

The Italians assigned the Superga Assault Division, reinforced by the Bafile Battalion, San Marcos Marines and the XLIII CCNN Battalion, to the Cipro landings. On Gozo's northern coast, Superga's 91st Regiment would land at six separate locations, each landing site having half a battalion of the 91st, a platoon of Guastatori and half a company of Bafile Marines:

- III/91st would land at Xwieni (Point Q) and Qbajjar (Point K); following their landing and reorganization, the battalion would lead the advance toward the capital of Rabat (aka Victoria).
- II/91st would land at Marsalforn (Point V) and Ramla (Point X), along with nineteen Semonvente L40/47s. They would advance on the village of Xaghra, then on to Rabat.

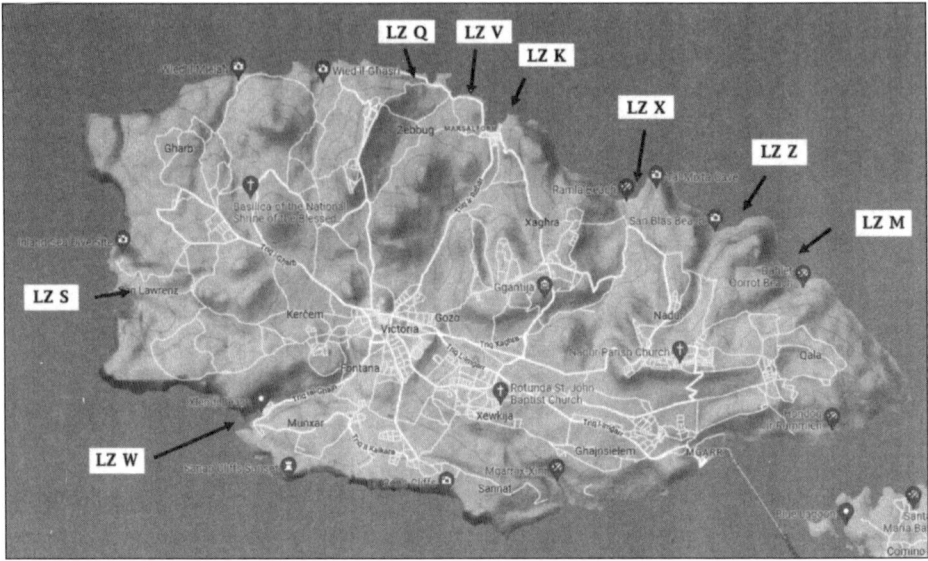

Figure VI-7: *CIPRO landing areas.*

- I/91st would land at San Bias (Point Z) and Dahlet Korrot (Point M), then advance toward the village of Nadur and from there to Mgarr harbour to seal the island from interference from Malta and to cut off any retreat from Gozo to Malta.
- Superga's 92nd Regiment, reinforced by the XLIII CCNN Battalion, was scheduled to land on the western side of Gozo at two locations. The I/92nd Battalion would land with at Ras id Dueira (Point S) and move uphill toward Rabat.
- Half of the II/92nd would land with nineteen Semovente L40/47s at the small Xlindi Bay (Point W) and join the drive for Rabat.
- Finally, the other half of II/92nd would take Camino Island, again cutting off access to the main island.

The III/92nd Battalion, 5th Artillery Regiment and Generale Lorenzelli's divisional command group were held in reserve.

Axis post-landing plans

It is axiomatic that no plan survives contact with the enemy; however, the planning staff did provide plans for the Axis *C3* forces to follow after landing. The *C3* invasion planners did not define the timing of these plans. For example, the amount of time needed to consolidate would depend heavily on the difficulty the divisions had in landing their troops, equipment and supplies (see logistics and terrain discussions below).

The base plan had the Friuli Division consolidate after landing, centred around the village of Bubakra, then drive eastward toward Hal Far airfield. Their next phase would be to link up with the Larnaca invasion forces covering Fort Benghajsa and clear the rest of the Marsaxlokk harbour area to open it up for Axis supply shipping. On their left flank, the Livorno Division would also push eastward to consolidate around the village of Gudia.[42] The Livorno would then sweep toward Marsa Scala and down the Delimara peninsula toward Fort Delimara.

Timing for the invasion called for all the first-wave troops and Livorno to be unloaded and ashore by 7.00 pm on X+1 day. The ships then would start the thirteen-hour journey back to Sicily to pick up the Assietta and Napoli divisions, which would be loaded in twelve hours and arrive off Malta on the morning of X+3.[43]

While the Livorno and Friuli swept the eastern section of Malta, the follow-up divisions, Assietta and Napoli, would be landing. Assietta planned to consolidate on the Dingli Plateau, then sweep through the town of Rabat and along the eastern edge of the Vittoria Lines to the northern coast. The Napoli Division would consolidate after landing around the village of Siggiewi. Once reorganized, the Napoli would sweep north on the right flank of the Assietta Division toward Malta's northern coast.

Figure VI-8: *Typical road on Malta.*

The Assietta Division's task would be the most challenging, as getting their troops, supplies and equipment – especially artillery – up to the plateau was problematical because of the width and condition of the roads. Figure VI-8 shows a typical road up to the plateau from the landing areas.

The final piece of the invasion was a single regiment of the Superga Assault Division which would land on Malta's north coast east of St Paul's Bay. This would take place after Gozo had been successfully captured.

Although not specified in the operational maps, the third phase of the *C3* operation would have been the convergence of the invading divisions on Valletta.

---

42. It is unclear from the operational planning maps whether the Livorno would be responsible for pushing the Axis perimeter out to encompass the consolidation area shown. This may have been a task of the paratrooper forces.
43. Gabriele, p.175.

Logistics

Supplying the invasion required substantial planning for both the 15,000 paratroops and the 80,000 seaborne troops.

Paratroops

Each paratroop landed with 6 litres of water and about 10kg of food and ammunition, with the water expected to last two days, by which time water from offshore tankers would be in place to provide this essential resource. Starting on X+2, the paratroops needed some 180 tons[44] dropped to them.

Since ammunition and other staples remained different for the Folgore troopers and the Fallschirmjäger, air drops were handled separately by each service.

The Italian Regia Aeronautica expected about 55 per cent of their SM.82 aircraft to have survived the initial paradrops, making some forty available for supply runs. The SM.82, the only Italian aircraft capable of airdropping supplies, could carry ten German supply containers, each with about 80kg of materiel, or seventeen of the Italian 'SP' model containers which could carry about 95kg. There were enough SP model containers to last five days. Each aircraft could carry about 1,600kg per flight for the first five days. The Italians expected to be able to average about two-and-a-half sorties per day, making their airdrop capability about 120 tons until day five and 80 tons thereafter.

The Germans expected to be able to have about 200 Ju52 transport aircraft available for supply runs. These smaller aircraft could only carry four of the German containers, with about 320kg per flight. Thus, the Germans could deliver about 160 tons if they averaged the same number of sorties per day.

Once a Maltese airfield was captured and secured,[45] air ferrying of supplies could begin. The Italians had a variety of aircraft available for this task, and could conceivably deliver about 333 tons per day if the two-and-a-half sorties per day goal could be achieved. However, this would mean an average of one aircraft landing and unloading each minute of daylight at a single airfield, creating a major bottleneck.

The other caveat to the air ferrying of supplies would have been if the *Spezia Aerotrasportabile* Division, in reserve for *C3*, had been needed. Just bringing in the division's personnel would have taken about three days, during which time no supplies could have been ferried.

Seaborne troops

The planners based the *C3* plan for the seaborne logistics on having enough supplies for the first five days delivered with the landing troops. Each man would land with 2 litres of water and 18kg of ammunition and food. Another 4 litres of water and 47kg per man would be landed with the troops and transported to the assembly locations. For the 10,000-strong Friuli Division, this meant that 470 tons of food and ammunition, plus 40 tons of water, would have to be unloaded from boats – along with support weapons, artillery, armour etc. – and carried up from the landing areas.

---

44. The plan's basis of supply calculations was in kilograms. For simple conversions: 3kg of water was 3 litres, each slightly smaller than a US quart. A kilogram is about 2.2lb, with 1,000kg (2,204lb) considered a ton.
45. Secured means runway obstructions and mines have been cleared and anti-aircraft interdiction of the field has been eliminated.

They expected the delivered water to last two days, after which water tankers offshore, carrying some 500 tons of water – enough for 50,000 men for three days – would be available. Two rope-tow systems designed to get the critical water off the landing sites to the top of the surrounding ridge had been planned;

Additional supplies for day six and onward, depending on how the invasion battle progressed, would hopefully be delivered through a captured port (Marsaxlokk). The second-best option would be a captured airfield, like Hal Far. The worst option was to continue to bring supplies off the beachhead. For the 80,000 seaborne troops, a minimum of 11.5kg of supplies,[46] or 920 tons in total, would be required per day.

The fact that their field kitchens required wood and very little existed on the island complicated the entire food issue for the Italians.

Factors favouring the attackers

Numbers

Numbers comprised the primary advantage the Axis had in the *C3* operation. They planned on throwing almost 100,000 troops against 26,000 nearly starved defenders, with complete air superiority. As planners determined, even if they lost 20 per cent of the force in the initial drops and landings, they would still hold an edge in numbers.[47]

The caveat with the numbers was the ability of the Axis to concentrate and apply those numbers. The highly trained Folgore and Fallschirmjäger and the better-trained Livorno and Fruili divisions would have operated effectively. The Assietta and Napoli divisions, standard Italian divisions, were questionable, as previous actions in France and Greece had proven. The key to victory on the island thus lay with the initial troops.

Time

Time should have been completely on the side of the Axis, for two reasons. First, Malta's isolation meant any incursion by the Royal Navy would have been of short duration, with daylight exposure to the Luftwaffe and Regia Aeronautica bombers. In addition, the island's isolation meant every bullet, every artillery shell and every mortar bomb expended could not be replaced.

However, while on the surface the Axis had all the time in the world to initiate and exploit their overwhelming numeric and logistics superiority, in truth they didn't. Hitler needed to have Malta behind him for two reasons. First, the Eastern Front *Fall Blau* offensive towards Stalingrad and the Baku oilfields was already under way and needed every ounce of Germany's resources. And second, Rommel's *PanzerArmee Afrika* and the Italians were sitting under intense pressure from Britain's Desert Air Force and American bombers on the Egyptian border. In both cases, the Germans needed to relocate Luftwaffe assets to the threatened areas as soon as possible.

---

46. The 11.5 kg of supply per day is broken down as follows: Water, 3 liters, Ammunition, 6 kg; food and firewood, 2 kg; gasoline and other fuel, 0.3 kg, mother, 0.2 kg.
47. Gabriele, 195, note 1.

Factors hindering the attackers

Terrain
The terrain on Malta has already been discussed as favouring the defenders, both for the island's small size and its ubiquitous stone walls. However, several other terrain considerations would also have impacted the attackers.

The landing site terrain made the initial landings difficult. For example, Figure VI-9 shows one of the Famagosta beaches. Troops landing by ladder would have been able to negotiate the transition from boat to land, but getting equipment ashore would have been significantly more difficult, especially under sporadic artillery fire. Add the initial landing being at night and the landings would have been chaotic at worst, delayed at best. As already noted, the plan called for the landing of 24,000 troops, forty-five armoured vehicles, forty-eight artillery pieces and 113,000 tons of supplies in fifteen hours. Given the terrain – and the nature of the landing sites – that timing was simply impractical.

Figure VI-9: *Famagosta, Point F, from the plateau top and from sea level.*

As mentioned earlier in the plans section, the narrow, rock-wall-lined roads on Malta made the effective use of supporting armour very difficult. The armoured vehicles or tractors brought ashore by the Axis would have only been able to use the main roads, which could be easily blocked by the defenders. Although the armour could bull through and over the walls, this would take its toll on the machines and slow progress significantly.

Furthermore, the plan called for the seizure of several villages by the paratroops. Urban warfare in the confined, narrow, rubble-choked streets would have been horrendous, both in time and casualties.

High-level apathy

Their own leadership's apathy about the project remained the single most damaging factor against the attackers. Hitler had other priorities and a denigrated view of Italian capabilities. He had opted not to attack Malta in 1941 and, although he had agreed to the operation at the end of April 1942, he had expected miracles from Rommel and *C3* in June. Although he had finally agreed with his Southern Commander to provide the fuel and paratroops needed for the invasion, his concerns were still prevalent.

There was concern too among the Italian commanders. As early as May 1942, Generale Rino Corso Fougier, who had replaced Generale Pricolo as Regia Aeronautica's Chief of Staff in November 1941, told Foreign Minister Ciano he viewed the eventual landing 'with much anxiety'. The chief of their Air Bureau, Colonnelle Giuseppe Casero, was even more pessimistic, noting Malta's anti-aircraft defence was very efficient and the interior of the island 'one solid nest of machine guns'.[48] Perhaps worse, Ciano also recorded a conversation with the Friuli's commander, Generale Carboni, expressing his fears:

> '[The generale was] convinced, technically convinced, that we are heading for an unheard-of disaster. Preparations have been childish, equipment is lacking and inadequate. The landing troops will never succeed in landing, or if they land, they are doomed to total destruction.'[49]

Carboni even sent a memorandum to Crown Prince Umberto, son of the Italian king and titular head of the operation, stating:

> '[T]he Malta operation was being carried out with the inadequate means at our disposal and is taking on the appearance of a new folly, the consequence of which will be not only a new loss of military and political prestige to us but will also have another effect. There is reason to fear that the enemy might take advantage of a defeat on Malta by landing in Italy and that our ally might seize upon this new confirmation of our strategic and tactical weakness to take over command.'[50]

---

48. Ciano Diary, 12 May 1942, p.485.
49. Ibid., 20 June 1942, p.499.
50. Malta at War, Vol 6, No XX, p.1,850.

Chapter VII

Saturday
15 August 1942[1]

Time	Wind (kn)	Sea	Notes		
8.00 am	0–1	calm	fog	sunrise	6.25 am
8.00 pm	2–3	mostly calm		sunset	7.48 pm

Saturday 15 August in Malta started like every other day in the past month, with air raid warnings as dozens of Axis fighters and bombers swarmed over the island. Turmoil from exploding bombs, mingled with the near-continuous crack of anti-aircraft gunnery, deadened everyone to the noise and dust, the islanders only occasionally cheered by an Axis plane falling from the sky. Smoke and dust clung in the air, with no wind to disperse it.

Rumours started flying early from cryptic comments made by Flight Lieutenant Harry Coldbeck, who had flown a photo-reconnaissance mission that morning. The results of his flight, interpreted in the Lascaris War Rooms underneath Valletta's massive walls, troubled Malta's leaders – tri-motor transports on Sicilian fields, concentrations of shipping in the southern Sicilian ports of Licata and Porto Empedocle, and a convoy of ships and naval vessels steaming south off the coast of Sicily, near Augusta. Gort and Scobie reluctantly agreed: invasion was imminent. They transmitted the code word *Volcano* to all defence headquarters, while Lieutenant Governor Jackson sent the code on the civilian side. Air Vice Marshal Park ordered his remaining seven fighters readied to oppose the airborne assault.

As the Volcano signal spread through the island, various organizations began a well-rehearsed and planned series of activities. At police stations throughout the island, on- and off-duty police gathered with members of the Air Raid Protection organization to begin preparing their locales for possible battle. Inhabitants were notified personally to stay in their homes or shelters and off the roads to allow critical traffic to move unimpeded. Medical personnel, aided by clergy, prepared casualty stations in churches, police stations and shelters. Home Guard units congregated to aid in the population control.[2]

As the morning wore on, with battalions and companies reporting into their battle stations, slowed by incessant interdiction from the air, the defence council became perplexed at the nature of the morning Axis air blitz. Reports consistently said that air attacks heavily targeted virtually all anti-aircraft sites along the south-western coast, unlike the previous days when the

---
1. Weather information comes from the Supermarina's Diary for August 1942.
2. Instructions from Civil Organization in the event of an enemy landing or attempted landing.

airfields had been the main targets. With invasion imminent, the men assumed the bombing targeted areas to support landings, but the rocky cliffs of the south-west coastline seemed unsuitable for a large-scale invasion force. Most of the targeted sites reported some disruption, but only one, the Bofors of F Battery/186/74, was destroyed when a Ju88 crashed on top of the site.

While trying to make sense of the air attacks, several naval sighting reports came in. HMS *Una* (Lieutenant C.P. Norman) off the eastern coast of Sicily reported a strong naval squadron – two older battleships and escorts – moving south. The submarine had been unable to get off a shot at the Italians. Two other submarines, P46 (Lieutenant J.S. Stevens) and HMS *Utmost* (Lieutenant L.W. Langridge), also reported flotillas moving out from the small southern Sicilian ports. They had expected the seaborne concentration of shipping at those ports, having been warned about them from Special Intelligence provided by London, but the ultimate destinations remained unknown.

Just after noon, the AMES radar stations warned of a massive air concentration beginning to build up over Sicily. With the naval reports taken into account, Air Vice Marshal Park, with the concurrence of his flight controller, Group Captain 'Woody' Woodall, scrambled their pilots. For the first time in three days, the RAF took to the skies. Squadron leader Lucas, Buerling, and the other pilots made a valiant effort to get in amongst the onrushing transports. There was confusion in Lascaris fighter control as two waves of aircraft, identified by the Spitfire pilots as transports, swung around the island; but the confusion ended as the waves turned to approach the island from the south.

Around 1.20 pm,[3] following a wave of bombers that struck the southern area with smoke bombs, more than 400 Axis transports – Ju52s and SM.82s – began discharging their passengers into the maelstrom over the island. Parachutes burst open all along the south-west coast from Dingli to Bubakra. The 1. Fallschirmjäger Regiment (FJR1) landed on the left on the Dingli Plateau, 3. Fallschirmjäger Regiment (FJR3) and Ramcke's battalions on the right flank in and around the village of Qrendi, and the Italians in the centre between them.

As the parachutes opened up, the code word *Cyclone* was transmitted throughout the island – the alert for general invasion action. Another sound added to the cacophony of anti-aircraft guns, bombs and low-flying aircraft: bells; hundreds of bells from every church on the island, announcing the arrival of enemy troops.[4]

1. Fallschirmjäger Regiment (Figure VII-1)

For the men of the 1. Fallschirmjäger Regiment, their drop onto the left flank of the drop zone became reminiscent of that on Crete the year before. Anti-aircraft fire led one troop of Ju52 aircraft to release their passengers early, causing many men of 6/II[5] to fall into the ocean, with the rest clinging to steep rocky cliffs as best they could. The remainder of I and II Battalion dropped on top of Malta's fully alerted 4 Brigade – an organization that Axis intelligence failed to identify. Third Company came down near the Verdala Palace and machine-gun fire from two troops of Malta's tanks cut them to pieces. Elsewhere, the two battalions sustained heavy

---

3. Time is Malta-local time. Malta was on Central European Summer Time, two hours ahead of normal.
4. Originally, church bells had been used to signal the 'All Clear' after an air raid, but at the beginning of 1942, the civilian authorities had decided that ringing the bells would be the fastest way to signal an invasion.
5. Unit designation will be generally by company/battalion; 6/II indicates 6th Company/II Battalion.

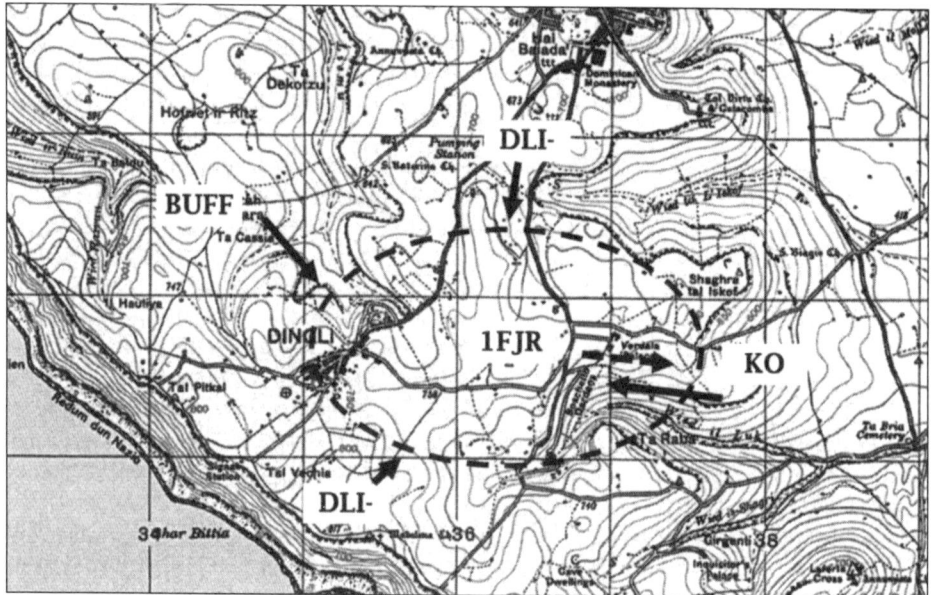

Figure VII-1: *The 1. Fallschirmjäger Rgt versus 4 Brigade.*

losses and scrambled to regroup, confused as much by the smoke as from the heavy ground fire of the Durham Light Infantry, veterans of the North African siege of Tobruk, and the King's Own Regiment. The capture of Oberst Karl-Lothor Schultz, their regimental commander who drifted into the battle station of D Company/8th King's Own, made matters worse. After the war, he recalled:

> 'The regimental command team stood at the door as the Maltese coast came back into view. A minute later, we jumped. As the plane receded, gunfire from the ground could be heard and we were fighting for our lives as we landed, some of us in the midst of the enemy. There were crashes and booms from every direction.'[6]

Both the 1st and 3rd companies of I Battalion were overrun. Near Dingli, two platoons of D Company/Durham Light Infantry waged a vicious and solitary battle with the Germans 2nd Company, with neither side giving way nor quarter. The British drove the rest of the two German battalions into a rocky area of about 150 acres.

The surge out to attack by 4 Brigade as the last of the parachutes drifted down had little organization; their orders had simply been to 'engage and utterly destroy the enemy'. Most of the action came at platoon level as each company's battle station had been organized into separate platoon strongpoints. But as the platoons charged out haphazardly to hit the just-landed paratroops, they learned a hard lesson. Their briefings had told them the Germans dropped lightly armed with just pistols and grenades, while their other weapons – rifles, machine guns

---

6. *Kurowski, Jump into Hell, p.230.

and mortars – were dropped separately in weapons containers.[7] But the Germans had learned from the bloody lessons of Crete; these Fallschirmjäger dropped with their more effective weapons, many armed with the Maschinenpistole (MP)38 submachine gun. With an effective range of 100 yards and a thirty-two-round magazine, the weapon gave the landing paratroops a potent punch, as the British found out to their cost.[8]

The Germans also managed to collect several of their 75mm recoilless LG40s from the regiment's 13th Company and used the guns to catch C Company of the 8th King's Own in the open, inflicting heavy casualties and potentially opening a way out of the trap. But British artillery fire fell on the advancing paratroops and drove them back, pinning them again in their enclave. To the west, the last battalion of 4 Brigade – 4th Battalion, the Buffs – moved east to join their comrades, but Luftwaffe interdiction on various road junctions slowed them. Their primary mode of transportation – bicycle – did not do well off-road.

A push south by the Malta Tanks and A Company from the DLI displayed the coordination difficulties not only inherent with a lack of training, but with self-inflicted command problems. Colonel Brittorious, 4 Brigade's commander, spent much of the afternoon racing from point to point, delivering orders to individual platoons, bypassing both company and battalion commanders. The effect became apparent when the DLI's battalion commander, Lieutenant Colonel Arderne, tried to concentrate two of his companies for a drive south with armour support, but could only find a single scattered company to make the attempt.

Arderne's troops moved slowly out across the rocky fields, while the tanks – A9 Cruisers of 2 Troop – stayed on the road and moved ahead of them, under a sporadic umbrella of artillery fire. But the Germans had one of their LG40 recoilless rifles set up and quickly slammed a 75mm round into the leading tank, brewing it up violently. Having been held in reserve, 7 Platoon moved out to support the tanks, but machine-gun fire caught them crossing a field and pinned them down with casualties. On the other flank, 8 Platoon ran into the same fire. Captain C.E. Fraser, the company commander, brought up a Vickers machine gun to support the infantry, while a second A9 added its machine-gun fire; its 2-pdr gun had no high explosive rounds to help against infantry. Another recoilless round slammed into the rock wall by the side of the second tank, spraying the tank commander with stone shrapnel and stunning him. Before he could recover, a second recoilless round struck the turret and exploded the tank.

The third A9 backed quickly out of danger. The Vickers machine-gun team, however, spotted the flashback from the German weapon and gunned down the crew. Artillery finally began impacting directly onto the Germans, and Lieutenant R.N. Simmons called for his 7 Platoon to charge across the field with bayonets fixed – only to run straight into a burst of short rounds from his own artillery, killing him and several of his platoon. The attack stalled, a costly lesson. Nevertheless, the paratroops pulled back, having suffered enough from the artillery.

---

7. The Ruckenpackung Zwangauslosung (RZ) 20 parachute used by the Fallschirmjäger attached with a strap on the back of the trooper's harness, rather than at the shoulders like other parachutes. The RZ20 allowed little control during descent and required a forward roll upon landing. Carrying weapons was problematic, but the disaster on Crete led to additional training to be able to land with weapons, although more weapons were also dropped in arms containers as before; http://www.fjr2.be/Pagina%20E-26-%20German%20parachutes.htm.

8. In addition to dropping with automatic weapons, the Germans also used a better jumpsuit and a better harness release that did not require them to stand erect to free them from the parachute. Student to Göring, 'Future of German Paratroop and Airborne Operations', November 1942.

Italian 1 Brigade Folgore (Figure VII-2)

In the centre, Tenente Colonnello Luigi Camossa's Folgore 1 Brigade dropped from Laferla Hill to the incomplete Qrendi airfield. Below the high ground, the Italians became more spread out than their German counterparts, due to the size of their transports. The SM.82 carried three times the troops a Ju52 could, but dropped them over a wider area; it took over a minute for the thirty-two men on the aircraft to jump out under normal conditions. The drop over Malta, with its heavy anti-aircraft fire, was anything but normal, and the Folgore paratroops fell over almost 2 miles of the island. The drop scattered heavily and sustained losses, especially from III Battalion, which lost several aircraft shot down and most of 9th Company that drifted into the village of Siggiewi, where troops of the Royal West Kents (RWK) hunted them down among the narrow streets and alleys.

One RWK officer, Lieutenant Jimmy James, wrote after the battle:

> 'One of the troop carriers was hit four square and came flaming down – a terrifying spectacle – with one parachute dragged behind it. The hunt through the town for the paratroops was pretty awful. Single snipers and small packets of them made going slow and caused a lot of casualties. Officers couldn't control anything in the ruined streets. Several fights between friendly squads made everyone nervous.'[9]

The paratroop survivors found themselves forced back toward the village square, dominated by the Church of Saint Nicholas and the saint's statue, before being surrounded.

On the left flank of the plateau, the King's Own Royals drove Italian Folgore paratroops of II Battalion's 5th Company off Laferla Hill[10] and down toward the flatlands below, further isolating the Germans from help in that direction.

The worst blow to the Italians and the defenders occurred in the walled city of Mdina, where a crippled SM.82 slammed its 30 tons of metal, fuel and men into the narrow streets of the ancient capital. The crash killed much of the Folgore's 8th Company as well as the III Battalion commander.[11]

On the ground, other Italian platoons coalesced, as they had been trained, into ad hoc companies and tried to overrun the F Battery/182 of light Bofors guns. But the Maltese of D Company from the King's Own Malta Regiment's (KOMR), 3rd Battalion, held them off, with the help of the battery's Bofors and point-blank fire from the nearby D Battery, 12th Royal Artillery's 25-pdr guns. The Italian attack was uncoordinated and without communications, which left other troops out of the battle despite being close at hand. The next Folgore surge, however, initially overran the battery when another platoon of Italians from II Battalion

---

9. *James, Attack on Malta, p.210.
10. Laferla Hill was named for the Laferla Cross, erected in 1900 to commemorate the Holy Year of the Catholic Church and named after Reverend Paul Laferla who took the initiative to have it put up. The plinth is a small chapel dedicated to Our Lady of Sorrows. The cross was blessed by the Archbishop in 1904, when a painting of Our Lady of Sorrows was added. It collapsed in 1946 but was re-erected in 1963. It is 16 metres (52ft) high and a landmark. There is a chapel next to it dedicated to the Annunciation, originally built in 1420, falling into ruin on several occasions and also collapsing in an earthquake in 1693, but rebuilt each time. The cross was removed in 1943 when Qrendi became an active field.
11. *Folgore Battle Diary, Malta, p.10.

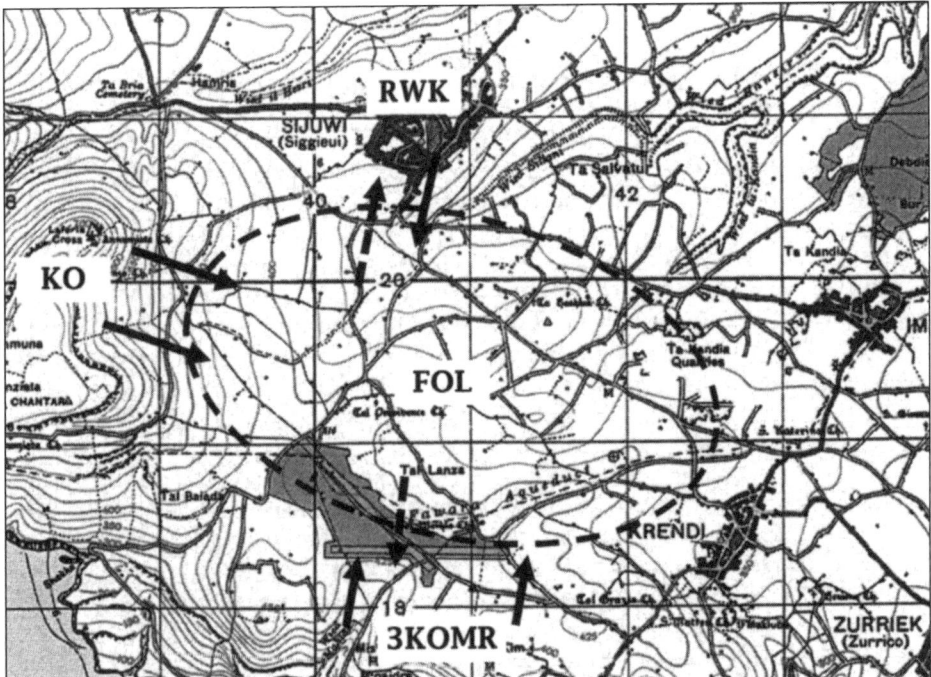

Figure VII-2: *Folgore versus Royal West Kents et al.*

attacked the Royal Artillery site. The gunners drove off the attackers, but the effort distracted their guns at a critical time.

Further north, Maggiore Mario Zanninovich, the II Battalion commander, collected several platoons from 4th and 6th companies and assaulted the outskirts of Siggiewi to regain contact with their missing comrades. The surge caught RWK's D Company in the middle of the earlier mop-up and initially pushed the British back past the church into the ruined village's northern end, the Italians rescuing some fifty-five of their captured comrades. But the British regrouped, and with 17 Platoon's Captain Bill Robinson leading the counter-attack, repulsed the continued push by the Italians into the village with heavy losses. The British attack finally lost steam after Robinson was killed; the rest of the troops halted at the edge of the village and consolidated. Zanninovich's Italians retreated nearly a kilometre south of the village and began to dig in. He also began an effort to reorganize the scattered Folgore paratroopers in the absence of Camossa, who had disappeared in the drop.[12]

Over the city of Mosta, more paratroops were spotted drifting down. Platoons from the 8th Manchesters and 11th Lancashire Fusiliers scrambled to react to the drops, initiating a strong search for the enemy paratroops within the city and up to the north coast. The battalions spent hours chasing hysterical reports only to find dummies had been dropped.

---

12. *Ibid., p.14.

3. Fallschirmjäger Regiment and Ramcke's Brigade (Figure VII-3)

Two battalions of the 3. Fallschirmjäger Regiment and two from Ramcke's brigade came down on the drop zone's right flank. Oberst Ludwig Heilmann's Third Regiment came down relatively intact, but scattered.

The II Battalion's Sixth Company drifted on top of Qrendi village and its defenders from 3rd KOMR. The defenders' cohesion had been nearly shattered when two Ju52s collided and fell into the village – one aircraft clipped a church tower and slammed into Triq it-torri (Tower Street) on top of the battalion's headquarters; Major H.D. Chaplin, the battalion's commander, and his staff were killed. Just south of Qrendi, C Company's commander, Major F.E. Tonna Barthet, and the members of his Headquarters Company stood on the grounds – and the roof – of Guarena Palace shooting skyward, causing heavy casualties as the paratroops drifted down. Several disappeared into the massive cave called Il Maqluba[13] near St Matthew's Church, while others vanished behind the high walls of farms south of the village. They had difficulty assembling, having little idea where their comrades had fallen.

In the village itself, the explosion and fire minimized the resistance to the falling Germans as many of the battalion's troops fought the flames. The leaderless paratroops, their own company commander having drifted into the inferno caused by the crash, overwhelmed the Maltese in several buildings, splitting the village in two, with the remnants of the defenders holding one end and the battered Germans the other. Fighting raged in the narrow winding streets.

On the far right of the drop zone, two Bofors light anti-aircraft batteries, G/225 and J/182, savaged the transports of General Ramcke's two battalions, enfilading the flight path with 40mm shells. Nearly thirty aircraft were shot down, showering the Maltese countryside with flaming wrecks and burning troops. Ramcke himself survived only because he jumped first from his transport, as was his usual habit; only three other paratroops got out of the aircraft after him before the plane was engulfed in flames and went down.[14]

One of the defending batteries, J/182, became surrounded by paratroops and was quickly overrun; the other repulsed several assaults on its position by paratroops as close-range 40mm fire against the rock walls of the Maltese countryside caused horrendous casualties to attacking Germans. Another company dropped in and around Bubakra, where the scattered Germans were driven off by the Maltese of 3rd KOMR's A Company, led by Captain Aumier.

Despite the horrific greeting, the scattered paratroops began their assigned mission – to kill anti-aircraft batteries. They quickly overran three heavy batteries from the 7th Heavy AA Regiment – C, D1 and D2 – along with Battery A/5 from the 4th Heavy AA Regiment.

The impact of nearly 100 aircraft crashing throughout the centre of the island added to the initial smoke barrage and disrupted the overall defensive reaction, causing both civilian and military casualties, and chaos in communications.

---

13. Il Maqluba (upside down) is a collapsed cave. Maltese tell the legend of a group of bad people living together in a hamlet. God warned the village, through a good woman living close by, against their bad ways. As they did not heed these warnings, God decreed that the land swallow the hamlet, sparing none except the good woman. Angels were then dispatched to dispose of the hamlet by dumping it at sea upside down. This legend was said to account for the formation of the island of Filfla off the south-west coast of Malta.
14. *Alcidi, Edgar, Fallschirmjager Brigade Ramcke in the Mediteranean, 1942–1943, p.22. REALITY: the actual name of the book is Fallschirmjager Brigade Ramcke in North Africa, 1942–1943.

As the last parachutes drifted down, between Zurrieq and Bubakra, Malta's 1 Brigade infantry moved out to engage Heilmann's and Ramcke's paratroops and learned the same harsh lesson their sister 4 Brigade had.

Intense fire from the German 3rd Regiment's 10th Company decimated the Hampshires' 11 Platoon before the rest of the company could arrive to flank and drive the paratroops south. Heilmann remembered:

> 'The enemy started launching immediate counter-attacks and the small unit was hard pressed. Another section joined us with a machine gun and we were able to drive the enemy to cover. But the situation was critical. I had no contact with my two other companies and we began receiving fire from several directions, forcing us to fall back. Fortunately, other sections arrived to reinforce our position, although many were already wounded.'[15]

To the east, though, the Hampshires' A and C companies, led by the battalion's second-in-command, Major Maurice French, along with the twin Lewis guns surrounding Kirkop Airfield, slaughtered Ramcke's 2nd Company of II Battalion which drifted onto the blocked airfield. The German commander von der Heydte, later wrote:

> 'As we passed the coastline of the island, I pushed with hands and feet, throwing my arms forward. Then the slipstream caught me and a jerk on my chest took my breath away as the parachute opened. Unlike the quiet drop on Crete last year, this time, there was noise all around. Black spots of anti-aircraft guns, tracers from below reached out among my troops. The fear I had felt nearly dropping into a reservoir in Crete was replaced by fear of being shot without being able to accomplish anything. Finally, I landed – hard but safely – and caught my breath behind a stone wall.'[16]

The two British companies then moved south by platoons in a rather uncoordinated fashion, before being stalled by Ramcke's troops and errant artillery fire called in from the Royal Artillery's E and G Batteries. Further south, the Hampshires' D Company attacked out of Zurrieq, overrunning and capturing the recoilless artillery of 3rd Regiment's 13th Company. Increasing pressure from Germans on all sides cut short the advance, especially when their commander, Captain T. Keene, went down, forcing a retreat back into the village. The company repulsed the initial half-hearted German probes into Zurrieq, but the assaults continued as more Germans converged on the village, led by II Battalion commander Major von der Heydte, and the fighting turned heavy, with losses on both sides.

Even as this drive stalled, Germans pushed further into Qrendi village, trying to take advantage of the chaos the crashed transports had caused. South of the beleaguered village, 3rd KOMR's B Company commander, Captain Charles Vella, without higher orders, attempted to gather his scattered platoons and move away from the cliffs to try to join their comrades

---

15. *Kurowski, p.233.
16. *von der Heydte, Daedalus Returned, p.209. REALITY: von der Heydte wrote of his experience on Crete with his book, but would have added the drop on Malta had it happened.

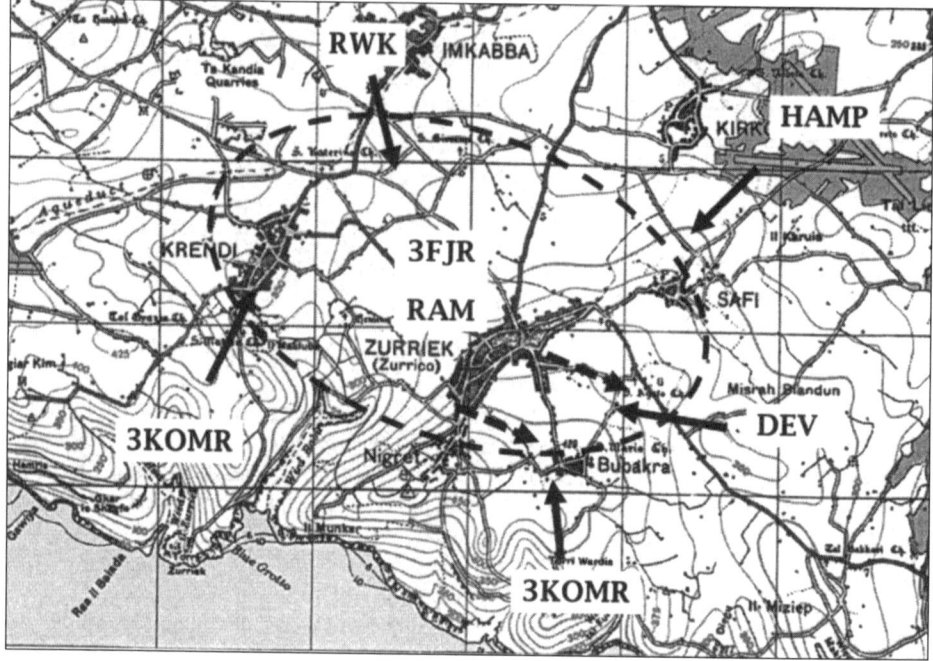

Figure VII-3: *3. Fallschirmjäger & Ramcke versus 1 Bde.*

in Qrendi. They ran into a concentration of German troopers of III Battalion/FJR3, under the command of a wounded Major Kratzert. The unexpected assault panicked some of the barely trained Maltese and only a portion of the company survived to join Major Barthet, who had assumed command of the battalion, outside Qrendi. Once united, the Maltese pushed into the village, trying to gather their scattered squads, but they found themselves again under heavy assault by converging paratroops. Morale plummeted as they lost more and more buildings to the Germans.

Further east, the Devonshires' A Company moved out from Hal Far and arrived just in time to drive off the Germans attacking G Battery. However, pursuing the retreating Germans cost the companies more casualties when they ran into two Gruppe that had their MG34 machine guns up and running. After rescuing the battery from its imminent overrunning, the Devons, pursuant to their training, consolidated their positions' and dug in and sent runners back to their battalion headquarters in Ghaxaq, requesting further instructions.

An hour later, orders from Colonel Valentine sent the company forward again, reinforced by a platoon from C Company, their goal being to relieve the surrounded troops (and their brigade commander and staff) in Bubakra, being probed by Germans in small but increasing numbers. With promised support from A Battery/26th Defense Regiment, the Devons again moved westward by 4.00 pm. Their pace proved slow and costly, as the time lost awaiting orders allowed the Germans to continue regrouping, interdicting the approach with heavy machine-gun fire. However, manoeuvres by the British did keep German attacks into Bubakra limited as more paratroops turned to fight them off. The 1 Brigade headquarters, located just west of the village in the large four-storey limestone Bubakra Tower, continued to hold off German probes.[17]

The Royal West Kents' A and B companies, led by the battalion's second-in-command, Major G.V. Shaw, moved to Luqa airfield's southern edge and engaged Ramke's decimated 3rd Company. The disjointed platoon-level attacks sustained severe casualties to the unexpected German firepower. However, they virtually destroyed the scattered Germans, capturing the company commander, Oberleutnant Büttner, and thirty-two of his men. One of the survivors recalled after the war:

> 'We fought for our lives in the ruined village, being attacked from three sides. Oberleutnant Büttner fell wounded and more and more of us fell as well. Our ammunition was running low, with only a few grenades and pistol bullets remaining. A grenade knocked me down and when I regained my senses, Tommy was disarming us.'[18]

Leaving a platoon to consolidate the prisoners, the two companies continued their advance, ordered to relieve the troops trapped in Zurrieq and Bubakra. The Royal West Kents suffered little delay in receiving new orders as Colonel Pulverman had also moved forward with his staff.

Despite the chaos caused by the drop and the crashed aircraft, Malta's Infantry Commander, General Scobie in Valletta, began to get reinforcements moving toward the drop area. Movement was slow as any troop concentration on a road attracted the attention of roving German fighters. Two companies of the Cheshires' machine-gun battalion started south with their Vickers machine guns in hand to bolster Luqa airfield's southern defences by 3.30 pm. They joined with the Royal West Kent C Company in digging in between Imbaqqa and Kirkop to hold the Germans off Luqa airfield by 5.00 pm, while their D Company regrouped in Siggiewi. In the north, the Royal Irish Fusiliers, 2 Brigade's mobile reserve, began their move across the Victoria Lines to get into the fight. An Irish officer wrote:

> 'We could see the parachutes from our battle positions, a load of them in pretty coloured parachutes coming down; although none was coming down near us, the lads had a go at them. But pretty soon they were lost in the haze of smoke and dust that hung over the middle of the island. We were eager to get into the fight, but it was a couple hours before we got the word to move out toward the fighting.'[19]

With the paratroops on Malta landed and fighting for control, Sicilian airfields dealt with the chaos of returning transports, many badly damaged. The airfield at Catania closed for an hour while the servicemen removed the wreckage of two crashed aircraft from the runway. Luftflotte XI officers and Regia Aeronautica staff worked to make sense of the confusion, trying to keep the tight schedule the *C3* invasion plans called for. They had planned three more full drops – one of troops and artillery, one of supply, and a third of glider-borne German pioneers – but

---

17. *Jary, Yells, Bells & Smells: 187.
18. *Kurowski, p.241.
19. *Johnson, Island Prize: Malta, p.130. REALITY: Royal Irish Fusiliers officer Johnson actually wrote the book Island Prize: Leros after participating in (and being captured during) the 1943 battle for the Aegean island.

despite the experience of Crete, the schedule had minimized the potential of damage. Aircraft had to be inspected, serviced and then loaded.

General der Flieger Kurt Student had to dealt with chaos of his own at Catania. He had only intermittent Luftwaffe radio contact with II/FJR1 battalion commander Major Kurt Gröschke, whose brief message had informed him that his 1. Fallschirmjäger Regiment fought for its life on the drop zone's left flank, with both regimental commander Schulz and the commander of the 1st Battalion listed among the missing. The trapped paratroops got no support from the Luftwaffe aircraft overhead as the two sides remained intermingled, creating the potential for friendly as well as enemy casualties. Other reports had more British troops moving toward the battle.

On the right, General Ramcke established contact with Student through the unit's only long-range radio set. He reported heavy casualties to anti-aircraft fire and strong counter-attacks from Hal Far but, with 3rd Regiment close at hand, his situation was stabilizing. Student contacted Kesselring, informing him of the situation, then turned his attention to motivating the aircraft turnaround to get his other three battalions airborne. Gone was the possibility of another coordinated airborne drop; the chaos of damaged aircraft that crash-landed upon return, the dust clouds covering the airfields and the delays in refuelling – which had to be done by hand, pumped from barrels – all contributed to delays.[20] As fifty Ju52s were inspected for damage, then refuelled, Student loaded a battalion of paratroops, regardless of air group, and sent them airborne.

In Rome, Generalfeldmarschall Kesselring met with his Italian counterparts to discuss the invasion's progress. With no radio contact with the Folgore paratroops, the Italians assumed things were going according to plan. Cavallero reminded Kesselring that 2nd Squadra's battleships had been tasked with troop support and would be off the southern Maltese coast by 6.00 pm. They had a bombardment allowance of 200 special 12.6in shells, each the size of a 1,000lb bomb, for use as needed, some for troop support, the rest set aside for the reduction of Fort Delimara.

At sea, around 2.30 pm, after the paratroops landed, 60-year-old Ammiraglio di Squadra Vittorio Tur, aboard the torpedo boat *Procione*, dealt with his own chaos as 300 ships in ten separate convoys converged in the Mediterranean about 18 nautical miles west of Gozo. Tur, in command of Forza Navale Speciale (FNS), carrying the first wave of the seaborne invasion – men of the Friuli and Livorno Divisions, plus units of the San Marcos Marines – felt overwhelmed. In command of the Albanian Naval Zone when the war had started, Tur had been assigned to FNS upon creation of the force, initially tasked with the invasion of Corfu in October 1940 as part of Italy's war with Greece. That invasion had been postponed due to bad sea conditions and ultimately cancelled when the situation ashore worsened for the Italians.

Nothing, however, had quite prepared him for the massive job he now had. The invasion convoy voyage to this point had been remarkably free of problems, with only two small cargo ships hit by lurking British submarines. Stevens's P46 had sunk one shortly after leaving Porto Empedocle, sending men from the Camicie Nere's LX Battalion into the water, along with most of their equipment. The other ship had been badly damaged by a torpedo from HMS *Utmost*, but able to return to its port, carrying Livorno troops of II/33rd Brigade away from their assigned landing.

---

20. *Kurowski, p.237. The Germans had the same problem during the battle for Crete.

North of Gozo, the ships and landing craft bearing the Superga Division had split into multiple separate columns, under Ammiraglio di Divisione Luigi Biancheri in his flagship *Orione*, to approach their assigned beach areas near that island.

On Malta, more paratroops arrived between 4.00 and 5.00 pm as the afternoon wore on, but this time, with the horrific lessons of the first drop learned, the aircraft flew west to east, limiting their losses significantly.

The III Battalion/FJR1 dropped north-west of the village of Dingli just after 4.00 pm, flanking the attackers of their beleaguered brethren and squarely in the path of the converging reinforcements. Two companies, the 9th and 10th, nearly landed on top of the outlying platoons of the Durham Light Infantry's D Company, regrouping after the solitary battle with the II Battalion's 6th Company. The new arrivals overwhelmed the exhausted British, capturing the survivors, who included company commander, Captain J.H. Thorpe, who recalled:

> 'We were still digging in when more Jerries dropped in. It was paralyzing for a long moment, almost an admiration to see this thing, but finally you started firing as they came down. You can imagine the chaos. We were taken prisoner and searched; our steel helmets snatched from our heads.'[21]

The Germans suffered casualties as well, but under the command of Hauptmann Karl-Heinz Becker, the battalion commander, consolidated all the survivors from the three paratroop companies and directed movement toward the nearby radar site and Dingli village. However, the defence had gained time for the radar technicians at the AMES 242 site to smash their equipment and arm the demolition charges left to ensure the destruction of the facility.

In Dingli village itself, casualties from both sides found themselves in the middle of a see-saw battle for control of the village. Dr Busuttil, the district medical officer, worked side by side in the church with German medics on civilians and casualties on both sides as fighting raged around them.

Further north, III Battalion's 11th Company landed nearly on top of two artillery batteries, C/26th and C/12RA, as well as two companies of the 4th Battalion, the Buffs. The Germans were able to pull back toward their comrades, but left half the company on the field as they did so. As III Battalion consolidated and pushed into the village, the battle for I and II Battalion continued, with King's Own Malta and Durham Light Infantry troops advancing against the Germans with some artillery support. But the uncoordinated attack failed to overrun the German defenders and the British pulled back to dig in as evening fell.

In the centre, the Regia Aeronautica's 1st Assault Battalion arrived half an hour later with the Loreto Battalion in the second drop in and around the inactive Qrendi airfield. The D Company Maltese inflicted casualties on the air force commandos as they floated down, but, surrounded on all sides and cut off from their fellows, their morale collapsed and they surrendered. Eight Go242 gliders bearing batteries of the Germans' artillery tried landing directly at the incomplete airfield at Qrendi. The first broke apart as it overshot the field and slammed into a stone wall. Another triggered an uncleared mine that destroyed the glider and caused another coming in behind it to veer, catching a wing and tumbling to its destruction. In all, only three of the eight weapons were salvaged.

---

21. *Thorpe, My Time on Malta, p.206.

During the second drop, resistance in Qrendi from the remnants of King's Own Malta 3rd Battalion, assaulted from all sides and now from above, completely collapsed. The Germans consolidated their hold on the village, while I Battalion/FJR3 and II Battalion/Ramcke floated down during the second drop closer to 6.00 pm to bolster the paratroops on the right flank. The loss of anti-aircraft sites limited aircraft losses, with only another ten shot down or damaged. Qrendi village became the Axis de facto headquarters as well as the collection point for the wounded from both sides. Ramcke met with the District medical officer, Dr Muscat, and the KOMR battalion's medical officer, Surgeon Captain H. Ferrente, at the village's police station to ensure coordination of casualty care, promising the Maltese that care was meant for all casualties – enemy, friendly or civilian.[22]

As the last of his battalions landed in the drop zone, General Student organised the final major operation of the day, sending twenty-one Go242 gliders into the air, carrying the four companies of Fallschirmkorps-Pioneer Bataillon, commanded by Major Rudolf Witzig. Their target was the peninsula creating the southern arm of Marsa Scirocco Bay. Half the force intended to land inside and take Fort Benghajsa and its 9.2in coastal guns, while the rest would land outside the fort and keep relieving forces at bay.

After sending off the gliders, Student again contacted Kesselring, who had obtained permission from the Supermarina to task 2nd Squadra's battleships with bombardment support. Student huddled with two of his staff officers and pilots from the Regia Aeronautica's 76th Gruppo, specialists trained in aerial spotting and reconnaissance who would be initially spotting for the battleships. The German outlined the areas he wanted interdicted, which stretched from Fort Bingemma through the city of Rabat to the outskirts of Siggiewi and Luqa, with the very specific targets of Fort Bingemma, which could interdict one of the primary landing zones, and Fort Delimara, which could impact the second landing zone. In between, troop concentrations and artillery sites were to be targeted. Shortly afterwards, two Caproni Ca.313 reconnaissance aircraft lifted off for Malta.

Just after 5.00 pm, fire control radar at Fort Bingemma picked up large targets some 40,000 yards off the southern coast, closing at 15 knots – the battleships spotted earlier by submarines had arrived. Although the fort's defenders manned its single 9.2in gun, there was little they could do unless the ships closed to under 21,000 yards.[23] However, Ammiraglio Bergamini, on the old battleship *Caio Duilio*, had no intention of giving them that satisfaction.

With the list of target areas to be bombarded, the *Duilio* and its sister *Andrea Doria* fired their first broadside from a range of 22,000 yards; twenty 1,100lb armour-piercing common shells screamed in, impacting in and around Fort Bingemma, shattering stone walls, destroying a hunter's hut and dismantling the fort's only coastal gun. A second broadside from both battleships slammed in and around the fort, ensuring its silence. Bergamini's ships continued their cruise to their next target.

Above the island, Italian reconnaissance aircraft recorded the fall of shot and radioed corrections to their on-board liaison officers to put the heavy rounds on what they saw as important targets, with the stipulation to stay away from beachhead area – the Axis ground commanders did not want (nor trust the ability of) the battleships for close support. Communications improved again when the battleships launched their own spotter planes, but

---

22. *Boog et al., Vol VI, p.425.
23. The Mk X 9.2in coastal gun on a Mk V mounting was limited to 21,000 yards; on a Mk VII mounting the range would have reached out to 29,000 yards. There had been plans for upgrading the 9.2in mounts on Malta, but it never happened. Rollo, Guns and Gunners of Malta, Appendix H, p.421.

the bombardment continued to be very slow and deliberate. However, the simultaneous impact of ten to twenty 1,100lb shells in a relatively small area proved a terrifying and disruptive experience for the nearby British. Despite the lack of hard results, the bombardment disrupted the defence's capability to close in and seal off the drop zone.

Unfortunately for the Axis, the survivors of the Folgore's 8th Company became major victims of the bombardment. These paratroops had been badly scattered away from their fellow troopers and had created a defensive zone to hold off probes from 4 Brigade units. Spotted and misidentified by the Ca.313s above, one full broadside landed across their perimeter, shattering the survivors. Two further broadsides fell across the embattled village of Siggiewi, wounding Major Shaw, disrupting the Royal West Kent defenders and filling the streets with more rubble.

As the Italian battleships pounded the interior of the island, other fighters and bombers gave a final work-over on the defenders in the Benghajsa peninsula; finally, the gliders released at 4,500ft altitude and 15 miles from their target, hoping to sweep in from the sea and surprise the supposedly suppressed defence.

The Luftwaffe fighters and bombers had not eliminated or disrupted all the anti-aircraft positions on the peninsula prior to the pioneers' arrival. Light Bofors 40mm guns from the 3rd Royal Maltese Artillery and 74th Light Anti-aircraft Regiment greeted the incoming gliders with a torrent of 2lb shells at 120 rounds a minute. The flak shot down five gliders, one exploding as a shell found its grenade locker; another, its wing damaged, slammed into the cliffs below Benghajsa, killing all aboard.

The remaining five gliders of the fortress assault force did sweep in on the fort. The first ploughed directly into the fort's right-hand coastal gun – 7 tons of men, equipment, tube steel, wood and canvas met 22 tons of gun and disintegrated, destroying the gun and the two squads. Three follow-on gliders tried to swerve from the destruction. One landed late and slid right out of the fort, spilling its human cargo into the moat around the fort; the other two tangled as they landed, causing casualties.

The fourth glider landed safely, but very close to the fort's limestone buildings. The fort's garrison consisted of the gun crews of the coastal artillery, members of the 23rd Heavy Coastal Battery, along with a partially trained platoon from the 10th Battalion, King's Own Malta Regiment. Despite the casualties, the remaining pioneers disentangled themselves from their gliders and attacked. The Germans took the remaining gun easily, laying satchel charges to destroy it. Another pioneer squad panicked the untrained artillery crews with a flamethrower, driving them from room to room in the fort before they surrendered. The vicious battle inside the fort did not last long, but only about fifteen of the Germans who landed escaped unscathed. Witzig himself had been seriously wounded when the satchel charge one of his men threw into a room came back out and exploded.[24]

Outside the fort, other pioneers overran a heavy anti-aircraft site (Battery C/5/4) and attacked an artillery battery from the 26th Regiment. They destroyed the battery's guns, but infantry from the Devonshires' D Company arrived to drive the remaining pioneers back toward the fort. As light faded, fighting subsided.

Off shore, the two Italian battleships rounded the south-western tip of Malta and trained their big guns at Fort Delimara. During the next half hour, heavy shells rained onto and around the fort, with its 6in and 12-pdr guns unable to reply. All the fort's guns were wrecked, as was the heavy anti-aircraft battery of G/11th Royal Malta Artillery. The 3rd RMA's Bofors site

---

24. *Boog et al., Vol VI, p.457.

close by received one close call; the shower of rocks thrown by the explosions temporarily put all guns out of operation. Bergamini's ships finally ceased fire and continued to sail around the island on their way back to Messina, content with their contribution to the invasion.

Darkness brought a lull to the fighting, except on the Dingli Plateau. There, the German III Battalion, under Hauptmann Becker, brought pressure from the west, but became entangled in the village. The remnants of the Durham Light Infantry's D Company, aided by members of the battalion's carrier platoon, fell back slowly among the rubble, holding road blocks and sniping from ruined buildings before falling back further into the narrow, choked streets. It took the Germans hours to push through and clear the village, exhausting the paratroops. Despite Colonel Brittorious's demands to retake the village, DLI commander Arderne pulled back his scattered platoons to reorganize.

While the battle for Dingli village continued, Major Groschke led an assault group of the trapped Fallschirmjäger survivors of I and II Battalion to surprise the infantry of King's Own C Company in the Girganti Valley near a large limestone dwelling[25] that housed the battalion's headquarters. The dusk assault initially pushed the British back. However, the seventeenth-century building and its walls channelled the attack onto clear roadways, allowing the British troops, led by their second-in-command, Major Davidson, to recover and decimate the attackers, driving them back in turn. Nevertheless, the surprise attack gained the Germans some breathing space. As full darkness fell, the new German arrivals contacted their beleaguered brethren to form a more solid defence, while III Battalion commander Becker assumed command of the regiment from a wounded Gröschke.[26]

Shortly before dark, the invasion convoys reached a point south-west of Malta, where Tur began the difficult job of organizing the ships into a line-ahead formation for the final run toward the island. He planned to place the ships in the order they would approach their designated landing sites, so that they could easily reach their position. Thus, the ships for the Larnaca beaches would head the long line. Daylight had faded into full darkness by the time the exasperated admiral was satisfied that the formation was ready. Then, leading the 7,000-metre-long column, he started the slow approach. At the column's overall speed of 5 knots, he expected to reach the island around 2.00 am – two hours later than he had planned. To make matters worse, the wind began picking up, followed by the sea. For most of the vessels, the worsening of the sea conditions meant little; however, for the 20,000 troops travelling in the flat-bottomed Motozatteras and Motolancias,[27] the voyage became very uncomfortable, overwhelming them with seasickness. As the ships' motion increased, so did the pre-invasion jitters of all involved.

On the island, combat had died down to sporadic firing as exhausted soldiers on each side gave in to the occasional paranoia that movement at night can generate. Water became the most pressing issue for all the combatants. Many of the paratroops had already run through their 3-litre ration, which had been expected to last two full days. One paratrooper recalled:

---

25. The Girganti Palace, built in 1625 for Inquisitor Onorato Visconti, and was the holiday and summer home for the Inquisition in Malta. It includes a chapel, dedicated to San Carlo Borromeo, built by Inquisitor (later Cardinal) Angleo Durini in 1763. It is now the summer home of Malta's Prime Minister.
26. *Boog, Vol VI, p.464.
27. A Motozattera (Motor raft) was the Italian copy of the German Marinefährprahm (MFP), a 200-ton marine ferry landing craft capable of carrying some 100 tons of troops or equipment. A Motolancia was a 36-ton landing craft similar to the Allies' Landing Craft, Mechanized (LCM), but could only carry troops.

'We were getting very hot – the air was nearly 50°C. Thirst was terrible. Just as at Crete, we had been sent into battle with full uniform and jump overalls. Absolutely crazy! And our rations of salty ham were not going to make things better.'[28]

In Qrendi, the wounded of both sides lay together as medics and Dr Muscat tried to tend to the overwhelming number of casualties. Only British artillery batteries moved in the dark, taking advantage of the cover that it provided against the predatory aircraft above to switch positions. The batteries displaced to add their power to those already ringing the paratroop drop zone on the southern coast. Additional machine-gun teams from the Cheshires' Machine-Gun Battalion also arrived to bolster the infantry surrounding the zone.

As daylight faded, Scobie and Gort became seriously concerned about the initial reports of casualties among their troops, as resistance from the Germans – and even the Italians – proved far stronger than they had expected and the haphazard assaults by their troops so costly. Both men knew part of the answer – poor or little training in the past year. Reports of the fighting on the Dingli Plateau – and the acrimonious complaints about Colonel Brittorious's chaotic interference with battalion operations – showed a further problem with brigade-level coordination. Scobie had already recalled Brittorious to headquarters to relieve that particular problem.

Overall, of the fourteen battalions on the island, seven had been heavily involved; two – the Royal Irish Fusiliers and 4th The Buffs – were in motion toward the fighting. Two others – the 8th Manchesters and 11th Lancashire Fusiliers – were only marginally involved as they chased reports of paratroops landing between Attard and Curmi, all of which proved to be dummies. Only the 1st and 2nd Battalions, King's Own Malta Regiment, stationed on the northern part of the island, and the 1st Battalion, Dorsetshires in the south had been left in place.

Gort considered two possibilities based on the paradrop, which had basically left him baffled.[29] First, that they had been dropped to pull troops away from the good landing beaches on the island's north-east coast, weakening the defences there; or second, that the Axis actually intended to send their seaborne contingent to the south-western coast, away from the coastal artillery that covered the north-east shore. The latter seemed unlikely, given the area's rocks and steep cliffs, unsuitable for large-scale landings. General Clifford T. Beckett, the island's overall artillery commander – having surveyed the entire coastline, including the south-west, while laying out the artillery grid references – noted only two places on the south-western coast where heavy equipment could be landed: the coves of Ghar Lapsi and Wied iz-Zurrieq, used by islanders to launch fishing boats. From his perspective, the paradrop had to be a feint to pull troops and attention away from the north.

Gort and Scobie reluctantly concurred with Beckett and, although their whole defence plan called for an immediate and unrelenting assault against the paratroops, they chose to leave the bulk of their unengaged troops where they were to cover other contingencies.

Elsewhere, more British activity brewed. A thousand miles to the west, the harbour at Gibraltar became frantic with activity as the massive armada of Forces Z and X under Vice Admiral Syfret got under way. Once clear of their moorings, the four aircraft carriers, two

---

28. *Poppel, Heaven & Hell, p.74. REALITY: this was paraphrased from Poppels' remembrance of Crete.
29. *Colville, Valour, p.227.

battleships and seven cruisers made their way into the roads and formed up for their journey. By midnight, both forces were at sea and heading east at 20 knots.

Meanwhile, at Alexandria, Admiral Philip Vian sat at dinner with all his captains to discuss strategy and his plans for the upcoming relief effort. The orders received from Churchill had been explicit: stop the invasion. Admiral Harwood's version of the orders, although similar, had major caveats: breakthrough to Malta if possible, and stop or disrupt invasion if possible.

Vian's tactical orders to his captains were similar to those he used in June – if engaged by enemy surface vessels, all cruisers would concentrate their fire against single enemy ships to force their retirement. The battle line would press forward, threatening torpedo attack.[30] Vian also reminded his captains to use measured firing in any battle, in order to conserve ammunition as they would have to fight at the end of their journey to Malta, as well as during both legs. Destroyer captains received reminders to use only half their torpedo stocks in any surface battle in order to have them available once they reached the island.

---

30. *15th Cruiser Squadron signals 00636/4, 15 August 1942.

Chapter VIII

Sunday
16 August 1942

Time	Wind (kn)	Sea	Notes		
8.00 am	17–21	slight chop	fog	sunrise	6.26 am
8.00 pm	22–27	rough		sunset	7.47 pm

Shortly after midnight, aides awoke Governor Gort with news of naval activity sighted off Gozo. By the time he and Admiral Leatham got back to the underground headquarters, the reports had multiplied. The sightings placed Axis ships threatening multiple positions around the 25 square mile island: Ramla, Dwejra, Xlendi, San Blas and Xwejni all reported activity.

While they pondered the reports, the officers manning the Coastal Defence Room in Lascaris underground control centre received a frantic call from Fort Bingemma – their fire control radar registered 'many ships bearing south-east, range decreasing'. They also reported their coastal gun still out of action.

Informed of Bingemma's warning, Gort and Leatham switched their attention to maps of their own island, intent on trying to determine where the blow would fall. As reports of the convoy heading west had been coming in the previous day, they began to assume a landing in and around Ghajn Tuffieha Bay, but the current mass of ships were too far south for that to be the case. Now it appeared the invasion was aimed at the recently overrun Fort Benghajsa. Leatham had a message sent to the 3rd Motor Launch Flotilla's section to move again. Four of the flotilla's motor launches had initially been at St Paul's Bay, but moved to Comino Island between Gozo and Malta when the convoy movement was all to the west. Now Leatham ordered them toward Ghajn Tuffieha and possibly further south. He left the remaining three launches stationed at St Thomas's Bay in place.

Some 10 nautical miles off Augusta, Sicily, the British achieved some payback for the invasion as HMS *Una* sighted Bergamini's squadron steaming north toward their anchorage at Messina. This time Lieutenant Norman's submarine, in perfect position, slammed a couple of torpedoes into the starboard side of the battleship *Andrea Doria*, tearing two huge holes in its side and bringing it to a halt as the boiler rooms flooded. Norman and *Una* escaped to the south, leaving an enemy squadron in chaos.

An hour later, the first vessel of the *C3* invasion reached the central south-west Maltese coast to start the horrendous job of getting ships where they needed to be, made far more difficult by the mist that had sprung up at sea. Aboard the torpedo boat *Procione*, which acted as his headquarters afloat, Admiral Tur could only fret as the chaos he had expected off the invasion beach code-named Famagosta turned much worse. His orders called for both the Friuli and Livorno Divisions – plus supporting troops, equipment and supplies – to be landed by noon on this rocky joke of a beach area, so he could return to Sicily to pick up the two follow-on divisions. But the mist made a mockery of the tight schedule. Landmarks carefully memorised from photographs became nearly impossible to distinguish in the grey murk. Pathfinders in small boats moved slowly next to the rocky coast trying to identify specific landing areas; fortunately for the scouts, the jutting sea arch near Landing Zone F helped orient the searchers. But each time they found a landmark, the pathfinders then had to find the right vessels with the designated troops. Calmer seas aided the invaders.

On the far left flank of the invasion, west of Ghar Lapsi at Hagra-is-Sewda, San Marco Marines pushed their boats nose-first against the rocks and set their ladders. At 3.56 am, Italian seaborne troops climbed the 25ft cliff and finally set foot on Malta's rocky soil. San Marco Marine Tenente Antonio Cagnolo became the first Italian to step ashore from the invasion fleet; a minute after he stepped off the ladder, he also became the seaborne attack's first casualty as he broke his ankle on Malta's uneven surface.[1] But others followed. Further west, two boatloads of combat engineers steered into Ghar Lapsi's small cove and immediately had their small boats' bottoms torn out by the rocks, leaving them to sink in the shallow water. In the pillbox overlooking the cove, three overwhelmed Maltese soldiers watched as an armada of boats appeared in front of them. They briefly discussed opening fire, but chose instead to simply report the boats and try to escape. They were captured moments later.

In Valletta, British military leaders began responding. Brigadier Beckett contacted his artillery batteries and designated the 6in howitzers at Gebel Ghawzara and Ghaxaq to initiate a slow but steady bombardment of the coastline, using the detailed maps of Malta's entire coast. Fifteen minutes after Beckett send out his order, several 6in howitzer shells struck the Ghar Lapsi area. The initial explosions rocked the landing troops of the III Battalion/87th Regiment, causing a couple of them to fall from their ladders into the sea, where their equipment pulled them under to drown.

All along the coastline, other Motozatteras (MZ) pushed their bows against the limestone rocks and the occupants manhandled the ladders to rest against the cliffs above. Around them, swift assault boats buzzed. Even as troops stepped off the heaving ladders onto dry ground, more chaos erupted at sea.

The Italian anti-submarine vedette, VAS 201, cruising slowly some 100 yards off shore on the assault beaches' left flank, initially thought the craft coming from the north were simply lost patrol craft from the convoy. Pre-launch briefings by Admiral Tur indicated he did not expect any Royal Navy presence, except for submarines, for several days. The VAS 201's commander, Tenente di Vascello Antonio Lombardo, illuminated the oncoming vessels with his searchlight in the light pre-dawn fog and prepared to hail them, when the lead boat of the 3rd Motor Launch flotilla, ML-126 (Lieutenant. G.W. Stead), opened fire with its 20mm Oerlikon cannon. The fire swept the Italian crew off their forward cannon and shattered the bridge, wounding Lombardo and killing the helmsman. ML-168 (Lieutenant C.E. Brookman), trailing the lead boat, then hit the vessel with a 57mm shell from its ancient 3-pdr gun, leaving the Italian craft burning.[2]

---

1. *Etruschi, Albion Defeated, p.168.
2. *Pack, Naval Battle of Malta, p.98. Lombardo survived to describe the experience. He was awarded the Medaglia d'Argento al Valore Militaire (Silver Medal for Valour) for getting his damaged craft back to Sicily.

The explosion and fire, though, caught the attention of the Italian minelayer *Eso* (formerly the Yugoslavian Royal Navy's minesweeper *Sokol*) some 400 yards further out at sea. Its captain, Tenente Giovanni Battista Garrone, broadcast a warning to Admiral Tur and the rest of the Famagosta escorts as it ramped up speed to close with the attackers.

Stead's four motor launches, which had closed on the invasion site at a quiet 10 knots, pushed throttles forward, passed the *Eso* – even as that vessel's 90mm gun barked out and exchanged fire with the trailing British launches – and got in among the mass of shipping standing motionless near shore. Machine-gun fire, 20mm rounds and 57mm cannon fire reached out to the Italian transports, chewing through men and supplies; one MZ exploded as a 20mm round struck a case of mortar rounds. Stead recalled:

> 'All our guns were firing as my coxswain weaved through the ships. There was a tremendous explosion on one of the landing craft – we had hit something important. As we passed, I could see soldiers leaping off the burning craft.'[3]

The Italians began to respond. Individuals with weapons fired at the speeding boats more out of something to do than for effect, while the landing craft's bigger weapons also started their return fire, some of it going astray and into friendly vessels, adding to the chaos. Tur wrote later:

> 'Confusion reigned when the British attacked. All our ships began moving in every direction and many came close to ramming each other. There was a lot of panicked firing that didn't help. Much time was lost afterwards getting the landing started again.'[4]

One lucky Italian shot shredded the cockpit of ML-135, killing its coxswain and wounding the commander, Lieutenant J. Peal. The launch, suddenly out of control, slammed straight into MZ 731; at 20 knots, the wooden hull punched a massive hole in the Italian transport's steel side. Its passengers, men of the II Battalion/87th and Guastatori from the lst/V Company, discarded their weapons to abandon the flooding vessel.[5]

Across from Ghar Lapsi, Stead's three remaining launches encountered VAS 203, which was responding to the crisis. The duel was one-sided as all three British launches poured their fire into the small patrol craft, but return fire from the VAS's own 20mm cannon disabled ML-134, leaving only two to continue their mad dash through the invasion fleet. That dash ended a few minutes later as the torpedo boats *Antares* and *Cascino*, having threaded their way through the invasion fleet, raked both boats with their numerous 20mm cannons: Brookman's ML-168 exploded and ML-126 lost its engine. Stead, the surviving launch's commander, recalled:

> 'The Italian fire was devastating to my boat. The forward Oerlikon was destroyed with a direct hit that killed the gunner. The aft 20mm jammed when splinters struck its magazine. Another burst struck the starboard ammunition locker and

---

3. *Stead, A Leaf Upon the Sea, p.100.
4. *Tur, Plancia Ammiraglio, p.98.
5. *Pack, Naval Battle of Malta, p.111.

started a fire. Another burst damaged our steering and engines and we started slowing down. I steered toward the coast in hopes my remaining crew could make it ashore.'[6]

Off Malta's eastern coast, the other naval intervention attempt was less successful. As reports of the invasion fleet filtered in, minesweepers HMS *Speedy*, *Hythe* and *Rye* led the Hunt-class destroyer *Badsworth* out of Grand Harbour and began to circle the island to the east. Once past the known minefields, Lieutenant Gray brought his destroyer to 25 knots and sailed due south. As he passed St Thomas's Bay, Lieutenant Commander Strowlger led his three motor launches south.

The moonless night made visibility extremely difficult, so Gray had his crew at general quarters with his Type 285 radar searching ahead. At 4.36 am, his radar picked up multiple contacts at some 3,000 yards, including one large contact. Even as that report came in, gunfire erupted at sea behind the destroyer.

Unknown to the British – and missed by the *Badsworth* – a small VAS boat carrying Italian special forces from 102^a Arditi Nuotatori, escorted by four German Schnellbootes, sailed north along the coast toward St Thomas's Bay. The Arditis' assignment was simply to land and spread as much chaos as they could. As they moved north, the S-boats spotted Strowlgers' motor launches and opened fire. Strowlger's own ML-121 was swept with 20mm and machine-gun fire almost before the British knew they were in danger; the external fuel tanks, still attached after their journey from Gibraltar, ruptured and caught fire. His two follow-on boats, ML-459 (Lieutenant C.E. Pearse) and ML-462 (Lieutenant. J.W. Main), tried manoeuvring to return fire but both were overwhelmed by the S-boats' heavier armament. As the sea battle unfolded, VAS 228, with its cargo of Arditi, reversed course and headed back toward the invasion fleet.

British and German radios blared the news of the engagement as it happened. Off Benghajsa Point, four more German S-boats and the German destroyer ZG3 (*Hermes*), with German Vizeadmiral Eberhard Weichold[7] aboard, responded quickly, increasing speed to head north. Aboard the *Badsworth*, the radar contact reflected the increased speed and Gray ordered his ship to open fire. He later remembered: 'We had missed something on radar, possibly clutter from the coastline, but I had a big target, close enough to hurt.'[8]

Badsworth's three turrets blasted the *Hermes* at the point-blank range of 2,500 yards, catching the German ship by surprise. The 4in shells destroyed a 37mm anti-aircraft position and caused a fire amidships. A shell also exploded in the engine room, rupturing steam pipes and putting a boiler off line, limiting the *Hermes*' speed. The German ship responded to the attack by firing a star shell, which illuminated their attacker, then returning fire with the forward 5in turret, but missed. Its escort of S-boats, though, changed direction and closed on the British ship.

Badsworth and *Hermes* traded gunfire as the lighter armament on the S-boats and the destroyer escort began to strike home. Gray remembered:

'The enemy return fire was effective; one of my aft turrets was damaged and my speed was slowing. My radar was showing other targets beyond the enemy ship and I decided, since it was already on fire, to switch my

---

6. *Lieutenant Stead was awarded the DSC for his Dash. Stead, p.110.
7. Weichold was the Kriegsmarine liaison to Italy's Supermarina.
8. *Gray, G., 'Reflections of my fight', After the Battle, Vol 3, #10 (1977), p.21.

guns to the further targets, hoping to damage invasion shipping. I distinctly recall seeing a hit in the distance from our fire, but couldn't tell what we had hit. Then my bridge was struck with a heavy barrage of 20mm fire and I was wounded and the helmsman killed. Before I could recover, there was a terrible explosion aft.'[9]

The *Badsworth* had taken a torpedo almost directly under one of its aft turrets; the massive explosion tore the stern off the destroyer and it began sinking. A wounded Gray ordered his crew to abandon ship. He and most of his crew were picked up by the S-boats and transferred to the damaged *Hermes*.

Further to the north, the minesweepers approached the battle site that had ended so disastrously for Strowlger's motor launches. *Speedy*'s captain, Commander A.E. Doran, spotted the idle S-boats, illuminated by the burning ML-121, and opened fire with his single 4in gun. At a range of 1,000 yards, its second shot exploded aboard the S 30 boat, killing its captain, Oberleutnant zur See Weber, and setting the boat on fire. Two of the remaining torpedo boats reacted, speeding toward the minesweeper, while another boat aided their damaged companion. The resulting battle between the 16-knot minesweeper and the 35-knot S-boats was never in doubt, as Doran couldn't manoeuvre quickly enough to avoid the Germans' deadly riposte. A torpedo tore the side out of the minesweeper and it went down quickly. Its companions, *Rye* and *Hythe*, reversed course and headed back to Grand Harbour, unwilling to battle the odds.

As the firing at sea died down, the Italians struggled to recover from the unexpected attacks and continue their mission. 'Stead's dash', as it came to be called[10], had caused casualties, especially among the 87th Regiment's first two battalions, and damaged some Motozatteras, but the landings went on. *Badsworth*'s battle with the *Hermes* had less effect on the situation. The unexpected attacks proved far more damaging to Tur's timetable – ships awaiting their movement to the shoreline had cranked up their engines and veered away from the threat, shattering the positioning Tur had enforced. One landing site off Ghar Lapsi became completely closed off, with a burning MZ still suffering explosions as ammunition on board cooked off. Assault boats plied the choppy dark waters picking up survivors.

As the ships offshore contended with the chaos, the actual landings had their own problems to deal with. Wave motion made climbing ladders tricky, and more than one soldier slipped and went into the water to drown. The struggle to haul crates of ammunition and food up the cliffs slowed everything; the division had five days of supplies with them – 470 tons – all of which had to be manhandled up from the boats. Further east, an assault boat tried to enter Wied iz-Zurrieq, only to have all its occupants swept into the sea by the unseen cable that closed the entrance to the creek.[11] Fire from the pillbox covering the inlet added to the carnage and kept the inlet closed until landing troops could deal with the blockhouse and cut the cable.

Into this chaos, Malta's defenders added their voice. Shells from the 26th Defence Regiment's guns slammed into the rocks up and down the coastline. The fire was sporadic and

---

9. *Ibid., p.22. Records show that no invasion transports were hit in this action, but a German Raumboote reported being hit.
10. *Roskill, The War at Sea, Vol II, p.324.
11. A cable was stretched across the entrance to Wied iz-Zurrieq creek throughout the war, and was lowered for a few daylight hours each day to allow fishermen to ply their trade. Caruana correspondence.

intermittent, generally causing little damage, but it slowed the landings and added to an already chaotic situation. Nevertheless, slowly, ever so slowly, Italian troops landed.

Fortunately for Tur and the Italians, daylight was fast approaching – the mist would dissipate and the Luftwaffe would be in the air to attack the British artillery. The admiral sent the word out to the vessels carrying the invasion's heavy equipment – guns and armour – not to attempt to land until the beachhead could be clearly observed. Infantry, though, continued to make the treacherous climb out of their boats.

As the confusion from the British attack subsided, Tur ordered his escorts to assume anti-submarine duties. Five miles offshore, the destroyers *Turbine* and *Sebenico*[12], running separate 6-mile circles at 5 knots, with their German-built Periphon sonars actively pinging the depths, created his first line of defence. Two miles closer to the transport area, two VAS boats and the destroyer escort *Pegaso* steamed slowly at 3 knots to overlap the destroyers' coverage. Tur assigned the flanks for the transport area to the Germans on the right and to the Gozo landing force escorts on the left, along with his VAS escorts.

To the south-east, the second part of the invasion plan, heading for the Larnaca beaches, also got under way, with the landings set to take place in Marsaxlokk Bay at Malta's south-eastern tip. The Larnaca landings had been planned to be less a mass transfer of troops and supplies than a stealthy attack. As soon as the transports came opposite Benghajsa Point, Blackshirt commandos from XLII Battalion, stiffened with companies of Guastatori from the Livorno and Superga Divisions as well as troops from a specially trained lanciafiamme (flamethrower) battalion, loaded into assault boats and motored in, landing on the north-east edge of Benghajsa Point. German pioneers loaded into Stb39s[13] for a long run around the point and into the bay to their assigned beaches. Some 200 pioneers were to be landed at three separate sites on the Delimara peninsula to attempt to take Fort Delimara, covering the north-west side of Marsa Scirocco Bay, by coup de main following its reduction by the Regia Marina.

Against an alerted garrison, the stealth manoeuvre never had a chance. As the Blackshirts and assault engineers started coming ashore, they ran into wire and fire from beach posts, which quickly drove the invaders to ground on Benghajsa Point. The posts radioed their sightings and laid fire to pin the attackers until artillery began hitting the point, further disrupting the Italians. The Italian assault engineers took heavy casualties cutting through the wire and the mines in an attempt to get close enough to the posts for the flamethrowers to eliminate them. Bren-gun fire at one point exploded the tank of one of the flamethrowers, stopping all forward progress on Larnaca's beaches O and P. The disruption gave the Devonshires' D Company under Captain Mike Howard, newly attached from the regiment's replacement company, time to move through the Kalafrana seaplane base and reinforce the beach post defenders.

Elsewhere, the Germans trying to land at two points around Tumbrell Point met fire from a platoon of the Dorsetshires' A Company and became pinned down almost immediately. One German group actually entered Marsa Scirocco Bay, with one of their craft shot up by the single working 40mm Bofors on Delimara Point. The survivors made it to their assigned beach (S), but found themselves stranded; what looked to be a scalable cliff proved not to be, completely blocked by rubble from the fort above's destruction.[14]

---

12. The Sebenico was the captured Yugoslavian Royal Navy's destroyer Beograd.
13. A leichtes sturmboot 39 (Stb39) was a small high-powered assault craft, capable of 30mph carrying six troops.
14. *Smith, Battle for Malta, p.205.

As the sky lightened, Vizeadmiral Weichold, in charge of the Larnaca landings aboard the damaged *Hermes*, had a hard decision to make – whether to continue to try to land or not. He had troops on Benghajsa Point and armour in his MFPs[15] to land inside the bay if he could. He chose to try.

As dawn burned off the light mist, two Raumboote (R-boote) minesweepers circled Benghajsa Point and made for the bay's mile-wide mouth. They were still 500 yards short of the mouth when the sole surviving searchlight in the ruins of Fort Delimara came on, illuminating them. A 12-pdr on Delimara Point hurled its first 3in shell at the boats, both of which responded with 37mm gunfire. The *Hermes* added its two forward 5in naval guns, determined to suppress the searchlights and any other response from the defenders.

After ten minutes of the duel, the fort's searchlight had been destroyed and the 12-pdr crew scattered; but one *R-boote* drifted afire.[16] A line of MFPs, with another R-boote leading the way, rounded the point to continue the assault.

Then two 18/25-pdr beach guns on the bay's southern shore opened fire over open sights. Despite Weichold's demand for progress, the landings on Benghajsa Point had failed to push through the Devonshires' D Company in time to clear the peninsula. The fire, from an unexpected direction, devastated the attack column. The lead R-boote took a round in its engine and went dead in the water on fire. An MFP took another 88mm shell from the 25-pdr that exploded against one of the T-34s it carried, killing crew and tankers around it; a second round disabled its steering.[17]

A second MFP swerved to miss the disabled landing craft and avoid the drifting R-boote. As it crossed the line between the points, the British set off one of the electrical mines that protected the entrance. Over 300kg of explosive erupted. The MFP wasn't directly over the mine when it went off, but close enough to heel the craft over away from the blast, then back as water poured through the huge tear in its side. Crew and passengers hastily abandoned ship. With mines still active, Weichold's bold attempt to force the bay had failed and he sent the recall. The beach guns hit another MFP several times more, sinking it, before salvos from the *Hermes* scattered the gunners and destroyed one of the guns. As Weichold's flagship retired, the other gun continued firing.[18]

The Larnaca portion of the invasion had been decisively repulsed. After his rescue from the sea, the *Badsworth*'s skipper, Lieutenant Gray, had been invited by Weichold to witness the landings. After the repulse, he recalled, 'I simply looked at the German admiral and said, "Welcome to Malta". He was not amused.'[19]

In the early morning hours, as the Forza Navale Speciale continued to sort out its landing, several command conferences took place on the island.

In the area outside the village of Dingli, the acting commander of the 1. Fallschirmjäger Regiment, Hauptmann Becker, conferred with his surviving company officers. His troops were low on supplies, water especially, with little to be looted from the Maltese inhabitants. His officers strongly suggested pushing east to regain contact with rest of the drop zone paratroops. But Becker argued that they had a good blocking position – stalling any strong attack onto

---

15. Marinefährprahms (MFPs) were 200-ton landing craft capable of carrying two tanks, 100 tons of supplies or troops.
16. *Pack, Naval Battle of Malta, p.125.
17. *Ibid., p.132.
18. *Ibid., p.138.
19. *Gray, G., 'Reflections', After the Battle, #XX (1967), p.23.

the drop zone's left flank, something that had not been considered probable in pre-invasion conferences. Allied prisoners identifying themselves as 4 Brigade troops had revealed they had expected to move in force against an invasion. Ultimately, Becker ordered consolidation of their defences, while he contacted the Luftwaffe for supply. Once resupplied and reorganised, the regiment would attack east far enough to capture the high ground overlooking the invasion area.[20]

On the drop zone's right flank, Ramcke and 3rd Regiment's commander, Heilmann, discussed their options. Scouts had informed them the British were dug-in south of the Luqa and Kirkop airfields, but they still had some pockets of resistance in Bubakra to deal with as well as pressure from Hal Far airfield in the west. The isolated Fallschirmjäger pioneers on the other side of Hal Far were being pressed back toward Fort Benghajsa, complicating their options as those troops needed to be relieved. Italian Blackshirts had landed on Benghajsa Point to support them, but were pinned down. The two men decided to wait for resupply and then have Ramcke's battalions push east against Hal Far, while Heilmann's troops held the centre of the line.

The Folgore paratroop commanders – Generale Enrico Frattini and interim 1 Brigade commander Tenente Colonnello Alberto Luserna, who had taken over for the still-missing Camossa – held their own conference near the Qrendi airfield, even as Loreto troops slowly made it unusable. The airfield troops had suffered casualties from the mines and booby traps left on the partially completed field, which made night-time operations difficult. The occasional artillery shell that impacted slowed things even more, although the advent of the invasion fleet had removed that hindrance – transferring the shelling to the seaborne contingent. As dawn lightened up, work resumed at a faster pace, but it became evident that the field would not be ready by the time of the first scheduled airdrop.[21]

The Folgore paratroops dug in south of Siggiewi. One full company – the unfortunate 8th Company – remained missing, and scouts had no contact with the Germans on their left flank; instead of their allies, the scouts ran into British troops. They decided they would call for supplies and the division's 2 Brigade for the morning drop, and move the Regia Aeronautica's assault battalion to the foot of the high ground to hold against any British move from that direction. Without radio contact with Sicily, Frattini sent their message to Ramcke for transmission to Sicily and beyond. They also gave the same message via air panels for the aircraft soon to be above them.[22]

Meanwhile, the mood beneath Valletta's walls in the Maltese command centre was even grimmer as they looked at the status of their island defences. Confirmation of troops landing on Gozo was streaming in. The good news from Delimara tempered the bad news of landings all along the south-western coast.

The Devonshire Regiment held Hal Far airfield and hoped to break into Bubakra long enough to extract the Maltese and 1 Brigade command group, but had two of its companies involved in firefights around the fallen Fort Benghajsa.

The Dorsetshires' A Company was mopping up small-scale landings around Tumbrell Point. Only part of the Royal Irish Fusiliers battalion had finally arrived at Siggiewi, having been badly disrupted by the battleship bombardment. Ironically, the stunned survivors of the

---

20. *Boog, Germany and the Second World War, Vol VI, p.401.
21. *Etruschi, Albion Defeated, p.201
22. *Folgore Battle Diary, Malta, p.18. Air panels were a non-radio means of communication with aircraft from the ground to identify friendly positions, similar to the more modern coloured smoke grenades.

Folgore's 8th Company had to be rounded up and marched away, further eroding the Irish combat power.

The Royal West Kents and Hampshires had developed a strong line of defences stretching from Siggiewi to Kirkop, while patrols in the night showed the Italians and Germans doing the same.

On the Dingli high ground, the King's Own battalion held Laferla Hill with Germans and Italians on either side. The battered Durham Light Infantry troops currently sealed the Germans off from Rabat/Mdina, but had suffered considerable casualties in doing so, including the loss of irreplaceable tanks. The Buffs were just coming into contact on the far left of the Germans position, but would be out of position for any concerted move toward the invasion area and would have to deal with the Germans holding Dingli village.

The Admiralty reported the Royal Navy's response fleet from Gibraltar at sea heading for the island, but it would not be off the coast until dawn on 18 August at the earliest – still two days away. They also reported Admiral Vian's Alexandria group was scheduled to leave later in the day for arrival after midnight on the 18th. Until then, they were on their own.

Both Gort and Scobie knew what needed to be done – break through to the invasion beaches – but the current line stretched their battalions, amidst scattered reports of exhaustion among the troops. They needed a concentrated force, which at present they did not have. Their pre-invasion plans of having a full brigade – the Fourth – available for a counter-attack had been thwarted when the Germans dropped on top of it. The Manchester and Lancashire battalions remained in reserve and relatively fresh, as were the two King's Own Malta battalions in the north beyond the Victoria Lines. They had most of the Dorsetshire battalion, with only A Company actively engaged at Tumbrell Point. But to pull in those troops against the paratroops and the southern coast invasion site meant leaving the north and its coast dangerously devoid of troops, defended only by scattered outposts and coastal guns. Furthermore, it would take time to concentrate the troops, given the Luftwaffe's air superiority. They remained concerned that landings at St Thomas's Bay, signalled by the capture of Sottotenente Guglielmo, might still be in the offing, especially after the naval battle near there. But the more time they took to concentrate – or reach a consensus to concentrate – the more Italian troops would be ashore.[23]

They decided to compromise, ordering the Manchesters and Lancashires to concentrate around their battalion headquarters, leaving the Dorsetshires to cover St Thomas's Bay and the surrounding sites, and for the Maltese of the 1st Battalion KOMR to pull back to the Victoria Lines, while their sister battalion split into platoons to cover the vacated positions. One company of the 2nd Battalion, though, had to be assigned to guard the small but growing number of Axis prisoners.

While Gort and Scobie began sending out their orders, Vice Admiral Leatham and the 10th Flotilla's Captain Simpson also reacted to the landings. Leaving *Una*, *Utmost* and P46 in place covering the Sicilian invasion ports, Simpson ordered the other U-class submarines to converge on the southern coast, with P31 near Pantelleria and P35 to approach from the north-west, around Gozo. P42, patrolling near the Medina Bank, would converge from the south. He ordered P34 and P44, covering Malta's northern coast, to circle around the island, avoiding the known Axis minefields, and join P42. Simpson left the timing of the attacks to the discretion of his captains.[24]

---

23. *Colville, Man of Valour, p.229.
24. *Wingate, The Fighting Tenth, p.215.

As the British leadership made their difficult decisions, Sicilian airfields roared into life once again. At Catania, the Germans loaded more Go242 gliders with artillery and supplies in preparation for take-off once the Loreto Battalion declared Qrendi cleared and open, while Ju52s were loaded with supplies – ammunition, food and extra weapons. General Student struggled to coordinate two separate drops: one to his isolated 1st Regiment, the other to Ramcke's and Heilmann's troops. At Gela and Castelvetrano air bases, the Italians loaded supplies into some of their S.82 aircraft, but most loaded with the three battalions of the Folgore 2 Brigade.

As news of the Larnaca repulse and the motor launch attack filtered through the command levels in Italy, a far more disturbing report came in. The Italian consul in the southern Spanish city of Algeciras had observed from the top of the Hotel Riena Cristina that Gibraltar harbour was nearly empty[25] – the fleet he had reported there in the past week was gone. The Royal Navy was now at sea.

As the sun started lightening the sky, Lieutenant Colonel Allen launched a probe with a company of his Irish Fusiliers at the edge of the Folgore line just west of Siggiewi, following a brief bombardment by F and B batteries (Figure VIII-1). With the A-13 Cruiser tanks from 3 Troop leading the way, Major Ben Barrington's C Company pushed the Folgore's 6th Company back half a kilometre. The commander of Barrington's 13 Platoon, Lieutenant Ted Johnson, wrote:

> 'My platoon's goal was to push over a line of stone walls then cover for 14 Platoon's move forward. I had to get my chaps organized and moving. This was my first proper action where live bullets were flying around. After a lot of unaimed covering fire, we moved forward by section flanking a tank. We had trouble negotiating the stone walls, with one section covering while another climbed over. I hadn't seen the opponents as yet and none of my men could give me any good sightings in spite of hostile fire cracking past us. Suddenly my section commander, Lance Sergeant John Caldwell, went down right beside me, shot cleanly through the head. That shook me. Most of us hit the ground immediately, forward movement stalled. It took a while to get them moving again.'[26]

The Folgore company commander, Capitano Marenco, rallied his troops and, aided by reinforcements from sister companies, stopped the push. In the attack, the British lost one precious tank when Folgore Private Drago Ricci sacrificed himself to plant explosives directly on the armoured vehicle.[27]

Even as the Irish attack slowed down, other British battalions were in motion. The Lancashire Fusiliers began to concentrate at Qormi. The two northern Maltese battalions began shifting position, with the 1st Battalion moving toward the Victoria Lines while the 2nd Battalion headed for the Melleiha Ridge high ground. The Manchester Battalion split their concentration, moving one company to Mdina, where C Company continued helping with the fires and disaster from the horrific S.82 crash of the day before. The rest of the battalion moved toward Mosta.[28]

---

25. *The hotel roof had a good view of the British anchorage; Farago, Ladisla, Burn after Reading, p.46.
26. *Johnson, Island Prize: Malta, p.152. REALITY: this was based on Johnson's description of his battle on Leros, where Sergeant Caldwell was killed.
27. *Private Ricci was awarded the Medaglia d'oro al Valore Militare for his actions. Etruschi, p.221.
28. *Smith, Battle for Malta, p.232.

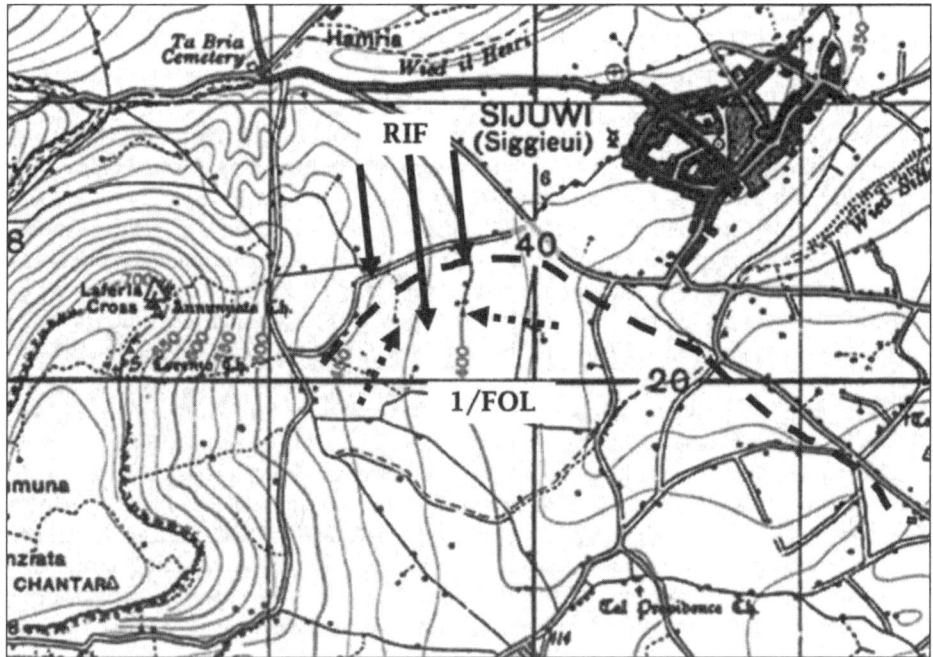

Figure VIII-1: *Royal Irish Fusilier attack west of Siggieui.*

As daylight fully broke, the mass of aircraft swept in from Sicily. Ju52s dropped supplies to both enclaves of German paratroops, but winds that were picking up hampered collection efforts. Becker's troops near Dingli managed to collect only about 30 per cent of the supplies dropped to them. The rest fell into the sea or into 4 Brigade's lines, where the British welcomed the extra weapons, ammunition and, especially, food rations. The supply drop to Ramcke proved more on target, with nearly 60 per cent recoverable.[29]

To the embattled Folgore, the S.82s that appeared overhead brought their sister brigade, with three battalions of 2 Brigade drifting down in and around Qrendi. The massive reinforcement brought the Irish attack to a standstill as the troops stared at mass of parachutes set to fill the hole they had hoped to punch in the Italian lines, then began shooting up at the descending figures. The winds drifted two Italian companies onto the already crowded beach area, disrupting the Friuli troops trying to come ashore and making many smaller boats move to rescue paratroops that landed in the water. Major Barrington called a halt to the Irish attack as the new situation developed. Lieutenant Johnson later wrote:

> Everyone stopped in place and seemed to be firing at the parachutes. I even fired my revolver. We must have killed a lot of them, but soon after we got the word to pull back to the village.'[30]

---

29. *Boog, Vol VI, p.410.
30. *Johnson, p.154.

As the Irish dealt with the distraction of the new paradrop, Maggiore Zanninovich led a Folgore counter-attack which pushed the exhausted British troops back to their start line.

While the Germans worked to collect the supply containers, the Buffs Battalion started closing in on Dingli village. Becker had already started his troops moving eastward out of the village, but left a rearguard in place under the wounded Major Gröschke that effectively stalled the Buffs with machine-gun and sniper fire for several hours, a vicious reprisal of the Durham Light Infantry's defence the previous day. The Buff's Colonel Iqqulden sent his A Company directly into the village while another company under Major Dyke moved to flank the defenders.

On the other side of the invasion zone, Ramcke's II Battalion commander, Major von der Heydte, led his 1st and 2nd companies as they assaulted into Bubakra after a flight of Stukas had pounded the village, inflicting demoralizing casualties on the defenders from the 3rd KOMR's A Company (Figure VIII-2). At the same time, Captain H. Duke led the Devonshires' C Company to also attack with artillery support into the village from the east, overrunning two MG34 machine-gun positions and opening an escape route for the village's British defenders. The vicious engagement among the limestone rubble took a heavy toll on both the Fallschirmjäger and British attackers. The German 1st Company commander, Oberleutnant Trebes, fell in the attack. Lieutenant Pat Anderson's 15 Platoon pushed their way through the village to Bubakra Tower and succeeded in withdrawing Brigadier General Smith and his 2 Brigade staff. Their primary task done and the Germans stalled for the moment, the Devonshires and the remnants of Captain Aumier's Maltese pulled out with the rescuers, leaving the village in enemy hands.[31]

Daylight gave Ammiraglio Tur a better glimpse of the chaos of the landings. Sporadic artillery fire was impacting the areas, but not concentrated enough to truly hamper the landing of the infantry, just to make them slow. The transfer of ammunition, food and other supplies from the boats onto the beach continued to be even slower than troops going up ladders; the seas were becoming choppier, making the transfers increasingly difficult.

Even as he assessed the information, his staff fielded a frantic message from the commander of III Battalion/88th Infantry, assigned to land at Wied il Bassasa, nearly a mile east of Wied iz-Zurrieq. The commander reported a single company landed and packed into the landing area with very little manoeuvring room; what had appeared to be an easily negotiable ravine leading up to the high ground proved virtually non-existent. With the single company ashore pinned down, under mortar and sniper fire, the battalion commander remained out of touch with his own 88th Infantry commander, scheduled to land later near Wied iz-Zurrieq. The message requested orders, but Tur understood the commander's plea to pull out from an untenable position.[32]

On Benghajsa Point, the survivors of the German Pioneer Battalion had been pushed back into the captured fort by the Devonshires' D Company, whose commander, Captain Howard, left his 18 Platoon to watch and pin the Germans in the fort and moved the rest of his company back towards the Kalafrana seaplane base. At the base, two platoons watched as the remaining Guastatori and lanciafiamme troops were evacuated from their slim Larnaca beaches. Howard then moved his reduced company back to Hal Far.

With Benghajsa Point essentially clear, Brigadier Smith was able to shore up his defensive line near Hal Far with the Devonshires' A and D companies. He also had the Dorsetshires' B Company (Captain Hamilton) concentrate near Birzebugia to act as his brigade reserve. With the Dorset A Company still busy mopping up the remnants of the abortive landings at Tumbrell

---
31. *Boog, Vol VI, p.416.
32. *Tur, p.110.

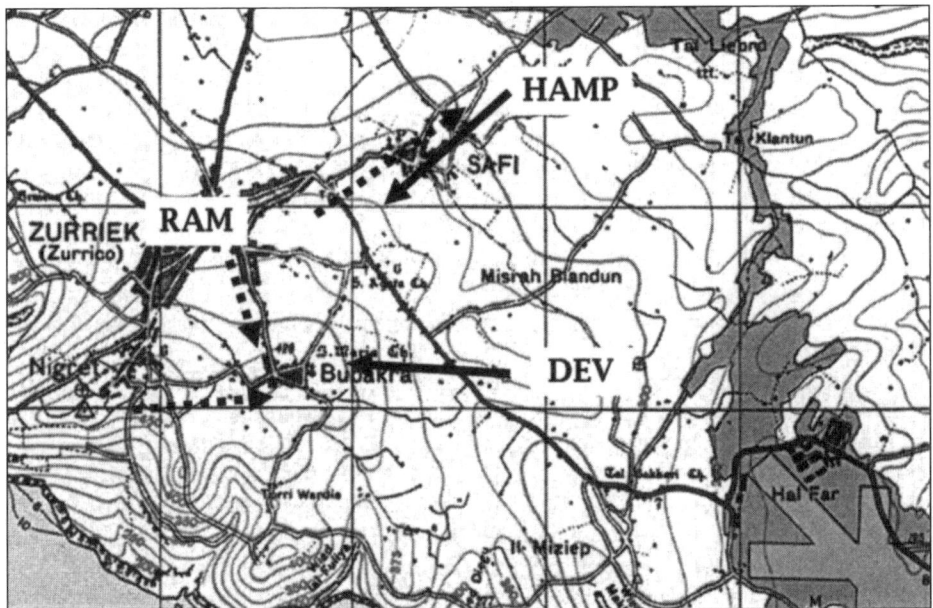

Figure VIII-2: *Battles at Bubakra and Safi.*

Point, the defence of St Thomas's Bay and the south-east coast, under Dorsetshire commander Lieutenant Colonel Ray, became very weak.

With the limited supplies collected, Hauptmann Becker launched his III Battalion/FJR1 eastward in an effort to shift his blocking force to the edge of the high ground at Laferla Hill (Figure VIII-3). His troops dislodged a platoon of King's Own troops holding the Girganti Palace and valley, but that small success became moot with the call for help from Major Gröschke, whose troops had been evicted from Dingli and remained under pressure from the Buffs. The Durham Light Infantry troops, having regrouped from their earlier engagements, were also probing more vigorously on their side of the defensive perimeter. Becker stopped his eastward move to reinforce his rearguard.

Another British assault materialized on Ramcke's perimeter, with the Hampshires' A and C companies, coordinated by A Company commander Captain R. King, attacking with some artillery support. The surge evicted the German III Battalion's 5th Company from Safi. However, a quick counter-attack led by the battalion commander, Major Rau, pushed the Hampshires back out of the little village and into their night defence positions, ending that threat by noon.[33]

On Sicily, with one major air drop finished and another loading, air crews turned their attention to close air support aircraft and started getting more of the Ju88s and Ju87s into the air to help their paratroops on Malta. Spotter aircraft had noted the new firing positions of British artillery and the Luftwaffe began attacking those positions. They suppressed some batteries temporarily – their crews finding cover – but the guns returned to work as the covering anti-aircraft batteries took a toll of the attacking planes.

---

33. *Smith, p.242.

At about the same time at sea, a Vichy French airliner passing over the Mediterranean sighted the British fleet from Gibraltar at sea and radioed their authorities. Two hours later, the Supermarina received notification of the sighting and passed the information onto its pack of submarines stationed in the western Mediterranean. They also received word that a force of cruisers and destroyers had left Alexandria that morning. Regia Aeronautica search planes from Rhodes and Crete launched soon after to locate the latter force.[34]

Off shore, Tur could only shake his head in frustration as the afternoon wore on. The invasion plan had called for him to land two divisions of assault troops plus armour in a single day, and then return to Sicily for more troops. By mid-afternoon, he had barely half the Friuli infantry ashore, with only some mortars landed for support. That support didn't matter, as the Italian troops were fully engaged in hauling supplies from the boats below and were unavailable and unready for combat.[35]

In Qrendi village, the Folgore commander, Generale Frattini, finally met with Oberst Heilmann of the Fallshirmjäger's 3. Regiment to discuss deployment of his reorganizing 2 Brigade. Ramcke also joined the meeting with news that his troops had been stymied on their initial drive to take the aifield by artillery and heavy defensive fire just west of Hal Far. Frattini reported that the tentative push by Irish troops had been repulsed by his reinforced 1 Brigade. The discussion was complicated by the conflicting orders for the paratroops; Frattini's orders were to hold his line and prevent any British incursion against the landing areas, while Ramcke had orders to capture Hal Far airfield. The three commanders eventually agreed to start shifting Heilmann's 3. Regiment east to take over Ramcke's right flank positions to free up more of his troops and have the Folgore move into the vacated German positions, thus extending their front.[36]

As the Axis commanders made their plans, the gunners of the Cheshires' C Company arrived at Hal Far in mid-afternoon and set about creating strongpoints to reinforce the western defences. The troops of C Company of the Devonshires, reinforced from their replacement company, dug in west of them, backed by B Company and anchoring their line on G Battery's Bofors; the light anti-aircraft guns had thus far been instrumental both in driving off Stukas and breaking up German assaults. The Devonshires' second-in-command, Major Guy Young, had overall command of the airfield's defences.

In the severe heat of late afternoon, the Buffs' attack west out of Dingli began to falter as exhaustion set in. The Germans suffered too as their water ran out.

They abandoned two of their anti-tank guns and many of their wounded, including Major Gröschke, to pull back into a tighter perimeter. Neither the Buffs nor the Durham troops had the energy to continue pushing, so they began to dig in. The medical facilities in the village were overwhelmed with casualties from both sides, captured German medics working side by side with their British counterparts and Maltese civilians.

On the beaches at sunset, Tur's staff reported two-thirds of the Friuli infantry ashore with some Legion troops, but no armour or artillery had started to land. Tur suspended all attempts to land equipment at night, but ordered infantry and supply landing to continue. Supply landings continued going well at Wied iz-Zurrieq, once the Italian engineers cut the cable closing the creek and reduced the defending pillbox. The deep water of the creek allowed the landing craft, one at a time, to sidle next to the concrete wharf. Manhandling the supplies up the steep hill proved the hardest problem, with all the Friuli troops landed there fully committed to the task.

---

34. *Pack, p.153.
35. *Tur, p.115.
36. *Boog, Vol VI, p.420.

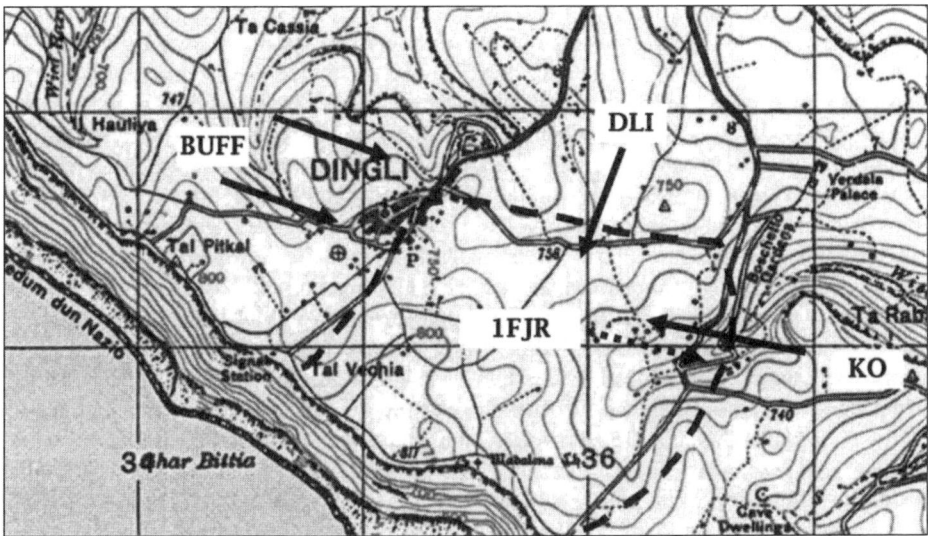

Figure VIII-3: *Battle on the Dingli Plateau.*

At Ghar Lapsi, the shallow cove stopped all but the small assault boats so supplies had to be hauled up from the boats by rope and muscle, made more difficult by the rough seas. East of the cove, where Tur wanted to land his Semovente assault vehicles, the 150 metres of rocky shore (designated Beach D) became clogged with supplies and troops, all which had to be moved before the armour landed. His most disturbing report was that his engineers complained there was no way to get the heavy equipment off the 2km landing area between the two fishing sites as they had only found a single 2ft-wide path between Beaches D and E, making it impossible for anything but infantry to move through those landing areas. They concluded that a road would have to be built, something they were not equipped to do.

The beachheads from the initial landings also reported that water continued to be a major problem for the paratroops, who subsisted by begging it off the Friuli troopers already landed. C3 planners had proposed a rope tow system to get water from the water tankers with the convoys up to the higher ground, with one rope tow scheduled to be built at Wied iz-Zurrieq and another at Ghar Lapsi. Tur sent word to his engineers ashore to speed up the creation of the system. He would move a tanker closer in the morning.[37]

Beach casualties due to artillery fire began to rise, partly a consequence of congestion and partly because of a change in artillery tactics by Brigadier Beckett, Malta's artillery commander. Rather than assign a portion of the beach to each battery of the 26th Artillery Regiment with guns that would reach the area, as he had originally, he switched to having all batteries fire five rounds at the same beach coordinates to maximize firepower, then switch to other coordinates. One lucky 6in round overshot the beach and struck MZ 750, carrying the Friuli's 65mm guns and ammunition, setting off a series of secondary explosions that tore the big landing craft apart. Nearby craft also suffered damage. Despite this, the Italians kept landing.[38]

---

37. *Tur, p.119.
38. *Etruschi, p.241.

To the east, four hours out of Alexandria, Axis search planes found Admiral Philip Vian's reaction force. At dusk, Captain Poland on the destroyer HMS *Jervis* notified the admiral of a 'Snowball' alert.[39] A few minutes later, HMS *Arethusa* reported radar contact with aircraft 50 nautical miles out and closing. The attack by ten escorted S.79 torpedo bombers flying out of Gadurra, Rhodes, split into two groups to come at the ships from both flanks. However, the Beaufighters of 252 Squadron out of Egypt's Idku airfield still flew cover for the force and bounced the Italians. Tangling first with the escorting Fiat G.50 Freccia fighters, the heavier British aircraft used their cannon to shoot down two of the six fighters, with one of their own damaged and sent flying south out of the fight. The remaining Beaufighters also brought down two of the attacking torpedo bombers, but the rest broke through. The surviving Italians concentrated their effort on the light cruiser HMS *Birmingham*, whose 9,100 tons made it the largest ship in Vian's force. Anti-aircraft fire from the force's three Dido-class cruisers hampered the attack and, although pressed home with great determination, the Italians inflicted no damage to the ships, other than the expenditure of anti-aircraft shells which Vian regretted.[40]

South of Malta, the three British U-class submarines rendezvoused, then proceeded north in a staggered line abreast with the surfaced P42 in the lead, with P44 and P34 following a mile apart and half-a-mile behind.

At approximately 10.35 pm, P42's hydrophones picked up the sounds of active sonar pinging ahead of them. Signalling his consorts, Lieutenant Alastair C.G. Mars took his boat down to periscope depth and, as worked out with his fellows, began the approach to the Italian anti-submarine line at 3 knots.

Ahead of him, the Italian destroyers *Turbine* (Capitano di Corvette Savatore Granato) and *Sebenico* (Capitano di Corvette Luca G. de'Flamini) made lazy 5 nautical mile ovals, some 10,000 yards off the beachhead. While the *Turbine* was moving away from the submarines, the *Sebenico* wasn't and an alert sonar operator announced contact at 10.53 pm.

The Italian ship followed up the contact with a depth-charge attack. Mars increased speed and depth, taking evasive manoeuvres and initiating a half-hour cat-and-mouse affair that had both Italian destroyers and VAS 211 (Guardiamarina Franco Nicasro) sequentially making contact after being disrupted by the depth charges and dropping charges themselves. P42 received a severe shaking but was not seriously damaged during these attacks.

During one of the brief interludes in the depth charging, with his ASDIC reporting all contacts at slow speeds (indicating problems re-establishing contact), Lieutenant Mars brought the boat up to periscope depth to see the *Turbine* moving slowly in front of him. He recalled:

> 'My hands were sweating badly from the depth-charge attacks, but were steady, and my heart thumped like a trip hammer. The tip of the periscope nosed out of the water. I could see a ship right in front of me.
> '"Fire One!" I yelled, then, "Down periscope, hard starboard, full ahead!"
> 'As we spiralled down, we head a great clattering explosion. A hit!'[41]

---

39. Snowball was the Jervis's unofficial mascot, a small dog they adopted in Alexandria. Snowball had an uncanny sense of enemy aircraft, generally alerting the crew before any aircraft were visible. Connell, Mediterranean Maelstrom, p.125.
40. *Pack, p.160.
41. *Mars, Unbroken, p.135.

The torpedo struck the destroyer amidships and it stopped dead in the water, listing badly. The explosion and chaos allowed the submarine to move toward the anchorage, but the *Sebenico* quickly re-established contact and aggressively prosecuted the submarine, leaving the smaller VAS boat to help with the sinking *Turbine*.

Further west, P44, next in line, had increased its speed to 5 knots when its hydrophone picked up the faint sounds of depth charges. However, its passage into the Italian anchorage was halted when detected by the destroyer escort *Pegaso* (Tenenti di vedette Mario De Petris). De Petris followed up the contact with a devastating depth charge attack that shattered some battery cells and damaged one of the engines. P44's commander, Lieutenant Thomas E. Barlow, took his sub deep and withdrew, hounded by the *Pegaso* until the torpedo explosion on the *Turbine*. The escort then turned back to aid the *Sebenico* in its hunt. Barlow later reported:

> 'A full pattern of depth charges came down on us. There was a big explosion and sharp cracks as a main motor fuse blew. Total damage: shallow gauges destroyed, wireless smashed, asdic gone, batteries broken. Thank God the destroyer left us soon after.'[42]

While Mars and P42 twisted and turned beneath the hunters, and P44 limped south, P34 (Lieutenant Peter R.H. Harrison) drifted toward the Italian anchorage undetected. Approaching to within 1,000 yards, he saw a large group of small ships in the throes of raising anchor and steam, alerted by the anti-submarine conflict nearby. Harrison fired all four of his forward torpedo tubes in a slight arc, then increased speed to turn and dove away from the expected retaliation. Two of the missiles missed the ships, one exploding harmlessly against Malta' rocks; the other did the same, but exploded between two ships landing their troops, sending troops on the ladders and supplies being hauled up into the water. The remaining two torpedoes did hit two ships, with one capsizing almost immediately, taking about half the II Battalion/34° Regiment of the Livorno Division with it. On the other ship, soldiers of the I Battalion/33° and the regiment command group abandoned ship. Two batteries of 20mm anti-aircraft guns and a company of mortars were also lost, along with several tons of supplies for the division. Despite the efforts of two VAS boats, Harrison and his crew escaped.[43]

Meanwhile, in Valletta, a dispirited Governor and his staff assessed the day's activities. The last words received from Gozo indicated that at least one column of Italian infantry of the several landed had entered the island's capital in the early afternoon. The skirmish with British submarines had been inconclusive. Some ships were sunk or damaged, but the landings continued, and the island could not rearm the submarines. Simpson ordered the five subs to make for Alexandria. All five arrived safely, but P44 showed up much later than expected, unannounced due to the loss of its wireless.[44]

Of their three primary offensive actions on Malta, only the Buffs' attack on the Germans near Dingli could be regarded as a victory as the village ruins had been reclaimed. The Irish assault on the Italians and the Devonshires' attempt to mop up Benghajsa Point had been effectively stymied.

Gort also realized from the battalion reports that exhaustion was setting in – the starvation diet forced on the defenders was having its effect on stamina. Beckett reported the scarcity of

---

42. *Wingate, p.210.
43. *Pack, p.170.
44. *Simpson had readied a signal to the Admiralty announcing P44's loss when it showed up. Wingate, p.220.

artillery shells at his defending batteries; they would have to resupply the batteries at night to escape the Luftwaffe's attention. He also noted that their inventory of artillery shells was shrinking fast, recalling that 'we were all keenly aware that our stock of ammunition for the guns was limited'.[45]

Without saying it, Gort and his leaders realized that doing nothing would give the Axis additional time to land troops and supplies. But they also knew that they needed to mass a large attack force to truly accomplish anything, something they couldn't do without significant risk. Gort made the decision to continue operating offensively against the Germans on the Dingli Plateau, but to shift completely to defence elsewhere, hoping that the Royal Navy's advance would affect the ability of the Axis forces to press home their attack.

---

45. *Beckett, The Fall of Malta, p.63.

Chapter IX

Monday
17 August 1942

Time	Wind (kn)	Sea	Notes		
8.00 am	22–27	rough	fog	sunrise	6.26 am
8.00 pm	22–27	rough		sunset	7.46 pm

At midnight, Vice Admiral Syfret's fleet sailed directly south of Dragonera point on Mallorca and was just entering the patrol box of five Italian and two German submarines. Pre-warned of the fleet's approach by shadowing Luftwaffe aircraft, the submarines were prepared and alerted.

The Italian submarine *Uarsciek* (Tenente di Vascello Gaetano Targia) became the first to make contact with the fleet. He radioed his position but before he could approach and attack, the fleet's screen of destroyer escorts detected his submarine and drove him away.

Less than an hour later, the fleet encountered the German U-73 (Kapitanleutnant Helmut Rosenbaum), who put four torpedoes into the carrier HMS *Eagle*. The old Mediterranean veteran sank within six minutes of the torpedoes striking, with the loss of over 400 of its crew and all its aircraft. Rosenbaum successfully escaped the escorts' wrath.

An hour later, HMS *Wolverine* struck back as it caught Italian submarine *Dagabur* (Tenente di Vascello Renato Pecori) on the surface and sank it by ramming.[1]

As reports of the night action came in, activity at Italy's western naval bases picked up. Ammiraglio di Squadra (designato d'Armata) Angelo Iachino, flagged in the battleship *Vittorio Veneto*, led the older battleship *Guilio Cesare* – transferred to take the place of the refitting *Littorio*[2] – and five destroyers out of Naples into the Tyrrhenian Sea, sailing toward Sardinia. On that island, Ammiraglio Alberto da Zara prepared his 7ᵃ Division of light cruisers and destroyers to join Iachino from Cagliari.

Axis reconnaissance flights took off from Crete and Sardinia at first light to search and locate the converging fleets. Shortly after 6.00 am, a Ju88 located Syfret's fleet 80 nautical miles north by north-east of North Africa's Cape Benngut.[3] Word quickly spread, and within the hour shadowing aircraft surrounded the fleet. On Sardinia, the Regia Aeronautica and Luftwaffe prepared a

---

1. *Naval details from Smith, The August Battle for Malta, pp.73–83. Reality: these events actually took place during Operation Pedestal.
2. The new Littorio was still in Taranto, finishing repairs from torpedo damage suffered during the attempt to intercept Operation Vigorous in June.
3. For the cartologists among us, 38° North 4° 32' East.

massive air attack. Gruppo Aerosilurasnte 105° from Stormo 46 and the two *gruppo* from Stormo 36 – 108° and 109° – would put twenty-four S.79 and nineteen S.84 torpedo bombers into the air from the Sardinian base at Decimomannu. They would be reinforced by another eight S-79s from Naval Air detachments 2° and 3° and escorted by thirty-four G.50 and Cr.42 fighters. The Luftwaffe contributed ten He.111Hs, loaded with two torpedoes each, from Kampfgeschwader 26. Another twenty-nine S.79s waited at Margano base on Pantelleria in reserve.

To the east, reconnaissance initially failed to find Admiral Vian's Alexandria fleet, thanks in part to the increase in speed Vian ordered after dark. He had planned to do so because of a suggestion made by Admiral Harwood, which he suspected was based on special intelligence he was not privy to.[4] Increasing his speed from 20 to 25 knots during the night put him 40 nautical miles closer to Malta and away from where the enemy expected to find him. Even as the Axis made contact with his ships at 7:20 am some 135 miles west by south-west of the island of Gavdos,[5] United States B.24 and B.25 bombers from the 12th and 98th Bombardment Groups in Egypt swept in to attack airbases on Crete and the Cyrenaica hump. Overall damage was negligible, but the attack disrupted German efforts to put anti-shipping units into the air.

Word of the Alexandria fleet's location passed through channels to the Supermarina and then on to Ammiraglio di Squadra Carlos Bergamini on the battleship *Caio Duilio*. His reduced 2nd Squadra – his battleship *Caio Duilio* and the three heavy cruisers of 3ª Division, minus the torpedoed *Andrea Doria* – left Messina before midnight and rendezvoused with the light cruisers of 8ª Division out of Augusta at 2:00 am, before proceeding south-east at 18 knots. The Supermarina's latest information led the Italians to expect contact with Vian's force around noon.

As dawn lightened the sky on 17 August, *C3*'s third day, with seas remaining high and rough, Ammiraglio Tur off the Famagosta beachhead assessed his situation as only slightly less chaotic than the previous day. He still had Friuli troops to be landed, with those of the Livorno suffering in their ships awaiting their turn, over twenty-four hours behind schedule. Friuli troops struggled to get themselves, their weapons, and supplies off the rocky shelves. Three of the beaches, between Ghar Lapsi and Wied-iz Zurrieq, proved nearly impossible with the clutter, with no easy way off for anything other than infantry, as his engineers had reported earlier. Tur heard that a single Friuli company had made it off the middle beaches E–H, exhausted and without any of their equipment.

All this, he thought, and the Royal Navy was on its way.[6]

He sent orders to the ship masters carrying the Livorno Division to be prepared to move, in case they needed to. Then he sent word to the railway ferry *Messina* to move up and start landing its equipment.

The big 1,300-ton ferry, loaded with nine Semovente armoured assault guns and seventeen 75mm guns, plus ammunition and fuel, moved forward, shoving its prow against the rocks, and lowered the ramp as much as it could against the higher rocks just east of Ghar Lapsi. The Semoventes of 10° Raggruppamento Corazzato Gruppo DLV began to unload. It was a slow process – each 15-ton vehicle had to negotiate a very steep ramp that rocked with ship and wave motion in the rough seas, then cross 100 yards of rough rocky ground before getting to the road that led up from Ghar Lapsi. The first two Semoventes actually made it to the narrow road before Malta's defenders began to respond. Scouts on the high ground notified Valletta

---

4. Detailed reconnaissance schedules had been intercepted since May 1942. Kew Ultra files. Operational commanders were not authorized to see Ultra intercepts.
5. 34° 6' North, 21° 12' East.
6. *Tur, p.125.

about the assault guns, but it was almost a half hour before Beckett ordered a battery of the 26th Defence Regiment to target the Ghar Lapsi beach area – delayed because of events coming out of Safi. The third Semovente threw a track 20 yards away from the ramp.

As the Italian armour struggled ashore, pickets for the Hampshires' B Company were surprised to see three Germans walking out of the ruins of Safi village, carrying a large white flag, flapping hard in the stiff wind. Captain H.D. Smith, the Hampshire company's commanding officer, came forward to meet the German delegation, shocked to be introduced to General Ramcke himself. The Fallschirmjägers' commander suggested a two-hour ceasefire to discuss terms. Smith duly reported the request up the chain of command.

Thirty minutes later, General Scobie, accompanied by the Hampshires' Lieutenant Colonel J.L. Spenser, arrived via Bren carrier, untroubled by the Luftwaffe aircraft already circling overhead. Maltese artillery continued its firing toward the beachhead area, but the morning attack planned by the Buffs held up in deference to the parley.

Scobie refused Ramcke's initial suggestion of a complete ceasefire, noting that the Italians were still landing troops and equipment onto the rocky southern shoreline and would be opposed until they stopped. He also noted no Italian delegate at the meeting. Miscommunication had left the Folgore's Generale Frattini, the highest-ranking Italian ashore, out of the proposed parley, while the Friuli's commander, Generale Carboni, had yet to land. Undeterred, Ramcke provided a clear recitation of the odds against the fortress defenders:

> 'Your troops have fought magnificently. But you are outnumbered and no rescue is possible. I recognize and respect your courage and determination, but to continue to fight will only lead to further losses to your men and the civilians under your protection. I urge you to surrender honorably. You will be well treated.'[7]

Scobie politely refused, noting that the Axis had landed on Malta's rocks and would 'lose teeth in that bite'.[8] Ramcke saluted and returned to his lines. Scobie conferred with Spencer briefly before doing the same.

With full daylight, and the offer of surrender refused, Axis activities picked up. Ju52s and S.82s roared over the invasion site, dropping another load of supplies to the paratroops. Winds scattered the drop, but on the main landing ground, Italian and German troops collected most of the dropped supply this time. On the Dingli Plateau, though, Hauptmann Becker and his beleaguered 1st Regiment troops managed to get only a small amount of what was dropped. Supplies dropped outside the Axis-held zone were scavenged by British troops and civilians, especially the food. Water remained a major problem for the exhausted Germans.

While the paratroops collected and distributed the meager collection of supplies, firing broke out near the cliffs in Becker's rear. It took several minutes and minor casualties before Fallshirmjägers from 11th Company realized the 'attackers' were actually San Marco Marines. A patrol of Grado Battalion's 2nd Company, scouting up a trail that had been designated for the follow-on Assietta Division's route off the beachhead, had found the path undefended before running into German pickets. Sending some of the German paratroops down the path, they returned loaded down with canteens from the Italians. They also reported the path as scalable

---

7. *Alcidi, Brigade Ramcke, p.56.
8. *Colville, Man of Valour, p.254.

for the lightly armed troopers to get out of the trap they were in, even though the path would not be useable by the Italian division as expected; there were too many sharp switchbacks for anything other than light troops.

As the paratroops resupplied and slaked their parched throats, a probe by the Durham Light Infantry troops forced the Germans to fall back, but an additional move by the Buffs was stalled with fire from massed MG34 machine guns from the I Battalion's 4th (heavy weapons) Company, keeping the perimeter mostly intact.

On the other side of the drop zone perimeter, Ramcke's brigade prepared to attack as soon as the ceasefire ended, moving east against the defenders protecting Hal Far airfield following a massed Stuka attack. Although Hal Far's anti-aircraft gunners blunted most of the air assault, the Stukas left the Devonshire defenders shaken. Part of Ramcke's attack never materialized because one Stuka, hit on its approach, dropped its bombs on two companies of his II Battalion, causing casualties and stopping any forward movement by those troops (Figure IX-1).

C Company of the Devonshires, dug in near the old ruins at Tal Bakkari, repulsed the weakened German attack, with the Germans' 1st Company bearing the brunt of the casualties in front of the Bofors of G Battery. Vickers machine guns raked the attackers from their newly created strongpoint on the ruin's tower. A German paratrooper recalled:

> 'Our objective was before us, but they spotted us and gave us hell. People were getting hit and I heard cries of pain. I saw Schindler, the company commander,

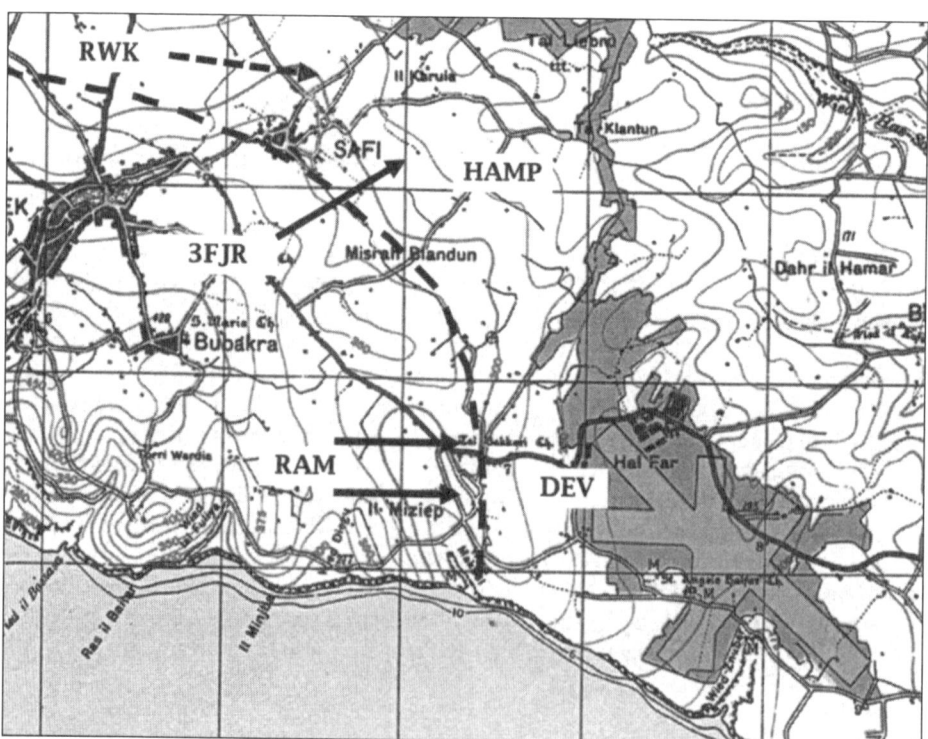

Figure IX-1: *German attacks on the eastern perimeter.*

go down. We were forced to halt the attack and withdraw, leaving many on the ground behind us.'⁹

Nevertheless, fire from the 75mm and 105mm recoilless rifles of the paratroops' artillery took their toll on the defenders, leaving the company a hollow shell of itself, Captain Duke being among the wounded. A second assault by the Fallschirmjäger, better coordinated but without Stuka support, was barely repulsed, with more casualties incurred.

Colonel A.W. Valentine now ordered Howard's D Company forward to help hold Hal Far, maintaining a single platoon to pin the Germans inside Fort Benghajsa. As the company moved forward, the exhausted C Company withdrew to regroup at Hal Far. The regiment's remaining replacements from E Company were sent to again reinforce the battered unit.

In the centre, the Royal Irish managed to infiltrate two platoons from their B Company, under Captain J. Salton, into flanking positions in the rough ground on Laferla Hill. A short barrage by three Royal Artillery 25-pdr batteries which slammed into the Folgore 1 Brigade defenders near Siggiewi was followed by a Royal Irish attack. The disrupted Italians held their ground tenaciously despite the bombardment and a close-range firefight ensued. Maggiore Zanninovich again led reinforcements from 4th and 5th companies to bolster the defenders. The attack broke off when the Irish came under fire from their flank by San Marco Marines, which stalled the advance and created some chaos when Captain Salton was killed. The Italian Marines were themselves unable to move forward as they became pinned by rifle fire on their flank from troops of the King's Own on Laferla Hill.¹⁰

As afternoon approached, little had been accomplished by either side, other than losing troops.

Battle of Cape Bougaroun (Figure IX-2)

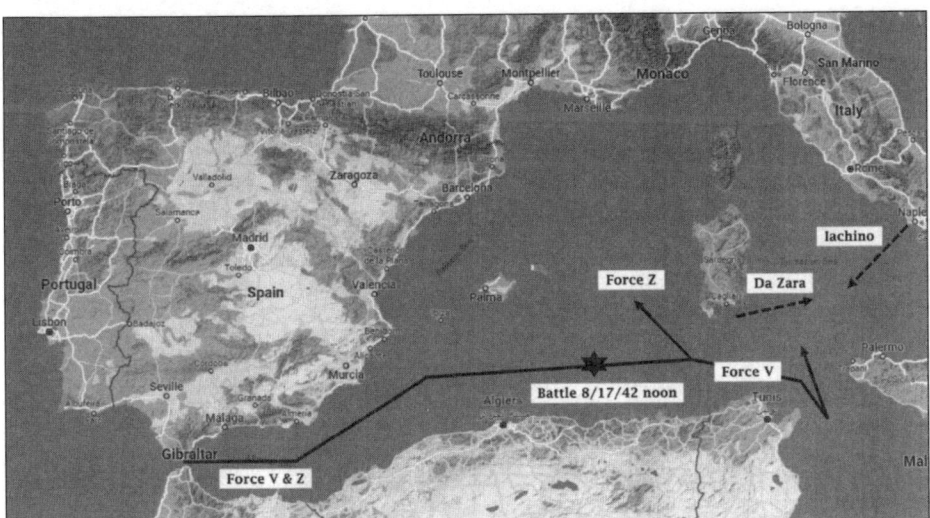

Figure IX-2: *British Force Z & V and battle off Cape Bougaroun.*

---

9. *Poppel, p.57. REALITY: another of the author's remembrances from Crete.
10. *Folgore Battle Diary, Malta, p.26.

Syfret's fleet had enjoyed a brief respite from alarms after passing through what had been the first submarine box the Axis had set up. After the initial sighting, aerial snoopers circled the fleet, but remained nimble enough to stay out of the way of the combat air patrols from the fleet's remaining carriers.

Royal Navy Cape Bougaroun Order of Battle*

Force Z – Gibraltar escort force –	
Vice Admiral E. Neville Syfret	
Battleships	
Nelson (flag), Captain H.B. Jacomb	*Antelope*, Lt Cmdr E.N. Sinclair
Rodney, Captain J.W. Rivett-Carnac, DSC	*Wishart*, Cmdr H.G. Scott
Aircraft Carriers – Rear Admiral A.L. Lyster	*Vansittart*, Lt Cmdr T. Johnston, DSC
Victorious, Captain H.C. Bovell	*Westcott*, Cmdr I.H. Bockett-Pugh, DSO
809 Squadron, 884 Squadron – 16 Fulmers	*Wrestler*, Lt Cmdr R.W.B. Lacon, DSC
885 Squadron – 6 Sea Hurricanes	
817 Squadron, 832 Squadron – 14 Albacores	**Force X – Malta Reaction Force**
Indomitable, Captain T.H. Troubridge	**Rear Admiral H.M. Burrough**
806 Squadron – 10 Martlets	
800 Squadron, 880 Squadron – 24 Sea Hurricanes	**Light Cruisers**
827 Squadron, 831 Squadron – 14 Albacores	*Manchester*, Captain H. Drew
Eagle, Captain L.D. Mackintosh, DSC (sunk)	*Kenya*, Captain A.S. Russell
801 Squadron, 813 Squadron – 16 Sea Hurricanes	*Nigeria* (flag), Captain H.S. Paton
Furious, Captain T.O. Bulteel	*Cairo*, Captain C.C. Hardy
804 Squadron, 807 Squadron – 24 Sea Hurricanes	
823 Squadron – 14 Albacores	**Destroyers**
Ashanti (6 DF), Captain (D) Cmdr R.G. Onslow	
Light Cruisers	*Tartar*, Cmdr St. J.R.J. Tyrwhitt, DSC
Phoebe, Captain C. P. Frend	*Eskimo*, Cmdr E.G. Le Geyt, DSC
Sirius, Captain P.W.B. Brooking	*Laforey* (19 DF), Captain(D) R.J. Hutton

Charybdis, Captain G.A.W. Voelcker	*Lightning*, Cmdr H.G. Waters, DSC
Destroyers	*Lookout*, Lt Cmdr C.P.F. Brown
Ithuriel, Lt Cmdr D.H. Maitland-Makgill-Crichton	
Iscarus, Lt Cmdr C.D. Maud, DSC	**Destroyer Escorts**
Intrepid, Cmdr E.A. de W. Kitcat	*Derwent*, Cmdr R.H. Wright, DSC
Foresight, Lt Cmdr R.A. Fell	*Bramham*. Lt. E.F. Baines
Fury, Lt Cmdr C.H. Campbell, DSC	*Bicester*, Lt Cmdr S.W.F. Bennets
Pathfinder, Cmdr E.A. Gibbs, DSO	*Ledbury*, Lt Cmdr R.P. Hill
Penn, Lt Cmdr J.H. Swain	*Zetland*. Lt J.V. Wilkenson
Quentin, Lt Cmdr A.H.P. Noble, DSC	*Wilton*, Lt. A.P. Northey, DSC

*Sources: Smith, Peter, PEDESTAL; website www.unithistories.com

Fifty nautical miles north of North Africa's Cape Bougaroun, just after 12.00 pm, air search radars lit up as the first major air assault approached.

The Axis plan had been to hit British from three directions at the same time, converging from east, north and south. From the east, ten S.84 bombers from 109°/36 Stormo, each armed with two *motobombas* – 880lb circling mines – would drop the weapons directly in front of the British. The twenty mines would hopefully throw the fleet into confusion, allowing the concentric attacks – seventeen S.79s and nine S.84s from the north, and fifteen S.79s and ten He111Hs of 6/KG26 from the south – to overload and penetrate the air defences and deliver their own torpedoes.

However, delays in launching from the various Sardinian airfields and forming up led the simultaneous attacks to be delivered sequentially.

The ten S.84s armed with *motobombas* arrived first. They had no escorts and the fleet's combat air patrol savaged them; only five managed to get within a couple nautical miles of the ships to drop their mines. In the absence of other attacks, the fleet simply sidestepped the threat to the south.

The sidestep, however, only brought the southern pincer arm of the Axis air attack closer. Scrambled fighters off the carriers tangled with the escorts – twenty-six Reggiane Re.2001 fighters. One Sea Hurricane was lost in the ensuing dogfight, while two Italian fighters went down.[11]

Other defending fighters broke up the incoming bombers, splitting them into smaller groups of three or four. Sweeping over the outlying destroyers, the bombers struggled through the anti-aircraft fire from the *Rodney* and light cruiser *Phoebe* trying to reach the carriers. One He111 flew directly into the shell of a 16in round from the battleship and disintegrated. Two others were shot down, while the rest delivered their torpedoes from 3,000–5,000 yards and beyond and with one exception all were easily avoided. That one exception slammed into *Rodney*'s thick armour; it expended most of its energy against the big ship's torpedo bulkhead,

---

11. *Pack, p.183.

176   Operation C3: Hitler's Plan to Invade Malta 1942

only creating minor flooding, not enough to stop the ship from operating.[12] The pilot, Capitano G. Ricciarini, remembered:

> 'The enemy fire was intense. I dropped my torpedo at about 800m just as a burst of fire struck the right engine, causing the fuel tank to burn. The blaze grew in intensity and I decided to ditch at once. My plane was completely wrapped in flame and smoke. I ditched almost by instinct. Unable to open the cockpit roof, I had to discard my parachute and crawl through the fuselage, then out into the sea. Several of my crew were on the port wing. We got the raft out before the plane sank.'[13]

Fifteen minutes later, the northern attack materialized. With time to reorient, the newly scrambled Sea Hurricanes and Fulmers again fought through the escorting fighters to break up the attacking formations. Defensive fire shot down several of the Sparvieros, one by the fighters and two by anti-aircraft fire, along with a Fulmer and an escorting Re.2001. This time, however, one S.79, already on fire, fought through the flak with determination and planted a torpedo in the stern of carrier HMS *Furious* before ditching. The hit jammed the carrier's rudder, damaged a propeller shaft and created moderate flooding. The 22,000-ton ship slowed and circled as its crew fought to contain the damage.[14]

In the aftermath of the attack and confusion from the circling carrier, none of the British lookouts noticed a single low-altitude S.79 coming toward the fleet, nor the Cant Z.1007 that followed it. Two combat air patrol Fulmers did spot the planes but the escorts of G.50 fighters took their immediate attention.

The oncoming Sparviero was from a special combat unit, conceived by Italian Generale Ferdinando Raffaelli[15] as a flying bomb – unmanned, radio-controlled and packed with high explosives.[16] Although originally intended to strike at one of the British battleships, the Cant pilot's attention was drawn to the slowly circling, wounded carrier. Belated anti-aircraft fire from the outlying destroyers failed to bring it down and the big plane slammed into the carrier's side, causing a massive explosion that engulfed half the ship in fire. Secondary explosions from burning fuel, planes and ammunition tore at the ship and left it burning fiercely and dead in the water, clearly doomed. Captain T.O. Bulteel ordered his ship abandoned.[17]

By 1.30 pm, the attacking aircrews had debriefed and reported their results. The exultation the pilots and crew felt at sinking a carrier was somewhat muted when the reconnaissance aircraft still surrounding the British reported that, after an hour of collecting the survivors from *Furious* and sinking the burning hulk with torpedoes, the British still sailed east.

---

12. *Smith, p.254.
13. *Etruschi, p.240. Ricciarini and the other survivors were rescued twenty-one hours later.
14. *Pack, p.165. The S.79 pilot, Tenente G. Barani, was awarded the Medaglia d'oro al Valore Militare for the attack.
15. General Ferdinando Raffaelli, trained as a pilot, started the Second World War as the commander of the Operations section of the Joint Chiefs of Staff, before taking command of Regia Aeronautica units in Libya. From March 1942 until the armistice, he directed Unit 5° (technical-military studies) of the General Staff of the Regia Aeronautica.
16. *Smith, August Battle for Malta, p.159. REALITY: this was an actual weapon used during Operation Pedestal against the convoy. However, the radio controls failed and the plane flew past the convoy to crash on the Algerian mainland. Smith, Pedestal, p.107.
17. *Pack, p.168.

Battle of Third Sirte (Figure IX-3)

Shortly after noon, about the same time as the air attack on Force Z, radar on the cruiser HMS *Arethusa* warned of several planes approaching Force V; visual sighting identified the planes as IMAM Ro.43 reconnaissance aircraft. Admiral Vian knew these planes were ship-based and ordered his single reconnaissance aircraft from the *Birmingham*, a Supermarine Walrus, launched.[18]

Third Sirte Order of Battle

2ª **Squadron** (A.S. Carlo Bergamini) at Messina	**Force V – Rear Admiral Sir P.L. Vian**
5ª Division	**Light Cruisers**
BB *Caio Duilio* [F] (C.V. Giorgio Conti)	*Arethusa*, Captain A.C. Chapman
	Birmingham, Captain H.B. Crane
15ª Destroyer Squadron at Reggio Calabria	*Euryalus*, Captain E.W. Bush
Pigafetta [F] (C.V. Enrico Valle)	*Cleopatra* (flag), Captain G. Grantham
Da Verazzano (C.F. Angelo Lo Schiavo)	*Dido*, Captain H.W.U. McCall
16ª Destroyer Squadron at Reggio Calabria	
Da Recco [F] (C.V. Aldo Cocchia)	**Destroyers**
Malocello (C.F. Mario Leoni)	*Napier* (RAN 7DF), Capt (D) S.H. Arliss
Premuda (C.F. Alessandro Mirone)	*Nizam* (RAN), Cmdr M.J. Clark
Norman (RAN), Cmdr H.M. Burrell	
3ª Division at Messina	*Sikh* (22 DF), Capt (D) St.J Macklethwait
CA *Gorizia* [F] (C.V. Paolo Melodia)	*Zulu*, Cmdr R.T. White
CA *Bolzano* (C.V. Mario Mezzadra)	*Jervis* (14 DF) Capt(D) A. L. Poland
CA *Trieste* (C.V. Umberto Rouselle)	*Javelin*, Lt Cmdr H.C. Simms
	Kelvin, Cmdr M.S. Townsend
7ª Destroyer Squadron at Augusta	*Pakenham* (12 DF), Capt (D) E. Stevens
Freccia [F] (C.F. Alvaro Minio Paluello)	*Paladin*, Cmdr A.F. Pugsley
Folgore (C.C. Renato D'Elia)	
Lampo (C.C. Antonio Cuzzaniti)	
Saetta (C.C. Enea Picchio)	
8ª Division at Augusta	

---

18. The Supermarine Walrus was a catapult-launched biplane amphibian with pusher propeller. The Arethusa had been built with a catapult as well, but it had been removed in 1941. The Dido-class cruisers had not been designed with an aircraft catapult.

CL *Garibaldi* [F] (C.V. Vittorio De Pace)	
CL *Duca d'Aosta* (C.V. Luciano Bigi)	
CL *Abruzzi* (C.V. Giovanni Viansino)	
13ª Destroyer Squadron at Augusta	
Alpino [F] (C.V. Ferrante Capponi)	
Fuciliere (C.F. Umberto Del Grande)	
Mitragliere (C.F. Silvio Garino)	
Bersagliere (C.F. Anselmo Lazzarini)	
Corazziere (C.F. Antonio Monaco di Longano)	

Twenty minutes later, his scout sent word of three cruisers directly ahead of his course. Confusion reigned on Vian's bridge when the Walrus reported a second set of three cruisers, some 40 degrees off the course of the ships previously spotted. Having been warned by the Admiralty of Italian heavy cruisers sighted heading south earlier, Vian realized he was facing heavier odds than expected. He ordered his chosen battle formation – all five cruisers in line abreast, with destroyers trailing on each wing.

Meanwhile, the Italians had received their own scouting reports and both Ammiraglio Angelo Parona's 3ª Divisione of heavy cruisers, flagged on *Gorizia*, and the *Caio Duilio*, trailing the cruisers by 15 nautical miles, changed course to intercept. Ammiraglio Raffaele De Courten's 8ª Divisione of light cruisers, which the British submarines missed reporting, continued on its course, closing in. They all launched more Ro.43 aircraft to provide gunnery support.

At 1.16 pm, *Arethusa* reported radar contact with ships at 36,500 yards and closing;[19] two minutes later, it reported more ships closing from the north. Worse was the news from the Walrus that a third group, this time with another cruiser or battleship, sailed astern of the first two.

Six minutes later, lookouts on the *Cleopatra*, in the centre of the British line, called out 'Ships at Green 0-1-2'[20] as the *Gorizia* led its line toward them. The range was about 26,000 yards, well beyond the extreme gunnery range of Vian's Dido-class cruisers with their Mk I 5.25in guns, but within the *Gorizia*'s range for its 8in guns. The British admiral signalled his squadron to assume line ahead, turning all his ships south to unmask all their guns. Minutes later, the Italians began to do the same.

At 1.28 pm, Vian recorded 'enemy engaged' as the Italians began firing, with HMS *Birmingham* and *Euryalus* returning fire at a range of 24,000 yards.[21]

Ronald Sired, an able seaman in the low-angle gun directory of HMS *Euryalus*, recalled:

---

19. *ADM 234/353: Battle summaries, Malta 1942, No. 18: Third Sirte.
20. British lookouts were taught to call out sightings as Green (starboard) or Red (port) and the bearing. In this case, Green 0-1-2 means ships to starboard bearing 12 degrees off the bow.
21. *ADM 234/353: Battle summaries, Malta 1942, No. 18: Third Sirte.

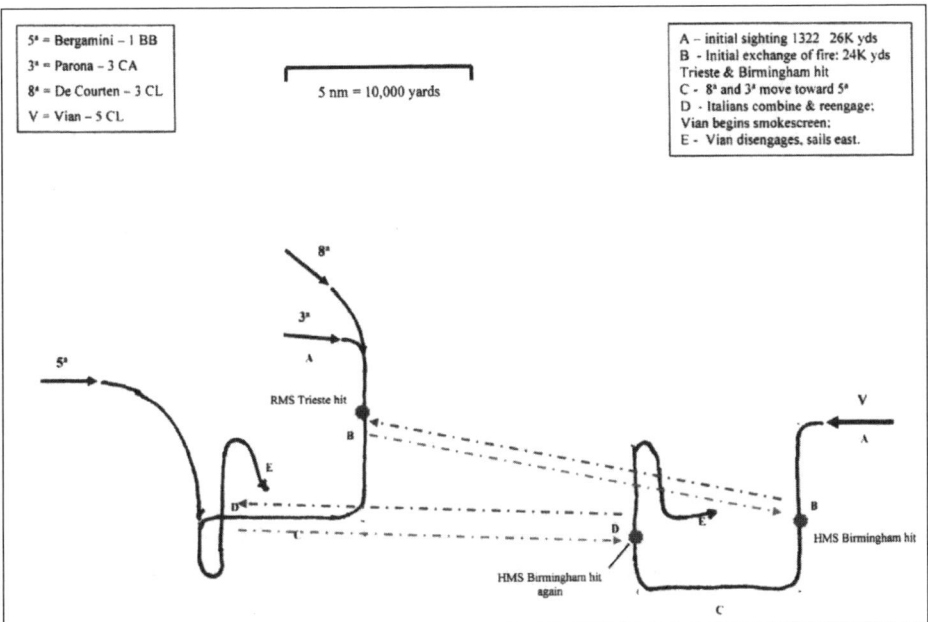

Figure IX-3: *Battle of Third Sirte.*

'Through the rangefinder, I saw three Italian 8in cruisers. I obtained ranges and passed them to the transmitting-stations. The *Euryalus* opened fire with "A" Turret on the middle cruiser and shook the ship. The range was over 20,000 yards. It was extremely difficult to hit a target at that range; several of our spotting shots were not even sighted.

'It was an awful moment when I saw the cruiser open fire on us knowing a salvo of 8in shells was coming toward us. I remembered feeling the same way when the Italian battleship *Littorio* had fired on us in March; the 8in shells dropped close to the ship and we had to take avoiding action.'[22]

Nominal British doctrine called for the ships to fire as fast as they could to overwhelm the enemy with shells.[23] Vian had previously ordered British fire to be slower, more measured and concentrated on single ships, adamant that his captains not fire as rapidly as they were used to in order to conserve ammunition to use both at Malta and on the way back to Alexandria.

Neither side scored anything other than straddles, as the British line weaved. One close call shook HMS *Dido* enough to cause several electrical circuits to open, disabling the aft turret for several minutes.

One shell finally hit the Italian cruiser *Trieste* amidships, close to its torpedo mounts; at first little damage was caused except for a fire that the crew started battling. Sired remembered:

---

22. *Sired, Enemy Engaged, p.47. REALITY: these are based on observations Sired made at the Battle of Second Sirte from aboard Euryalus.
23. The Dido-class light cruisers' nominal rate of fire was 100 shells per minute. Ibid., p.22.

'I saw a good straddle on the target cruiser, and seconds later a vivid red flash which I believed to be a hit. A few minutes later I saw a bigger explosion on the ship.'[24]

The fire cooked off the torpedoes in the mount, setting off a massive explosion that rocked the 10,000-ton vessel. The explosion killed many of the damage control party fighting the fire and the flames spread. The cruiser reeled out of the line.

British optimism faded a minute later as an 8in shell hit *Birmingham*'s aft Y turret, ripping it open and putting it out of action and on fire.

Vian signalled a shift to line abreast, sailing directly towards the Italians. With *Trieste* on fire, Parona ordered *Gorizia* and *Bolzano* to turn away and regroup back with the oncoming *Caio Duilio*. De Courten's light cruisers manoeuvred to join the other ships. Light cruisers *Abruzzi* and *D'Aosta* both traded salvos with HMS *Dido* as they manoeuvered, rocking the British ship with straddles but inflicting little damage. Vian optimistically reported the Italians retreating.[25] However, at about the same time his scout finally identified the oncoming ship as a Duilio-class battleship.

Just after 2.00 pm, the Italian ships finally converged, and Ammiraglio Bergamini, onboard the *Caio Duilio*, assumed command of the battle. His ship, with Parona's heavy cruisers in front and de Courten's light cruisers manoeuvring behind to form a full line of battle, re-engaged at 2.12 pm.[26]

Vian, still running in line abreast due west, shifted his force to line ahead as the battleship engaged, moving north, opposite the Italian's current course. He had to revise his initial assessment, noting, 'engaged with battleships and five cruisers, wind against us, four hours daylight remaining'. He sent a signal at 2.15 pm to Harwood, citing the battle odds and asking: 'Continue Mission? Immediate response needed.'[27]

With the firing general between the two lines some 23,000 yards apart, he ordered his ships to make smoke, deciding to try to outmanoeuvre the Italians behind the screen. Sired wrote:

> 'When we started making smoke, it was like March all over again. *Euryalus*, with dense grey-black smoke pouring from her funnels, heeled from side to side as she changed course. We were firing mostly by radar as I could only spot the Italians momentarily through the smoke.
>
> 'A column of spray and water shot up on our port side only 80 yards away, and others dropped off our starboard side some 40 yards away. The ship trembled with the explosions and dirty black spray that fell on board. One large splinter hit us on our port side, but didn't do much damage. We recovered it later and added it to the big hundredweight splinter we had collected in March.'[28]

---

24. *Ibid., p.48.
25. *ADM 234/353: Battle summaries, Malta 1942, No. 18: Third Sirte.
26. *Etruschi, p.255.
27. *15th Cruiser Squadron signals 00723/5 17 August 1942; ADM 234/353: Battle summaries, Malta 1942, No. 18: Third Sirte.
28. *Ibid., p.50.

As the smokescreen built, fire continued, but any British hits scored (two)[29] proved nearly useless as their shells could not penetrate the Italian armour at that range. The Italians, after reversing course to parallel Vian's line, had less trouble. Ten minutes after re-engaging, the battleship hit the *Birmingham* with a 12.6in shell on the aft X Turret, killing all the Royal Marines inside and forcing Captain H.B. Crane to flood his aft magazines, veering out of the battle line. Vian immediately ordered his cruisers to reverse course behind the smokescreen and head south while the burning *Birmingham* withdrew.

His hope that his course reversal could allow his ships to circle around the Italians proved useless as the Ro.43 spotter aircraft reported the course change and Vian's own spotter radioed the Italians turning south as well.

The manoeuvre having failed, Vian realized that continuing the running battle was only depleting his ammunition and delaying any arrival off Malta, as well as continuing to run his destroyers low on fuel. Showing an uncharacteristic hesitancy,[30] he stalled by querying his navigator as to potential landfall at Malta should the Italians break off the action immediately. The officer gave him the bad news that they'd arrive near dawn – with little time to do anything before the whole Axis air force came down on them.

A little after 3.00 pm, having not heard from Alexandria, Vian ordered his line to turn east and sent the following cryptic signal to his home base: 'Ammunition running low, fuel running low, enemy persisting in blocking approach. Unable to complete mission. Returning to base.'[31]

The British cruisers turned away from the Italians, keeping the smokescreen between them. Bergamini sailed on, but ordered the four destroyers of 7ª Squadriglia Cacciatorpediniere to move between his line and the smokescreen, as he sent his last scout plane to see what lay behind the smokescreen. He remembered Iachino's experience from the Second Battle of Sirte, when British destroyers loomed out of the weather and smoke to attack with torpedoes. Vian, however, did not order such a move, knowing his destroyers were running short of fuel.

Bergamini heard from his scout plane that the British were disengaging and sailing due east. He began moving north-east back toward Malta and Sicily, sending an exultant signal to Supermarina: '*Ritiro nemico. La vittoria è il nostro!*' (Enemy withdrawing. Victory is ours!).[32]

In Alexandria, Harwood received Vian's first message just after 3.30 pm. Harwood immediately sent his reply: 'Continue if possible; your decision.' Half an hour later, Vian's second signal arrived and Harwood sent it on to the Admiralty, adding only his note that he 'concurred with his onsite commander'.[33]

In his post-war memoirs, Vian wrote:

> 'I had chided myself for not being resolute enough to push the *Vigorous* convoy through to Malta in June. I had fewer doubts about my decision to withdraw

---

29. *Etruschi, Cesare, p.258.
30. Vian's hesitancy had been noted by observers during June's Operation Vigorous, but it wasn't until well after the war that it was learned he had been suffering from an infected cyst on his head that made him less decisive. Hore, p.165.
31. *15th Cruiser Squadron signals 00724/5 17 August 1942.
32. *Etruschi, Cesare, p.261.
33. *ADM 234/353: Battle summaries, Malta 1942, No. 18: Third Sirte.

182   Operation C3: Hitler's Plan to Invade Malta 1942

in August. There was little else I could do except sacrifice good men and good ships for little gain.'³⁴

On Malta that same afternoon, massed Luftwaffe bombers made a tremendous effort to suppress the British artillery positions around Ta'Qali airfield, but did little damage and lost several aircraft to the intense anti-aircraft fire. However, a Stuka attack on one battery (F/12RA) disrupted it enough to keep it from helping defend the Tal Bakkari position. The third assault by Ramcke's I Battalion troops, led by battalion commander Major Kroh and preceded by a barrage of smoke from battalion mortars, successfully overran the position, destroying the Bofors of G Battery as well as the Cheshires' strongpoint of machine guns. The Devonshires' D Company pulled back in some disarray, but the steadfastness of their commander Howard brought the unit under control. Further penetration onto Hal Far was stopped cold, though, as Valentine's A Company struck the penetration from the flank and halted the German momentum.

To the north, however, another crisis developed as Heilmann's 3rd Regiment attacked out of Safi, pushing back the Hampshires' A Company and killing the company commander, Captain King. Their momentum carried through the positions of C Company of the Hampshires. Only a quick counter-attack onto their flank by the neighbouring Royal West Kents forced the Germans to halt. However, the attack opened a big hole in the defensive perimeter. Colonel Spenser combined the exhausted troops of A Company with the remnants of C Company, all under Captain Van Lessen, to fill the gap and dig in. The Kent's Colonel Pulverman, after pulling back his counter-attack, shifted some of his reserve troops while more Cheshire machine-gun units were dispatched from Valletta. The twin setbacks left only a thin line of platoon positions and machine-gun strongpoints between the enemy and Luqa airfield, indeed the whole centre of the island.³⁵

The Irish, re-formed after their morning attack, were preparing to hit the Folgore again, hoping to catch the Italians in a troop shift as they reinforced their line south of Siggiewi and pulled out the battered 4th Company. But the crisis in the Hampshires' defensive zone made Scobie rethink another Irish attack, and Colonel Allen was told to hold his troops back for a more concerted effort. More Irish units continued to straggle in from the north.

On the Dingli Plateau, Buffs and Durham Light Infantry troops tried to coordinate their assault on the Fallschirmjägers there, but multi-battalion manoeuvres proved difficult for troops not trained for them and the coordination was only partially successful. The Buffs overran the remnants of the German 6th Company, but were again stopped by heavy machine-gun and mortar fire. Pursuit became complicated by the capture of many wounded Germans.

Offshore, Tur got all nine Semoventes ashore from the *Messina*, but three were disabled, two with thrown tracks from the rocky terrain and one from an artillery near miss. Efforts to unload the guns and ammunition from the big ferry were disrupted as the ship took a direct hit from a 6in howitzer shell, causing a fire. Only the concerted effort of the crew and passengers kept the fire from spreading to the ammunition aboard. Tur wrote:

---

34. *Vian, p.98.
35. *Smith, p.276.

'I was relieved when the fire was reported out – had it reached the ammunition still on board the anchorage would have been devastated and the whole landing disrupted.'[36]

Unloading the Friuli troops, equipment and supplies continued to be slow as the beaches contended with crowded, chaotic conditions as the troops brought up supplies from the boats, as well as bodies.

In the Tyrrhenian Sea, aboard the battleship *Vittorio Veneto*, Admiral Angelo Iachino followed events in both the east and west. The cruisers of Admiral Da Zara had made contact an hour earlier out of Cagliari and now steamed 15 nautical miles ahead of him. The last report he had received placed the British at 60 nautical miles south-west of Cape Spartivento[37] at 3.00 pm with two carriers and three battleships on a course of 85 degrees, speed 20 knots. However, the signal had not been received for a full two hours and staring at the plot, Iachino realized now – at 5.00 pm – the British could be only 80 nautical miles from da Zara's cruisers and less than 100 from his two battleships. Given his experiences off Cape Matapan in March 1941, when British carrier aircraft had hit both his flagship and the cruiser *Pola*, he made the only choice available to him – he reversed course, ordering da Zara to do the same.

His decision was based on outdated information, however. A second air attack on the British had struck Force Z an hour earlier. The smaller attack by fifteen S.79s and five He111s was easily disrupted by the remaining combat air patrol and their torpedoes all missed. Shortly after the attackers left the scene, Admiral Syfret turned Force H around, splitting off the four cruisers and six destroyers of Rear Admiral Borrough's Force X to continue the run for Malta. Iachino did not receive that information until almost 7.00 pm, putting him several hours steaming away from the much smaller – and outgunned – British force. The chance for 1st Squadra to intercept the British had been lost.[38]

However, the Italians had several other lines of defence ready. At dusk, the S.79s from 130° and 132° Stormo out of Pantelleria swept in from the darkened eastern sky. Burrough's force twisted and turned its way through the attack, shooting down one bomber and sending three others smoking into the dark, without sustaining a hit. But their luck ran out with the last trio of aircraft that pushed home their attack relentlessly, planting two torpedoes into HMS *Cairo*, bringing it to a listing halt. A short conversation with Captain Hardy on the stricken vessel told Borrough that the cruiser was doomed, so he ordered Hardy to abandon ship and get his crew onto the accompanying destroyers as fast as possible. A half hour later, Force X was on its way again after sinking the *Cairo* with a torpedo.[39]

In London, the Admiralty reacted quickly to the news that Vian had disengaged. They sent an urgent message to Syfret not to detach Borrough's force, since alone they could not hope to achieve anything. Half an hour later, Syfret reported the alarming news that Burrough had already been detached. Frantic messages went out to Force X on all channels to withdraw.

A furious Churchill exploded when told the news, railing about the decision that would cause the fall of the fortress. Sir Charles Wilson, his personal physician, recalled the moment:

---

36. *Tur, p,131.
37. 38° North 7° 55' East.
38. *Etruschi, p.273.
39. *Pack, p.175.

'PM in an explosive mood. Harwood does not care about the fate of Malta.'[40] Later, Churchill railed at his cowed staff: 'Battles are not won by arithmetic calculations of the strength of the opposing force, they are won by resolute action.'[41]

Off Malta, Tur received the welcome news that the Royal Navy in the east had been beaten off and that Bergamini was returning to take station off the island. He ordered the transports to continue the unloading process, though still hampered by rough seas.

While the Italians were struggling to unload off their objective, Force X entered the operating zone of the next barrier to their passage following the final air attack – five Italian submarines. The first to contact the British was the *Alagi* (Tenente di Vascello S. Puccini), but his attack went awry as the torpedoes malfunctioned after leaving the tubes. The abortive attack warned Force X of the danger, and the destroyers of 6th and 19th Flotillas began actively hunting. Another attack, this one by the *Axum* (Tenente di Vascello R. Ferrini), although it failed to hit its target, had an unintended consequence; manoeuvring to avoid the oncoming torpedoes, HMS *Lightning* ran into a mine. The massive explosion holed the destroyer. Its two consorts, *Laforey* and *Lookout*, forced Ferrini to go deep, away from the scene, but the *Lightning*'s captain, Commander H.G. Waters, warned the two destroyers away. Admiral Burrough, in contact with Waters, made the hard decision and ordered the two destroyers to depart, leaving Waters and his crew to fend for themselves.[42] Shortly after that engagement, Burrough received the withdraw command. After confirming the order, Force X reversed course and headed back to rendezvous with Syfret, who circled back himself to provide air cover.[43]

In the Lascaris War Rooms under Valletta, Gort and his commanders stared at an uncomfortable map, made more so by the news that the Royal Navy had been repulsed in its attempt to get to the island. The pressure on Hal Far was building, and their centre was weakening too, putting Kirkop and Luqa at risk. The 1st Battalion, King's Own Malta troops were finally at Rabat, and the Lancashire Fusiliers and the 8th Manchesters were concentrated at Ta'Qali. From there, night marches would place the troops in position for what they hoped was a concerted effort against the Italians near Siggiewi. The crisis was near.

While the counter-attack took priority, Gort had to make time to discuss the secret orders he had received from the Admiralty. London was concerned about the Maltese Dockyard falling intact into enemy hands. Gort and his naval team met with Yard Machinery Manager Joseph Spiteri to map out the drilling and placing of explosives around the dockyard to deny the facilities to the Axis should Malta surrender. After the war, he would recall the difficulty of remaining positive about the counter-attack's possibility for success while having to plan for the destruction of Malta's harbour.[44]

---

40. *Smith, p.286, REALITY: Wilson wrote this during the arguments with Auchinleck over attacking at Gazala. The Harwood reference was for Auchinleck.
41. *Churchill, Second World War, Vol IV, p.345. REALITY: part of this statement was made in May 1942 as Churchill tried to persuade General Auchinleck to attack the Germans at Gazala.
42. *An hour later, Ferrini and the Axum returned to find the destroyer still afloat, and sank it with another torpedo. Smith, p,187.
43. *Pack, p.182.
44. *Colville, p.283.

Chapter X

Tuesday
18 August 1942

Time	Wind (kn)	Sea	Notes		
8.00 am	22–27	rough	fog	sunrise	6.27 am
8.00 pm	0–1	almost calm		sunset	7.45 pm

Shortly after midnight, Gort, Scobie and Beckett arrived in Siggiewi to meet with the commanders of the counter-attack battalions. Awaiting them at the Church of Saint Nicholas ta Bari were Lieutenant Colonel Page from the Lancashire Fusiliers, Lieutenant Colonel Westropp from the King's Own, Lieutenant Colonel Newell from the 1st Battalion, King's Own Malta Regiment, and the designated coordinator of the counter-attack, the Irish Fusiliers' Lieutenant Colonel Allen. Also attending were Brigadier Smith from 1 Brigade, whose troops fought to keep the Germans out of Hal Far, Major S. Longworth, commander of the Maltese tanks which would be accompanying the attack, and Lieutenant Colonel French, whose Manchester Battalion would be the final reserve. The initial report from Allen stated he had a little over ten British companies from the Royal Irish, Lancashire Fusiliers and King's Own regiments, plus the entire 1st Battalion of the King's Own Malta Regiment, pulled out en masse from the north. The 8th Manchesters were concentrated in reserve at Ta'Qali airfield.

Scobie started the conference with a review of the current situation while the commanders studied the large map laid out for them. Italian and German paratroops were dug-in from the area south of Laferla Hill to Zurrieq, with many Italians continuing to land within the protected area. The landings had included some armour – Semovente assault guns – in the Ghar Lapsi area. On the beachhead's southern flank, German Fallschirmjäger troops continued to push and probe at the defences in place near Hal Far airfield. Fort Benghaisa was occupied by Germans, but pinned in place by a Devonshire platoon. Activity along the north-east coast had quietened, but was still being patrolled by the Dorsets' A and C companies.

Next to talk was Scobie's artillery commander, General Beckett. The initial plans had earmarked seven of the island's ten artillery batteries to launch the attack with a massive half-hour barrage aimed at the Italian line south-west of Siggiewi. The remaining artillery would strike the beachhead's right flank near Hal Far to both pin the Germans there and disrupt any attempt to reinforce the assault sector.

But Beckett had bad news for the conference, based on the reports just received from his quartermaster in charge of resupplying the artillery batteries that night. Basically, their supply of artillery shells was dwindling; he noted that his twenty-eight guns, firing five rounds per minute – a standard barrage rate – would burn through over 4,000 rounds in half an hour. That

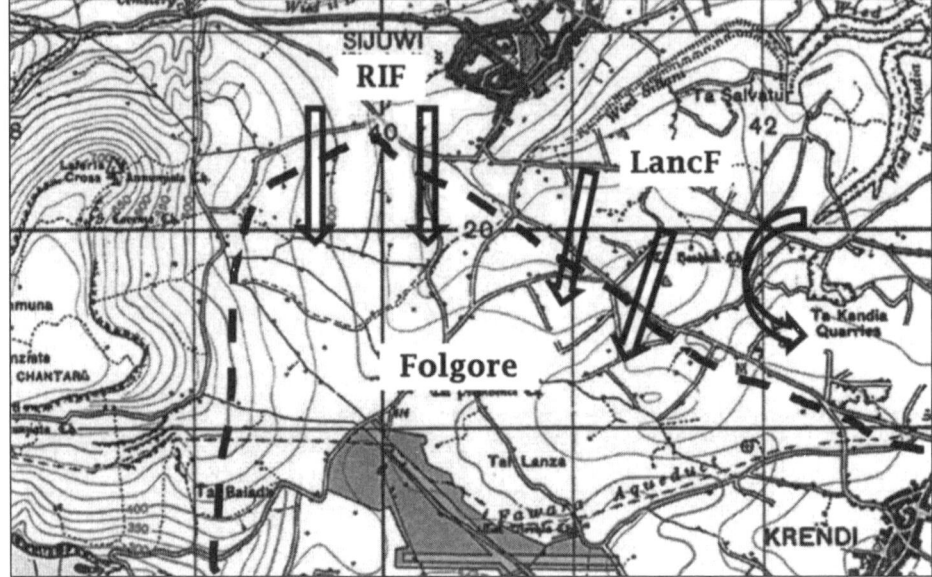

Figure X-1: *British Counter-attack Plans.*

would, he noted, leave virtually nothing to support defensive measures if the counter-attack failed.[1] He stated he could support a fifteen-minute barrage at most, unless ordered to expend it all, pointedly looking at Gort, who quickly agreed to the shorter barrage. In addition, he noted that delays were beginning to creep in as night movement of artillery ammunition from the ammunition storage caves in the Victoria Lines, to the scattered battery sites, ran behind schedule, so the proposed kick-off of the attack – 3.30 am – would be pushed back.

The plan itself was simple (Figure X-1). The two primary assault battalions – the Irish and Lancashire Fusiliers – would punch through a 1,000-yard portion of the defensive border to open a gap to the high ground over the beachhead, with the King's Own providing pressure from the high ground. The reserve battalion of the King's Own Malta Regiment would push through the gap, sweep east across the Qrendi airfield and, hopefully, shatter the Italians.

Originally, Longsworth's tanks were to accompany both Fusilier battalions, with a combined troop of his four remaining Cruisers on the better roads with the Lancashire battalion and his two heavier Matilda tanks going with the Irish. However, the tank commander noted the roadless terrain in front of the Irish would make tank movement slow and risky due to the many rock walls that covered the intended battle area – one of his Matildas had already been lost, breaking a track on rocky soil. He recommended strongly that all his tanks move with the Lancashire Fusiliers on the roads in their sector, with the Matildas switching west once the Lancashires had pushed through the initial Italian defensive line. Gort approved the change, but also ordered some mobile anti-tank weaponry be given to the Irish in place of the tanks. That mobile weaponry consisted of two Breda 47mm anti-tank guns captured earlier in the war from the Italians in North Africa.

---

1. *Beckett, p.86.

The Lancashires' commander, Lieutenant Colonel Page, interjected that as planned, the assault would create a bulge that would be vulnerable to an Axis attack from the east; he proposed having his D Company dig in facing that direction to defend that flank once they were in the area south of the Ta Kandia Quarry. Scobie and Allen approved the change.

Finally, on the right flank, the Buffs and Durham Light Infantry would continue to clear the Dingli Plateau of the Germans and put pressure on the beachhead's western flank. To the east, 1 Brigade would continue to act as an anvil, holding the Germans at bay and creating a block for any Italians trying to escape the attack.

Both Gort and Scobie knew they were probably asking too much of troops who had been fighting for three days after years of near-starvation and little training. Their primary hope was that the Italians would display the same fragility they had in North Africa. But they also knew the alternative was to continually defend and fall back, until there was only Valletta to fall back into. Gort ended the conference with a quiet note of encouragement, expressing his confidence in their ability to break through and succeed in their mission.[2]

Unknown to them, other conferences were being held. Generaloberst Alfred Jodl, chief of the Operations Staff of the OKW, arrived from the Eastern Front, ostensibly to get a status on the *C3* operation from Kesselring. In reality, he was there to pass along Hitler's anger that the operation had not concluded. The Führer, from his primary headquarters in Vinnitza in the Ukraine (code-name Werewolf), was involved in personally commanding his eastern armies as they drove in multiple directions – due east across the Don River toward Stalingrad and the Volga River, and south-east from Rostov into the Caucasus toward Maikop and Baku, where Soviet oil fields tantalized him. Jodl reported to his Italian commanders that Hitler was livid about the slow pace of the Malta invasion, with his diatribes switching between demands for resolution and vitriolic complaints about the Italians. He wanted his paratroops withdrawn immediately – he wanted those elite troops in the East.

After Jodl left, Kesselring continued talking to Student. Both knew that a precipitous withdrawal of German troops from Malta would severely impact Italian resolve. Kesselring recalled:

> 'The lecture by Jodl worried Student, a man who always appeared calm, but was quite passionate about his men and their task. I told him not to worry so much; I had been trying to remove this hornet's nest of an island since my arrival in Italy the previous September. I wasn't about to give up.'[3]

But the point was moot as they had no way of getting their troops off the island. The only airfield they held was the incomplete one at Qrendi, which the Italian Loreto Battalion was trying to make useable for supply flights, not troop withdrawals. The field remained under artillery threat, as the main drive across the island would begin only after the Italian Friuli and Livorno divisions were ashore and organized. The fact that only the Friuli was currently ashore was a key problem, and until the Italian infantry were ready, the paratroops were pinned in place protecting the beachhead area.

---

2. *Colville, p.291.
3. *Kesselring, Memoirs, p.112. REALITY: Kesselring in November 1941 referred to his primary objective being to 'safeguard our supply lines by smoking out that hornet's nest [Malta]', p.105.

From the island they had a report that the Germans' 1st Regiment was retreating under pressure back into the beachhead, down a tortuous path that had been flagged for a follow-on Italian division. Elsewhere the situation remained static, with Generale Carboni, the Friuli commander, reporting his troops were still coming ashore and working on landing the tons of supplies they had brought with them. His division, he stated flatly, was not combat-ready.

Ramcke, the German onsite commander, reported he felt the defences at Hal Far weakening, and could be broken with a strong attack. The plan called for Hal Far to be taken by the Friuli Division once it was combat-ready, but Student, knowing he needed that airfield to withdraw his paratroops if ordered, asked Ramcke if his brigade could take the field. Ramcke told him he could if a massed Luftwaffe strike on the field prepared the way. Further discussion between the two was interrupted by a sudden roar from the east.

At 4.35 am, five batteries of the 12th Royal Artillery Regiment's 25-pdrs and two batteries of the 26th Defence Regiment's 6in howitzers opened fire on a 2-mile stretch south of Siggiewi, occupied at that moment by dug-in Folgore paratroopers.

The targeted area lay some 500 yards south of the Fusiliers' line of departure. The Folgore paratroopers had dug in behind existing stone walls, with heavy Breda 38 machine guns and 47/32mm anti-tank guns covering the main roads. Their part of the *C3* plan was simply to isolate the beachhead, allowing no British counter-attack, especially armour, known to be on the island, to get to the landing areas. Following standard defensive deployment, the battalions had two companies on the front line and one some 200 yards behind, supported by Guastatori assault engineers and battalion mortars, available for quick counter-attacks. Each company, in turn, had two platoons on the front line, with another close behind for quick response. Malta's rock walls, separating fields, provided most of the cover for the defenders.

Although the Italians had been under intermittent artillery fire since landing on Malta, the barrage was anything but intermittent. The paratroops were engulfed in a whirlwind of flying steel shards, rock fragments, concussive sound, smoke, dust and, most of all, percussive force. Worst of all, they had nothing to respond with; all of their artillery was still being unloaded and the Luftwaffe hadn't flown night missions once friendly troops landed on the island. The Folgore could only huddle in their scraped-out fighting positions and bear it.

Fifteen minutes after the barrage started, it lifted – sending shells deeper into the Axis beachhead area, but at a much-reduced rate of fire. In its place came the British troops.

On the attack's left flank, the Lancashire Fusiliers' A and C companies, coordinated by the battalion's second-in-command, Major Garnet Hicks, had begun moving forward during the artillery barrage, pausing when they reached the road to Zurrieq. The two companies were astride the road south where Longworth's Cruiser tanks rumbled. The tanks moved slowly to allow the infantry, hampered by having to clamber over rock walls, to keep pace. The obstacles delayed the advance, with the exertion of climbing the walls depleting the physical reserves of the advancing soldiers. B Company, with Lieutenant Colonel Page, followed the lead companies, while Captain E. Walker's D Company moved diagonally toward the quarries to guard the Fusiliers' left flank. Walker established the centre of his defences around Ta Banblask Church.

The Folgore's IV Battalion had been in place when the attack started, with their 10th and 12th companies in line. Both the battalion commander, Maggiore Vincenzo Padella, and 10th Company commander Capitiano Simoni were killed almost immediately, nearly decapitating the battalion. Both companies took heavy casualties, and when the artillery barrage lifted most of the troopers moved back to their second line, leaving the dead and wounded in place with destroyed equipment.

As the Fusiliers approached the initial Italian line of resistance, they came under fire from a single light machine gun. A wounded Folgore paratrooper, Sergente Maggiore Mario Giaretto, caught one platoon in the open field with several bursts, causing the British to go to ground and follow-on troops to take cover behind stone walls to return fire. Giaretto held up the advance by almost 15 minutes, until a 2-pdr shell from a Cruiser tank struck the wall directly in front of him, killing him instantly.[4]

Giaretto's defence and the slow progress of the infantry had a fatal impact on the entire attack. Even as A and C company troops passed through the main Italian line, they came under fire from 81mm mortars and rifles from the second Italian line. The IV Battalion's 11th Company had moved up to bolster the barrage survivors. Page had his own battalion mortars move forward to blanket the new Italian defenders with smoke and allow his troops to move under cover across the open fields between walls. Capitano Constantino Ruspoli, the 11th Company's commander, led a spirited counter-attack on C Company's flank which pushed the British back momentarily, until Captain D. Lister, C Company's commander, stopped the retreat and, with the help of the tanks, repulsed the Italians, killing Ruspoli in the action.

According to the Folgore battle diary:

> 'The advanced position held by Captain Simoni's 10th Company was first subjected to a heavy pounding by artillery, then assaulted. With the death of their commander, the paratroops fell back. But Capitan Ruspoli rallied them and led an aggressive counter-attack. The enemy was thrown off by the unexpected counter-attack, which stopped them.'[5]

With resistance increasing, Page sought to break the apparent stalemate by having the four British Cruiser tanks surge forward. Almost immediately one threw a track trying to burst through a stone wall. When the second was destroyed by a flamethrower – Italian Guastatori assault engineers had arrived to bolster the defence – Page had to order the tanks to remain back covered by his infantry. As the sky continued to lighten, the Fusiliers had gained only 200 yards. After the battle, Page would lament that 'it had taken too long for his starved troops to take advantage of the artillery barrage's disruption – too many walls to cross between line of departure and the Italian defensive position'.[6]

On the Lancashires' right, the Royal Irish Fusiliers moved forward, following the initial barrage in much the same manner as their Lancashire brethren. A and B Company led the way, with Major Barrington's C Company following. Having attacked before, the Irish were familiar with the stone walls that obstructed their advance and were able to move somewhat quicker to reach the Italian main line, past wrecked anti-tank guns, and then push further south.

C Company's Lieutenant Johnson recalled:

> 'My platoon was tasked with following Captain Mason's B Company, moving two Italian anti-tank guns forward. The bloody guns weighed nearly 40 stone [560lb] and it was exhausting trying to manhandle the things over the walls. We finally got permission to abandon one just to keep moving with the other,

---

4. *Giaretto was awarded the Medaglia d'oro al Valore Militare for his 'undaunted courage'. REALITY: Giaretto was actually killed under similar circumstances on the Deir Alinda Ridge in North Africa.
5. *Folgore Battle Diary, Malta, p.29.
6. *Hallam, p.68.

trading off squads, one to drag the gun and ammunition, another to break down a wall ahead, and the other to rest.'[7]

Ahead of the Irish, the Italians of 4th and 6th Company/II Battalion fell back, but began regrouping at their secondary line 250 yards in the rear, where 6th Company's Capitano Marenco rallied the barrage's survivors. Battalion commander Maggiore Zanninovich brought more troops forward and got their 81mm mortars into action, which slowed, then stopped, the Irish advance. The stalemate began to go in the Italians' favour as the Irish second-in-command, Major W. Shepard, and B Company commander Captain C. Mason were both wounded by mortar fire. Lieutenant Johnson remembered:

> 'Wood's 15 Platoon had to go forward to help with casualties. Mortar fire was bad. It was hard to keep the lads focused on moving forward when the casualties were coming backwards.'[8]

The stalemate was broken when two Matilda tanks arrived to begin firing on the Italian flank. The tanks could only fire solid shot, but their machine guns forced the Italians to pull further back, allowing the Irish to once again advance. As before, though, the Italians simply regrouped behind another stone wall, and their mortar fire continued to hamper the attack.

The Italian withdrawal in front of the Irish led to a similar pulling back by the Italian IV Battalion in front of the Lancashire Fusiliers, allowing them to move forward again; but as they did, with dawn breaking, their flank came under pressure from the east, just as Lieutenant Colonel Page had predicted.

The British attack initially created chaos in the Axis beachhead. Casualties from the barrage and attack streamed back toward Qrendi airfield, where they quickly swamped the Axis medical teams. Into the mix, Friuli infantry scrambled to break out weapons and ammunition from the supplies they had manhandled up from the shore, and to sort themselves out into a semblance of combat readiness.

The Axis commanders quickly huddled in Qrendi village. Ramcke had arrived after informing Student of the attack. Friuli commander Generale di Divisione Carboni, always a sceptic about the possibility of *C3*'s success, was close to declaring the invasion a failure, with the Folgore's Frattini attempting to mollify him. Ramcke's appearance put an end to that discussion, and under the German's forceful personality, the three worked out a response. Carboni would concentrate his troops at Qrendi to be ready to counter any British breakthrough, while the Folgore 2 Brigade would attack toward the flank of the British attack. German paratroops would provide a counter-attack force from Heilmann's 3rd Regiment to help the Italians, but also continue to prepare for an assault on Hal Far.

The commander of the Folgore 2 Brigade, Colonello Tandillo, gathered his VII Battalion under Tenente Colonello Carlo Ruspoli to advance east against the defensive line that Walker's D Company of the Lancashire Fusiliers had established. Major Kratzert, Heilmann's III Battalion commander, sent his 10th Company of Fallschirmjägers to bolster the Italians.

The initial advance by Capitano Carlo Mautino's 19th Company enabled Kratzert to spot the British machine-gun positions anchoring the Lancashire defensive line in the early light.

---

7. *Johnson, p.167.
8. *Ibid., p.168.

He focused his mortars on those positions, knocking each out. When they went silent, he ordered a switch to smoke shells, then personally led his company forward. Fusilier Lieutenant Colonel Page recalled: 'Our flank was counter-attacked heavily and led to hand-to-hand combat with heavy casualties on both sides. We began running out of ammunition and started to pull back.'[9] Although Kratzert was wounded during the assault's exchange of hand grenades, the Germans broke through, forcing the Fusiliers back.[10] Ruspoli's battalion began to exploit the gap.

With his flank now crumbling, Page's Fusiliers had to stop their forward progress. Furthermore, the 1st Battalion of the King's Own Malta Regiment, expected to exploit the Fusilier breakthrough, was forced to move to support the flank defence.

On the attack's right, the Irish continued to move forward but ran into major trouble as Italian armour made its appearance, coming up from the beachhead area. Three M41 assault guns arrived to lead an Italian counter-attack, forcing the British troops back. Lieutenant Johnson recalled:

> 'We met several troops running back, yelling about tanks. We pushed our gun into a gap in a wall, and loaded it. In the pre-dawn light, we could just make out a big ugly vehicle, a few hundred yards away. It turned toward our tanks and we got off a shot at it. The first missed, but the second struck it but appeared to do nothing, except turn it toward us. The lads got off another shot. Suddenly, there were men bailing out as smoke rose from it. The sight cheered us as Bren fire cut them down. But a second armoured vehicle appeared around the first and a big explosion threw our gun backwards and stunned me senseless for a moment.'[11]

An exchange of fire between the remaining Semoventes and the Matildas led to another of the Italian assault guns brewing up. Two more arrived, however, and kept the British tanks under fire with their 75mm guns. The heavy 3in frontal armour of the Matildas shrugged off the hits, and another Semovente began to smoke. Its companions finally damaged the lead Matilda's main gun and it began to pull back. Another Italian hit damaged its track and the crew bailed out.

The loss of the anti-tank gun forced the Fusiliers to fall back. The remaining Matilda, bereft of infantry support, had to slowly withdraw. Backing down the road was not an option because of the infantry withdrawal, but as it tried going cross-country it broke a track and its crew abandoned the vehicle.

As the Irish withdrew, the Italians surged forward on the Fusiliers' right flank, led by the San Marco Marines of Grado Battalion. But fire into the Marines' flank from the King's Own battalion on the Laferla Cross ridge soon slowed their attack.

With the sun now fully up, the British attack had come to a stop. Some ground had been taken, but the breakthrough Gort had counted on had failed to materialize. The Folgore had held their ground tenaciously, despite the casualties from the initial barrage. Troop exhaustion and lack of continued artillery support had halted the attack.

By mid-morning, the initial crisis for the Axis forces seemed to have passed. The beachhead perimeter had shrunk by about 600 yards, but each assault by the British became weaker as

---

9. *Hallam, p.75.
10. *Kurowski, p.129.
11. *Johnson, p.171.

their conditioning gave out in the face of the heavy exertion and the rising heat of the day. The only real gain came on the Dingli Plateau, where the Buffs and Durham Light Infantry soldiers finally broke the last rearguards left by the Fallschirmjägers' 1st Regiment, overrunning the machine guns and empty recoilless rifles left by the withdrawing Germans.

In Valletta, Gort and Scobie assessed the results of the counter-attack and the future they now faced due to its failure to break through. It was not an optimistic assessment. Troop exhaustion was increasing as the enemy's presence was growing. General Beckett informed them they did not have the artillery reserves available for another assault – the gunners needed what they had to continue sporadic pressure on the beachhead to slow the Italians' arrival and to support any location under pressure. Both the Lancashire and Irish Fusiliers were a spent force, ordered to pull back into reserve at Ta'Qali while the fresh Manchester battalion and the 1st Battalion KOMR took their place in the front defensive line. Both Fusilier battalions had suffered 150 casualties, dead and wounded. The Church of Saint Nicholas was crowded with the wounded, with medical supplies running appallingly short. With outside support now out of the question, Gort and his command staff knew it was only a matter of time before the end came. The Lieutenant Governor, Sir Edward St John Jackson, was the first to mention out loud the suggestion of surrender.

As the disruption caused by the British attack subsided, Axis operations continued. Tur began landing the Livorno Division as Generale Carboni organized his Friuli troops into battalion battle groups. General Ramcke radioed Sicily that his assault toward Hal Far would commence following his requested attack by Luftwaffe bombers. His chosen attack force, Major von der Heydte's II Battalion, had been busy patrolling and probing toward the British defensive positions, laying out red recognition panels to identify friendly positions for the airmen.

Ahead of them, most of the 2nd Battalion of the Devonshires lay in wait. Major Young's Hal Far defensive force now concentrated four companies from the Devons, plus Captain G.W. Hamilton's Dorsetshire B Company and the Maltese from A Company, 3rd KOMR. Supporting them were two sections from the Cheshires' machine-gun battalion and the Devons' regimental mortars.

While von der Heydte marshalled his men to await the Luftwaffe attack, another consultation took place off Malta's shore. Ammiraglio Tur heard from his Gozo counterpart, Ammiraglio di Divisione Luigi Biancheri, that affairs on the smaller island were under control. Biancheri suggested that he move his reserve – most of the Superga Division's 92nd Regiment – to their secondary invasion site: Malta's coast east of Salina Bay. Tur concurred, having heard the British attack that morning had petered out. Biancheri led the five small ships south in his flagship, the torpedo boat *Orione*.

As the small convoy began crossing the mouth of Mellieha Bay, it came under unexpected fire. Pre-invasion aerial reconnaissance had noted the fortification on Mellieha ridge, but had only identified it as a 'centre of fire with a dome' (*centro di fuoco con cupola*). Unknown to them, Fort Campbell was armed with two 6in naval guns. Those guns quickly ranged the Italian vessels, straddling one small ship, the *Principessa Mafalda*, before a shell struck home. Troops from the 92nd's 3rd Battalion abandoned the boat, struggling to reach other vessels. The *Orione*'s three 4in guns began firing at the fort, while its commander, Tenente di Vascello Carlo Bambilla, manoeuvred his ship to protect the hundreds of men going into the water.

The Maltese gunners finally acknowledged the Italian torpedo boat's fire, switching their aim to it. As the *Orione* manoeuvred to avoid the fire, Biancheri ordered the remaining boats to reverse course and head back to Gozo. His own ship continued to fire as other escorts tried to rescue as many men as they could from the sinking *Principessa Mafalda*. He finally called off the attempt after his ship was hit by a 6in shell, destroying one of its turrets and starting a fire. Some of the remaining Superga soldiers actually made it to the shore they were planning on reaching, but soaked, without weapons and under the guns of the converging KOMR's 2nd Battalion troops.

Further south, the Luftwaffe launched its pre-assault bombardment of the Hal Far defences. Stukas swarmed through the anti-aircraft fire to pound the area, while trios of Ju88s flew low to do the same. Me109s followed to strafe the area. The four remaining Bofors batteries of the 74th Light Anti-aircraft Regiment did their best to mitigate the attack, knocking three Stukas out of the sky and sending two Ju88s off trailing smoke. Their fire drew the attention of the German fighters, which strafed the batteries and caused casualties. By the time the Luftwaffe withdrew an hour after the initial bombs dropped, the area was clouded with smoke and dust and its defenders severely disrupted.

As the aircraft left, von der Heydte's Fallschirmjägers opened up on the defenders with 81mm high explosive mortar rounds and 50mm smoke bombs. Feinting on the left, the Germans focused their main assault on the right, nearer the coast. Their 2nd and 3rd companies moved forward under the covering fire (Figure X-2). A feldwebel recalled:

> 'We advanced by leaps and bounds, with our MG34s hammering the enemy ahead of us. Return fire shot past our heads. Rapid bursts of fire, joined by individual rounds from snipers, whizzed all around us. Lungs were bursting, our hearts hammering wildly in our chests. Suddenly, enemy fire slackened as we overran the first position.'[12]

The attack struck the seam between the Devons' B Company and A Company of the 3rd KOMR, forcing a wedge between the units. B Company's Major Benbow led a counter-attack to retake the position and close the gap, but it was repulsed by German machine-gun fire, wounding him in the process. In the shower of hand grenades from both sides, 2nd Company commander Oberleutnant Lauk was killed, but Hauptmann Straehler-Pohl, 3rd Company's commander, rallied the paratroops and they continued their drive. The survivors of the two defending companies fell back and the Germans moved to expand the gap.

The Devons' Major Young, in charge of the airfield's defence, made the hard decision to pull all the defenders back inside the wire that surrounded the base, covering the move with rapid fire from his regiment's 81mm mortars. The Devons and Maltese fell back, stone wall by stone wall. The Germans followed, continuing to cover their move with smoke, pausing only to bring more high explosive fire down on the withdrawing defenders and consolidate their hold on the abandoned positions. The Dorsets' commander, Lieutenant Colonel Grimley, moved his A Company into the gap between Kirkop and Hal Far to forestall any Axis move directly against Birzebbugia – such a move would trap the Hal Far defenders.

Further west, as the Manchester battalion moved into the front line, replacing the Irish Fusiliers, the Folgore they faced surged forward, supported by the four remaining Semovente M41s. High explosive fire from the assault guns' 75mms, along with a barrage of mortar fire, caught French's troops before they could adjust to their new positions. They retreated to the positions held by the Irish before the morning's counter-attack. The move back exposed the flank of the 1st Battalion, KOMR, and Lieutenant Colonel Newell also pulled his troops back. All the ground gained by the Fusiliers had been lost again. The defenders in front of Siggiewi also came under heavy pressure from the Italian surge. Maggiore Zanninovich concentrated his

---

12. *Kurowski, p.133. REALITY: based on the experience of Feldwebel Graindl on Crete assaulting Fortress Hill.

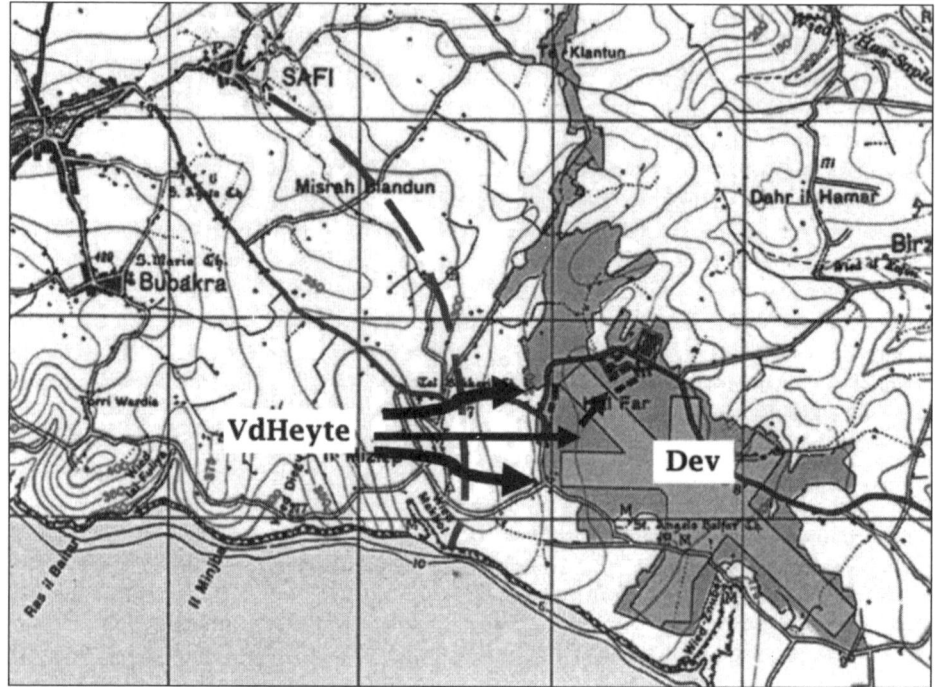

Figure X-2: *Von der Heydte's assault on Hal Far Airfield.*

remaining 1 Brigade of the Folgore, along with San Marco Marines, for the push, leaving his left flank facing the Dingli Plateau heights in the hands of the depleted German 1st Regiment.

The twin pressure points, Siggiewi and Hal Far, caused more consternation in Valletta, which was added to as reports came in from Fort Campbell. Artillery support was limited – resupply of ammunition depleted by the morning's barrage from the magazines under the Victoria Lines was slowed by roaming Luftwaffe fighters. The only bright spot in Gort and Scobie's opinion was the evacuation of the Dingli Plateau by the Germans. That would allow them to move two battalions – the Buffs and DLI – down toward Rabat to strengthen the island's centre, leaving the King's Own in place to guard against any flanking move out of the beachhead. It would take some time to get the two exhausted battalions down, with most movement being done at night to avoid Luftwaffe attention. With the naval action off Mellieha Bay, Gort decided to concentrate the DLI and the Irish Fusiliers near Gargur to be able to react if the aborted landing on the northern shore was repeated.

As those orders went out, Gort sent a signal back to Britain:

> 'Counter-attack failed, enemy continuing to land. Defensive lines under pressure, ammunition stores severely depleted. Issue in doubt. If no relief received soon, the result is inevitable.'[13]

---

13. *Gort telegram, HE/829 18 August 1942.

The Admiralty, upon receiving Gort's signal, sent it on to Middle East Headquarters in Cairo, marked 'Urgent', for Churchill, who had returned the previous day from Moscow.[14] Churchill reacted quickly, demanding action; his tirade, delivered personally to Harwood and by signal to Pound, was harsh:

> 'That we could not forestall the invasion of Malta is a most serious and disastrous failure in responsibility. The negativism and undue yielding to difficulties and a woeful lack of appreciation for the island's importance is contributing to a potential disaster far worse than the loss of Tobruk. If we cannot get through to Malta, the doom of the fortress cannot be long deferred.'[15]

Harwood complained bitterly that the Prime Minister was ignoring the efforts made by Vian in his attempt to get to the island and the heavy weight of broadsides and ships that had blocked his way. He gave Churchill copies of Vian's signals, adding that Vian's squadron was under heavy air attack on its return to Alexandria. The loss of a cruiser and destroyer in the attacks, plus damage to three other ships was, in Harwood's words, 'proof of their effort as well as an indictment of their unrealistic orders'.[16]

From London, Admiral Pound, involved in the upcoming large raid at Dieppe[17] scheduled for the following day, also complained about the diatribe, citing the loss of two aircraft carriers, a cruiser and destroyer in the western attempt to aid Malta. His signal to Churchill came as close to a rebuke of the Prime Minister as anyone recalled the First Sea Lord making: 'We have done our best. I would sincerely hope there will be no lasting criticism of our attempt to reach the island given the losses we have suffered.'[18]

Near Hal Far, the German advance had finally paused outside the wire defences around the airfield. Von der Heydte spent an hour consolidating his troops, with his lead companies having suffered over 100 casualties. British mortar fire continued to harass the paratroops as they reorganized.

Shortly after 1.00 pm, the tempo of high explosive and smoke shells increased on the Hal Far defences, heralding another push by the Germans. Blind rifle and machine-gun fire tried covering the wire, but despite casualties, several gaps were cut in it. Then the Devon defenders got a shock as flamethrowers lit up the terrain, probing for their positions. Italian Guastatori from the Folgore VIII Battalion's 22nd Company (Capitano Felice Laffredo) had joined von der Heydte's troops for this new push.

---

14. Churchill had been in Cairo since early August to deal with command issues in the Middle East that ultimately saw Lieutenant General Bernard Montgomery assume command of Eighth Army, replacing General Claude Auchinleck. He then travelled to Moscow to personally notify Stalin that there would be no Second Front (i.e. invasion of France by British and American forces) in 1942. Reid, pp.219–28.
15. *Roskill, Churchill and the Admirals, p.192. REALITY: Churchill used similar words in relation to the Admiralty's reluctance to invade the island of Pantelleria in 1941. Roskill, pp.167–72.
16. *The damaged cruiser HMS Birmingham and destroyer HMS Kelvin were sunk, while cruisers Dido and Arethusa, plus destroyer Zulu, were damaged. ADM 234/353: Battle summaries, Malta 1942, No. 18: Third Sirte, and Hore, p.175.
17. Operation Jubilee was a large raid on the German-held French port of Dieppe by over 6,000 Canadian and Allied troops, supported by tanks. The goal was to gain intelligence, destroy defences and show the Soviets a commitment to opening a second front.
18. *Gilbert, vol 4, The Worst of Times, 18 August 1942, p.1,102.

The terrifying gush of flame broke the defensive line, allowing the Germans to exploit the hole. Once again, the defenders on either side of the hole were forced back as their flanks were attacked. The Devons fell back to the buildings on the edge of the airfield, followed closely by Straehler-Pohl's paratroops. Savage close-order fighting in the buildings raged as Young's Devons were pushed out. Von der Heydte was trying to reinforce Straehler-Pohl's troops in the buildings with his 1st Company, when a strong counter-attack from his flank by the Dorsets' B Company forced them to ground. The attack, led by Lieutenant D. Wakely, the company's second-in-command, led two platoons against the Germans, who responded quickly to the threat with machine-gun fire.

The spirited attack began to falter in the face of the return fire. Wakely, leading from the front, was cut down, followed quickly by 11 Platoon's leader, Lieutenant D. Worral. Twelve Platoon commander Lieutenant W. Durden took charge, stopping the costly advance and having his Dorsets dig in to try and cover the approach to the airfield.

While von der Heydte was occupied with the assault on his left flank, Major Young was briefly able to break contact with the Germans in Hal Far's western buildings and pull the survivors back to those on the airfield's northern corner. The Germans were left holding four ruined buildings – two in flames – with more than eighty casualties from both sides.

Fighting all across the defensive line settled down as the afternoon wore on. Near Siggiewi, the Italians were content to re-establish their defences, while von der Heydte's Germans near Hal Far consolidated their hold on their portion of the airfield. Exhaustion and thirst in the hot August sun did much to suppress the fighting.

In Cairo, a fuming and frustrated Churchill commented: 'I feel like I'm fighting with my hands tied behind my back.'[19] Then he sent Gort the unwelcome news: 'No relief possible. Hold the Fortress as long as you can.'[20]

That night, Gort sat with his commanders to discuss their options. General Scobie led off the discussion, noting that his troops still held the perimeter around the beachhead as well as the centre of the island. But they had suffered some 3,000 dead and wounded in the four-day battle. Medical facilities were crowded and overwhelmed, especially with the addition of wounded Italian and German prisoners. There was minimal artillery support available. Malnutrition from their enforced starvation diet was taking its toll, but they were holding firm. He said his troops could make virtual fortresses of every village between the beachhead and Valletta if need be, making the Axis bleed for every one in costly urban combat.

Lieutenant Governor Jackson conceded that the urban strategy would delay the Axis, but pointed out the horrendous impact it would have on the island's civilian population, especially the closer the fighting got to Valletta. He reminded the group of the food situation: 'After the June convoys we set a Target Date – September – after which bread would be gone unless we were revictualled. Would fighting for two more weeks before full starvation gain us anything useful?'[21]

Gort summarised the discussion succinctly: they could hold out until their food ran out, but only by devastating the island and its inhabitants, whom they were trying to protect. 'It was,' he said later, 'the hardest – but also the easiest – decision I had made since the retreat in France. I told them to prepare for surrender.'[22]

---

19. *Reid, p.222. REALITY: Churchill made the comment following the loss of the island of Leros in November 1943.
20. *Rogers, Churchill's Last Defeat, p.223.
21. *Ibid., pp.225–30.
22. *Colville, Man of Valour, p.252.

Chapter XI

Battle
Aftermath – August 1942

As the sun rose on 19 August 1942, many in Valletta and the Three Cities were awakened by the sound of huge explosions from the harbour area. Smoke from the blasts and large fires floated in the slight breeze over the cities, as Royal Engineers troops continued the process of destroying critical equipment and secret files. Others travelled to Malta's forts to prepare their magazines and armament for destruction.

At a little after 6.00 am, Gort sent a final message to London and Cairo:

> 'Regret that without possibility of relief, defence of the island can only continue for a short time before food and ammunition are exhausted. Further resistance only delays inevitable and costs lives. Island armament, facilities and documents being destroyed. I am surrendering the island to avoid further bloodshed among troops and civilians.'[1]

He left Valletta in a Bren carrier, heading toward the village of Safi. From there, accompanied by Monsignor Edgar Salome, the parish priest of Mgarr and considered the most prominent Catholic pastor on the island, he approached the German lines sporting a large white flag. Half an hour later, General Ramcke and the Friuli's Generale Carboni walked out of Bubakra. After the military formalities had been completed, Gort asked for a ceasefire while 'terms of surrender' were discussed. He told Ramcke he was prepared to surrender the island fortress but wanted assurances that the troops would be well treated, and that food supplies would be brought to Malta for the civilian population. The German told the duo treatment would be in accordance with the Geneva Conventions, but he would need to confer with his own headquarters on the latter requirement. He agreed to a ceasefire until 10.00 am while the discussion took place. He then invited them to his temporary headquarters in Zurrieq while he conferred with higher authority.

News of the ceasefire and the possible surrender quickly spread. A wounded Lieutenant Johnson, being treated in Siggiewi, was depressed:

> 'Despite the setback the day before, we thought we were winning, but the word was no rescue, no supplies and no hope. We were pretty bitter.'[2]

---

1. *Colville, p.217.
2. *Johnson, p.180.

198   Operation C3: Hitler's Plan to Invade Malta 1942

At 10.30 am, Gort, in company with Ramcke, returned to Valletta to begin the process of standing down. There, he radioed to the island:

> 'Because no relief is possible and our supplies are running out, I have decided accept the inevitable and surrender the island to our enemies to avoid further needless casualties. No further resistance is to be attempted.'[3]

At 1 Brigade headquarters in Birzebbugia, Brigadier Smith radioed his commanders more bluntly:

> 'You are now all prisoners. The Governor has surrendered the island. Destroy your weapons and gather at your company command posts, where you will remain until collected by German or Italian troops.'[4]

At the embattled Hal Far airfield, Major Young left his defence post, with his batman carrying a white flag, and approached the buildings held by the Germans. Hauptmann Straehler-Pohl emerged and the two officers conferred to ensure that no further fighting would occur during the surrender. At Siggiewi, General Scobie and Generale Carboni drove between the two opposing lines to ensure the same. On all sides, but particularly in the front lines, soldiers felt the gamut of emotions: some the fears of their pending imprisonment status, others the exhilaration of winning, but all the relief at the end of the fighting and surviving.

Meanwhile, the German High Command issued the following announcement:

> 'The combined air and sea operation, led by our elite parachute troops, against the British island of Malta has been concluded. Enemy resistance has ended. The Central Mediterranean is now under our complete control.'[5]

The Italians, angered by the German announcement, which seemingly took full credit for the victory and made no mention of their involvement, issued their own declaration:

> 'The strongly fortified British base on our island of Malta has been reclaimed from under the heel of British domination with unequalled daring by our land and sea forces led by our fierce Folgore paratroops.'[6]

In England, the announcement was quieter:

> 'His Majesty regrets to announce the fall of the George Cross island fortress of Malta after a spirited and gallant defence against overwhelming Axis forces.'[7]

---

3. *Colville, p.219.
4. *Jary, p.117. REALITY: this was the announcement of surrender at Leros given to the Royal West Kents battalion. Peakman, p.196.
5. *Kurowski, p.136.
6. *Etruschi, Albion Defeated, p.205.
7. *Rogers, Churchill's Last Defeat, p.215.

On Malta, the announcement in Mabel Strickland's *Times of Malta* on 20 August was even briefer, but more acerbic:

> 'CAPITULATION! – Gort gives up.'

The initial bitterness on the island and hostility toward their new Italian masters was mollified somewhat three days later when two Italian ships arrived to deliver 10,000 tons of food.[8]

After his return to Sicily, General Ramcke reported to Student the losses accrued by the Fallschirmjäger during the invasion: 105 officers and 851 enlisted men killed, 111 officers and 1,801 enlisted men wounded in action. He noted that the 1st Regiment was the hardest hit, having dropped onto the unexpected concentration of British troops on the Dingli Plateau. He recommended the division be moved back to France for rebuilding before another assignment.[9]

In Italy, casualties to the Folgore's two regiments amounted to 390 killed and 780 wounded. Losses in the Friuli Division came to some 300, with most of those casualties lost at sea.[10]

On Malta, Gort reported 1,200 dead during the invasion, with the Durham Light Infantry, Royal Irish Fusiliers, Lancashire Fusiliers and Devonshire battalions taking the brunt of the casualties. Over 23,000 men went into captivity.[11]

The biggest casualty of the battle proved to be Winston Churchill. Upon his return to London, he faced his third vote of no confidence in Parliament, stemming not only from the loss of Malta but the disastrous raid at Dieppe.[12] This time the measure passed by 280–220, and Churchill was forced to resign as Prime Minister.

The Tories initially suggested Lord Halifax (Edward F.L. Wood), currently UK Ambassador to the United States, as Churchill's replacement, but the Labour Party members of the government – Clement Atlee and Arthur Greenwood – refused to work with him, citing his previous suggestions that Britain negotiate with Hitler as unacceptable. Halifax himself declined, as he had in 1940, citing his membership of the House of Lords rather than House of Commons. Ultimately, the choice fell on Anthony Eden, the Foreign Secretary and Tory Leader in the House of Commons. While a solid leader in the confines of meetings, Eden lacked Churchill's ability to generate confidence in the public.

Upon leaving office, Churchill said:

> 'Given the almost unbroken series of military defeats, galling links in a chain of misfortune and frustration to which no parallel could be found in our history, I cannot be surprised by this turn of events. I was like a bomber pilot, going out night after night, knowing one night I would not return. Losing Malta was one loss too much.'[13]

---

8. *Ibid., p.216.
9. *Ibid., p.218.
10. *Folgore war diary, Friuli war diary.
11. *Rogers, p.220.
12. On 19 August 1942, over 3,300 Canadians soldiers and nearly 250 British commandos were lost raiding the French seaport of Dieppe. The RAF lost over 100 aircraft and the Royal Navy a destroyer, more than thirty landing craft and over 550 dead.
13. *Reid, p.2,237. REALITY: this is an amalgam of various Churchill thoughts made in 1942. Reid, pp.192–97.

Chapter XII

Reality & Analysis

Everything written in this book up to the start of Operation *Theseus* is historical, as is much of the history until Rommel's capture of Tobruk. However, in reality, despite the agreement reached between Hitler and Mussolini to attack Malta following Rommel's taking of Tobruk, Operation *C3* was not initiated. Hitler had decided three weeks after the Klessheim meeting that *C3* would (or could) not be initiated in 1942. The Führer was convinced that the operation would be a failure, but he did not want to signal his opinion to the Italians, so his order to the *C3* planners was simply to 'only mentally prepare' the invasion. He justified breaking his word to the Italians by rationalizing that Mussolini was 'overvalued' due to the many Italian defeats and that they would accept the change since they could not invade the island without German help.[1] He ordered Student NOT to return to Rome on 20 May 1942.

German representatives in Italy protested the decision, noting that it was folly to make plans for African offensives solely on the 'hope' that Malta's neutralization would be enough.

When Rommel took Tobruk in a single day, Hitler initiated the Axis change in plans with a telegram to Mussolini which stated:

> 'Duce, at this time, when historic military events are in the offing, I would like to explain my thoughts as concisely as possible regarding a decision that may have decisive impact on the course of the war. Destiny, Duce, has given us an opening that will never again become available in the same theater of operations. The fastest and most totalitarian exploitation of this advantage is our best military opportunity at this time. Up to this moment I have always ordered our forces to pursue a defeated enemy in retreat for the longest possible time as our troop strength would allow. The British Eighth Army is virtually destroyed.
>
> 'At Tobruk, with its practically intact harbor and piers, you have, Duce, an auxiliary base that is all the more important in that the British themselves have built a railroad line all the way to Egypt. If we fail to pursue the remains of this British army now with the utmost effort of each soldier, we will follow the fate identical to that of the British when they lost their advantage very close to Tripoli because they diverted troops into Greece. Only this capital mistake of the British high command made our effort in reconquering Cirenaica [*sic*] a success.

---

1. Weichold, Chapter 5.

'If our forces do not march forward to the extreme limit, into the heart of Egypt, we will be faced with new, long range American bombers able to reach Italy. At the same time, British and American forces can link together from all sides. In a short time, the situation would turn against us. But the continued pursuit of the enemy will provoke its disintegration. This time, Egypt can, under certain conditions, be taken from England. The consequences of such an event will have repercussions all over the world. Our own offensive, helped by the occupation of Sevastapol, will determine the fall of the entire eastern structure of the British Empire.

'If I, Duce, can give you, in this historic moment which will not be repeated, my most heartfelt advice, it would be this: order the continuation of operations to seek the complete destruction of British forces to the very limits of what your high command and Marshal Rommel think is militarily possible with their existing troops. The goddess of war in battle comes to commanders only once, and he who fails to seize the opportunity at such a moment will never be given a second chance. The fact that the British, contrary to every rule of the art of war, decided to interrupt their advance on Tripoli and divert their units to another battlefield was enough to save us. Please Duce, accept this request only as the advice of a friend, who has considered for many years that his fate is tied to your own and is acting in consequence.'[2]

Mussolini took Hitler's advice, although with caveats. He noted, in particular, the difficult supply situation, Malta's continued resistance and the dire shortage of naval fuel oil. But *C3* was officially postponed to September and the rush for Suez was on.[3]

On 22 June, Rommel unleashed his forces eastward. Four days later, he struck the Eighth Army, now under General Auchinleck, at Mersa Matruh, forcing another retreat all the way to the El Alamein narrows, a 36-mile-wide stretch of desert between the coast and the impassible Qattara Depression. Axis forces had advanced another 300 miles in ten days and once again outpaced their supplies; the army was run into the ground – Rommel arrived at El Alamein with only 125 operational tanks (fifty-five German and seventy Italian).[4]

Despite his weakness, he attacked and initiated a three-week battle of attrition. Both sides lost heavily, but the British could make up their losses better (and faster) than could Rommel. His supply situation became critical. Allied bombing reduced Tobruk's ability to handle cargo, putting the strain back on getting supplies over the road from Tripoli and Benghazi to the front lines. After building up some strength throughout August, Rommel attacked at the end of the month (the Battle of Alam el Halfa) with 200 German tanks and 243 Italian tanks, and once again failed to break through.[5] The British had built up their forces tool, had a new commander in General Bernard Montgomery and knew in advance what Rommel's plans were through Ultra intercepts.

In mid-August, with the Regia Marina hampered by a lack of fuel oil, the British ran Operation *Pedestal* through to Malta. Despite heavy losses to air attacks – the aircraft carrier HMS *Eagle*,

---

2. Corvaja, pp.204–05.
3. Boog, p.709.
4. Greene & Massignani, Rommel's North Africa Campaign, pp.193–94.
5. Playfair, Vol III, p.383, footnote 1.

two cruisers and nine of fourteen merchant ships were sunk – 40,000 tons of supplies and a tanker load of fuel arrived on the island. Although rationing continued until December, and a brief but bitter air offensive was launched in October, the siege of Malta had been broken.

On 23 October 1942, the Eighth Army attacked Rommel at El Alamein with a superior force – a two-to-one advantage in tanks, guns and men – and after a hard-fought battle sent Rommel into retreat once more. British and American troops landed in Morocco and Algeria (Operation *Torch*) to the west on 8 November, and the race for Tunisia was on.

Ultimately, Tunisia was lost to the Axis in early 1943, helped in part by air units stationed on Malta. The island hosted the headquarters of the combined Allied forces as they prepared to take the war onto Italian soil for the first time with the July 1943 invasion of Sicily (Operation *Husky*). That September, the Italian fleet, surrendered by their government, sailed unopposed into Malta's harbours.

Why didn't the Axis invade Malta as planned?

In much the same way that Malta was saved by the stubbornness of one man – Winston Churchill – the Axis didn't invade the island because of the stubbornness (and differing priorities) of another man – Adolf Hitler.

As far back as early 1941, when his naval staff was suggesting a strong push for the Suez Canal to cut Britain off from easy access to its resources in the Far East, Hitler's focus was on his impending fight with the Soviet Union. He only became involved in the Mediterranean when Italian misfortunes threatened his southern flank, and more importantly, his Romanian oil sources. His choice to unleash his paratroops on Crete in May 1941 showed his priorities. Using them to attack Malta, which most of his staff recommended, would have helped the North African campaign's logistics; however, using them to attack Crete kept British bombers away from Romania's oil fields.[6]

Aside from his differing strategic priorities, Hitler also had little faith in his Italian allies. For one thing, he felt their plans were too grandiose to be coordinated effectively. But more to the point, he doubted their military capability to successfully invade. As noted previously, although he agreed with plans to invade Malta at the 30 April summit at Schloss Klessheim after Tobruk was captured, he pointedly raged at General Student three weeks later that:[7]

- Italian security was poor so no surprise was possible;
- their offensive capability was inadequate;
- the Regia Marina would run if the British Royal Navy intervened; and
- the sea lanes would still be threatened even if Malta fell.

Some of his commanders felt differently. Kesselring knew that as soon as the Luftwaffe was pulled out of Sicily to either Africa or the Eastern Front, Malta would recover, as it had previously. Student, despite concerns about the current planning process, agreed. But General Alfred Jodl, chief of the Army Operations Staff, agreed with his Führer and ultimately, Hitler got what he wanted.

---

6. Ansel, Walter, Hitler and the Middle Sea, p.197.
7. Boog, p.657.

Would the *C3* invasion have succeeded?

An analysis by the German Militarrgeschichliches Forschungsamt (Research Institute for Military History) posited that Malta could not have been taken in the summer of 1942.[8] Many senior Italian officers felt the same way; the Friuli's commander Generale di Divisione Giacomo Carboni, expressed his fears, stating he was 'convinced, technically convinced, that we are heading for an unheard-of disaster. Preparations have been childish, equipment is lacking and inadequate. The landing troops will never succeed in landing, or if they land, they are doomed to total destruction.'[9]

Nevertheless, when the conditions of the defenders are taken into account, an invasion would likely have succeeded. Air Vice Marshal Hugh Lloyd stated, just before he left as the island's air commander in July 1942, that 'after two days of stiff fighting on our siege rations, I doubt if anyone would have been able to walk a mile in half an hour, let alone fight'.[10]

What would have happened had Malta been successfully invaded in 1942?

If Malta had fallen in 1942, very little would have changed in the immediate course of the Second World War. Granted, this runs counter to normal thoughts on the subject, but there are three key reasons why this was so: the Soviet Union, the United States and logistics.

First: the Soviet Union. The Soviets were Hitler's primary focus and his biggest problem in 1942. His blitzkrieg assault in June 1941 had failed and the Soviets had counter-attacked the overextended and weakened German armies during the winter and pushed them back. Hitler's 1942 plans for the East were less grandiose than 1941, but nonetheless included a huge investment in men and materiel, not only to hold onto the territory he had taken, but to continue offensive operations and prepare for the next phase – the Caucasus oil fields. He had little else remaining to share with what he considered an Italian theatre.

When Mussolini requested help in early 1941 as his African legions were streaming westward out of Cyrenaica, Hitler gave him an armoured corps under Rommel to use as a mobile strike force. Rommel's initial orders were to defend offensively. Hitler and the Army staff expected Rommel to beat the British using 'surprise, skillful troop handling, well-coordinated, flexible leadership, good intelligence and superior weapons'.[11] He was not expected to win Italy's battle for them. Thus, even as Rommel arrived in Africa, Hitler's primary focus remained the Soviet Union.

Second: the United States. With the advent of the United States into the Second World War, the British had an ally that would simply not let them be defeated. The impact of the US had already been felt in the Mediterranean when the aircraft carrier USS *Wasp* helped deliver Spitfire fighters to beleaguered Malta in April and May 1942. Consider also the effect that the loss of Tobruk had on the United States. Prior to the fortress's fall, the United States had been adamant about not becoming too involved in the Mediterranean; the Joint Chiefs of Staff pressed for a quick invasion of France and assault on Germany. They felt the Mediterranean

---

8. Boog, Vol VI, p.720.
9. Ciano Diary, 20 June 1942, p.499.
10. Lloyd, Hugh, Briefed to Attack: Malta's Part in African Victory, p.199.
11. Ibid., p.718.

was simply a distraction and at best a diversion of resources. After Tobruk fell, US resistance to landings in North Africa – a plan Churchill and his chiefs were proposing – dwindled. In addition, the United States authorized the immediate transfer of 300 tanks and 100 self-propelled guns to the British in Egypt.[12]

With the United States involved, Germany now faced two nations whose sole focus was the Mediterranean, even if torn between multiple fronts.

The final reason for the likelihood of the loss of Malta not being decisive was logistics. If Malta had fallen, the Axis convoy route from Italy to Tripoli would have been secure for the moment. However, Rommel was still a thousand miles away from Tripoli. He needed a supply base closer to the front lines. Tobruk helped, but it was within bombing distance of the British Desert Air Force as well as the arriving bombers of the American Army Air Corps. Thus, its cargo capacity was at risk. Benghazi was too small, leaving Tripoli as the supply base. All supplies had to be transported by truck from there to wherever Rommel stood. And he didn't have enough trucks. At one point Rommel demanded 8,000 more trucks, heedless of the fact that all four panzer corps in the Soviet Union had only 14,000 for themselves.[13]

While more supplies would make it to Tripoli if Malta had been taken, that didn't help get them to where it would help the Axis armies.

What would the impact of Malta's loss have been in 1942? The primary effect would have been on the Allies themselves, as the Axis reinforcement route from Europe to Tunisia would have been easier until Allied airpower moved closer from east and west. That could have made the battle for Tunisia harder on the Allies, but no less certain. But after Tunisia had been taken, the route to Sicily and Italy lay through Malta. Would the Allies have attacked Malta to neutralize Axis air power the same way the Axis had tried? Strategically, it would have been necessary; politically, to have bombed an island that had held out so long under another bombardment would have been a difficult choice to make. It is conceivable that the Allies would have not made that choice. Instead, they could have attacked Sardinia and Corsica (the proposed Operation *Brimstone* May 1943), then on to southern France or Italy north of Rome. Or they could have acceded to American military demands that they go straight into France. Whatever the case, Allied plans would have been impacted by Malta's fall.

What would have happened if the Axis had attacked earlier?

There are a considerable number of options here. First, the Italians might have tried in 1940 as one of their opening moves after declaring war. An immediate attack would have caught the island with little defence and probably would have been successful. However, as noted previously, Mussolini declared war almost on the spur of the moment and no real plans for an invasion of Malta existed.

If the Germans had attacked Malta in 1941, as most of the Staff had wanted, the war might have changed for the better for the Axis.

Even before Germany became actively involved in the Mediterranean, several key Nazi leaders stressed the need to take Malta and remove the 'thorn in the flesh of Italian sea warfare'. Both Vizeadmiral Eberhard Weichold, Germany's naval liaison officer in Rome, and General

---

12. Boog, p.703.
13. van Creveld, Martin, Supplying War, p.193.

Franz Halder, Chief of Staff to the German Army's overall commander, General Walther Brauchitsch, separately made that recommendation in August and November 1940.[14]

After Mussolini's call for help in early 1941, the island received a much closer look. Both the Staff of the Landesverteidigung (L or Defence Section) of the OKW under General Walter Warlimont and the planning Staff of the Seekriegsleitung, the Naval Operations office, recommended taking the island. L Section's report in particular recommended Malta as the only real long-term solution to success in the Mediterranean. They pointed out that if Africa was lost to the Axis, Malta could be used to spearhead the invasions of Sicily and Europe itself; taking the island would give the Luftwaffe additional airfields to shut the British out of the central Mediterranean.[15]

The main dissenting voice was Reichsmarschall Hermann Göring, commander-in-chief of the Luftwaffe. When the time came to choose between Crete and Malta, his Luftwaffe planners felt that Malta's terrain and stone walls would not allow paratroops to paralyze key points on the island as they had at Fort Eben-Emael in Belgium and Rotterdam in Holland.[16] Hitler ultimately chose Crete, since its capture would protect his vital Romanian oil fields. He told Student and the other leaders: '*Malta hat spater noch zeit*' (There'll be time for Malta later).[17]

If Hitler's advisors (other than Göring) had won their case, the German Fallschirmjäger would have found an island only partially defended in May 1941, compared to its strength a year later. Specifically, there were three fewer battalions of infantry, eight fewer tanks and forty fewer light anti-aircraft guns. In addition, the island's garrison was still wedded to a rigid coastal defence scheme, developed by Major General Scobell early in the war when there were far fewer troops available; there was no reserve brigade. Reaction to an air or sea invasion would have been significantly slower in 1941 than in 1942. The only factor in the garrison's favour was that they had not been subjected to the starvation conditions that existed later on in the war.

---

14. Ansel, pp.18, 51.
15. Ibid., p.111.
16. General Kurt Student, the father of the German Fallschirmjäger, stressed the doctrine of handstreich (coup de main) with its elements of Uberraschung (surprise) and schlagartig (paralysis) for his troops. Ibid., p.195.
17. Ibid., p.199.

Bibliography

I. Archives

Maltese
Malta Defence Scheme – May 1942

British – Public Records Office, National Archives, Kew, United Kingdom
(Note: The British war diaries are a mixed bag of information. Some contain daily comments on air raids, etc. Some contain order of battle strength, officer lists etc; others don't.)

Second World War War Diaries
WO 169/7395 – Malta Tanks, Royal Tank Regiment
WO 169/7396 – 1 (Northern Infantry Brigade
WO 169/7397 – 2 (Southern) Infantry Brigade
WO 169/7398 – 3 (Central) Infantry Brigade
WO 169/7399 – 4 (Western) Infantry Brigade
WO 169/7420 – 1st Bn. King's Own Malta Regiment
WO 169/7421 - 2nd Bn. King's Own Malta Regiment
WO 169/7422 – 3rd Bn. King's Own Malta Regiment
WO 169/7424 – 4th Bn. The Buffs
WO 169/7425 – 1st Bn. Cheshire Regiment
WO 169/7426 – 2nd Bn. The Devonshire Regiment
WO 169/7427 – 1st Bn. The Dorsetshire Regiment
WO 169/7428 – 1st Bn. Durham Light Infantry
WO 169/7429 – 1st Bn. The Hampshire Regiment
WO 169/7430 – 2nd Bn. Royal Irish Fusiliers
WO 169/7431 – 2nd Bn. Queen's Own Royal West Kents
WO 169/7432 – 11th Bn. The Lancashire Fusiliers Regiment
WO 169/7433 – 8th Bn. The Manchester Regiment
WO 169/7434 – 8th Bn. King's Own Royal Regiment

Italian
Archivio dell'Ufficio Storico dello Stato Maggiore dell'Esercito (AUSSME), Via Damiata 14, 00192 Roma. http://www.esercito.difesa.it/root/Storico/uff_norme.asp
Archivio dell'Ufficio Storico della Marina Militare (AUSMM), Via Taormina 4, 00135 Roma. http://www.marina.difesa.it/storia/ufficiostorico/Ufficio001.asp

Archivio dell'Ufficio Storico dello Stato Maggiore dell'Aeronautica (AUSSMA), Viale dell'Università 4,00185 Roma. http://www.aeronautica.difesa.it/SitoAM/Default.asp?idsez=2748&idente=74

Biagini, Antonello and Frattolillo, Fernando (eds), *Diario Storico del Comando Supremo, Volume I (11.6.1940–31.8.1940); Volume II (1.9.1940–31.12.1940); Volume III (1.1.1941–30.4.1941); Volume IV (1.5.1941–31.8.1941); Volume V (1.9.1941–31.12.1941); Volume VI (1.1.1942–30.4.1942); Volume VII (1.5.1942–31.8.1942); Volume VIII (1.9.1942–31.12.1942); Volume IX (1.1.1943–30.4.1943)* (Ufficio Storico dello Stato Maggiore dell'Esercito, Roma, 1986–2002).

Biagini, Antonello, Frattolillo, Fernando and Saccarelli, Silvio (eds), *Verbali delle Riunioni Tenute dal Capo di SM Generale, Volume I (1939–40); Volume II (1941); Volume III (1942); Volume IV (1943)* (Ufficio Storico dello Stato Maggiore dell'Esercito, Roma, 1983–85).

Mattesini, Francesco and Cermelli, Mario (eds), *Le Direttive Tecnico-Operative di Superaereo, Volume I: Aprile 1940 – Dicembre 1941; Volume II: Gennaio 1942–Settembre 1943* (Ufficio Storico dello Stato Maggiore dell'Aeronautica, 1992).

Mattesini, Francesco (ed.), *Corrispondenza e Direttive Tecnico-Operative di Supermarina, Volume I, Tomo I: Maggio 1939 – Luglio 1940; Tomo II, Agosto 1940 – Dicembre 1940; Volume II, Tomo I: Gennaio 1941 – Giugno 1941; Tomo II: Giugno 1941 – Dicembre 1941* (Ufficio Storico della Marina Militare, (2000–01).

II. Memoirs

Alcidi, Edgar, *Fallschirmjager Brigade Ramcke in North Africa, 1942–1943* (Schiffer Publishing Ltd, Atglen, PA, 2009).

Badoglio, Pietro, *Italy in the Second World War: Memories and Documents* (Oxford University Press, London, 1948).

Barnham, Denis, *Malta Spitfire Pilot: A Personal Account of the Ten Weeks of War, April – June 1942* (Frontline Books, South Yorkshire, UK, 1956).

Bodriti, Sisto, *'I Grifi' della 6ª Compagnia del II Battaglione Paracadutisti* (privately published, undated).

Bonner, Robert A., *The Ardwick Boys went to Malta: A British Territorial Battalion during the Siege 1940–1943* (Fleur de Lys Publishing, Macclesfield, Cheshire, 1992).

Bucciante, Giuseppe, *I Generali della Dittatura* (Mondadori, Milano, 1987).

Buerling, George and Roberts, Leslie, *Malta Spitfire: Diary of an Ace Fighter Pilot* (Grub Street, London, 2011).

Carboni, Giacomo, *Memorie Segrete 1935–1948* (Parenti, 1955).

Cavallero, Ugo and Bucciante, Giuseppe (ed.), *Diario 1940–1943* (Ciarrapico, Roma, 1984).

Cavallero, Ugo and Cavallero, Carlo (ed.), *Comando Supremo* (Cappelli, Bologna, 1948).

Churchill, Winston, *The Second World War: The Hinge of Fate* (Houghton Mifflin Company, Boston, 1950).

Churchill, Winston, *The Second World War* (London, Cassel & Co. Ltd, 1959; Italian trans. by Arturo Barone *et al.*, *La Seconda Guerra Mondiale*, Rizzoli, Milano, 2000).

Ciano, Galeazzo, De Felice, Renzo (ed.), *Diario 1937–1943* (Rizzoli, Milano, 2000).

Douglas-Hamilton, James, *The Air Battle for Malta: The Diaries of a Spitfire Pilot* (Pen & Sword, London, UK, 1981).

Galea, Michael, *Malta: Diary of a War, 1940–1945* (Publishers Enterprises Group Ltd, San Gwann, Malta, 1992).
Gerard, Francis W., *Malta Magnificant* (Whittlesey House, New York, 1943).
Gibbs, Patrick, *Torpedo Leader on Malta* (Grubb Street, London, 1992).
Grech, Charles, *Raiders Passed: The Wartime recollections of a Maltese Youngster* (Midsea Books, Valletta, 2002).
Gregory-Smith, Frank, *Red Tobruk: Memoirs of a World War II Destroyer Captain* (Pen & Sword, South Yorkshire, UK, 2009).
Hughes, Jimmy Quentin, *Who Cares Who Wins: The Autobiography of a World War II Soldier* (Charico Press, Liverpool, UK, 1998).
Iachino, Angelo, *Le Due Sirti: Guerra ai Convogli in Mediterraneo* (Arnold Mondadori, Italy, 1953).
Iachino, Angelo, *Tramonto di una Grande Marina* (Arnoldo Mondadori, Milano, 1959).
Kesselring, Albrecht, *The Memoirs of Field Marshal Kesselring* (Presidio, Novato, 1989).
Lamb, Charles, *To War in a Stringbag* (Bantam Books, New York, 1980).
Lloyd, Air Marshal Sir Hugh, *Briefed to Attack: Malta's Part in African Victory,* (Hodder & Stoughton, London, 1949).
Lucas, Laddie, *Malta, the Thorn in Rommel's Side: Six Months that Turned the War* (Stanley Paul, London, 1992).
Mars, Alistair, *UNBROKEN: The Story of a Submarine* (Pen & Sword Military Classics, South Yorkshire, UK, 2006).
Mizzi, Laurence, *The People's War: Malta 1940/43* (Progress Press, Valletta, 1998).
Simpson, George, *Periscope View: A Memoir of the 10th Submarine Flotilla at Malta, 1941–1943* (Seaforth Publishing, London, 1972).
Simpson, Michael (ed.), *The Cunningham Papers: Selections from the private and official correspondence of Admiral of the Fleet Viscount Cunningham of Hyndhope, O.M., K.T., G.C.B.,D.S.O. and two bars, Volumes I (The Mediterranean Fleet, 1939–1942) and II (The triumph of Allied Sea Power, 1942–1946)* (Ashgate for the Navy Records Society, Aldershot, 1999).
Sired, Ronald, *Enemy Engaged: A Naval Rating with the Mediterranean Fleet, 1942–1944* (William Kimber, London, 1957).
Stead, Gordon W., *A Leaf upon the Sea: A Small Ship in the Mediterranean, 1941–1943* (University of British Columbia Press: Vancouver, 1988).
Tedder, Arthur W., *With Prejudice: The War Memoirs of Marshal of the Royal Air Force, Lord Tedder, G.C.B.* (Little, Brown & Company, Boston, 1966).
Tur, Vittorio, *Plancia Ammiraglio* (Edizioni Moderne, Roma, 1959–960, and Canesi, Roma, 1963).
Warlimont, Walter, *Inside Hitler's Headquarters 1939–45* (Presidio Press, Novato, 1964).
Weldon, H.E.C., *Drama in Malta: A Personal Flash-back* (The Naval and Military Press Ltd, East Sussex, UK).
Williams, Raymond, *The Defenders of Malta* (private publication, 1988).
Woodhall, Martin, *Soldier, Sailor & Airman, Too: The Fighting Life of Group Captain A.B. 'Woody' Woodhall* (Grubb Street Publishing Ltd, London, 2008).

III. General Histories

Allen, Bruce W., *The Great Siege of Malta: Epic Battle between the Ottoman Empire and the Knights of St. John* (ForeEdge, Lebanon, NH, 2015).
Ansel, Walter, *Hitler and the Middle Sea* (Duke University Press, Durham, NC, 1972).

Austin, Douglas, *Churchill and Malta: A Special Relationship*, (Spellmount, London, 2006).
Austin, Douglas, *Churchill and Malta's War, 1939–1943* (Amberley, London, 2011).
Austin, Douglas, *Malta and British Strategic Policy, 1925–1943* (Frank Cass: London, 2004).
Ballou, Martin, *The Story of Malta* (Houghton, Mifflin and Company, Boston, 1893).
Bennett, Ralph, *Ultra and Mediterranean Strategy* (Wm Morrow & Company: New York, 1989).
Blouet, Brian W., *The Story of Malta (Revised Edition)* (Progress Press Co. Ltd, Valletta, 2000).
Boffa, Charles A., *The 'Illustrious' Blitz: Malta in Wartime, 1940–1941* (Progress Press Co. Ltd, Valletta, 1995).
Boffa, Charles A, *The Second Great Siege: Malta 1940–1943* (Progress Press Co. Ltd, Valletta, 1992).
Berg, Warren G., *Historical Dictionary of Malta* (Scarecrow Press, Lanham, MD, 1995).
Boog, Horst, *et al.*, *Germany and the Second World War, Vol. III: The Mediterranean, South-East Europe, and North Africa 1939–1941; Vol. VI: The Global War* (Claredon Press, Oxford, 2001).
Bradford, Ernie, *Siege: Malta, 1940–1943* (Wm Morrow & Company: New York, 1986).
Castillo, Dennis, *The Maltese Cross: A Strategic History of Malta* (Praeger Security International, Westport, CT, 2006).
Cernuschi, Enrico, *Malta, 1940–1943: La Storia Inconfessabile* (Edibus Comunicazione, Vincenze, IT, 2016).
Corvaja, Santi, *Hitler & Mussolini: The Secret Meetings* (Enigma Books, New York, 2008; trans. edition of *Mussolini nella tana del lupo*).
De Belot, Raymond, *The Struggle for the Mediterranean, 1939–1945*, (Greenwood Press, New York, 1951).
Ehlers, Robert S., *The Mediterranean Air War: Airpower and Allied Victory in World War II* (University Press of Kansas, Lawrence, KS, 2015).
Elliott, Peter, *The Cross and the Ensign: A Naval History of Malta, 1798–1979* (USNI, Annapolis, MD, 1980).
Forty, George, *Battle for Malta* (Hersham, Ian Allam Publishing, 2003).
Gabriele, Mariano, *Operazione C3: Malta*, 2nd rev. ed. (Ufficio Storico della Marina Militare, Roma, 1990).
Gooch, John, *Mussolini and his Generals: The Armed Forces and Fascist Foreign Policy, 1922–1940* (Cambridge University Press, Cambridge, UK, 2007).
Goodwin, Stephan, *Malta: Mediterranean Bridge* (Bergin & Garvey, Westport, CT, 2002).
Gregory, Desmond, *Malta, Britain, and the European Powers, 1793–1815* (Associated University Presses, London, 1996).
Harrison, Mark (ed.), *The Economics of World War II: Six Great Powers in International Comparison* (Cambridge University Press: Cambridge, UK, 1998).
Hinsley, F.H., *British Intelligence in the Second World War, Volume 1 and 2* (HMSO, London, 1981).
Hogan, George, *Malta: The Triumphant Years, 1940–1943* (Robert Hale, London, 1978).
Holland, James, *Fortress Malta: An Island Under Siege 1940–1943* (Orion Books Ltd, London, 2003).
Hughes, Quentin, *Fortress: Architecture and Military History in Malta* (Progress Press, Valletta, Malta, 2001).
Jacobs, Peter, *Fortress Island Malta: Defence and Re-Supply During the Siege* (Pen & Sword, South Yorkshire, UK, 2016).

Jacobsen, Hans-Adolf and Smith, Arthur, W*orld War II Policy and Strategy: Selected Documents with Commentary* (Clio Books, Santa Barbara, CA, 1979).

Jellison, Charles A., *Besieged: the World War II Ordeal of Malta, 1940–1942* (University Press of New England, Hanover, NH, 1984).

Joseph, Frank, *Mussolini's War: Fascist Italy's Struggles from Africa and Western Europe to the Mediterranean and Soviet Union, 1935–1945* (Helion & Company, West Midlands, UK, 2010).

Kertzer, David, *The Pope and Mussolini: The Secret History of Pius XI and the rise of Fascism in Europe* (Random House, New York, 2014).

Lutton, Wayne Charles, *Malta and the Mediterranean: A Study in Allied and Axis Strategy, Planning and Intelligence during the Second World War*, (unpublished DSS, Southern Illinois University, 1983).

Malizia, Nicola, *Inferno su Malta* (Ugo Mursia, Milano, 1976).

Rogers, Anthony, *Churchill's Folly: Leros and the Aegean – The Last Great British Defeat of World War II* (Cassel, London, 2003).

Rollo, Denis, *The Guns and Gunners of Malta* (Mondial Publishers, Valletta, Malta, 1999).

Salerno, Reynolds M., *Vital Crossroads: Mediterranean Origins of the Second World War, 1935–1940* (Cornell University Press, Ithaca, NY, 2002).

Spiteri, Stephen C., *British Military Architecture in Malta* (Stephen C. Spiteri, Valletta, 1996).

Spooner, Tony, *Supreme Gallantry: Malta's Role in the Allied Victory, 1939–1945* (John Murray, London, 1996).

Vella, Philip, *Malta: Blitzed but not Beaten* (Progress Press, Valletta, Malta, 1985).

Wragg, David, *Malta: The Last Great Siege 1940–1943* (Pen & Sword Books Ltd, Barnsley, 2003).

IV. Land Warfare

Bond, Brian and Murray, Williamson, 'The British Armed Forces, 1918–1939', in Millett, Alan and Murray, Williamson (eds), *Military Effectiveness, Vol. 2: The Interwar Period (Mershon Center Series on International Security and Foreign Policy)* (Routledge, London, UK, 1990).

Botti, Ferruccio, *La Logistica dell'Esercito Italiano (1831–1981), Volume III: Dalla Guerra Totale alla Guerra Integrale (1919–1940); Volume IV: Dalla Guerra Integrale alla Guerra Nucleare (1940–1981), Tomo 1: La Logistica nella Seconda Guerra Mondiale (1940–1943)* (Ufficio Storico dello Stato Maggiore Dell'Esercito, Roma, 1994–95).

Bradford, George, *British Armored Fighting Vehicles (World War II AFV Plans)* (Stackpole Books, Mechanicsburg, PA, 2008).

Ceva, Lucio, *La Condotta Italiana della Guerra: Cavallero e il Comando Supremo 1941–1942* (Feltrinelli, Milano, 1975).

Chamberlain, Peter and Doyle, Hilary, *Encyclopedia of German Tanks of World War Two* (Silverdale Books, Wigston, 2004).

Chamberlain, Peter and Ellis, Chris, *British and American Tanks of World War Two* (Silverdale Books, Wigston, 2004).

Hughes, David *et al.*, *The British Armies in World War Two: an Organisational History* (George F. Nafziger, West Chester, 1999–2003).

Knox, MacGregor, *Hitler's Italian Allies: Royal Armed Forces, Fascist Regime, and the War of 1940–1943* (Cambridge University Press, Cambridge, 2000); Italian trans. by Sergio Minucci, *Alleati di Hitler: Le Regie Forze Armate, il Regime Fascista e la Guerra del 1940–1943* (Garzanti, Milano, 2002).

Madej, W. Victor, *German Army Order of Battle, 1939–1945, Volume 1, 2, Supplement* (Game Marketing Company, Allentown, PA, 1981).

Madej, W. Victor, *Italian Army Order of Battle, 1939–1943* (Game Marketing Company, Allentown, PA, 1981).

Micallef, Joseph, *When Malta Stood Alone (1940–1943)* (Interprint Limited, Malta, 1981).

Messe, Giovanni, *Operazioni Italo-Tedesche in Tunisia (11 Novembre 1942 – 13 Maggio 1943), Tomo I: La I^a Armata Italiana in Tunisia* (Ufficio Storico dello Stato Maggiore dell'Esercito, Roma, 1950).

Montanari, Mario, *Le Operazioni in Africa Settentrionale, Volume 3: El Alamein (Gennaio–Novembre 1942)* (Ufficio Storico dello Stato Maggiore dell'Esercito, Roma, 1989, 2nd ed. 1993).

Montanari, Mario, *L'Esercito Italiano alla Vigilia della 2^a Guerra Mondiale* (Ufficio Storico dello Stato Maggiore dell'Esercito, Roma, 1982).

Montanari, Mario, *Politica e Strategia in Cento Anni di Guerre Italiane, Volume 3: Il Periodo Fascista, Tomo II: La Seconda Guerra Mondiale* (Ufficio Storico dello Stato Maggiore dell'Esercito, Roma, 2007).

Nafziger, George F., *Italian Order of Battle World War II: An Organizational History of the Italian Army in World War II* (George F. Nafziger, West Chester, 1996).

Niehorster, Leo W.G., *German World War II Organizational Series* (11-plus volumes) (Dr Leo W.G. Niehorster, Hannover, 1988–94; The Military Press, Milton Keynes, 2004–005).

Pignato, Nicola and Cappellano, Filippo, *Gli Autoveicoli da Combattimento dell'Esercito Italiano, Volume I: Dalle Origini fino al 1939; Volume II: 1940–1945* (Ufficio Storico dello Stato Maggiore dell'Esercito, Roma, 2002).

Pignato, Nicola and Cappellano, Filippo, *Gli Autoveicoli Tattici e Logistici del R. Esercito Italiano fino al 1943* (Ufficio Storico dello Stato Maggiore dell'Esercito, Roma, 2005).

Playfair, I.S.O. et al., *History of the Second World War: The Mediterranean and Middle East – Volume III: British Fortunes Reach their Lowest Ebb (September 1941 to September 1942)* (HMSO, London, 1960; reprint by The Naval & Military Press Ltd, Uckfield, 2004).

Quarrie, Bruce, *German Airborne Divisions: Blitzkrieg 1940–41*, Osprey Battle Orders 4 (Osprey Publishing, London, 2004).

Quarrie, Bruce, *German Airborne Divisions: Mediterranean Theatre 1942–45*, Osprey Battle Orders 15 (Osprey Publishing, London, 2005).

Rochat, Giorgio, *Le Guerre Italiane 1935–1943: Dall'Impero d'Etiopia alla Disfatta* (Torino, Einaudi, 2005).

Ryan, David A., Hughes, David and Rothwell, Steve, *The British Armies of the Second World War: an Organizational History* (George F. Nafziger, West Chester, 1990).

Sogno, Vittorio, *Operazioni Italo-Tedesche in Tunisia (11 Novembre 1942 – 13 Maggio 1943), Tomo II: Il XXX Corpo d'Armata Italiano in Tunisia* (Ufficio Storico dello Stato Maggiore dell'Esercito, Roma, 1952)

Stefani, Filippo, *La Storia della Dottrina e degli Ordinamenti dell'Esercito Italiano, Volume II, Tomo 1: Da Vittorio Veneto alla 2^a Guerra Mondiale; Volume II, Tomo 2: La 2^a Guerra Mondiale (1940–1943)* (Ufficio Storico dello Stato Maggiore dell'Esercito, Roma, 1985)

Various authors, *Armor in Action* (Squadron Signal Publications, Carrolton, 1972).
Various authors, *Combat Troops in Action* (Squadron Signal Publications, Carrolton, 1973).
Various authors, *Schiffer Military History* (Schiffer Military History, West Chester, 1990).

V. Naval Warfare

Ufficio Storico della Marina Militare published a comprehensive history of Italian naval war (*La Marina Italiana nella Seconda Guerra Mondiale*) spanning twenty-two volumes. The ones relevant to C3 operations are:

I – Fioravanzo, Giuseppe, *Dati Statistici*, 2nd ed. (Ufficio Storico della Marina Militare, Roma, 1972).
II – Fioravanzo, Giuseppe, *Navi Militari Perdute*, 5th ed. (1975).
III – Notarangelo, Rolando and Pagano, Gian Paolo, *Navi Mercantili Perdute*, 3rd rev. ed. (1997).
IV – Fioravanzo, Giuseppe, *Le Azioni Navali in Mediterraneo dal 10 Giugno 1940 al 31 Marzo 1941*, 3rd ed. (1976).
V – Fioravanzo, Giuseppe, *Le Azioni Navali in Mediterraneo dal 1° Aprile 1941 all'8 Settembre 1943*, 2nd ed. (1970).
VI – Cocchia, Aldo, *La Difesa del Traffico con l'Africa Settentrionale dal 10 Giugno 1940 al 30 Settembre 1941*, 2nd ed. (1977).
VII – Cocchia, Aldo, *La Difesa del Traffico con l'Africa Settentrionale dal 1° Ottobre 1941 al 30 Settembre 1942*, 2nd ed. (1976).
VIII – Fioravanzo, Giuseppe, *La Difesa del Traffico con l'Africa Settentrionale dal 1° Ottobre 1942 alla caduta della Tunisia* (1964).
IX – Lupinacci, Pier Filippo, *La Difesa del Traffico con l'Albania, la Grecia e l'Egeo* (1965).
XIII – Bertini, Marcello, *I Sommergibili in Mediterraneo*, 2nd ed. (1972).
XVIII – Lupinacci, Pier Filippo and Pagano, Gian Paolo, *La Guerra di Mine*, 2nd rev. ed. (1988).
XIX – Franti, Massimino, *Il Dragaggio* (1969).
XXI – Fioravanzo, Giuseppe, *L'Organizzazione della Marina durante il Conflitto, Tomo I: Efficienza all'Apertura delle Ostilità; Tomo II: Evoluzione Organica dal 10.6.40 all'8.9.43* (1972–78).
XXII – Rauber, Vitaliano, *La Lotta Antisommergibile* (1978).

Ufficio Storico della Marina Militare published a series of seven volumes about its ships (*Le Navi d'Italia*). These books are now being thoroughly revised and expanded in a new series of seven volumes published so far, with more forthcoming:

I – Giorgerini, Giorgio and Nani, Augusto, *Le Navi di Linea Italiane 1861–1969*, 3rd ed. (Ufficio Storico della Marina Militare, Roma, 1969).
II – Pollina, Paolo M. and Bertini, Marcello, *I Sommegibili Italiani 1895–1971*, 3rd ed. (1971).
III – Giorgerini, Giorgio and Nani, Augusto, *Gli Incrociatori Italiani 1861–1975*, 4th ed. (1976).
IV – Pollina, Paolo M., *Le Torpediniere Italiane 1881–1964*, 2nd ed. (1974).

V – Fioravanzo, Giuseppe, *I Cacciatorpediniere Italiani 1900–1971*, 3rd ed. (1971).
VI – Bagnasco, Erminio, *I M.A.S. e le Motosiluranti Italiane 1906–1968*, 2nd ed. (1969).
VII – Bargoni, Franco, *Esploratori, Fregate, Corvette ed Avvisi Italiani 1861–1974*, 3rd ed. (1974).
I (new series) – Bagnasco, Erminio, *M.A.S. e Mezzi d'Assalto di Superficie Italiani* (1996).
II – Bargoni, Franco and Gay, Franco, *Esploratori Italiani* (1996).
III – Bagnasco, Erminio, *Unità Veloci Costiere Italiane: Motosiluranti, Motocannoniere, V.A.S., Motomissilistiche e Aliscafi Lanciamissili* (1998).
IV – Turrini, Alessandro and Miozzi, Ottorino Ottone, *Sommergibili Italiani* (1999).
V – Bargoni, Franco and Gay, Franco, *Navi a Vela e Navi Miste Italiane* (2001).
VI – Bargoni, Franco and Gay, Franco, *Corvette e Pattugliatori Italiani* (2004).
VII – Gay, Franco, *Le Torpediniere Italiane 1875–1917* (2008).

Bagnasco, Erminio and Cernuschi, Enrico, *Le Navi da Guerra Italiane 1940-1945*, (Ermanno Albertelli Editore, Parma, 200) (2nd ed. 2005)
Ball, Simon, *Bitter Sea: The Struggle for Mastery in the Mediterranean, 1935–1949* (Harper Press, London, 2009).
Barrett, Corelli, *Engage the Enemy More Closely: The Royal Navy in the Second World War* (W.W. Norton & Company, New York, 1991).
Borghese, J. Valerio, *Sea Devils: Italian Navy Commandos in World War II* (Naval Institute Press, Annapolis, MD, 1995).
Brown, David K. (ed.), *Nelson to Vanguard: Warship Design and Development 1923–1945* (Chatham Publishing, London, 2000).
Brown, David K. (ed.), *The Design and Construction of British Warships 1939–945: the Official Record* (Conway Maritime Press, London, 1995).
Brown, Les, *British Destroyers A-I and Tribal Classes (Shipcraft #11)* (Seaforth Publishing, South Yorkshire, UK, 2009).
Campbell, John, *Naval Weapons of World War Two* (Conway Maritime Press, London, 1985).
Caruana, Joseph, *Malta Maritime Diary, September 1939 – January 1943* (TBP).
Farquharson-Roberts, Mike, *A History of the Royal Navy in World War I* (I.B. Tauris, London, 2014).
Frothingham, Thomas G., *The Naval History of the World War: The Stress of Sea Power, 1915–1916* (Books for Library Press, Freeport, NY, 1971).
Gardiner, Robert (ed.), *Conway's All the World's Fighting Ships 1922–1946* (Conway Maritime Press, London, 1980).
Gay, Franco et al., *Orizzonte Mare: Navi Italiane nella 2ª Guerra Mondiale*, Ed. Bizzarri, Roma, 1972–75; Ed. Dell'Ateneo, Roma, 1977–85 (Ermanno Albertelli, Parma, 1994–98).
Giorgerini, Giorgio, *La Guerra Italiana sul Mare: La Marina tra Vittoria e Sconfitta 1940–1943* (Arnoldo Mondadori, Milano, 2001).
Giorgerini, Giorgio and Nani, Augusto, *Almanacco Storico delle Navi Militari Italiane: La Marina e le sue Navi dal 1861 al 1995*, 2nd rev. ed. (Ufficio Storico della Marina Militare, 1996).
Greene, Jack and Massignani, Alessandro, *The Naval War in the Mediterranean 1940–1943* (Chatham Publishing, London, 1998).
Grehan, John and Mace, Martin, *The War in the Mediterranean 1940–1944: Despatches from the Front* (Pen & Sword, London, 2014).

Gröner, Erich, *Die Deutschen Kriegschiffe 1815–1945* (Bernard & Graefe Verlag, Bonn, 1998).
Gröner, Erich *Die Schiffe der Deutschen Kriegsmarine und Luftwaffe 1939–1945 und ihr Verleib* (Bernard & Graefe Verlag, Bonn, 2001).
Gröner, Erichand Jung, Dieter, *German Warships 1815–1945* (Conway Maritime Press, London, 1991).
Hore, Peter, *Henry Harwood: Hero of the River Plate* (Seaforth Publishing, Barnsley, UK, 2018).
Konstam, Angus, *British Battlecruisers, 1939–1945* (Osprey Publishing, Oxford, UK, 2003).
Konstam, Angus, *British Battleships, 1939–45 (1)* (Osprey Publishing, Oxford, UK, 2009).
Konstam, Angus, *British Light Cruisers, 1939–45* (Osprey Publishing, Oxford, UK, 2012).
Konstam, Angus, *Taranto 1940: The Fleet Air Arm's Precursor to Pearl Harbor (Campaign 288)* (Osprey Publishing, Oxford, UK, 2015).
Lumby, E.W.R., *Policy and Operations in the Mediterranean, 1912–1914* (Navy Records Society, London, 1970).
Mattesini, Francesco, *La Battaglia Aeronavale di Mezzo Agosto* (Edizioni dell'Ateneo, Roma, 1986).
Mawdsley, Evan, *The War for the Seas: A Maritime History of World War II* (Yale University Press, ,New Haven CT, 2019).
O'Hara, Vincent P., *In Passage Perilous: Malta and the Convoy Battles of June 1942* (Indiana University Press, Bloomington, 2012).
O'Hara, Vincent P., *On Seas Contested: The Seven Great Navies of the Second World War* (USNI, Annapolis, 2010).
O'Hara, Vincent P., *Six Victories: North Africa, Malta and the Mediterranean Convoy War – November 1941 – March 1942* (USNI, Annapolis, 2019).
O'Hara, Vincent P., *Struggle for the Middle Sea: The Great Navies at War in the Mediterranean Theater, 1940–1945* (USNI, Annapolis, 2009).
Page, Christopher (series ed.), *The Royal Navy and the Mediterranean; Volume 1: September 1939 – October 1940, Volume 2: November 1940–December 1941* (Frank Cass, London, 2002).
Paterson, Lawrence, *U-boats in the Mediterranean 1941–1944* (Chatham Publishing, 2007).
Perrett, Bryan, *The Hunters and the Hunted: The Elimination of the German Surface Warships around the World, 1914–1915* (Pen & Sword, South Yorkshire, UK, 2012).
Rohwer, Jurgen, *Chronology of the War at Sea: The Naval History of World War II* (USNI, Annapolis, MD, 2005).
Roskill, S.W., *Churchill and the Admirals* (Wm Morrow & Co., New York, 1978).
Roskill, S.W., *The War at Sea 1939–1945 – Volume II: The Period of Balance* (HMSO, London, 1956; reprint by The Naval & Military Press Ltd, Uckfield, 2004).
Sadkovich, James J., *The Italian Navy in World War II* (Greenwood Press, New York, 1994).
Scarpaci, Wayne, *Italian Battleships, 1928–1957: An Illustrated Technical Reference* (Art by Wayne, Gardenerville, NV, 2009).
Simmons, Mark, *The Battle of Matapan 1941: The Trafalgar of the Mediterranean* (Spellmount, Glouscestershire, UK, 2011).
Smith, Peter C., *Fighting Flotilla: Royal Navy Laforey-class Destroyers in World War II* (Pen & Sword Military, South Yorkshire, UK, 2010).
Smith, Peter C., *Pedestal: The Malta Convoy of August 1942*, rev. ed. (Crecy Books, Manchester, 1994).

Smith, Peter C. and Walker, Edwin, *The Battles of the Malta Striking Forces* (USNI, Annapolis, 1974).
Stephen, Martin, *The Fighting Admirals: British Admirals of the Second World War* (USNI, Annapolis, 1991).
Stern, Robert, *The Battleship Holiday: The Naval Treaties and Capital Ship Design* (Seaforth Publishing, Barnsley, UK, 2017).
Stille, Mark, *Italian Battleships of World War II* (Osprey Publishing, Oxford, UK, 2011).
Stille, Mark, *Italian Cruisers of World War II* (Osprey Publishing, Oxford, UK, 2018).
Stille, Mark, *Italian Destroyers of World War II* (Osprey Publishing, Oxford, UK, 2021).
Thomas, David, *Malta Convoys, 1940–42* (Leo Cooper, London, 1999).
Various authors, *Warships in Action* (Squadron Signal Publications, Carrolton, 1977).
Williamson, Gordon, *German E-boats 1939–45* (Osprey Publishing, Oxford, UK, 2002).
Wingate, John, *The Fighting Tenth: The Tenth Submarine Flotilla and the Siege of Malta* (Leo Cooper, London, UK, 1991).
Wiper, Steve, *German S-Boats (Shipcraft #6)* (Chatham Publishing, London, 2006).
Zapoticzny, Walter S., *Decima Flottiglia MAS: The Best Commandos of the Second World War* (Fonthill, Stroud, UK: 2017).

VI. Air Warfare

Air Battle for Malta: Official Account of the RAF in Mata, June 1940–November 1942. Prepared for Air Ministry by the Ministry of Information (HMDO, London, 1944), http://ww2lairfronts.org/theaters/mto/hmso-malta/hmso).html.
Angelucci, Enzo and Matricardi, Paolo, *Complete Book of World War II Combat Aircraft* (The Military Press, New York, 1988).
Angelucci, Enzo and Matricardi, Paolo, *Guida agli Aeroplani di Tutto il Mondo* (Arnoldo Mondadori, Milano, 1976–78).
Angelucci, Enzo and Matricardi, Paolo, *The Rand McNally Encyclopedia of Military Aircraft 1914–1980* (The Military Press, New York, 1983).
Arena, Nino, *La Regia Aeronautica 1939–1943, Volume I: 1939–1940, Dalla Non Belligeranza all'Intervento; Volume II: 1941, L'Anno della Riscossa; Volume III: 1942, L'Anno della Speranza; Volume IV, 1943: L'Anno dell'Armistizio* (Ufficio Storico dello Stato Maggiore dell'Aeronautica, Roma, 1981–84 and Napoli, 1994).
Bowyer, Chaz, *Royal Air Force Handbook 1939–1945* (Ian Allan Ltd, Shepperton, 1984).
Brotzu, Emilio, Caso, Michele and Cosolo, Gherardo, *Dimensione Cielo: Aerei Italiani nella 2ª Guerra Mondiale, Volume I, II, III: Caccia-Assalto; Volume IV, V, VI: Bombardieri-Ricognitori; Volume VII, VIII, IX: Trasporto; Volume X, XI: Scuola-Collegamento* (Edizioni Bizzarri, Roma, 1971–76; Edizioni dell'Ateneo, Roma, 1977).
Buchner, Alex, *Weapons and Equipment of the German Fallschirmtruppe* (Schiffer Military History, Atglen, PA, 1996).
Caruana, Richard, *Malta George Cross: Victory in the Air* (Modelaid International Publications, Valletta, Malta, 1996).
Craven, Wesley F. and Cate, James L. (eds.), *The Army Air Forces in World War II, Volume I: Plans and Early Operations, 1939–August 1942; Volume II: Europe: Torch to Pointblank, August 1942 to December 1943* (University of Chicago Press, Chicago, IL, 1948, Vol I; 1949, Vol II).

Cull, Brian and Galea, Frederick, *Screwball Buerling: Malta's Top Scoring Fighter Ace* (Wise Owl Publications, Rabat, 2010).
D'Avanzo, Giuseppe, *Ali e Poltrone* (Ciarrapico, Roma, 1976).
Delve, Ken, *Malta Strikes Back: The Role of Malta in the Mediterranean Theatre, 1940–1942* (Pen & Sword, London, 2018).
De Zeng, Henry L. IV, Stankey, Douglas G. and Creek, Eddie J., *Bomber Units of the Luftwaffe 1933–1945: A Reference Source* (Midland Publishing, Hinckley, 2007–08).
Donald, David (ed.), *British Warplanes of World War II* (Aerospace Publishing, London, 1998).
Donald, David (ed.), *Warplanes of the Luftwaffe* (Aerospace Publishing, London, 1994).
Dunning, Christopher, *Courage Alone: The Italian Air Force, 1940–1943* (Hikoki Publications, Manchester, UK, 1998).
Hooton, E.R., *Eagles in Flames: The Fall of the Luftwaffe* (E.R. Hooton, London, 1997; Brockhampton Press, London, 1999).
Hooton, E.R., *Phoenix Triumphant: The Rise and Rise of the Luftwaffe* (E.R. Hooton, London, 1994; Brockhampton Press, London, 1999).
Jones, Ben (ed.), *The Fleet Air Arm in the Second World War: Volume I 1939–1941: Norway, Mediterranean and the Bismarck* (Ashgate, Farnham, UK, 2012).
Mattioli, Marco, *Savoia-Marchetti S.79 Sparviero Torpedo Bomber Units* (Osprey Publishing, Oxford, UK, 2014).
Noppen, Ryn K., *Malta: 1940–42: The Axis's air battle for Mediterranean Supremacy* (Osprey Military, London, 2018).
Price, Alfred, *The Luftwaffe Data Book* (Greenhill Books, London, 1997).
Prien, Jochen *et al.*, *Die Jagdfliegerverbände der Deutschen Luftwaffe 1934 bis 1945, Teil 8: Einsatz in Mittelmeerraum Novembre 1941 bis Dezember 1942* (Struve Druck, Eutin, 2004).
Shores, Christopher, Cull, Brian and Malizia, Nicola, *Malta: The Hurricane Years, 1940–1941* (Grub Street, London, 1987); revised as Cull, Brian and Galea, Frederick, *Hurricanes Over Malta, June 1940–April 1942* (Grub Street, London, 2001).
Shores, Christopher, Cull, Brian and Malizia, Nicola, *Malta: The Spitfire Year, 1942* (Grub Street, London, 1991; reprint 2002); revised as Cull, Brian and Galea, Frederick, *Spitfires Over Malta: The Epic Air Battles Of 1942* (Grub Street, 2005).
Shores, Christopher, Cull, Brian and Malizia, Nicola, *Regia Aeronautica, Vol 1: A Pictorial History of the Italian Air Force 1940–1943* (Squadron/Signal Publications, Carrollton, TX, 1976).
Santoro, Giuseppe, *L'Aeronautica Italiana nella Seconda Guerra Mondiale* (Edizioni Esse, 1950–57).
Various authors, *Aircraft in Action* (Squadron Signal Publications, Carrollton, 1971).

VII. Other Sources

Addison, Paul and Calder, Angus, *Time to Kill: The Soldier's Experience of War in the West, 1939–1945* (Pimlico, London, 1997).
Alberto, Giovanni, *Il dramma di Malta* (Milano, Mondadori, 1991).
Alexander, Harold and North, John (ed.), *The Alexander Memoirs, 1940–1945* (Thomson Newspapers Ltd, London, 1961); Italian translation by Enzo Peru, *Le Memorie del Maresciallo Alexander 1940–1945* (Garzanti, Milano 1963).

Amè, Cesare, *Guerra Segreta in Italia 1940–1943* (Gherardo Casini, Roma, 1954).
Andò, Elio and Bagnasco, Erminio, *Navi e Marinai Italiani nella Seconda Guerra Mondiale* (Ermanno Albertelli Editore, Parma, 1977; 2nd ed. 1999).
Apostolo, Giorgio (ed.), *Ali d'Italia* (La Bancarella Aeronautica, Torino, 1995).
Arena, Nino, *Assalto dal Cielo: Storia delle Truppe Aviotrasportate 1939–1945* (Ugo Mursia, Milano, 1975).
Arena, Nino, *Folgore: Storia del Paracadutismo Militare Italiano* (Centro Editoriale Nazionale, Roma 1965).
Arena, Nino, *I Caccia a Motore Radiale* (Stem Mucchi, Modena, 1979).
Arena, Nino, *I Paracadutisti* (Stem Mucchi, Modena, 1972).
Arena, Nino, *I Paracadutisti: Aerei, Armi, Uniformi* (Stem Mucchi, Modena, 1994).
Arena, Nino, *I Paracadutisti: Storia, Cronaca, Immagini del Paracadutismo Militare Italiano* (Ermanno Albertelli, Parma, 1996).
Arena, Nino, *Il Radar* (Stem Mucchi, Modena, 1976–77).
Arena, Nino, *Mimetizzazione dei Velivoli dell'Aeronautica Italiana* (Ufficio Storico Dello Stato Maggiore dell'Aeronautica, Roma, 1983).
Arena, Nino and Pini, Giorgio, *Schemi e Colori Mimetici dell'Aeronautica Militare Italiana* (Stem Mucchi, Modena, 1994).
Attard, Joseph, *The Battle of Malta* (William Kimber, London, 1980).
Bagnasco, Erminio, *Le Armi delle Navi Italiane nella Seconda Guerra Mondiale* (Ermanno Albertelli Editore, Parma, 1978).
Bagnasco, Erminio, *Le motosiluranti della Seconda Guerra Mondiale* (Ermanno Albertelli Editore, Parma, 1977).
Bagnasco, Erminioand Rastelli, Andrea, *Sommergibili in Guerra* (Ermanno Albertelli Editore, Parma, 1989).
Bagnasco, Erminio and Spertini, Marco, *I Mezzi d'Assalto della Xa Flottiglia MAS 1940–1945* (Ermanno Albertelli Editore, Parma, 1991).
Barbieri, C., *I Caccia della Seconda Guerra Mondiale* (Ermanno Albertelli Editore, Parma, 1970).
Bean, Tim and Fowler, Will, *Russian Tanks of World War II: Stalin's Armoured Might* (Amber Books, London, 2002).
Beckett, C.T., 'The Siege of Malta', in Duncan, William Edmonstone (ed.), *Royal Artillery Commemoration Book, 1950* (Royal Artillery Institution, Wilts, UK, 1950).
Bedeschi, Giulio, *Fronte d'Africa: C'ero Anch'Io* (Ugo Mursia, Milano, 1979).
Benussi, Giulio, *Armi Portatili, Artiglierie e Semoventi del Regio Esercito Italiano 1900–1943* (Intergest, Milano, 1975).
Benussi, Giulio, *Carri Armati e Autoblindate del Regio Esercito Italiano 1918–1943* (Intergest, Milano, 1970).
Beevor, Antony, *Crete: The Battle and the Resistance* (John Murray, London, 1991).
Bellis, Malcolm, *British Armoured and Infantry Regiments, 1939–1945* (Malcolm Bellis, Cheshire, 1988).
Benussi, Giulio, *Armi Portatili, Artiglierie e Semoventi del Regio Esercito Italiano 1900–1943* (Intergest, Milano, 1975).
Benussi, Giulio, *Carri Armati e Autoblindate del Regio Esercito Italiano 1918–1943* (Intergest, Milano, 1970).
Benvenuti, Bruno and Colonna, Ugo F., *Fronte Terra: l'Armamento Italiano nella 2ª Guerra Mondiale* (Edizioni Bizzarri, Roma, 1972–74).

Benvenuti, Bruno and Miglia, Fulvio, *Guida ai Carri Armati* (Arnoldo Mondadori, Milano, 1981).
Bernardi, G., *Il Disarmo Navale tra le Due Guerre Mondiali* (Ufficio Storico della Marina Militare, Roma, 1975).
Bharucha, P.C., *Official History of the Indian Armed Forces in the Second World War, 1939–1945; Campaigns in the Western Theater: The North African Campaign, 1940–1943* (Combined Inter-services Historical Section, New Delhi, 1956).
Blumenson, Martin, *Kasserine Pass: Rommel's Bloody, Climactic Battle for Tunisia* (Houghton Mifflin, Boston, 1967); Italian translation by Emma Castellano Credazzi, *Tre Giorni per la Sconfitta* (Gherardo Casini, Roma, 1969).
Bohmler, Rudolf and Haupt, Werner, *The German Paratroops: A Documentary in Words and Photographs 1939–1945* (Almark International, New Malden, Surrey, 1971).
Boffa, Charles A., *The Saga of the French Occupation: Malta 1798–1800* (Progress Press Co. Ltd, Valletta, 1998).
Bowen-Jones, H., Dewdney, J.C. and Fisher, W.B., *Malta: Background for Development* (Department of Geography, Durham Colleges, Durham, 1961).
Bradford, Ernie, *The Great Siege* (Harcourt, Brace & World, Inc., New York, 1961).
Bragadin, Marc'Antonio, *La Marina Italiana nella Seconda Guerra Mondiale (1940–1943)* (Lega Navale Italiana, 1948); English translation by Gale Hoffman, *The Italian Navy in World War II* (USNI, Annapolis, MD, 1957).
Bragadin, Marc'Antonio, *Il Dramma della Marina Italiana: 1940–1945* (Mondadori, Milano, 1968; reprint, 1982).
Bridgman, Leonard (ed.), *Jane's Fighting Aircraft of World War II* (Jane's Publishing Company, London, 1947; reprint Backen Books, London, 1989).
Burgwyn, H. James, *The Legend of the Mutilated Victory: Italy, the Great War and the Paris Peace Conference, 1915–1919* (Greenwood Press, Westport, 1993).
Burgwyn, H. James, *Italian Foreign Policy in the Interwar Period, 1918–1940* (Praeger, Westport, 1997).
Cappellano, Filippo, *Andare Contro i Carri Armati: L'Evoluzione della Difesa Controcarro nell'Esercito Italiano dal 1918 al 1945* (Gaspari Editore, Udine, 2007).
Cappellano, Filippo, *Le Artiglierie del Regio Esercito* (Ermanno Albertelli Editore, Parma, 1998).
Cappellano, Filippo and Pignato, Nicola, *Il Regio Esercito alla Vigilia dell'8 Settembre 1943* (Ermanno Albertelli, Parma, 2003).
Cappellano, Filippo and Termentini, Fernando, *Le Mine Antiuomo e Anticarro nelle Guerre Italiane del '900* (Museo Storico Italiano della Guerra, 2000; reprint 2006).
Carr, John, *The Knights Hospitaller: A Military History of the Knights of St John* (Pen & Sword Military, South Yorkshire, 2016).
Cassano, Mario, *Maledette Benedette Stellette* (Bacchilega Editore, Imola, 2005).
Cernuschi, Enrico, *I Sette Minuti di Punta Stilo: Analisi Comparata di una Battaglia Navale* (Ufficio Storico della Marina Militare, Roma, 1998).
Cervi, Mario, *The Hollow Legions: Mussolini's Blunder in Greece, 1940–1941* (Doubleday & Company, New York, 1971).
Ceva, Luigi and Curami, Andrea, *La Meccanizzazione del Regio Esercito fino al 1943* (Ufficio Storico dello Stato Maggiore dell'Esercito, Roma, 1989).

Chant, Christopher, *Encyclopedia of World Aircraft* (Brian Todd Publishing Ltd, London, 1990).
Chant, Christopher, *World War II Aircraft* (Orbis Books, London, 1975); Italian translation by Silvia Castorina, *Aerei della Seconda Guerra Mondiale* (Istituto Geografico de Agostini, Novara, 1976).
Chaplin, H.D., *The Queen's Own Royal West Kent Regiment, 1920–1950* (Naval & Military Press Ltd, Uckfield, East Sussex).
Christensen, Ben, *The 1st Fallschirmjager Division in World War II, Volume I: Years of Attack; Volume II: Years of Retreat* (Schiffer Publishing Ltd, Atglen, 2007).
Civoli, Massimo, *S.A.S.: I Servizi Aerei Speciali della Regia Aeronautica 1940–1943* (Gribaudo, Cavallermaggiore, 2000).
Cohen, R., *Knights of Malta, 1523–1798* (Aegypan Press, 1920).
Colville, J.R., *Man of Valour: The Life of Field-Marshal The Viscount Gort, VC, GCB, DSO, MVO, MC* (Collins, London, 1972).
Comitato per la Storia dell'Artiglieria Italiana, *Storia dell'Artiglieria Italiana, Parte V (Dal 1920 al 1943), Volume XV: L'Evoluzione dei Concetti d'Impiego, del Tiro, della Tecnica e dei Materiali; Volume XVI: L'Artiglieria Italiana nelle Operazioni Belliche dal 1920 al 1945* (Biblioteca d'Artiglieria e Genio, Roma, 1953–55).
Craven, Wesley F. and Cate, James L. (eds), *The Army Air Forces in World War II, Volume I: Plans and Early Operations, 1939 – August 1942; Volume II: Europe – Torch to Pointblank, August 1942 to December 1943* (University of Chicago Press, Chicago, 1948–49).
Crociani, P. and Battistelli, P.P, *Italian Blackshirt 1939–45* (Osprey Publishing, Oxford, UK, 2010).
Cruikshank, Charles, *Greece, 1940–1941* (Associated University Press, Cranbury, NJ, 1979).
D'Ascia, Renato, *Storia dell'Arma del Genio, Volume VI: Dalla Fine della Prima Guerra Mondiale alla Vigilia della Campagna in Africa Orientale (1918–1935); Volume VII, Tomo I: Dalla Campagna in Africa Orientale alla Vigilia della Seconda Guerra Mondiale (1935–1939)* (Ufficio Storico dello Stato Maggiore dell'Esercito, Roma, 2002–07).
De Felice, Renzo, *Mussolini il Duce: Volume II, Lo Stato Totalitario 1939–1940* (Giulio Einaudi, Torino, 1981; reprint 1996).
De Felice, Renzo, *Mussolini l'Alleato: Volume I, L'Italia in Guerra 1940–1943, Tomo I: Dalla guerra 'Breve' alla Guerra Lunga; Tomo II: Crisi e Agonia del Regime* (Giulio Einaudi, Torino, 1990; reprint 1996).
De Grand, Alexander, *Italian Fascism: Its Origins and Development* (University of Nebraska Press, Lincoln, 1982).
De la Sierra, Luis, *Buques Suicidas* (Luis de Caralt, Barcelona, 1958); Italian translation by Franco Bissocoli, *Gli Assaltatori del Mare* (Ugo Mursia, Milano, 1971; reprint 2002).
De la Sierra, Luis, *La Guerra Naval en el Mediterráneo (1940–1943)* (Editorial Juventud, Barcelona, 1976); Italian translation by Alfredo Brauzzi, *La Guerra Navale nel Mediterraneo 1940–1943* (Ugo Mursia, Milano, 1987; reprint 1998).
De Risio, Carlo, *Generali, Servizio Segreto e Fascismo: La Guerra nella Guerra 1940–1943* (Mondadori, Milano, 1978).
Di Terlizzi, Maurizio, *Aviolibri* (IBN Editore, Roma, 2000).
Dicorato, Giuseppe *et al.*, *Storia dell'Aviazione* (Fratelli Fabbri, Milano, 1973–76).
Dobie, Edith, *Malta's Road to Independence* (University of Oklahoma Press, Norman, 1967).

Donolo, Luigi, *Storia della Dottrina Navale Italiana* (Ufficio Storico della Marina Militare, Roma, 1996).
Edwards, Roger, *German Airborne Troops* (Doubleday & Company, Garden City, 1974).
Ellis, Chris, *7th Flieger Division: Student's Fallschirmjäger Elite* (Ian Allan, Hershaw, 2002).
Emiliani, Angelo, Gergo, Giuseppe F. and Vigna, Achille, *Immagini e Storia dell'Aeronautica Italiana 1935–1945* (Intergest, Milano 1975–79).
Emiliani, Angelo, Gergo, Giuseppe F. and Vigna, Achille, *Regia Aeronautica: i Fronti Africani* (Ermanno Albertelli, Parma, 1979).
Emiliani, Angelo, Gergo, Giuseppe F. and Vigna, Achille, *Regia Aeronautica: il Settore Mediterraneo* (Intergest, Milano, 1976).
Emiliani, Angelo, Gergo, Giuseppe F. and Vigna, Achille, *Regia Aeronautica: Periodo Prebellico e Fronti Occidentali* (Intergest, Milano, 1975).
Ezell, Edward, *Small Arms of the World* (Stackpole Books, Harrisburg, 1977); Italian translation by Carlo Camarlinghi, *Armi Leggere di Tutto il Mondo* (Ermanno Albertelli Editore, Parma, 1988).
Falessi, Cesare and Pafi, Benedetto, *Veicoli da combattimento dell'Esercito Italiano 1939–1945* (Intyrama Books, Bologna, 1976).
Favagrossa, Carlo, *Perchè Perdemmo la Guerra* (Rizzoli, Milano, 1946).
Fletcher, David, *Matilda Infantry Tank 1938–45*, Osprey New Vanguard 8 (Osprey Publishing, London, 1994).
Forty, George, *British Army Handbook 1939–1945* (Chancellor Press, London, 2000).
Forty, George, *World War Two AFVs: Armoured Fighting Vehicles & Self-Propelled Artillery* (Osprey Automotive, London, 1995).
Forty, George, *World War Two Tanks* (Osprey Automotive, London, 1995).
Foss, Christopher F. (ed.), *The Encyclopedia of Tanks and Armoured Fighting Vehicles* (Spellmount, Staplehurst, 2003).
Fowler, Will, *The Balkans and North Africa 1941–1942* (Ian Allan, Hershaw, 2003).
French, David, *Raising Churchill's Army: The British Army and the War against Germany, 1919–1945* (Oxford University Press, Oxford, 2000).
Fulvi, Luigi *et al.*, *Le Fanterie di Marina Italiane*, 2nd rev. ed. (Ufficio Storico della Marina Militare, Roma, 1998).
Galuppini, Gino, *Guida agli Incrociatori dalle Origini a Oggi* (Mondadori, Milano, 1982).
Galuppini, Gino, *Guida ai Sommergibili dalle Origini a Oggi* (Mondadori, Milano, 1985).
Galuppini, Gino, *Guida alle Corazzate dalle Origini a Oggi* (Mondadori, Milano, 1978).
Galuppini, Gino, *La Portaerei* (Mondadori, Milano, 1979).
Georgiano, G.N., *World War Two Military Vehicles: Transport & Halftracks* (Osprey Automotive, London, 1994).
Gilbert, Martin (ed.), *The Churchill War Papers, Volume I: At the Admiralty, September 1939 – May 1940; Volume II: Never Surrender, May 1940–December 1940, Volume III, 1941* (William Heinemann Ltd, London, 1993)Gilbert, Martin (ed.), *Winston Churchill's War Leadership* (Random House, New York/Fratelli Fabbri, Milano, 1978).
Giorleo, Aldo, *Palestra Azzurra: L'Aeronautica Militare e il Paracadutismo* (Ufficio Storico dello Stato Maggiore dell'Aeronautica, Roma, 1975).

Green, William, *War Planes of the Second World War* (Macdonald, London, 1960–68); partial Italian translation by Gianni Burla, *Dimensione Cielo: Aerei Stranieri nella 2ª Guerra Mondiale* (Edizioni Bizzarri, Roma, 1971–76).

Greene, Jack and Massignani, Allessandro, *Rommel's North Africa Campaign, September 1940–November 1942* (Combined Books, Conshohocken, PA, 1994).

Greene, Jack and Massignani, Allessandro, *Mare Nostrum: The War in the Mediterranean* (Typesetting Inc., Watsonville, 1990).

Grove, Eric, *World War II Tanks* (Orbis Books, 1976); Italian translation by Silvia Castorina, *Mezzi Corazzati della Seconda Guerra Mondiale* (Istituto Geografico DeAgostini, Novara, 1977).

Gunby, David and Temple, Pelham, *RAF Bomber Losses in the Middle East and Mediterranean 1939–1942* (Midland Publishing, Hinckley, 2006).

Gunston, Bill, *The Illustrated Directory of Fighting Aircraft of World War II* (Greenwich Editions, London, 2004).

Hallem, John, *The History of the Lancashire Fusiliers, 1939–1945* (Alan Sutton Publishers, Gloucestershire, UK, 1993).

Halpern, Paul G., 'French and Italian Policy in the Mediterranean, 1898–1945' in Hattendorf, John B. (ed.), *Naval Policy and Strategy in the Mediterranean* (Frank Cass, London, 2000).

Hamlin, John F., *Military Aviation in Malta G.C., 1915–1993: A Comprehensive History* (GMS Enterprises, Peterborough, 1994).

Hardie, Frank, *The Abyssinian Crisis* (B.T. Batsford Ltd, London, 1974).

Hart, Sydney, *Submarine Upholder* (Amberley Publishing, Gloucestershire, 2008).

Harrison, Mark (ed.), *The Economics of World War II: Six Great Powers in International Comparison* (Cambridge University Press, Cambridge, 1998).

Hay, Ian, *Malta Epic* (Appleton-Century Company Inc., London, 1943).

Hildebrand, K., *The Third Reich* (George Allen & Unwin, London, 1984).

Hogan, George, *Malta: The Triumphant Years, 1940–1943* (Robert Hale, London, 1978).

Hogg, Ian V., *Allied Artillery of World War Two* (Crowdood Press, Ramsbury, 1998).

Hogg, Ian V., *German Artillery of World War Two* (Greenhill Books, London, 2002).

Hogg, Ian V., *The Encyclopedia of Infantry Weapons of World War II* (Bison Books, London, 1977).

Hogg, Ian V., *The Guns 1939–1945* (Macdonald, London, 1969); Italian translation by Nicola Pignato, *I Cannoni 1939–1945* (Ermanno Albertelli, Parma, 2005).

Humble, Richard (ed.), *Naval Warfare: An Illustrated History* (Orbis Books, London, 1983); Italian translation by Franco Lenzi and Riccardo Nassigh, *25 Secoli di Battaglie Navali* (Istituto Geografico de Agostini, Novara, 1981).

Hurst, David, *Force for Freedom: The Legacy of the 98th Bombardment Group (H)* (Turner Publishing Company, Paducah, 1990).

Jary, Christopher, *They Couldn't have Done Better: The Story of the Dorset Regiment in War and Peace 1939–67* (Semper Fidelis Publications, UK, 2014).

Jary, Christopher, *Yells, Bells & Smells: The Story of the Devons, Hampshires & Dorsets in the Siege of Malta 1940–43* (Bluemoon Print, UK, 2017).

Jowett, Philip S., *The Italian Army 1940–45 (1): Europe 1940–43*, Osprey Men-at-Arms 340 (Osprey Publishing, London, 2000).

Jowett, Philip S., *The Italian Army 1940–45 (2): Africa 1940–43*, Osprey Men-at-Arms 349 (Osprey Publishing, London, 2001)
Kavanaugh, Stephen L.W., *Comparison of the Invasion of Crete and the Proposed Invasion of Malta* (U.S. Army Command and General Staff College, Fort Leavenworth, 2006).
Keegan, George, *The Second World War* (Century Hutchinson Ltd, London, 1989); Italian translation by Maurizio Pagliano, *La Seconda Guerra Mondiale* (Rizzoli, Milano, 2000).
Kennedy, Greg, 'Sea Denial, Interdiction and Diplomacy: the Royal Navy and the Role of Malta, 1939–1943', in Speller, Ian (ed.), *The Royal Navy and Maritime Power in the Twentieth Century* (Frank Cass, London, 2005).
Kershaw, Ian, 'Rome: Summer & Autumn 1940 – Mussolini Decides to Grab his Share', in *Fateful Choices: Ten Decisions that Changed the World, 1940–1941* (Penguin Press, New York, 2007).
Kitchen, Martin, *Europe between the Wars: A Political History* (Longman Group, Essex, 1988).
Kitchen, Martin, *Rommel's Desert War: Waging World War II in North Africa, 1941–1943* (Cambridge University Press, Cambridge, 2009).
Knox, MacGregor, *Mussolini Unleashed, 1939–1941: Politics and Strategy in Fascist Italy's Last War* (Cambridge University Press, Cambridge, 1982).
Kuhn, Volkmar, *German Paratroops in World War II* (Ian Allan Ltd, London, 1978).
Lazzero, Ricciotti, *La Decima Mas* (Rizzoli, Milano, 1984).
Lembo, Daniele, *Le Portaerei del Duce: Le Navi Portaidrovolanti e le Navi Portaerei della Regia Marina* (Grafica Ma.Ro Editrice, Copiano, 2004).
Liddell Hart, Basil H., *The Other Side of the Hill* (Hamilton & Co., London, 1956); Italian translation by Mario Bonini and Oreste Rizzini, *Storia di una Sconfitta: La Seconda Guerra Mondiale Attraverso le Testimonianze dei Generali Tedeschi* (Rizzoli, Milano, 1998).
Longo, Luigi Emilio, *I Reparti Speciali Italiani nella Seconda Guerra Mondiale* (Ugo Mursia, Milano, 1991).
Lucas, James, *German Army Handbook 1939–1945* (Sutton Publishing, Stroud, 1998).
Lucas, James, *Storming Eagles: German Airborne Forces in World War Two* (Arms and Armour, London, 1988).
Lundari, Giuseppe, *Paracadutisti Italiani 1937/45* (Editrice Militare Italiana di Ivo Fossati, Milano, 1989).
Lyon, D.J. and Lyon, H.J., *World War II Warships* (Orbis Books, London, 1976); Italian translation by Silvia Castorina and Laura Mori, *Mezzi Navali della Seconda Guerra Mondiale* (Istituto Geografico de Agostini, Novara, 1977).
Mack Smith, Denis, *Mussolini* (Weidenfeld & Nicholson Ltd, London, 1981); Italian translation by Giovanni Ferrara degli Uberti, *Mussolini* (Rizzoli, Milano, 1990).
Mack Smith, Denis, *Mussolini's Roman Empire* (The Viking Press, London, 1976); Italian translation by Giovanni Ferrara, *Le Guerre del Duce* (Arnoldo Mondadori, Milano, 1993).
Macksey, Kenneth, *Kesselring: German Master Strategist of the Second World War* (Greenhill Books, London, 1996).
Mallett, Robert, *Mussolini and the Origins of the Second World War, 1933–1940* (MacMillan Palgrave, New York, 2003).
Mallett, Robert, *The Italian Navy and Fascist Expansion, 1935–1940* (Frank Cass, Portland, OR, 1998).
March, Daniel J., *British Warplanes of World War Two* (Grange Books plc, London, 2002).
Marcon, Tullio, *I Muli del Mare* (Ermanno Albertelli Editore, Parma, 1982).

Markham, George, *Guns of the Reich: Firearms of the German Forces, 1939–1945* (Arms and Armour, London, 1991); Italian translation by Piero Schino, *Armi del III Reich: Armi Tedesche 1939–1945* (Fratelli Melita Editori, La Spezia, 1992).

Martel, Gordon (ed.), *The Origins of the Second World War Reconsidered: The A.J.P. Taylor Debate after Twenty-five Years* (Allen & Unwin, London, 1986).

Massimello, Giovanni and Apostolo, Giorgio, *Italian Aces of World War 2*, Osprey Aircraft of Aces 34 (Osprey Publishing, London, 2000).

Mattesini, Francesco, *Il Giallo di Matapan* (Edizioni dell'Ateneo, Roma, 1985).

Mattesini, Francesco, *La Battaglia di Punta Stilo* (Ufficio Storico della Marina Militare, Roma, 1990).

Mattesini, Francesco, *L'Operazione Gaudo e lo Scontro Notturno di Capo Matapan* (Ufficio Storico della Marina Militare, Roma, 1998).

Maurer, M. (ed.), *Air Force Combat Units of World War II* (Office of Air Force History, Washington, 1983).

May, Ernest (ed.), *Knowing One's Enemies: Intelligence Assessment before the Two World Wars* (Princeton University Press, Princeton, 1984).

Megargee, Geoffrey P., *Inside Hitler's High Command* (University Press of Kansas, 2000); Italian translation by G. Simone, *Il Comando Supremo di Hitler* (Libreria Editrice Goriziana, Gorizia, 2005).

Micallef, Joseph, *When Malta Stood Alone (1940–1943)* (Interprint Limited, Malta, 1981).

Migliavacca, Renato, *Assalti e Contrassalti: I Paracadutisti Italiani in Africa* (Auriga, Milano, 1996).

Migliavacca, Renato, *Nel Vivo della Battaglia: Testimonianze Dirette di Uomini della Folgore in Combattimento ad El Alamein* (Auriga, Milano, 2002).

Miller, David, *The Illustrated Directory of 20th Century Guns* (Salamander Books, London, 2001).

Miller, David, *The Illustrated Directory of Submarines of the World* (Greenwich Editions, London, 2004).

Miller, David, *The Illustrated Directory of Tanks of the World* (Greenwich Editions, London, 2004).

Miller, David, *U-Boats: History, Development and Equipment, 1914–1945* (Conway Maritime Press, London, 2000).

Mommsen, Wolfgang J., and Kettenacker, Lothar (eds), *The Fascist Challenge and the Policy of Appeasement* (George Allen & Unwin, London, 1983).

Morewood, Steven, *British Defence of Egypt: Conflict and Crisis in the Eastern Mediterranean* (Frank Cass, London, 2004).

Morgan, Philip, *Italian Fascism, 1919–1945* (MacMillan, New York, 1995).

Morisi, Paolo, *The Italian Folgore Parachute Division* (Helion & Company, West Midlands, UK, 2016).

Morse, Stan (ed.), *The Illustrated Encyclopedia of Aircraft* (Orbis Publishing Ltd, London, 1981–85); Italian translation by Achille Boroli *et al.* (eds), *Mach 1: Enciclopedia dell'Aviazione* (Edipem, Novara, 1978–82).

Musto, Francesco, *Storia della Tecnologia Radar: L'Avventura di Argo* (Bariletti, Roma, 1990).

Nassigh, Riccardo *et al.*, *La Battaglia dei Convogli 1940–1943* (Ufficio Storico della Marina Militare, Roma, 1994).

Nesi, Sergio, *Un Alcione dalle Ali Spezzate* (Arti Grafiche Elleci, Bologna, 1989).

Pack, S.W.C., *Night Action off Cape Matapan* (USNI, Annapolis, 1972).
Pack, S.W.C., *The Battle for Crete* (USNI, Annapolis, 1973).
Pack, S.W.C., *The Battle of Sirte* (USNI, Annapolis, 1975).
Pafi, Benedetto and Pignato, Nicola, *Storia dei Mezzi Corazzati: Tecnologie, Profili, Battaglie* (Fratelli Fabbri, Milano, 1976).
Pasetti, Aldo, *Omega 9* (Bietti, Milano, 1968).
Pegg, Martin, *Luftwaffe Ground Attack Units 1939–45*, Osprey Air War 4 (Osprey Publishing, London, 1977).
Perowne, Stewart, *The Siege within the Walls: Malta, 1940–1943* (Hodder & Stoughton, London, 1970).
Pesce, Giuseppe, *Guerra Attraverso l'Etere nel Teatro Mediterraneo* (Stem Mucchi, Modena, 1978).
Petacco, Arrigo, *La Battaglie Navali del Mediterraneo nella Seconda Guerra Mondiale* (Arnoldo Mondadori, Milano, 1976).
Petacco, Arrigo et al. (eds), *La Seconda Guerra Mondiale* (Armando Curcio, Roma, 1980).
Pickles, Tim, *Malta 1565: Last Battle of the Crusades*, Osprey Campaign 50 (Osprey Military Publishing, Oxford, 1998).
Pignato, Nicola, *Atlante Mondiale dei Mezzi Corazzati, Volume 2: I Carri dell'Asse* (Ermanno Albertelli, Parma, 1971).
Pignato, Nicola, *Gli Autoveicoli del Regio Esercito nella Seconda Guerra Mondiale* (Ermanno Albertelli, Parma, 1998).
Pignato, Nicola, *Italian Armored Vehicles of World War Two* (Squadron Signal Publications, Carrollton, 2004).
Pignato, Nicola et al. (eds), *Gli Eserciti del Ventesimo Secolo* (Armando Curcio, Roma, undated).
Pope, Dudley, *Flag 4: The Battle of Coastal Forces in the Mediterranean 1939–1945* (Chatham Publishing, London, 2006).
Price, Alfred, *Bomber Aircraft* (Arms and Armour, London, 1989), Italian translation by Anna Strambo, *Bombardieri della Seconda Guerra Mondiale* (Fratelli Melita, Spezia, 1992).
Price, Alfred, *Instruments of Darkness: The History of Electronic Warfare, 1939–1945*, rev. ed. (Greenhill Books, London, 1977; reprint 2005).
Price, Alfred, *Spitfire Mark V Aces 1941–45*, Osprey Aircraft of Aces 16 (Osprey Publishing, London, 1997).
Quarrie, Bruce, *German Airborne Troops 1939–45*, Osprey Men-at-Arms 139 (Osprey Publishing, London, 1983).
Quarrie, Bruce, *Hitler: The Victory that Nearly Was* (David & Charles, London, 1989).
Ramsey, Winston G. (ed.), *Malta G.C.*, After the Battle 10 (Battle of Britain Prints International, London, 1975).
Rastelli, Achille, *La Portaerei Italiana: Cento Anni di Dibattiti e Progetti* (Ugo Mursia, Milano, 2001).
Raven, Alan and Roberts, John, *British Cruisers of World War Two* (USNI, Annapolis, 1980).
Reid, Walter, *Churchill under Friendly Fire, 1940–1945* (Birlinn Limited/Casemate Publishing, Edinburgh, 2008).
Restayn, Jean et al., *Blindés de la Seconde Guerre Mondiale* (Histoire et Collection, Paris, 1995); Italian translation by Giorgio Pini, *Corazzati della Seconda Guerra Mondiale* (Ermanno Albertelli Editore, Parma 1996).
Reuth, Ralf G., *Entscheidung im Mittelmeer: Die Südliche Peripherie Europas in der Deutschen Strategie des Zweiten Weltkrieges 1940–1942* (Bernard & Graefe, Bonn, 1985).

Rissik, David, *The D.L.I. at War: The History of the Durham Light Infantry, 1939–1945* (Naval & Military Press Ltd, Uckfield, East Sussex, 2004).
Roatta, Mario, *Otto Milioni di Baionette* (Mondadori, Milano, 1946).
Rocca, Gianni, *Fucilate gli Ammiragli* (Arnoldo Mondadori, Milano, 1987).
Rocca, Gianni, *I Disperati: La Tragedia dell'Aeronautica Italiana nella Seconda Guerra Mondiale* (Arnoldo Mondadori, Milano, 1991).
Rössler, Eberhard, *Geschichte des Deutschen U-Bootbaues* (Bernard & Graefe Verlag, Koblenz, 1996); Italian translation by A.M. Carbone, *U-Boat: I Sommergibili Tedeschi, Tecnica ed Evoluzione* (Fratelli Melita Editori, La Spezia, 1993).
Rotassio, Gianrodolfo and Ruffo, Maurizio, *L'Armamento Individuale dell'Esercito Italiano dal 1861 al 1943* (Ufficio Storico dello Stato Maggiore dell'Esercito, Roma, 1995; 2nd ed. 1997).
Ruge, Friedrich, *Der Seekrieg* (K.F. Koehler Verlag, Stuttgart, 1954); Italian translation by Carlo De Angelis, *La Guerra sul Mare 1939–1945* (Garzanti, Milano, 1964).
Salvadó, Francisco J., *The Historical Dictionary of the Spanish Civil War* (Scarecrow Press, Plymouth, UK, 2013).
Santoni, Alberto, *Il vero Traditore* (Mursia, Milano, 1981).
Santoni, Alberto, *Le Operazioni in Sicilia e Calabria (Luglio – Settembre 1943)*, 2nd rev. ed. (Ufficio Storico dello Stato Maggiore dell'Esercito, Roma, 1989; reprint 2004).
Santoni, Alberto, 'The Italian Navy at the Outbreak of World War II and the Influence of British ULTRA Intelligence in Mediterranean Operations', in Love, Robert William and Bogle, Laurie (eds), *New Interpretations in Naval History: Selected Papers from the Tenth Naval History Symposium 11–13 September 1991* (USNI, Annapolis, 1991).
Santoni, Alberto and Mattesini, Francesco, *La Partecipazione Tedesca alla Guerra Aeronavale nel Mediterraneo 1940–1945* (Ermanno Albertelli, Parma, 2005).
Schermerhorn, Elizabeth. W., *Malta of the Knights* (Wm Heinemann Ltd, London, 1929).
Schreiber, Gerhard, 'Italy and the Mediterranean in the Power-Political Calculations of German Naval Leaders, 1919–1945', in Hattendorf, John B. (ed.), *Naval Policy And Strategy in the Mediterranean* (Frank Cass, London, 2000).
Scutts, Jerry, *Bf 109 Aces of North Africa and the Mediterranean*, Osprey Aircraft of Aces 2 (Osprey Publishing, London, 1994).
Scutts, Jerry, *German Night Fighter Aces of World War 2*, Osprey Aircraft of Aces 20 (Osprey Publishing, London, 1998).
Scutts, Jerry, *German Night Fighter Units 1939–45*, Osprey Air War 9 (Osprey Publishing, London, 1978).
Sgarlato, Nico, *I Grandi Aerei Storici* (Delta Editrice, Parma, 2002).
Sgarlato, Nico, *La Regia Aeronautica nella Seconda Guerra Mondiale* (Delta Editrice, Parma, 2000).
Shores, Christopher and Cull, Brian, *Luftwaffe Fighter Units: Mediterranean 1941–44*, Osprey Air War 20 (Osprey Publishing, London, 1978).
Showell, Jak P. Mallmann, *Fuehrer Conferences on Naval Affairs, 1939–1945* (Greenhill Books, London, 1990).
Showell, Jak P. Mallmann, *The German Navy in World War Two* (Arms and Armour Press, London, 1979); Italian translation by L. Cambiaso and C. Albano, *La Marina Tedesca nella Seconda Guerra Mondiale* (Fratelli Melita Editori, La Spezia, 1993).
Simpson, Michael, 'Superhighway to the World Wide Web: The Mediterranean in British Imperial Strategy, 1900–1945', in Hattendorf, John B. (ed.), *Naval Policy and Strategy in the Mediterranean* (Frank Cass, London, 2000).

Sire, H.J.A., *The Knights of Malta* (Yale University Press, London, 1996).
Smith, Peter C. and Walker, Edwin, *The Battles of the Malta Striking Forces* (USNI, Annapolis, 1974).
Spertini, Marco and Bagnasco, Erminio, *I Mezzi d'Assalto della X^a Flottiglia MAS* (Ermanno Albertelli, Parma, 1991).
Spick, Mike, *Air Battles in Miniature: A Wargamers' Guide to Aerial Combat 1939–1945* (P. Stephens, London, 1978); Italian translation by Maurilio Tamaio, *Combattaimenti Aerei in Miniatura* (Ugo Mursia, Milano, 1980).
Spick, Mike, *The Illustrated Directory of Fighters* (Greenwich Editions, London, 2004).
Stephenson, Charles, *The Fortifications of Malta 1530–1945*, Osprey Fortress 16 (Osprey Publishing, London, 2004).
Strang, G. Bruce, *On the Fiery March: Mussolini Prepares for War* (Praeger, Westport, 2003).
Taylor, Michael J.H. (ed.), *Jane's Encyclopedia of Aviation* (Studio Editions, London, 1989).
Thiele, H., *Luftwaffe Aerial Torpedo Aircraft and Operations in World War II* (Hikoki Publications, Manchester, 2004).
Thomas, Andrew, *Beaufighter Aces of World War 2*, Osprey Aircraft of Aces 65 (Osprey Publishing, London, 2005).
Thomas, David, *Malta Convoys, 1940–42* (Leo Cooper, London, 1999).
TM30-410, *Handbook on the British Army; with Supplement on the Royal Air Force and Civil Defence Organization* (US War Department, September 1942).
Trizzino, Antonino, *Navi e Poltrone* (Longanesi, Milano, 1973).
Trovato, Battista G., *Ritorno a El Alamein* (Ugo Mursia, Milano, 1983).
Vajda, Ferenc A. and Dancey, Peter, *German Aircraft Industry and Production 1933–1945* (Airlife Publishing Ltd, West Sussex, 1998).
Vanderveen, Bart H., *The Observer's Fighting Vehicles Directory, World War II* (F. Warne, London, 1969); Italian translation by Eugenio Torre, *Automezzi della Seconda Guerra Mondiale* (Ermanno Albertelli, Parma, 1997).
Vella, Philip, *Malta: Blitzed but not Beaten* (Progress Press, Valletta, Malta, 1985).
Walker, Ian W., *Iron Hulls, Iron Hearts: Mussolini's elite Armoured Divisions in North Africa* (The Crowood Press, Wiltshire, UK, 2003).
Weal, John, *Jagdgeschwader 27 'Afrika'*, Osprey Aviation Elite 12 (Osprey Publishing, London, 2003).
Weal, John, *Junkers Ju 87 Stukageschwader of North Africa and the Mediterranean*, Osprey Combat Aircraft 6 (Osprey Publishing, London, 1998).
Weal, John, *Messerschmitt Bf 110 Zerstörer Aces of World War 2*, Osprey Aircraft of Aces 25 (Osprey Publishing, London, 1999).
Williamson, Gordon, *Wolf Pack: The Story of the U-Boat in World War II* (Osprey Publishing, London, 2005).
Wingate, John, *The Fighting Tenth: The Tenth Submarine Flotilla and the Siege of Malta* (Leo Cooper, London, 1991).
Winton, John, *Cunningham* (John Murray, London, 1998).
Wismayer, J.M., *The History of the King's Own Malta Regiment and the Armed Forces of the Order of St John* (Said International Ltd, Valletta, 1989).
Worth, Richard, *Fleets of World War II* (Da Capo Press, Cambridge, 2001).
Wragg, David, *Fleet Air Arm Handbook 1939–1945* (Sutton Publishing, Stroud, 2001).

Wragg, David, *Junkers Ju 87 Stukageschwader of North Africa and the Mediterranean* (Osprey Publishing, London, 1998).
Wragg, David, *Messerschmitt Bf 110 Zerstörer Aces of World War 2* (Osprey Publishing, London, 1999).
Zaloga, Steven J., *KV-1 & 2 Heavy Tanks 1939–1945* (Osprey Publishing, London, 1995).

4.0 Internet links

12 O'Clock High, http://forum.12oclockhigh.net/index.php?
A Military History of Malta, http://www.educ.um.edu.mt/militarymalta/index.html
Air of Authority – A History of RAF Organisation, http://www.rafweb.org/Menu.htm
Aircraft of World War II, http://www.ww2aircraft.net/forum/
British Aircraft of World War II, http://www.jaapteeuwen.com/ww2aircraft/
Chronik des Seekrieges 1939–1945, http://www.wlb-stuttgart.de/seekrieg/chronik.htm
Commonwealth Orders of Battle 1939–45, http://home.adelphia.net/~dryan67/orders/army.html
Elevon: Aviation on the Internet, http://www.csd.uwo.ca/Elevon
Fleet Air Arm Archive 1939–1945, http://www.fleetairarmarchive.net/Home.html
Flightline Malta, http://www.flightlinemalta.com/
German Naval History, http://www.german-navy.de/
Greendevils, http://www.greendevils.com/greendevils/
Italie 1939–1945, http://italie1935-45.fr.tc/
Luftwaffe Resource Center, http://www.warbirdsresourcegroup.org/LRG/index.html
Malta GC, http://www.killifish.f9.co.uk/Malta%20WWII/Index.htm
Naval History Information Center, http://www.hazegray.org/navhist/
Navweaps, http://www.navweaps.com/
RAF Commands, http://www.rafcommands.currantbun.com/
Regio Esercito, http://regioesercito.dns1.us/../index.htm
Royal Air Force, http://www.raf.mod.uk/
The Luftwaffe 1933–45, http://www.ww2.dk/
The National Archives, http://www.nationalarchives.gov.uk/
The World War II Encyclopedia, http://www.lemaire.happyhost.org/
Ubootwaffe.net, http://www.ubootwaffe.net/index.html
USAF Historical Studies, http://www.au.af.mil/au/afhra/numbered_studies/studiesintro.asp
Warsailors.com, http://www.warsailors.com/
World War II Armed Forces, http://niehorster.orbat.com/
Worldwar.it, http://www.worldwar.it/

4.2 Discussion forums

Axis History, http://www.axishistory.com/
Comando Supremo, http://www.comandosupremo.com/
Feldgrau, http://www.feldgrau.com/

Appendix A

Axis Land Order of Battle

**Operazione *C3*
OOB of Axis Land Forces[1]**
(by Davide Pastore, 2006)

CTS (*Comando Tattico Superiore*)[2] – Gen Vecchiarelli[3]
  HQ Troops
  10° Ra.Co. (Raggruppamento Corazzato)
  3° Reggimento Artiglieria Contraerea
  LIII Gruppo Artiglieria

XXX Corpo d'Armata – Gen Sogno
  HQ Troops
  1ª Divisione di Fanteria (d'Assalto) 'Superga'
  4ª Divisione di Fanteria (d'Assalto) 'Livorno'
  20ª Divisione di Fanteria (d'Assalto) 'Friuli'
  29° Raggruppamento Artiglieria

XVI Corpo d'Armata – Gen Rossi
  26ª Divisione di Fanteria 'Assietta'
  54ª Divisione di Fanteria 'Napoli'

Corpo d'Armata di Aviosbarco – Gen Kurt Student
  7. Fallschirmjäger-Division – Gen Petersen
  4. Fallschirmjäger-Regiment
  1ª Divisione Paracadutisti – Gen Frattini
  80ª Divisione Aerotrasportabile 'Spezia' – Gen Pizzolato
  I Battaglione d'Assalto Paracadutisti dell'Aeronautica
  Battaglione Riattatori 'Loreto'
  Battaglione Speciale Arditi

---

1. The following list includes all combat units but omits any and all HQ, motor transport, medicals, services, etc. However, I included Artieri (road engineers) and Pontieri (bridge engineers).
2. Comando Tattico Superiore (Superior Tactical Command) was the (not very imaginative) name for the army-level C3 land forces.
3. Commander-in-Chief of all C3 land forces (including Student's paratroops and other German units). He was also Deputy Army Chief-of-Staff.

Italian Amphibious Troops (under Regia Marina control)[4]
    Reggimento '*San Marco*'
    Raggruppamento Battaglioni 'M' da Sbarco

German Amphibious Troops
    66. Panzer-Abteilung z.b.V.
    German Pionier Abteilung

CTS HQ Troops
    VIII Battaglione Artieri (road engineers)[5]
        3x Cp. Artieri
    CXI Battaglione Territoriale Mobile[5]
        3x Cp. Fucilieri
    CXII Battaglione Territoriale Mobile (details as CXI)[5]

10° Ra.Co. (Raggruppamento Corazzato)
    DLV Gruppo Artiglieria Semovente
        2x Batteria   4x Semovente M41 da 75/18
    LXX Battaglione Motomitraglieri
        2x ('light') Cp.
        3x ('heavy') Cp.

3° Reggimento Artiglieria Contraerea
    XXXV Gruppo Artiglieria[6]
        3x Batteria   4x 75/46 HAA gun (tractors)
    DIV Gruppo Artiglieria[6]
        2x Batteria   4x 90/53 HAA gun (tractors)

XXX Corps HQ Troops
    XXII Battaglione Artieri
        3x Cp. Artieri[7]
    One Pontieri (bridge engineers) ad hoc Cp.[6]
    7ª Compagnia Chimica (chemicals)[8]
    II Battaglione Lanciafiamme
        3x Cp. Lanciafiamme[9]

---

4. Only until the landing. Afterwards, under C.T.S. control.
5. Part of 2nd wave. Static infantry, probably to be used as HQ defence.
6. Part of 2nd wave.
7. One company with 1st wave, two with 2nd wave.
8. With smoke dischargers and, probably, some poison gas too (to be used only after the enemy did). Some elements (1st wave) attached to Superga and Livorno, bulk of the company available as reserve.
9. Flamethrower battalion parcelled into various detachments:
  Livorno 1 company
  Friuli 1 company
  Superga ½ company
  Larnaca beachhead ½ company

1ª Divisione di Fanteria (d'Assalto) 'Superga'[10]
  91° Reggimento Fanteria 'Basilicata'
    I/91° Battaglione Fanteria
      3x Cp. Fucilieri
      Cp. Armi d'Accomp.[11]   4x 47/32 gun, 6x 81mm, 6x flamethrower
    II/91° Battaglione Fanteria (details as I/91°)
    III/91° Battaglione Fanteria (details as I/91°)
  92° Reggimento Fanteria 'Basilicata' (details as 91°)
  I Battaglione Mortai
    3x Cp. Mortai
  5° Reggimento Artiglieria 'Superga'
    I/5° Gruppo Artiglieria
      3x Batteria[12]
    II/5° Gruppo Artiglieria (details as I/5°)[13]
    CXXXIII Battaglione Semoventi
      2x Cp. Semoventi   8x Semovente L40 da 47/32
    21ª Batteria Antiaerea
    34ª Batteria Antiaerea
  I Battaglione Controcarro Semovente[13]
    2x Cp. Semoventi   8x Semovente L40 da 47/32
    Cp. Anticarro
  I Battaglione Guastatori
    4x Cp. Guastatori[14]
  CI Battaglione Misto Genio
    14ª Compagnia Artieri
    101ª Compagnia Pontieri

4ª Divisione di Fanteria (d'Assalto) 'Livorno' (all details as Superga)
  33° Reggimento Fanteria 'Livorno'
  34° Reggimento Fanteria 'Livorno'
  IV Battaglione Mortai
  28° Reggimento Artiglieria 'Monviso'
    I/28° Gruppo Artiglieria
    II/28° Gruppo Artiglieria
    CXXXII Battaglione Semoventi
    68ª Batteria Antiaerea
    80ª Batteria Antiaerea
    364ª Batteria Antiaerea

---

10. Full 'Divisione d'Assalto' OOB. 47mm guns and 81mm mortars towed by three-wheel motorcycles. A few days after the invasion of Gozo (expected to be bloodless), a reinforced regiment from Superga would have landed on the north-west coast of Malta.
11. Normally parcelled out among the rifle companies.
12. Two batteries with 1st wave, one battery with the 2nd.
13. Part of 2nd wave.
14. Two companies of Superga, and one company of Livorno, detached to Larnaca beachhead.

IV Battaglione Controcarro Semovente[15]
XI Battaglione Guastatori[14]
LVII Battaglione Misto Genio
    20ª Compagnia Artieri
    104ª Compagnia Pontieri

20ª Divisione di Fanteria (d'Assalto) 'Friuli'[16]
87° Reggimento Fanteria 'Friuli'
    I/87° Battaglione Fanteria
        3x Cp. Fucilieri
        Cp. Mitraglieri
    II/87° Battaglione Fanteria (details as I/87°)
    III/87° Battaglione Fanteria (details as I/87°)
    Cp. Cannoni d'Accomp.[17]   4x 65/17 gun
    Cp. Mortai[17]
88° Reggimento Fanteria 'Friuli' (details as 87°)
XX Battaglione Mortai
    4x Cp. Mortai[18]
35° Reggimento Artiglieria 'Friuli'
    I/35° Gruppo Artiglieria[19]
        3x Batteria   4x 100/17 howitzer (tractors)
    II/35° Gruppo Artiglieria
        3x Batteria   4x 75/27 gun (tractors)
    III/35° Gruppo Artiglieria
        3x Batteria   4x 75/18 howitzer (tractors)
    320ª Batteria Antiaerea   8x 20/65 LAA gun (trucks)
    356ª Batteria Antiaerea   8x 20/65 LAA gun (trucks)
III Battaglione Controcarro
    3x Cp. Controcarro   8x 47/32 gun
V Battaglione Guastatori (details as Superga)
52ª Compagnia Artieri
88ª Legione Camice Nere 'Cappellini'
    LXXXVIII Btg. Camice Nere
        2x Cp. Fucilieri   12x LMG
    XCVI Btg. Camice Nere (details as LXXXVIII)
    96ª Cp. Armi di Accomp.[17]

---

15. ATR company with 1st wave, two L40 companies with 2nd wave.
16. Friuli never completed the transition to full 'Divisione d'Assalto' OOB, and remained a mix of old and new assets. The presence of the 65/17 guns is noteworthy. 47mm guns and 81mm mortars towed by three-wheel motorcycles.
17. Normally parcelled out among the rifle companies
18. One extra company present
19. Part of 2nd wave.

29° Raggruppamento Artiglieria
    LVII Gruppo Artiglieria[19]
        3x Batteria   4x 105/32 gun (tractors)
    LVIII Gruppo Artiglieria (details as LVII Gruppo)[19]
    CXXI Gruppo Artiglieria[19]
        3x Batteria   4x 149/13 howitzer (tractors)

26ª Divisione di Fanteria 'Assietta'[20]
    29° Reggimento Fanteria 'Pisa'
        I/29° Battaglione Fanteria (details as Friuli)
        II/29° Battaglione Fanteria (details as Friuli)
        III/29° Battaglione Fanteria (details as Friuli)
        Cp. Cannoni d'Accomp.[21]   8x 47/32 gun
        Cp. Mortai[21]
    30° Reggimento Fanteria 'Pisa' (details as 29°)
    CXXVI Battaglione Mortai
        3x Cp. Mortai
    25° Reggimento Artiglieria 'Assietta'
        III/35° Gruppo Artiglieria
            3x batteria   4x 75/18 howitzer (tractors)
        IV/35° Gruppo Artiglieria
            3x batteria   4x 75/13 pack howitzer (mule-pack)
        326ª Batteria Antiaerea   8x 20/65 LAA gun (trucks)
    126ª Compagnia Cannoni Anticarro   *8x 47/32 gun*
    64ª Compagnia Artieri   (no details)
    17ª Legione Camice Nere 'Cremona' (details as Friuli)
        XVII Battaglione Camice Nere
        XVIII Battaglione Camice Nere
        259ª Compagnia Armi di Accompagnamento

54ª Divisione di Fanteria 'Napoli' (all details as Assietta)[20]
    75° Reggimento Fanteria 'Napoli'
    76° Reggimento Fanteria 'Napoli'
    LIV Battaglione Mortai
    54° Reggimento Artiglieria 'Napoli'
        III/54° Gruppo Artiglieria
            3x batteria   4x 75/18 howitzer (tractors)
        IV/35° Gruppo Artiglieria
            2x batteria   4x 75/18 howitzer (tractors)
        354ª Batteria Antiaerea
    54ª Compagnia Cannoni Anticarro
    71ª Compagnia Artieri
    173ª Legione Camice Nere 'Salso'
        CLXIX Battaglione Camice Nere
        CLXXIII Battaglione Camice Nere
        174ª Compagnia Armi di Accompagnamento

---

20. Normal infantry divisions, part of 2nd wave. 47mm guns and 81mm mortars manhandled.
21. Normally parcelled out among the rifle companies

Axis Land Order of Battle   233

7. Fallschirm-Jäger Division (Gen Petersen)[22]
  1. Fallschirm-Jäger Regiment (Ob Karl Lothar Schulz)
    I/1. Battalion
      3x Rifle Coy (1., 2., 3.)
      4. (MG) Coy
    II/1. Battalion   (5. to 8. companies, as I/1.)
    III/1. Battalion (9. to 12. companies, as I/1.)
      13. (IG) Coy   (6x lg40 75mm and 2 x 105mm recoilless guns)
      14. (PaK) Coy   (12x sPzB41 anti-tank guns)
  3. Fallschirm-Jäger Regiment (Ob R. Heidrich) (as 1. FJR)

  Ramcke Fallschirm-Jäger Regiment (Generalmajor B. Ramcke)
    I/RAM (ex I/FJR2)
      3x Rifle Coy (1., 2., 3.)
      4. (MG) Coy
    II/RAM (ex I/FJR3)
      4x Rifle Coy (1., 2., 3., 4.)
      5. (MG) Coy
    III/RAM (ex II/FJR5)
      4x Rifle Coy (5., 6., 7., 8.)
      9. (MG) Coy

  FJ Panzer-Jäger Abteilung
    2. Coy   (12x PaK36, 18x MG34 LMGs)[23] [#2]
    4. Coy
    5. Coy

  1. Fallschirm-Jäger Artillerie Regiment
    I./1. FJ Artillery Battalion
      1. Battery   (4x 75mm GebG36 mountain guns)
      2. Battery   (4x 75mm GebG36 mountain guns)
      4. Battery   (4x 75mm GebG36 mountain guns)
    II./1 FJ Artillery Battalion
      7. Battery   (4x 75mm GebG36 mountain guns)
      8. Battery   (4x 75mm GebG36 mountain guns)

  Fallschirm-Korps-Pioneer-Battalion (Maj. Rudolf Witzig)
    4x Pionier Coy (1., 2., 3., 4.)   (36x MG34 LMGs, 8x flamethrowers)
    (8x MG34 HMGs, 12x anti-tank rifles)

---

22. As per Kesselring's plan. Total of twelve rifle battalions shown, however only nine (plus the two pionier units) were included into the airdrop timetable, hence it is possible this was the maximum number of rifle battalions available amongst the four regiments.

23. Some 42mm PjK41 anti-tank guns were probably available, but unknown numbers.

1ª Divisione Paracadutisti (Gen Frattini)[24]
  1° Reggimento Fanteria Paracadutista
    II Battaglione Fanteria Paracadutista
      Cp. Comando[25]   6x m.35 ATR, 6x HMG, ?x 45mm
      3x Cp. Fucilieri (4ª, 5ª, 6ª)
    III Battaglione Fanteria Paracadutista (details as X Btg.)
    IV Battaglione Fanteria Paracadutista (details as X Btg.)
    Compagnia controcarro   8x 47/32 gun
  2° Reggimento Fanteria Paracadutista (V, VI, VII Btg., details as 1°)
  3° Reggimento Fanteria Paracadutista (IX, X, XI Btg., details as 1°)[26]
  Compagnia Mortai
  1° Reggimento Artiglieria Paracadutista
    I/1° Gruppo Artiglieria
      2x Batteria (1ª, 2ª)   4x 47/32 gun
    II/1° Gruppo Artiglieria (3ª and 4ª Batteria, details as I/1°)
    III/1° Gruppo Artiglieria (5ª and 6ª Batteria, details as I/1°)
  VIII Battaglione Guastatori
    3x Cp. (22ª, 23ª, 24ª)   12x flamethrower

80ª Divisione Di Fanteria Aerotrasportabile 'Spezia' (Gen Pizzolato)[27]
  125° Reggimento Fanteria 'Spezia'
    I/125° Battaglione Fanteria (details as Friuli)
    II/125° Battaglione Fanteria (details as Friuli)
    III/125° Battaglione Fanteria (details as Friuli)
  126° Reggimento Fanteria 'Spezia' (details as 125°)
  80° Reggimento Artiglieria
    I/80° Gruppo Artiglieria
    2x Batterie (1ª, 2ª)   4x 65/17 gun
    II/80° Gruppo Artiglieria (3ª and 4ª Batteria, details as I/80°)
    III/80° Gruppo Artiglieria (5ª and 6ª Batteria, details as I/80°)
    7ª Batteria Contraerea   8x 20/65 LAA gun
    8ª Batteria Contraerea   8x 20/65 LAA gun
  LXXX Battaglione Anticarro
    3x Compagnia Controcarro   8x 47/32 gun
  XXXIX Battaglione Esplorante
    2x ('light') Cp.
    3ª ('heavy') Cp.
  LXX Battaglione Misto Genio
      5ª Compagnia Guastatori
      102ª Compagnia Artieri

---

24. All heavy weapons manhandled.
25. Normally parceled out among the rifle companies.
26. Not earmarked for C3 (reasons not stated).
27. Part of 2nd wave, to be air-lorried on a captured airfield. All heavy weapons towed by three-wheel motorcycles.

Special Forces

I Battaglione d'Assalto Paracadutisti dell'Aeronautica (Air Force's special forces)
    3x Cp.

Battaglione Riattatori 'Loreto' (Air Force, airfield repairers)
    Cp. Servizi   6x 20/65 LAA gun
    4x Cp.

Battaglione Speciale Arditi (special forces)
    101ª Cp. Arditi Paracadutisti   (paratroops)
    102ª Cp. Arditi Nuotatori   (swimmers)

Reggimento 'San Marco'[28]
    San Marco – Battaglione Fanteria 'Grado'
        3x Cp. Fucilieri
    San Marco – Battaglione Fanteria 'Bafile'
        3x Cp. Fucilieri
    San Marco – Swimmers [300 men, probably two companies]
    San Marco – Parachuted swimmers [160 men, probably one company]

Raggruppamento Battaglioni 'M' da Sbarco
    CC.NN. – XLII Battaglione 'M' da Sbarco 'Vicenza'
        3x Cp. Fucilieri[29].
    CC.NN. – L Battaglione 'M' da sbarco 'Treviso' (details as XLII)
    CC.NN. – LX Battaglione 'M' da sbarco 'Pola' (details as XLII)
    CC.NN. – XLIII Battaglione 'M' da sbarco 'Belluno' (details as XLII)
    CC.NN. – Heavy weapons[30]   16x 47/32 gun, 9x 81mm

German Land Units
Larnaca Beachhead[31]
        66. Panzer Abteilung z.b.V.
            1. Coy   12x Pz IV G, 5x Pz I F, 5x Pz II J
            2. Coy   at least 10x KV, ?x T-34
        Unidentified German Pionier Battalion
            3x Coy

---

28. Very strong rifle companies (400 men) with additional units attached.
29. Strong rifles companies (300 men) with additional units attached.
30. To be attached to rifle companies.
31. Larnaca beachhead included also:
    from C.T.S.½ flamethrower company
    from Superga2 Guastatori companies
    from Livorno1 Guastatori company

Summary

	CTS	XXX 29°	Superga	Livorno	Friuli	Assietta	Napoli	Folgore	Spezia	F.N.S.	S.F.
Rifle & m/c coy	3-6-0	n/a	18-0-0	18-0-0	22-0-0	0-22-0	0-22-0	18-0-0	0-21-0	n/a	n/a
Landing Rifle coy	n/a	n/a	n/a	n/a	n/a	n/a	n/a	n/a	n/a	18-0-0	n/a
Guast. Coy	n/a	n/a	2-0-0	3-0-0	4-0-0	n/a	n/a	3-0-0	0-1-0	6-0-0	n/a
Road & bridge eng. Coy	0-0-3	1-3-0	2-0-0	2-0-0	1-0-0	0-1-0	0-1-0	n/a	0-1-0	n/a	n/a
Flame & chemic. Coy	n/a	0-0-1	½-0-0	1-0-0	1-0-0	n/a	n/a	na	na	½-0-0	n/a
Special forces coy	n/a	n/a	n/a	n/a	n/a	n/a	n/a	n/a	n/a	n/a	12-0-0
German Tanks	n/a	n/a	n/a	n/a	n/a	n/a	n/a	n/a	n/a	34/44-0-0	n/a
Semov. M40	8-0-0	n/a	n/a	n/a	n/a	n/a	n/a	n/a	n/a	n/a	n/a
Semov. L40	n/a	n/a	16-16-0	16-16-0	n/a	n/a	n/a	n/a	n/a	n/a	n/a
152/37	0-0-8	n/a	n/a	n/a	n/a	n/a	n/a	n/a	n/a	n/a	n/a
149/13	n/a	0-12-12	n/a	n/a	n/a	n/a	n/a	n/a	n/a	n/a	n/a
105/32	n/a	0-24-12	n/a	n/a	n/a	n/a	n/a	n/a	n/a	n/a	n/a
105/28	n/a	0-0-12	n/a	n/a	n/a	n/a	n/a	n/a	n/a	n/a	n/a
100/17	n/a	n/a	n/a	n/a	0-12-0	n/a	n/a	n/a	n/a	n/a	n/a
90/53	0-8-8	n/a	n/a	n/a	n/a	n/a	n/a	n/a	n/a	n/a	n/a
75/46	0-12-12	n/a	n/a	n/a	n/a	n/a	n/a	n/a	n/a	n/a	n/a
75/27	n/a	n/a	n/a	n/a	12-0-0	n/a	n/a	n/a	n/a	n/a	n/a
75/18	n/a	n/a	8-16-0	24-0-0	12-0-0	0-12-0	0-20-0	n/a	n/a	n/a	n/a
75/13	n/a	n/a	n/a	n/a	n/a	0-12-0	n/a	n/a	n/a	n/a	n/a
65/17	n/a	n/a	n/a	n/a	8-0-0	n/a	n/a	n/a	0-24-0	n/a	n/a
47/32	n/a	n/a	24-0-0	24-0-0	24-0-0	0-24-0	0-24-0	40-0-0	0-24-0	28-0-0	n/a
20/65	n/a	0-0-16	16-0-8	24-0-0	16-0-0	0-8-0	0-8-0	n/a	0-16-0	n/a	n/a
81mm	n/a	n/a	63-0-0	63-0-0	54-0-0	0-45-0	0-45-0	9/12-0-0	n/a	15-0-0	n/a
ATR	n/a	n/a	0-12-0	12-0-0	n/a	n/a	n/a	36-0-0	n/a	n/a	n/a

Numbers are: 1st wave (Day Y, from 13 July afternoon to 14 July morning)
2nd wave (about, more or less, five days after day Y)
3rd wave / reserve (not scheduled, but available if required)

The only units in this list not part of any of the above are the horse-towed artillery in Assietta and Napoli (totally useless), and the 3° Italian parachute regiment (very useful; unaware of the reason it was not included). However, I listed them all for sake of completeness.

Readers familiar with the similar table included in Mariano Gabriele's book (*Operazione C3: Malta*), pp.162–65 of my edition, will note a number of differences: these are due to Gabriele's typos. I can say this because I utilized the same original archive papers Gabriele utilized as his source.

'F.N.S.' includes the spearheads in all landing beaches. I counted the German Pionieren amongst the Guastatori companies. Note that the 'Landing rifle coys' are stronger than the normal 'Rifle coys'.

'S.F.' includes all the Special Forces units (swimmers, saboteurs, reactivators, etc.).

7. FjD not included, since I know very little about its intended equipment.

Appendix B

Axis Naval Order of Battle

Operazione *C3*
OOB of Axis Naval Forces (August)
© Davide Pastore 2008

These are the Axis naval assets that would have been employed in *C3*, according to plans formalized in May 1942 and taking into account actual ship availability on the August new moon, my chosen landing date.

Exact unit assignment is tentative, since the picture has changed since the May list had been prepared. I tried to maintain the spirit of the original plan as far as possible.

The list includes every military ship from torpedo boats up, plus every submarine, MS, MAS and VAS. Of the large number of small subchasers I listed only those attached to F.N.S. (the best ones), and of the still larger number of minesweepers I listed only the parent units (Flottiglie dragamine).

Major ships (where the captain's name is given) are listed with division or squadron flagship first, thereafter in order of decreasing captain's seniority. Minor (numbered) ships are listed by number, irrespective of seniority. Submarines are listed from older to newer.

Squadra and Divisione HQs include the names of both the commanding admiral and his CSM (Capo di Stato Maggiore, Chief of Staff). Squadriglie were commanded by the senior captain.

Some Italian ships had very long names (including the two longest-named ships of the war: the cruisers *Luigi di Savoia Duca degli Abruzzi* and *Emanuele Filiberto Duca d'Aosta*). These ships were usually referred to in a short form (in the two cases above, *Abruzzi* and *Aosta*). I listed the complete names in the text, highlighting in bold the short form *(Luigi di Savoia Duca degli **Abruzzi** and Emanuele Filiberto Duca d'**Aosta**)*.

Ships unavailable (being at works for repairs *et al.*) have been removed from the OoB.

A (?) means the presence of the ship is arguable, for reasons explained in the note.

A [F] means the ship acts as flagship for his formation.

A * means the ship has a sonar, called ECG (*ecogoniometro*) by Italians. Note that, for some reasons hard to fathom, some heavy cruisers had it at a time when many escort vessels had not.

A [2 a/c] or [3 a/c] means the ship carries either two or three Ro.43 aircraft.

Note that while in English it is common to consider ship names as feminine-gendered ('her'), through the centuries Italian sailors have always considered their ships as males ('him').

Supermarina

Supermarina (telegraphic abbreviation for Gruppo Operativo dello Stato Maggiore Marina) was the highest naval operative command, located inside the navy department in Roma. It collected information and passed them to the naval formations; it also coordinated the air cooperation.

A heavily centralized command structure (reflecting the centralized nature of fascist Italy), it sent detailed (sometimes over-detailed) orders to the naval formations but, as a general rule, it did so only as long as they were not in the proximity of the enemy. Normally it relinquished command to the man on the spot as soon as a battle was approaching. Although this doctrine was well-intentioned (the combat being best controlled from an engaged ship), it nevertheless left the impression of Supermarina playing the game only as long as there was no risk, discarding any responsibility whenever one could get hurt – so that if a defeat will occur, it will not be its fault.

It was a collegial organ whose members at the time were:

- Sottocapo di Stato Maggiore (deputy Chief of Staff)   A.S. Luigi Sansonetti
- Capo Ufficio Piani (chief of planning bureau)   A.D. Emilio Brenta
- one of the following admirals, rotating in shifts every twenty-four hours:
  A.D. Enrico Accorretti
  C.A. Amedeo Nomis di Pollone
  C.A. Carlo Pinna
  C.A. Angelo Varoli Piazza

X Flottiglia Mas

Cover name for the Regia Marina special force unit. It was commanded by C.F. Ernesto Sforza (HQ La Spezia) and included a Reparto di superficie (surface group) under C.C. Salvatore Todaro with small motor boats, and a Reparto Subacqueo (underwater group) under C.C. Junio Valerio Borghese with human torpedoes and swimmers (the latter part of Gruppo Gamma under T.V. Eugenio Wolk) carried by submarine motherships (at the time *Ambra* and *Scirè*).

The Reparto di Superficie was to contribute to *C3* with a few boats in anti-surface ambush along Malta coasts. Previously it had carried observers there (including the famous Carmelo Borg Pisani). The Reparto subacqueo was unavailable since *Ambra* was at works and *Scirè* had been lost on 10 August during an unlucky attempt to attack Haifa harbour.

Abbreviation[1]	Definition	Translation
Csmg	Cacciasommergibili	Subchaser
CT	Cacciatorpediniere	(Torpedo boat-)Destroyer
CV	Corvetta	Sloop
IL	Incrociatore leggero	Light cruiser
IP	Incrociatore pesante	Heavy cruiser

---

1. Official papers show abbreviations either capitalized or not ('CT', 'Ct', 'ct') as well as with a dot or not ('C.T.', 'C.t.', 'c.t.'). There was not a definite guideline.

Abbreviation[1]	Definition	Translation
MAS	Motoscafo armato silurante	'Armed torpedo motorboat' (small MTB)
MC	Motocisterna	Diesel-engine tanker (actually akin to LST)
MF	Motoscafo	Motorboat
MFP	Marinefährprahm	'Navy ferry' (actually akin to LCT)
ML	Motolancia	'Motor launch' (actually akin to LCM)
MN	Motonave	Diesel-engine cargo ship
MS	Motosilurante	Motor torpedo boat (large MTB)
MV	Motoveliero	'Motor sailing boat' (actually a trawler)
MZ	Motozattera	'Motor raft' (Italian copy of MFP)
NB	Nave da battaglia	Battleship
NPA	Nave portaerei	Aircraft carrier
NT	Nave traghetto	Railway ferry
PF	Piroscafo	Steam-engine cargo ship
PM	Posamine	Minelayer
NPA	Nave portaerei	Aircraft carrier
Smg g.c.	Sommergibile da grande crociera	Long-range submarine
Smg p.c.	Sommergibile da piccola crociera	Short-range submarine
TP	Torpediniera	Torpedo boat
VAS	Vedetta antisommergibili	ASW patrol boat

Ranks					
Regia Marina		Kriegsmarine		Equivalent	
Abbr.	Rank	Abbr.	Rank	RN & USN	British Army
G.A.	Grande Ammiraglio[2]	GrA	Grossadmiral	Admiral of the Fleet	Field Marshal
A.A.	Ammiraglio d'Armata[3]	GA	Generaladmiral	Admiral	General
A.S.d.A.	Ammiraglio di Squadra designato d'Armata[4]	- / -	- / -	- / -	- / -

2. There had been only one Grande Ammiraglio (Paolo Thaon di Revel, retired at the time).
3. There was at the time only one Ammiraglio d'Armata (Domenico Cavagnari, retired).
4. Admiral 'nominated' for the higher rank. A mechanism somewhat akin to the ACW brevet system.

A.S.	Ammiraglio di Squadra	AD	Admiral	Vice Admiral	Lieutenant General
A.D.	Ammiraglio di Divisione	VA	Vizeadmiral	Rear Admiral	Major General
C.A.	Contrammiraglio	KA	Konteradmiral	Commodore	Brigadier General
C.V.	Capitano di Vascello	KS	Kapitän zur See	Captain	Colonel
C.F.	Capitano di Fregata	FK	Fregattenkapitän	Commander	Lieutenant Colonel
C.C.	Capitano di Corvetta	KK	Korvettenkapitän	Lieutenant Commander	Major
T.V.	Tenente di Vascello	KL	Kapitänleutnant	Lieutenant	Captain
S.T.V.	Sottotenente di Vascello	OS	Oberleutnant zur See	Sublieutenant	Lieutenant
G.M.	Guardiamarina	LS	Leutnant zur See	Midshipman / Ensign	Second Lieutenant

1ª Squadra (A.S.d.A. Angelo Iachino, Comandante in Capo delle Forze Navali; CSM A.D. Emilio Ferreri)[5]

9ª Divisione (A.D. Giuseppe Fioravanzo; CSM C.F. Mario Gerini) at Napoli[6]
    NB   *Vittorio **Veneto*** [7] [F]   (C.V. Corso Pecori Girardi)   [3 a/c]
    NB *(?)* *Giulio **Cesare***[8]   (C.V. Sesto Sestini)   (attached from 5ª Div.)

  10ª Squadriglia cacciatorpediniere (C.V. Riccardo Pontremoli) at Napoli[9]
    CT   **Maestrale* [F]   (C.V. Riccardo Pontremoli)

---

5. Located in western waters, for action against Gibraltar forces. Iachino was always very cautious even under the best circumstances, and exceedingly so after the Matapan disaster.
6. Normally based at Taranto.
7. Veneto was the normal flagship for 9ª Divisione, but at the time was also flagship for both 1ª Squadra and Comando Forze Navali. Admiral Fioravanzo (post-war head of the navy historical office) was freshly embarked after having spent the beginning of the war at Supermarina.
8. Without either Littorio nor Roma, 9ª Divisione was a bit on the weak side. Due to its outdated AA armament, Cesare would not have taken part in the preliminary naval bombardment of Malta, and probably (sources are unclear on this point) not even joined 5ª Divisione at Messina; so he might have been employed here, although somewhat slowing Veneto. However, it is more likely he would have just been left in port at Taranto.
9. On paper all destroyers were subordinate to 1ª Squadra (grouped into a Gruppo cacciatorpediniere di squadra whose administrative HQ was embarked onboard a unit at works, currently Granatiere) and assigned to tasks on ad hoc basis; the structure listed here (with the escorting Squadriglia subordinate to the escorted Divisione) is just for sake of clarity. The assignement of a particular Squadriglia to a particular Divisione is my guess, based upon ship characteristics.

CT	*Legionario*[10]	(C.F. Corrado Tagliamonte)	(attached from 11ª Sqd. Ct.)
CT	Alfredo **Oriani**	(C.F. Paolo Pesci)	
CT	*Vincenzo **Gioberti**[11]	(C.F. Vittorio Prato)	
CT	***Grecale**	(C.F. Luigi Gasparrini)	

7ª Divisione (A.D. Alberto Da Zara; CSM C.F. Giovanni Onnis)[12] at Cagliari

IL	Eugenio di **Savoia**[13] [F]	(C.V. Franco Zannoni)	[2 a/c]
IL	Raimondo **Montecuccoli**	(C.V. Arturo Solari)	[2 a/c]
IL (?)	Attilio **Regolo**[14]	(C.V. Pietro Sandrelli)	
IL	*Muzio **Attendolo**	(C.V. Mario Schiavuta)	[2 a/c]

11ª Squadriglia cacciatorpediniere (C.V. Gastone Minotti) at Cagliari

CT	**Aviere** [F]	(C.V. Gastone Minotti)	
CT	**Corsaro**	(C.F. Lionello Sagamoso)	(attached from 17ª Sqd. Ct.)
CT	**Legionario**	(C.F. Corrado Tagliamonte)	(detached to 10ª Sqd. Ct)
CT	**Ascari**	(C.F. Teodorico Capone)	(attached from 12ª Sqd. Ct.)
CT	**Geniere**	(C.F. Marco Notarbartolo)	
CT	**Camicia Nera**	(C.F. Adriano Foscari)	

2ª Squadra (A.S. Carlo Bergamini; CSM C.V. Ernesto Ciurlo)[15]

5ª Divisione (A.S. Carlo Bergamini; CSM C.V. Ernesto Ciurlo) at Messina[16]

NB	Caio **Duilio**[17] [F]	(C.V. Giorgio Conti)	
NB	Giulio **Cesare**	(C.V. Sesto Sestini)	(detached to 9ª Div.)
NB	Andrea **Doria**	(C.V. Mario Bussola)	

---

10. Legionario was at the time the only Italian ship carrying (since May 1942) a radar on board (FuMO 24/40 G).
11. One screw damaged, strong vibrations at full speed.
12. Da Zara, at the other end of the spectrum compared to Iachino, was easily the most aggressive Italian admiral in active service.
13. The original May plan listed Eugenio amongst Augusta forces, but I believe it a typo since this would have upset some long-established divisional structures.
14. Brand-new little Regolo was currently finishing is shakedown at La Spezia, Supermarina being probably a bit puzzled about how to best employ this one-of-a-kind animal (officially classified as Esploratore Oceanico, oceanic scout). The May plan listed him amongst light cruisers so I followed the example, however in practice Regia Marina seemed to have considered Regolo and its classmates more as very large destroyers.
15. Located in eastern waters, for action against Alexandria forces. Bergamini had long been advocating a more active use of battleship than Iachino's standard, leading them at sea in a number of convoy escort missions during the past months.
16. Normally based at Taranto. This formation would have bombarded Maltese targets.
17. Duilio was flagship for both 2ª Squadra and 5ª Divisione.

Axis Naval Order of Battle 243

15ª Squadriglia cacciatorpediniere (C.V. Enrico Mirti della Valle) at Reggio Calabria[18]
    CT   *Antonio **Pigafetta** [F]*   (C.V. Enrico Mirti della Valle)
    CT   **Giovanni Da Verazzano*   (C.F. Angelo Lo Schiavo)

16ª Squadriglia cacciatorpediniere (C.V. Aldo Cocchia) at Reggio Calabria[19]
    CT   **Nicoloso **Da Recco** [F]*   (C.V. Aldo Cocchia)
    CT   *Lanzerotto **Malocello***   (C.F. Mario Leoni)
    CT   ***Premuda***   (C.F. Alessandro Mirone)

Attached: **2° Gruppo torpediniere** (C.C. Emanuele Campagnoli) at Messina[20]
    TP   *Enrico **Cosenz** [F]*   (C.C. Emanuele Campagnoli)
    TP   *Generale Achille **Papa***   (T.V. Giuseppe Sardelli)

Attached: **4° Gruppo torpediniere** (T.V. Nicola Ferrone) at Messina[21]
    TP   *Giuseppe **Sirtori** [F]*   (T.V. Nicola Ferrone)
    TP   *Giuseppe Cesare **Abba***   (T.V. Antonio Narducci)(attached from 9° Gr. Tp.)

3ª Divisione (A.D. Angelo Parona; CSM C.V. Francesco Camicia) at Messina[22]
    IP   ***Gorizia*** [F]   (C.V. Paolo Melodia)   [2 a/c]
    IP   ***Bolzano**   (C.V. Mario Mezzadra)   [2 a/c]
    IP   ***Trieste**[23]   (C.V. Umberto Rouselle)   [2 a/c]

7ª Squadriglia cacciatorpediniere (C.F. Alvaro Minio Paluello) at Augusta[24]
    CT   ***Freccia*** [F]   (C.F. Alvaro Minio Paluello)
    CT   ***Folgore***   (C.C. Renato D'Elia)   (attached from 8ª Sqd. Ct.)
    CT   ***Lampo**   (C.C. Antonio Cuzzaniti)   (attached from 8ª Sqd. Ct.)
    CT   ***Saetta***   (C.C. Enea Picchio)   (attached from 8ª Sqd. Ct.)

---

18. Shortly before the war, most ships of this class (Navigatori) were reconstructed as convoy escorts, rendering them too slow for fleet action. However, they are listed here since there were insufficient modern destroyers to cover the battle fleet (minimal requirement was two to each battleship and one to each cruiser).
19. See previous note.
20. Attached from Basso Tirreno departmental forces. To be employed as running minesweepers for the battleships during the bombardment.
21. Attached from Sicilian departmental forces. See previous note.
22. Based at Messina for most of the war. About Parona's character I unfortunately know nothing.
23. Historically, Trieste rejoined 3ª Divisione (after torpedo damage repairs) only on 12 August; it had been ready to move since late June and didn't do so only to save fuel.
24. After 1941, these older ships had been employed only as convoy escort and the May plan has them assigned to FNS. However, they are listed here since there were insufficient modern destroyers (see Navigatori note above).

8ª **Divisione** (A.D. Raffaele De Courten; CSM C.V. Ubaldino Mori Ubaldini) at Augusta[25]
    IL   *Giuseppe* **Garibaldi** [F]   (C.V. Vittorio De Pace)   [2 a/c]
    IL (?) *Luigi* **Cadorna**[26]   (C.V. Leone Riccati di
                                              Ceva e di San Michele)   [2 a/c]
    IL   *Emanuele Filiberto*
                *Duca d'***Aosta**   (C.V. Luciano Bigi)   [2 a/c]
    IL   *Luigi di Savoia Duca*
                degli **Abruzzi**   (C.V. Giovanni Viansino)   [2 a/c]

    13ª **Squadriglia cacciatorpediniere** (C.V. Ferrante Capponi) at Augusta
    CT   **Alpino** [F]   (C.V. Ferrante Capponi)
    CT   *****Fuciliere**   (C.F. Umberto Del Grande)
    CT   **Mitragliere**   (C.F. Silvio Garino)   (attached from 12ª
                                                                                                   Sqd. Ct.)
    CT   **Bersagliere**   (C.F. Anselmo Lazzarini)
    CT   *****Corazziere**   (C.F. Antonio Monaco di
                                                  Longano)   (attached from 12ª
                                                                                                    Sqd. Ct.)

F.N.S. (Forza Navale Speciale) (A.S. Vittorio Tur; CSM C.V. Temistocle D'Aloia)[27]

11ª **Divisione** (A.S. Vittorio Tur; CSM C.V. Temistocle D'Aloia) at Porto Empedocle[28]
    IL   **Taranto**   (C.V. Temistocle D'Aloia)
    TP   *****Procione**[29] [F]   (C.C. Marco Sacchi)   (attached from 4ª
Sqd. Tp.)

12ª **Divisione** (A.D. Luigi Biancheri; CSM C.V. Paolo Mengarini) at Siracusa[30]
    IL   **Bari**   (C.V. Paolo Mengarini)
    TP   **Orione**[31] [F]   (T.V. Carlo Bambilla)   (attached from 42ª
                                                                                                             Sqd. Tp.)

---

25. Normally based at Taranto. Historically, moved to Navarino (Greece) in mid-July, but only after C3's shelving. De Courten was a popular admiral, later becoming Chief of Staff.
26. The plan listed Cadorna (as well as Eugenio) amongst Augusta light cruisers. However, this old ship had been employed as crew schoolship at Pola since January, and so it was far from being combat ready (and probably not a very useful addition to begin with).
27. 'Special Naval Force', controlling all landing ships and crafts as well as their escorts. Tur commanded it for most of the war (eventually invading Corsica in November 1942). He was rumoured to be hostile to fascism, having a French wife.
28. Controlling 'Famagosta' beachhead (Ghar Lapsi and Wied iz-Zurrieq).
29. During the actual landing, Tur would have transferred his flag from Taranto to Procione. The old cruiser would have remained at Augusta, probably acting as administrative HQ.
30. Controlling 'Cipro' beachhead (Gozo).
31. During the actual landing, Biancheri would have transferred his flag from Bari to Orione. (He had planned to transfer to the brand new Ciclone, but the ship was sunk on 8/3/1942 when it hit a mine.) The old cruiser would have remained at Augusta, probably acting as administrative HQ.

Axis Naval Order of Battle 245

German forces (VA Eberhard Weichold) at Licata[32]
    Zerstörer **ZG 3** [F] (KS Johannesson)

F.N.S. Escort forces[33]

1ª Squadriglia cacciatorpediniere[34]
CT	*Sebenico*	(C.C. Luca Goretti de' Flamini)
CT	*Turbine*	(C.C. Salvatore Granato)

4ª Squadriglia torpediniere[35]
TP	*Orsa	(T.V. Enrico Bucci)
TP	*Pegaso	(T.V. Mario De Petris)

11ª Squadriglia torpediniere[36]
TP	*Centauro	(C.C. Luigi Zerbi)
TP	*Climene	(C.C. Raffaele Cerqueti)
TP	*Castore	(T.V. Gaspare Tezel)

12ª Squadriglia torpediniere (C.C. Antonio Biondo)[37]
TP	*Antares* [F]	(C.C. Antonio Biondo)	
TP	*Aretusa*	(C.C. Egidio Cioppa)	
TP	*Cassiopea*	(T.V. Massimiliano Sigismondi)	(detached to 1ª Sqd. Tp.)
TP	Generale Antonio *Cascino*	(T.V. Gustavo Galliano)	(attached from 3° Gep. Tp.)

14ª Squadriglia torpediniere (C.C. Pasquale Senese)[38]
TP	*Partenope [F]	(C.C. Pasquale Senese)
TP	*Pallade	(C.C. Giuseppe Pasquinelli)
TP	*Polluce	(T.V. Tito Burattini)

6° Gruppo torpediniere (T.V. Umberto Manacorda)[39]
TP	Antonio *Mosto* [F]	(T.V. Umberto Manacorda)
TP	Giacomo *Medici*	(T.V. Antonio Furlan)
TP	Francesco *Stocco*	(T.V. Mario Corradino)

---

32. Controlling 'Larnaca' beachhead (Benghaisa). The units were subordinate to Deutsches Marinekommando Italien (Weichold's territorial command).
33. These forces would be split between the two Italian beachheads (under 11ª and 12ª Divisione). Starting ports for the invasion convoys were Catania, Siracusa, Licata and Porto Empedocle.
34. From Basso Adriatico departmental forces.
35. From Basso Tirreno departmental forces.
36. From Sicilian departmental forces.
37. From Basso Adriatico departmental forces.
38. From Marimorea departmental forces.
39. From Basso Adriatico departmental forces.

1ª Squadriglia VAS (T.V. Antonio Lombardo)
    VAS **Vas 201 [F]**   (T.V. Antonio Lombardo)
    VAS **Vas 203**   (?)
    VAS **Vas 209**   (S.T.V. Erasmo Speduto)
    VAS **Vas 216**   (G.M. Eugenio Bologna)
    VAS **Vas 225**   (?)

2ª Squadriglia VAS (T.V. Aldo Pucci)
    VAS **Vas 204**   (T.V. Aldo Pucci)
    VAS **Vas 210**   (G.M. Paolo Poletti)
    VAS **Vas 215**   (?)
    VAS **Vas 221**   (?)
    VAS **Vas 227**   (S.T.V. Giovanni Giamone)

3ª Squadriglia VAS (C.C. Enrico Berlucchi)
    VAS **Vas 211**   (T.V. Enrico Varoli Piazza)
    VAS **Vas 218**   (G.M. Franco Nicastro)
    VAS **Vas 228**   (C.C. Enrico Berlucchi)

attached from 4° Gruppo antisom
    Csmg *AS 96 *Quarnaro*   (T.V. Eugenio Grilli)
    Csmg *AS 98 *Frangipane*   (T.V. Antonino La Nasa)

attached from 8° Gruppo antisom
    Csmg *AS 101 *Malinska*   (?)

attached from 10° Gruppo antisom
    Csmg *AS 110 *Unie*   (T.V. Aristide Tomatis)
    Csmg *AS 112 *Vergada*   (C.C. Gastone Cantalupi)

attached from 15° Gruppo antisom
    Csmg *AS 111 *Eso*   (T.V. Giovanni Battista Garrone)
    Csmg *AS 118 *Selve*   (T.V. Umberto Miele)
    Csmg *AS 120 *Oriole*   (T.V. Alberto Bertacca)

attached from Gruppo addestramento antisom
    Csmg *AS 114 *Cyprus*   (T.V. Bruno Bonetta)
    Csmg *AS 122 *Zagabria*   (T.V. Filippo Rosada)

F.N.S. Landing Forces[40]

Gruppo Flottiglie Motolancie (ML 601 – ML 700)
    1ª Flottiglia ML
        1ª Sqd. ML (1ª Sez.: ML 601–605, 2ª Sez.: ML 606–610, 3ª Sez. ML 611–615)
        2ª Sqd. ML (4ª Sez.: ML 616–620, 5ª Sez.: ML 621–625)

---

40. This is the paper, administrative organization.

2ª Flottiglia ML
    3ª Sqd. ML (6ª Sez.: ML 626–630, 7ª Sez.: ML 631–635, 8ª Sez. ML 636–640)
    4ª Sqd. ML (9ª Sez.: ML 641–645, 10ª Sez.: ML 646–650)

3ª Flottiglia ML
    5ª Sqd. ML (11ª Sez.: ML 651–655, 12ª Sez.: ML 656–660, 13ª Sez. ML 661–665)
    6ª Sqd. ML (14ª Sez.: ML 666–670, 15ª Sez.: ML 671–675)

4ª Flottiglia ML
    7ª Sqd. ML (16ª Sez.: ML 676–680, 17ª Sez.: ML 681–685, 18ª Sez. ML 686–690)
    8ª Sqd. ML (19ª Sez.: ML 691–695, 20ª Sez.: ML 696–700)

Gruppo Flottiglie Motozattere (MZ 701 – MZ 765) (C.V. Orazio Bernardini)
    1° Flottiglia MZ (C.C. Leonardo Arrivabene Valenti Gonzaga)
        1ª Sqd. MZ (1ª Sez.: MZ 701–705, 2ª Sez.: MZ 706–710)
        2ª Sqd. MZ (3ª Sez.: MZ 711–715, 4ª Sez.: MZ 716–720)

    2° Flottiglia MZ (C.F. Manlio Lazzeri)
        3ª Sqd. MZ (5ª Sez.: MZ 721–725, 6ª Sez.: MZ 726–730)
        4ª Sqd. MZ (7ª Sez.: MZ 731–735, 8ª Sez.: MZ 736–740)

    3° Flottiglia MZ (C.C. Gino Azzo Del Pin)
        5ª Sqd. MZ (9ª Sez.: MZ 741–745, 10ª Sez.: MZ 746–750)
        6ª Sqd. MZ (11ª Sez.: MZ 751–755, 12ª Sez.: MZ 756–760, 13ª Sez.: MZ 761–765)

Flottiglia Motoscafi (MF 801 – MF 824) (T.V. Giuseppe Cicchioni)
    1ª Sqd. MF (1ª Sez.: MF 801–806, 2ª Sez.: MF 807–812)
    2ª Sqd. MF (3ª Sez.: MF 813–818, 4ª Sez.: MF 819–824)

First Wave Landing Ships (*Friuli* plus supports)

MN	831 *Aquileia*	(?)
MN	832 *Altino*	(?)
PM	833 *Pelagosa*	(T.V. Giovanni D'Aste)
PM	834 *Buccari*	(T.V. Raimondo Morpurgo)
PM	835 *Durazzo*	(T.V. Gianbattista Musante)
MC	841 *Scrivia*	(?)
MC	842 *Tirso*	(C.C. Francesco Geraci)
MC	843 *Sesia*	(?)
MC	844 *Garigliano*	(T.V. Umberto Cinquegrani)
NT	851 *Messina*	(?)
NT	852 *Aspromonte*	(?)
PF	861 *Principessa Mafalda*	(?)
PF	862 *Capitano Sauro*	(?)

PF	863 *Tabarca*	(?)
PF	864 *Punte Bianche*	(?)
PF	865 (?)[41]	(?)
PF	866 (?)[42]	(?)
PF	867 (?)[43]	(?)

Second Wave Landing Ships (*Livorno* plus supports)

PF	868 (?) *Rosandra*	
PF	869 (?) *Crispi*	
PF	870 (?) *Italia*	
PF	871 (?) *Viminale*	
PF	872 (?) *Milano*	
PF	873 (?) *Quirinale*	
PF	874 (?) *Aventino*	
PF	875 (?) *Donizzetti*	
PF	876 (?) *Calino*	
PF	877 (?) *Città di Tunisi*	

Gruppo Flottiglie Motovelieri (MV 901 – MV 949)

1ª Flottiglia MV (C.C. Conti)
    1ª Sqd. MV (1ª Sez.: MV 901–903, 2ª Sez.: MV 904–906)
    2ª Sqd. MV (1ª Sez.: MV 907–909, 2ª Sez.: MV 910–912)
    3ª Sqd. MV (1ª Sez.: MV 913–915, 2ª Sez.: MV 916–918)
2ª Flottiglia MV
    4ª Sqd. MV (1ª Sez.: MV 919–921, 2ª Sez.: MV 922–924)
    5ª Sqd. MV (1ª Sez.: MV 925–927, 2ª Sez.: MV 928–930)
3ª Flottiglia MV
    6ª Sqd. MV (1ª Sez.: MV 931–933, 2ª Sez.: MV 934–936)
    7ª Sqd. MV (1ª Sez.: MV 944–946, 2ª Sez.: MV 947–949)
    8ª Sqd. MV (1ª Sez.: MV 937–940, 2ª Sez.: MV 941–943)

Water tankers	5 units[44]
Gasoline tankers	3 units[45]
Minesweepers	12 units[46]

Tugs

Tug	*Salvatore Primo*	(C.C. Edoardo Kraus)
Tug	*Ciclope*	(T.V. Alcide Tomicich)
Tug	*Titano*	(C.C. Giuseppe Cascio)

---

41. Either Stamura or Veglia, exact one not yet chosen.
42. Either Spalato Jadranska or Lissa Jadranska, exact one not yet chosen.
43. Either Punta Amica or Punta Planca, exact one not yet chosen.
44. To be chosen amongst: Adige, Po, Tevere, Stura I, Bormida, Sarno, S. Luigi, Sile, N°84.
45. To be chosen amongst: Edgardo, Pontelongo, Fiamma, Intava, Liri, Shell II, Scaparro, Mina.
46. Taken from the Flottiglie dragamine in Sicily (13ª–19ª, see Departmental forces).

Tug	*Marittimo*	(?)
Tug	*Luigi Ferdinando **Marsigli***	(?)
Tug	*Nereo*	(?)
Tug	*Vigoroso*(?)	
Tug	*Tenace*	(?)
Tug	*Porto Sdobba*	(?)
Tug	*Senigallia*	(?)

Armed Rafts
Raft	**GM 216**[47]	(T.V. Silvio Zumino)
Raft	**GM 239**[48]	(T.V. Aldo Fontanelli)

German Forces

3. Schnellbootflotille (KK Friedrich Kemnade) at Licata[49]

Schnellboot	**S 30**	(OS Horst Weber)
Schnellboot	**S 33**	(?)
Schnellboot	**S 40**	(?)
Schnellboot	**S 54**	(?)
Schnellboot	**S 55**	(OS Klaus-Degenhard Schmidt)
Schnellboot	**S 56**	(OS Gunther Brauns)
Schnellboot	**S 57**	(?)
Schnellboot	**S 58**	(OS Siegfried Wupperman)
Schnellboot	**S 59**	(OS Albert Müller)
Schnellboot	**S 61**	(?)

6. Räumbootflotille (KL Reischauer) at Licata[50]

Räumboot	**R 9**	(?)
Räumboot	**R 10**	(?)
Räumboot	**R 11**	(?)
Räumboot	**R 12**	(?)
Räumboot	**R 13**	(?)
Räumboot	**R 14**	(?)
Räumboot	**R 15**	(?)
Räumboot	**R 16**	(?)

2. Landungsflotille (FK Dr. Franz Flesche) at Licata[51]

10x MFP typ A1 (F 343–347, F 353–357)
21x MFP typ A (F 147, F 149, F 150, F 152–159, F 348–352, F 358–362)

---

47. Armed with two 190/45 (18,900m range).
48. Armed with two 149/47 (20,600m range).
49. Normally based at Augusta and Porto Empedocle. It is unknown how many boats were inefficient at the time.
50. Normally based at Trapani and Tripoli (although official HQ was at Pola).
51. Official HQ was at Arenzano.

5. Kompanie / Bau-Btl. 85 (?) at Licata
   12x Siebelfähr 40 / 41
   6x Pionier-Landungsboot 40 / 41
   6x Pionier-Landungsboot 39

? Kompanie (?) at Licata
   81x Sturmboot 39

Available, from Sicilian departmental coastal forces (channel blockade)[52]

1ª Flottiglia Vedette MS (?) at Marsala

    1ª Squadriglia motosiluranti (C.F. Agostino Calosi) at Marsala
Ms	**Ms 11**	(?)
Ms	**Ms 12**	(T.V. Vittorio Daviso di Charvensod)
Ms	**Ms 13**	(S.T.V. Fiorenzo Semini)
Ms	**Ms 14**	(?)
Ms	**Ms 15**	(?)
Ms	**Ms 21**	(T.V. Vittorio Barenghi)

    2ª Squadriglia motosiluranti (C.C. Giorgio Manuti) at Marsala
Ms	**Ms 16**	(C.C. Giorgio Manuti)
Ms	**Ms 22**	(S.T.V. Franco Mezzadra)
Ms	**Ms 23**	(S.T.V. Giacomo Patrone)
Ms	**Ms 24**	(?)
Ms	**Ms 25**	(T.V. Franco La Pera)
Ms	**Ms 26**	(S.T.V. Alberto Bencini)
Ms	**Ms 31**	(T.V. Antonio Calvani)

2ª Flottiglia MAS (C.C. Massimo Alesi[53]) at Marsala[54]

    2ª Squadriglia MAS (T.V. Luigi Sala) at Messina
Mas	**Mas 547**	(?)
Mas	**Mas 556**	(T.V. Luigi Sala)

    15ª Squadriglia MAS (T.V. Andrea Giufra) at Marsala
Mas	**Mas 543**	(?)
Mas	**Mas 548**	(G.M. Miro Karis)
Mas	**Mas 549**	(T.V. Andrea Giufra)

    17ª Squadriglia MAS (S.T.V. R. Castello) at Marsala
Mas	**Mas 557**	(G.M. Giovanni Cafiero)

---

52. To be employed as anti-surface night blockade force in the Sicilian narrows, against Gibraltar forces.
53. Alesi was transferred on 12 August, replacement unknown.
54. According to the May plan, a number of MAS were to escort F.N.S., but by August the much more suited VAS were available in enough number to permit MAS to return to offensive duties.

Mas	**Mas 560**	(?)
Mas	**Mas 563**	(?)
Mas	**Mas 564**	(?)

18ª Squadriglia MAS (S.T.V. G. Pezzini) at Marsala

MAS	**Mas 562**	(G.M. Francesco Luciano)
MAS	**Mas 574**	(?)
MAS	**Mas 575**	(?)
MAS	**Mas 576**	(?)

20ª Squadriglia MAS (T.V. Carlo Paulizza) at Marsala

Mas	**Mas 552**	(?)
Mas	**Mas 553**	(?)
Mas	**Mas 554**	(?)

Squadra Sommergibili (A.S. Antonio Legnani; CSM A.D. Romeo Oliva)[55]

I Grupsom (C.F. Gino Spagone) at La Spezia[56]

Smg p.c.[57]	**H.1**	(S.T.V. Luigi Ginocchio)
Smg p.c.	**H.4**	(T.V. Giuseppe Simonetti)
Smg p.c.	**H.6**	(T.V. Renzo Fossati)
Smg p.c.	*Antonio **Bajamonti***	(C.C. Raffaello Allegri)
Smg p.c.	*Francesco **Rismondo***	(C.C. Virgilio Spigai)

II Grupsom (C.F. Emilio Francardi) at Napoli

Smg p.c.	*Topazio*	(T.V. Mario Patanè)

III Grupsom (C.F. Ferdinando Calda) at Messina

Smg p.c.	*Asteria*	(T.V. Dante Morrone)

IV Grupsom (C.F. Riccardo Boris) at Taranto[58]

Smg p.c.	**H.8**	(T.V. Ugo Gentili)
Smg p.c.	*Marcantonio **Bragadin***	(T.V. Adriano Pini)
Smg p.c.	*Santorre **Santarosa***	(C.C. Emilio Olivieri)
Smg p.c.	*Narvalo*	(T.V. Ludovico Grion)

---

55. The OOB of submarines is particularly complicated, since some boats had a paper dependence from one Grupsom (Gruppo Sommergibili), were attached to another one, and were operating from the base of a third one! The structure below shows the actual position. The boats are listed from older to newer.
56. The Spezia boats were employed in ASW patrol outside the harbour.
57. 'p.c.' for 'piccola crociera' (small cruise) were boats under 1,000 tons, 'g.c.' for 'grande crociera' (great cruise) were boats over 1,000 tons.
58. Most of the Taranto boats (either old or former minelayers) were cargo units, mainly used to transport gasoline to Africa.

Smg p c.	*Filippo* **Corridoni**	(T.V. Armando Rosso)
Smg g.c.	*Zoea*	(T.V. Rino Erler)
Smg g.c.	*Atropo*	(C.C. Pietro Abate)

V Grupsom (C.F. Bartolini Bardelli) at Lero

Smg p.c.	*Sirena*	(T.V. Vittorio Savarese)
Smg p.c.	*Ametista*	(T.V. Francesco Caprile)
Smg p.c.	*Nereide*	(C.C. Pasquale Terra)

VII Grupsom *(C.F. Alfredo Criscuolo)* at Cagliari

Smg g.c.	*Otaria*	(T.V. Alberto Gorini)
Smg p.c.	*Dagabur*	(T.V. Renato Pecori)
Smg p.c.	*Velella*	(T.V. Giovanni Febbraro)
Smg g.c.	*Dandolo*	(C.C. Alberto Campanella)
Smg g.c.	*Brin*	(T.V. Luigi Andreotti)
Smg g.c.	*Emo*	(T.V. Giuseppe Franco)
Smg p.c.	*Cobalto*	(T.V. Raffaele Amicarelli)
Smg p.c.	*Granito*	(T.V. Leo Sposito)
Smg p.c.	*Avorio*	(T.V. Mario Priggione)
Smg p.c.	*Volframio*	(T.V. Giovanni Manunta)

at La Maddalena

Smg p.c.	*Uarsciek*	(T.V. G. Arezzo della Targia)
Smg p.c.	*Giada*	(T.V. Gaspare Cavallina)
Smg p.c.	*Acciaio*	(T.V. Ottorino Beltrami)
Smg p.c.	*Bronzo*	(T.V. Cesare Buldrini)

VIII Grupsom (C.F. Pietro Scammacca) at Trapani

Smg p.c.	*Axum*	(T.V. Renato Ferrini)
Smg p.c.	*Alagi*	(T.V. Sergio Puccini)
Smg p.c.	*Dessiè*	(T.V. Renato Scandola)
Smg p.c.	*Ascianghi*	(T.V. Rodolfo Bombig)

IX Grupsom (C.F. Emilio Olivieri) at Brindisi
No units

X Grupsom (C.F. Francesco Murzi) at Augusta
No units

XII Grupsom (C.F. Alberto Agostini) at Pola[59]

Smg p.c.	*Vettor* **Pisani**	(C.C. Athos Fraternales)
Smg p.c.	*Fratelli* **Bandiera**	(C.C. Mario Vannutelli)
Smg p.c.	*Luciano* **Manara**	(C.C. Antonio De Giacomo)
Smg p.c.	*Ciro* **Menotti**	(C.C. Ugo Gelli)
Smg p.c.	*Squalo*	(C.C. Mario Resio)

---

59. Submarine training group, formed with older boats retired from front service.

Smg p.c.	*Delfino*		(C.C. Alberto Avogadro di Cerrione Trotti Bentivoglio)
Smg p.c.	*Serpente*		(C.C. Alberto Torri)
Smg p.c.	*Diaspro*		(C.C. Antonio Dotta)

Kriegsmarine forces in the Mediterranean

Marinegruppenkommando Süd (AD Karlgeorg Schuster) HQ Sofia

- **Admiral Schwarzes Meer** (VA Hans-Heinrich Wurmbach) HQ Costanza[60]
- **Admiral Ägäis** (VA Erich Förste) HQ Atene[61]
- **Comando Gruppo Navale Egeo Settentrionale [Marisudest]** (C.A. Catalano Gonzaga) HQ Atene[62]

Deutsches Marinekommando Italien (VA Eberhard Weichold)[63]
Deutscher Seetransportchefs Italien (KA Günther Horstmann) HQ Roma[64]
F.d.U. (Führer der Unterseeboote) Italien (KA Kreisch) HQ Roma

29. U-Flotille (KK Fritz Frauenheim) HQ La Spezia

At La Spezia
Unterseeboote	U 73	(KL Helmuth Rosenbaum)
Unterseeboote	U 83	(KL Hans-Werner Kraus)
Unterseeboote	U 205	(KL Franz-Georg Reschke)
Unterseeboote	U 331	(KL Hans-Dietrich Freiherr von Tiesenhausen)
Unterseeboote	U 431	(KL Wilhelm Rudolf Dommes)

At Salamis
Unterseeboote	U 77	(KL Heinrich Schonder)
Unterseeboote	U 97	(KL Friedrich Bürgel)
Unterseeboote	U 375	(KL Jürgen Könenkamp)
Unterseeboote	U 565	(KL Wilhelm August Franken)

---

60. Controlled all Kriegsmarine (and R.M.) units in the Black Sea.
61. Controlled all Kriegsmarine units in Greece and the Aegean.
62. An Italian naval command subordinate to a German HQ. Already listed above.
63. Controlled all surface forces, land troops and other offices of the Kriegsmarine in Italy and North Africa. Operationally subordinate to Supermarina. The units are listed under F.N.S.
64. Controlled German sea transportation in Italy and North Africa.

Appendix C

Axis Air Order of Battle

**Operazione *C3*
OoB of Axis Air Forces
© Davide Pastore 2007**

This is the Order of Battle for Axis air forces (Italian complete list in all theatres, plus German units in the Mediterranean area for Operazione *C3*).

The OOB generally refers to the day the air battle was originally scheduled to start (23 June 1942, day Y-30), taking exceptions for some cases.

Unfortunately, the last useful days of the July new moon (original day Y) were plagued by very bad weather, so *C3* had to be postponed to the August new moon. This means the air battle had to last nearly two months, probably bleeding white the involved units, and so requiring some replacements (to be taken amongst the ones listed as re-equipping and training in mainland Italy in June).

Air strength in Africa is quite a bit lower than the historical level during the El Alamein campaign, meaning Panzerarmee Afrika[1] would have been hard-pressed (and probably thrown back).

By the time *C3* is launched (15 August, as explained elsewhere), every unit involved in the air battle is expected to be much depleted. The Italians would have first swapped the bomber units in Sicily with those in Puglia, and later with the ones re-equipping, and those training in northern Italy (but there were precious few of them). Modern fighter units appear to be in short supply, as the African cauldron would have took the lion's share of available reinforcements.

The Germans had a stronger replacement service and probably did not need to swap units.

Regia Aeronautic

Armata Aerea *C3* is listed according to Superaereo letter n. 5571 of 20 June 1942 and subsequent variations. The name of the commander was not stated; however, a likely candidate was Gen. S.A. Ferruccio Ranza, commanding 4" Squadra Aerei involved in the operations.

Format for Italian units:

> Stormo [St.] (name of the commander*)* or 'independent' if the subordinate unit was Autonomo [Aut.].

---

1. At the time, Rommel's force, on paper (only) subordinated to Italians, bore the official name Armata Corazzata Italo-Tedesca (ACIT) Needless to say, today only Italian historians know this term. Germans invariably used Panzerarmee Afrika instead (Panzergruppe Afrika until early 1942), and since they were the senior partner I obliged them.

Gruppo [Gr.] as above.
Squadriglia [Sq.] as above.
(Aircraft quantity x aircraft type.)
Airfield for *C3*, according to planning.
(Airfield from where the unit was to be transferred, and/or historically used at the time, if applicable.)

A question mark means 'just a guess'.

With very few exceptions, two (three in fighter units) Squadriglie formed a Gruppo (plural Gruppi) and two Gruppi formed a Stormo (plural Stormi). Fighter units had an extra aircraft for both Gruppo and Stormo commander, as well as transport and liaison aircraft assigned (other units used their larger machines for these duties instead).

In theory, upper echelons included the Brigata Aerea (plural Brigate Aeree) and Divisione Aerea (Divisione Aeree), but by 1942 the aircraft were so few that these levels had been discontinued. At the top there was the Squadra Aerea (Squadre Aeree), four in Italy and a fifth one in Africa, plus smaller independent commands in the main islands and abroad.

Each Squadriglia was identified by an Arabic number followed by the figure 'a' (being feminine gendered). Each Gruppo and Stormo had the figure 'o' instead (male gendered). So both 1ª and 1° means '1st'. In theory, a Gruppo should have had its number written in Roman numbers (as per Regio Esercito standard of alternate styles in alternate command layers), but Regia Aeronautica rarely conformed to this rule.

The paper TOE was twelve aircraft per Squadriglia (plural Squadriglie) for smaller types (fighters etc.) and nine for larger one (bombers etc.). These levels were rarely attained while involved in front-line service, and as shown below average strength was about 70 per cent of that. On the other hand, units in quiet sectors could easily exceed them.

The aircraft quantities listed show the total quantity present in line, including inefficient aircraft. The numbers are only indicative, being largely referred to as 'strength during June' or even 'during summer'. A value preceded by a '~' means then is no historical source, so it is just a guess and the average of similar units.

Efficiency rate was usually about 60 per cent of total present, but occasionally could be worse (and, rarely, better). As a general rule the larger the aircraft, the lower the efficiency rate. For a large important operation like *C3*, the rate would probably be at least 75–80 per cent of the available total at the beginning of the air battle, shrinking thereafter (but likely 90–100 per cent for the airdrop Gruppi in their first mission).

Most of the units in training in mainland Italy are listed with a consistent '~' value about 60 per cent of their paper strength (meaning 'undergoing re-equipment'); actually, some had their full complement already, while others had scarcely a single aircraft.

For the Gruppi Complementary and Nuclei Addestramento, it is impossible even to try to quantify their detailed strength or the aircraft type.

About Aerosilurante (torpedo bombing, A.S.) units, it must be added that during the entire war they experienced a continuous and severe shortage of torpedoes.[2] As an intelligent assessment, the approximate total for Regia Aeronautica is as follows: 2,441 aircraft (618 in Armata Aerea *C3* alone).

---

2. According to Santoro, against Harpoon seventy-seven A.S. aircraft were deployed with sixty-six torpedoes. Against Pedestal there were 110 A.S. aircraft with 103 torpedoes. This means each unit had enough weapons to fly exactly two combat missions: the first one at the 60 per cent efficiency strength explained above and the second one with half such force, deducting lost and damaged aircraft. Thereafter they were toothless until replenished from the factories, at a very slow rate.

Luftwaffe

German units are listed according to OBS letter n. 7170/42 of 31 May 1942 (Kesselring's Plan), with the same format as above.

On paper, each Staffel (plural Staffelri) had twelve aircraft and was identified by an Arab number. Three Staffeln plus a Gruppestal of two aircraft formed a Gruppe of thirty-eight aircraft (Gruppen) identified by a Roman number. Three or four Gruppen plus a Geschwaderstab of four aircraft formed a Geschwader of 118–156 aircraft.

Similarly to Heer standard, I., II., III. and IV. Gruppe included 1. to 3., 4. to 6., 7. to 9. and 10. to 12. Staffel respectively. Note that in German, the dot is the numeral ('1.', meaning 1st).

The upper levels were the Fliegerführer (brigade), Fliegerdivision, Fliegerkorps and lastly Luftflotte.[3] All air units in the Mediterranean came under 2. Luftflotte.[4] As in Italian usage, alternate command layers used alternate Roman and Aral numbers.

The near-totality of the German units are listed here with their paper strength (grand total: 1,382 aircraft plus glider tugs) at twelve aircraft per Staffel, two per Gruppestab, four per Geschwaderstab and fifty-three for a complete Transportgruppe. Historical strength varied, but typically most units had about 90 per cent of the paper aircraft present in line.

Actual availability for *C3* may have been up to paper strength, slightly lower or quite lower, depending upon the whimsies of OKL: at the time, the air units in southern Russia were being rebuilt for the upcoming Caucasus offensive, so plenty of material was at hand, if diverted. In theory at least, all units *could* have been reinforced. This was a marked difference compared to the Regia Aeronautica, which was scratching the bottom of the barrel and had not even the hope of reaching paper strength.

Efficiency rate was typically about 70 per cent of the total present during a sustained campaign, but possibly up to 90–100 per cent at the beginning of the air battle, shrinking thereafter.

Regia Aeronautica – Armata Aerea *C3* [618 aircraft] (HQ Palermo ?) (Gen. S.A. Femiccio Ranza ?)

Al) **Comando Bombardamento Puglie**[5] [105 aircraft] (HQ Lecce) (?)

part of 16° Stormo B.T.[6] (Col. Enrico Cigerza)
   50° Gruppo B.T. (Ten. Col. Ugo Grossi)
      210ª, 211ª Squadriglia B.T. (10x CZ.1007bis) Manduria
   30° St. B.T. (Col. Umberto Fiore)
      87° Gr. B.T. (Ten. cV Mario Giuliani)
         192ª, 193ª Sq. B.T. (18x CZ.1007bis) Manduria (from Forli)
      90° Gr. B.T. (Magg. Emulo Paris)
         194ª, 195ª Sq. B.T. (18x CZ.1007bis) Manduria (from Forli)

---

3. Sometimes specialized units reflected it in their names: Jagdfiihrer, Jagddivision, etc.
4. Some German sources use the form Luftflotte 2 instead.
5. Basically this command was to act as replacements reservoir for depleted units in Sicily.
6. Also including 51° Gruppo in Sardinia (although, according to some sources, the two Gruppi were Autonomi by now).

Axis Air Order of Battle 257

    32° St. A.S.[7] (Col. Leone Leonello)
        38° Gr. B.T. (Magg. Tommaso Folinea)
            49^a, 50^a Sq. B.T. (18x SM.84) Crotone (from Gioia del Colle)
        89° Gr. A.S. (Ten. Col. Antonio Fadda)
            228^a, 229^a Sq. A.S. (16x SM.84) Crotone (from Gioia del Colle)
    37° St. B.T. (Col. Giuseppe Sgarlata)
        55° Gr. B.T. (Ten. Col. Renato DiJorio)
            220^a, 221^a Sq. B.T. (~12x BR.20/M) Lecce
        116° Gr. B.T. (Ten. Col. Luigi Fabiani)
            266^a, 267^a Sq. B.T. (13x BR.20/M) Lecce

A2) Comando Bombardamento Sicilia [98 aircraft] (HQ Palermo) (Col. Giuseppe Gaeta)

    7° St. A.S.[8] (Col. Domenico Ludovico)
        4° Gr. A.S. (Magg. Gastone Valentini)
            14^a, 15^a Sq. A.S. (15x SM.84) Sciacca
        25° Gr. A.S. (Magg. Gabriele Rivalta)
            8^a, 9^a Sq. A.S. (12x SM.84) Sciacca
    9° St. B.T. (Col. Giovanni D'Auria)
        29° Gr. B.T. (Ten. Col. Cesare De Porto)
            62^a, 63^a Sq. B.T. (13x CZ.1007bis) Trapani-Chinisia[9]
        33° Gr. B.T. (Ten. Col. Ercole Savi)
            59^a, 60^a Sq. B.T. (16x CZ.1007bis) Trapani-Chinisia
    10° St. B.T. (Col. Pasquale D'lppolito)
        30° Gr. B.T. (Magg. Giuseppe Noziglia)
            55^a, 56^a Sq. B.T. (11x SM.79) Palermo-Boccadifalco (from Sciacca)
        32° Gr. B.T. (Magg. Carlo Alberto Capitani)
            57^a, 58^a Sq. B.T. (11x SM.79) Palermo-Boccadifalco
    Independent
        173^a Sq. Aut. R.S. (8x CR.25) Palermo-Boccadifalco
    Independent
        88° Gr. Aut. B.T.[10] (Magg. Eduardo Agnello)
            264^a, 265^a Sq. B.T. (~12x BR.20/M) Castelvetrano

A3) Comando Assalto Sicilia [157 aircraft] (HQ Belpasso) (?)
part of 3° St. C.T.[11] (Ten. Col. Tito Falconi) 18° Gr. C.T. (Magg. Gino Lodi)

---

7. 32° Stormo was to operate in coordinated anti-ship attacks, using the traditional torpedo in 89° Gruppo A.S. and the new Motobomba F.F.F. in 38° Gruppo B.T. The latter weapons were first used in combat in August against Pedestal, vut they had been available since July.

8. 7° Stormo B.T. was officially converted to A.S. on 1 May 1942, but apparently never operated in (nor was trained in) the torpedo role and eventually reverted to B.T. on 1 October 1942.

9. As commonly done both at the time and now, I listed airfields located in small towns near large cities as 'Trapani-Chinisia', meaning ''location is Chinisia, probably not shown on most charts, but quite near to Trapani'.

10. According to some sources, 88° Gruppo was part of 43° Stormo (along with 98° and 99° Gruppo).

11. Also including 23° Gruppo re-equipping and training at Mirafiori.

258   Operation C3: Hitler's Plan to Invade Malta 1942

        83ª, 85ª, 95ª Sq. C.T. (18x MC.200/b.a.) Belpasso ? (from Mirafiori)
    5° St. Tuff. (Col. Guido Nobili)
        101° Gr. Tuff. (Magg. Carlo Alberto Rizzi)
            208ª, 238ª Sq. Tuff. (~20x CR.42/b.a.) Belpasso ? (from Gela)
        102° Gr. Tuff. (Magg. Giuseppe Cenni)
            209ª, 239ª Sq. Tuff. (15x Ju 87R) Belpasso ? (from Gela)
    15° St. Ass.[12] (Col. Silvio Napoli)
        46° Gr. Ass. (Magg. Giovanni Morbidelli)
            20ª, 21ª Sq. Ass. (~20x CR.42/b.a. ?) Lentini ? (from Vicenza)
        47° Gr. Ass. (Magg. Giovanni Masoero)
            53ª, 54ª Sq. Ass. (~12x Ca.313 & Ca.314 ?) Lentini ? (from Vicenza)
    53° St. C.T. (Ten. Col. Rolando Prate Hi)
        151° Gr. C.T. (Ten. Col. Antonio Giachino)
            366ª, 367ª, 368ª Sq. C.T. (38x G.50bis/b.a.) Lentini ? (from Caselle)
        153° Gr. C.T. (Magg. Andrea Favini)
            372ª, 373ª, 374ª Sq. C.T. (34x MC.200/b.a.) Lentini ? (from Caselle)

A4) **Comando Caccia Sicilia** [205 aircraft] (HQ Comiso) (Gen. B.A. Mario Piccini)
    51° St. C.T. (Ten. Col. Aldo Remondino)
        20° Gr. C.T. (Magg. Gino Callieri)
            151ª, 352ª, 353ª Sq. C.T. (35x MC.202) Gela
        155° Gr. C.T. (Magg. Duilio Fanali)
            351ª, 360ª, 378ª Sq. C.T. (35x MC.202) Gela
    54° St. C.T.[13] (Col. Carlo Calosso)
        7° Gr. C.T. (Magg. Alberto Beneforti)
            76ª, 86ª, 98ª Sq. C.T. (11x CR.42, 27x MC.200, 3x MC.202) Gela
        16° Gr. C.T. (Magg. Francesco Beccaria)
            167ª, 168ª, 169ª Sq. C.T. (11x CR.42, 27x MC.200, 3x MC.202) Gela Independent
            Sezione Caccia Fotografica (3x MC.202/r.f.) Gela
    Independent
        2° Gr. Aut. C.T.[14] (Ten. Col. Aldo Quarantotti)
            150ª Sq. C.T. (9x Re.2001) Pantelleria ? (from San Pietro di Caltagirone)
            152ª Sq. C.T. (9x Re.2001) Trapani-Chinisia ? (from S P di Caltagirone)
            358ª Sq. C.T. (9x Re.2001) Sciacca ? (from S P di Caltagirone) Independent

---

12. 15° Stormo spent long disappointing months from mid-1941 to early 1942 trying to find some use for the useless Ca.313 and Ca.314 they had been equipped with, finally giving up and receiving CR.42/b.a. fighter-bombers instead from mid-1942. Historically, the entire Stormo was converted to the 'new' planes during the summer (changing from 'Comb.' to 'Ass.'); however, according to June C3 papers, one Gruppo of Ca.314s was to be equipped with smoke dischargers (probably the only combat mission the type could fulfil). This assumes all the Caproni were to be concentrated into a Gruppo, and the biplanes into another one. The respective Gruppo identification is just a guess.
13. 54° Stormo was being gradually re-equipped with MC.202s, discarding the older types by the end of August. Actually Italian plans had it located at San Pietro, but this would have been difficult since that airfield was reserved for German units.
14. Actual Squadriglia allocation is just a guess. It seems 2° Stormo was to be used for convoy protection, since the air timetable lists four fighter Gruppi. This also reflects the flying characteristics of the Re.2001 compared to the MC.202 (slower but longer-ranged).

Axis Air Order of Battle 259

377ª Sq. Aut. C.T. (6x CR.42, 8x Re.2000) Palermo-Boccadifalco
Sezione I.[15] (4x CR.42/c.n.) Palermo-Boccadifalco
Sezione I. (3x CR.42/c.n.) Castelvetrano
Sezione I. (2x CR.42/c.n.) Pantelleria

A5) **Comando Divisione Trasporti** [155 aircraft] (HQ Palermo) (Gen. D.A. Vincenzo Velardi)

A5a) **Paradrop** (72 aircraft)[16] at Castelvetrano
  part of 44° St. T. (Ten. Col. Giovanni Buonamico) 146° Gr. T. (Magg. Mario Medina)
    603ª, 609ª Sq. T. (24x SM.82/P)
  45° St. T. (Col. Emilio Draghelli)
    37° Gr. T. (Magg. Pietro Lauri Filzi)
      47ª, 48ª Sq. T. (24x SM.82/P)
    147° Gr. T. (Magg. Felice Santini)
      601ª, 602ª Sq. T. (24x SM.82/P)

A5b) **Air ferry** (83 aircraft)[17] at Sciacca
  part 18° St. T.[18] (Col. Paolo Allan)
    56° Gr. T. (Ten. Col. Luigi Marini)
      222ª, 223ª Sq. T. (25x SM.81/T)
    57° Gr. T. (?)
      224ª, 225ª Sq. T. (no aircraft ?)[19]
  part of 44° St. T. (Ten. Col. Giovanni Buonamico)
    149° Gr. T. (Magg. Nicola Fattibene)
      607ª, 608ª Sq. T. (16x SM.82)
  48° St. T. (Ten. Col. Michele Scattaglia)
    144°Gr. T. (?)
      617ª, 618ª Sq. T. (no aircraft)[20]
    148° Gr. T. (Ten. Col. Mario Ferruzzi)
      605ª Sq. T. (4x SM.73)
      606ª Sq. T. (7xG.12)

---

15. The many Sezioni Inlercettori stationed on many airfields were (on paper) night fighter units.
16. Only seventy-two SM.82s were equipped for airdrop (SM.72/P). Apparently the remaining twenty could not be converted before C3 since they would be grounded for modifications for some time while they were deeply needed. The airdrop aircraft were to be organized into three reinforced Gruppi as shown. This seems to indicate each was to carry an infantry battalion (eighteen aircraft) plus heavy supports (two aircraft for each 81mm mortar platoon or 47mm gun platoon). Alternatively, they could carry a total of four infantry battalions without any heavy support (but disrupting the Gruppi organization). Actually, Italian plans had them divided between Castelvetrano and Gela airfields, but this is in conflict with the army paratroops' dispositions: front echelon near Castelvetrano, rear echelon near Gela.
17. According to a different source, there was a total of seventy-seven ferry aircraft, all types.
18. Also including 245°, 246" and 247" Squadriglie in Russia.
19. 57° Gruppo on 11 or 25 June. According to conflicting sources, either it was a skeleton unit scheduled to receive new SM.82s or it had old SM.81/Ts retired from bomber service (in the latter case, the twenty-five aircraft listed were to be divided amongst two Gruppi).
20. 144° Gruppo formed on 30 June without aircraft, scheduled to receive new SM.82s.

Attached from civilian airlines[21]
  N.C.A.L. (Nucleo Comunicazioni Ala Littoria)
    12x SM.75
    2x SM.82/C
  N.C.A. (Nucleo Comunicazioni Aviolinee)
    3x G.12/C
    4x G.18/V
  N.C.L. (Nucleo Comunicazioni L.A. T.I.)
    2x G.12/C
    6x SM.75
    2x SM.82/C

A6) **Comando Soccorso** [17 aircraft] (HQ Catania) (?)
  612ª Sq. Aut. Socc. (~6x CZ.506/C & /S) Marsala-Stagnone
  615ª Sq. Aut. Socc. (~6x CZ.506/C & /S) Siracusa
  Sezione Aut. Socc. (4x CZ.506/C, 1x CZ.509) ? (from Roma-Lido)

A7) **Unattached** (directly under Armata Aerea C3) [53 aircraft]
  part of 46° St. A.S.[22] (Col. Sirio Fossatl)
    104° Gr. A.S. (Magg. Virginia Reinero)
      252ª, 253ª Sq. A.S. (~14x SM.79) Reggio Calabria (from Decimomanni)
    Independent
    130° Gr. Aut. A.S. (Magg. Giorgio Grossi)
      280ª, 283ª Sq. A.S. (15x SM.79) Pantelleria (from Elmas)
    132° Gr. Aut. A.S. (Magg. Carlo Emanuele Buscaglia)
      278ª, 281ª Sq. A.S. (14x SM.79) Pantelleria (from Gerbini)
    Independent
      detachment from 1°, 2°, 3° N.A.S.[23] (~10x SM.79) Reggio Calabria ?

B) **Aviazione Ausiliaria per la Regia Marina (Marinavia)** [251 aircraft] (HQ Roma)[24] Gen. B.A. Francesco Man

Bl) **Units directly involved in C3**
  Comando in Capo Dipartimento MM. Basso Tirreno (HQ Napoli)
    182ª Sq. Aut. R.M. (10x CZ.501, 2x CZ.506) Napoli-Nisida

---

21. The exact strength of each Nucleo is a matter of guess, since my source only shows totals per aircraft type.
22. Also including 105° Gruppo in Sardinia.
23. Not included in the plan, but probably available as a reinforcement. See below.
24. Independent from Superaereo (which only provided men and aircraft) and operating under Supermarina orders, with naval observers on board. Deployment as per C3 plan, under the relative territorial navy command. The five Squadriglie in Alto Tirreno and Alto Adriatico were too far to be of use in the operation, but they would have acted as reserve. The ones in Egeo would not have taken part at all, recon work east of 20° E longitude being a Luftwaffe task. The remaining twenty-one fielded a total of ninety recon aircrafts (77x Cant Z.506 plus 13x RS.14 plus 123 convoy escort aircraft [Cant Z.501]). Another source lists twelve recon aircraft at Napoli instead of two, but this is probably a typo. Note, however, that these numbers are a paper total: roughly only 60–80 per cent of them were efficient and available at any given time.

Comando in Capo Dip. M.M. Jonio e Basso Adriatico (HQ Taranto)
    141ª Sq. Aut. R.M. (12x CZ.501) Brindisi
    142ª Sq. Aut. R.M. (10x CZ.501) Taranto
    288ª Sq. Aut. R.M. (10x CZ.506) Taranto

Comando M.M. in Sicily (HQ Messina)
  83° Gr. Aut. R.M. (Magg. Fgino Bianchini)
    140ª Sq. R.M. (9x CZ.501) Augusta (from Torre del Lago)
    170ª Sq. R.M. (10x RS.14) Augusta
    184ª Sq. R.M. (10x CZ.501) Augusta
    186ª Sq. R.M. (11x CZ.506) Augusta
    189ª Sq. R.M. (9x CZ.501) Augusta
  85° Gr. Aut. R.M. (Magg. Gennaro Venditti)
    144ª Sq. R.M. (11x CZ.506, 3x RS.14) Marsala-Stagnone
    187ª Sq. R.M. (9x CZ.501) Marsala-Stagnone (from Cadimare)
    197ª Sq. R.M. (9x CZ.501) Marsala-Stagnone

Comando M.M. in Sardegna (HQ La Maddalena)
    138ª Sq. Aut. R.M. (9x CZ.501) Olbia
    146ª Sq. Aut. R.M. (11x CZ.506) Cagliari-Elmas
    148ª Sq. Aut. R.M. (7x CZ.501) Olbia (from Vigna di Valle)
    171ª Sq. Aut. R.M. (9x CZ.506) Cagliari-Elmas (from Taranto)
    188ª Sq. Aut. R.M. (9x CZ.501) Cagliari-Elmas
    287ª Sq. Aut. R.M. (10x CZ.506) Cagliari-Elmas

Comando Superiore Regia Marina in Libia (HQ Tripoli)
    145ª Sq. Aut. R.M. (8x CZ.501, 7x CZ.506) Pisida
    196ª Sq. Aut. R.M. (5x CZ.501) Bengasi

Comando M.M. Grecia Occidentale (HQ Patrasso)
    139ª Sq. Aut. R.M. (7x CZ.501, 6x CZ.506) Prevesa

Real Situation on 15 August[25]

B1) Units directly involved in *C3*

Comando in Capo Dipartimento M.M. Basso Tirreno (HQ Napoli)
    182ª Sq. Aut. R.M. (13/9x CZ.501, 5/1x CZ.506, 1/lx RS.14) Napoli-Nisida

Comando in Capo Dip. M.M. Jonio e Basso Adriatico (HQ Taranto)
  141ª Sq. Aut. R.M. (11/10x CZ.501) Brindisi
  142ª Sq. Aut. R.M. (13/4x CZ.501) Taranto
  171ª Sq, Aut. R.M. (listed at Cagliari-Elmas)
  288ª Sq. Aut. R.M. (11/2x CZ.506) Taranto

---

25. Real aircraft availability on the morning of 15 August, as per Navy returns. '13/9' means thirteen aircraft present in line but nine efficient ones.

Comando M.M. in Sicily (HQ Messina)
   83° Gr. Aut. R.M. (Magg. Igino Bianchini)
      140ª Sq. R.M. (5/4x CZ.501) Augusta (actually at Torre del Lago)
      170ª Sq. R.M. (10/8x RS.14) Augusta
      184ª Sq. R.M. (10/8x CZ.501, 2/1x Ro.44) Augusta
      186ª Sq. R.M. (10/8x CZ.506, 6/5x RS.14) Augusta
      189ª Sq. R.M. (10/8x CZ.501) Augusta
   85° Gr. Aut. R.M. (Magg. Gennaro Venditti)
      144ª Sq. R.M. (5/3x CZ.501, 5/1x CZ.506, 6/3x RS.14) Marsala-Stagnone
      187ª Sq. R.M. (6/5x CZ.501, 6/4x CZ.506) Marsala-Stagnone (actually at Cadimare)
      197ª Sq. R.M. (9/5x CZ.501, 4/2x CZ.506, 1/lx RS.14, 1/lx Ro.43) Marsala-Stagnom

Comando M.M. in Sardinia (HQ La Maddalena)
   138ª Sq. Aut. R.M. (9/7x CZ.501, 1/1x Ro.43) Olbia
   146ª Sq. Aut. R.M. (12/8x CZ.506) Cagliari-Elmas
   148ª Sq. Aut. R.M. (7/2x CZ.501) Olbia (actually at Menelao)
   171ª Sq. Aut. R.M. (10/7x CZ.506) Cagliari-Elmas (actually at Taranto)
   188ª Sq. Aut. R.M. (9/4x CZ.501) Cagliari-Elmas
   287ª Sq. Aut. R.M. (11/10x CZ.506) Cagliari-Elmas

Comando Superiore Regia Marina in Libya (HQ Tripoli)
   145ª Sq. Aut. R.M. (3/3x CZ.501, 4/4x CZ.506) Pisida
   148ª Sq. Aut. R.M. at Menelao (listed at Olbia)
   196ª Sq. Aut. R.M. (9/6x CZ.501) Bengasi

Comando M.M. Grecia Occidentale (HQ Patrasso)
   139ª Sq. Aut. R.M. (11/5x CZ.501, 5/3x CZ.506) Prevesa

C) **2. Luftflotte** [1,382-plus aircraft][26] (HQ Frascati) Genfeldm Albert Kesselring

Cl) II. Fliegerkorps [700 aircraft] (HQ Taormina) Genob Bruno Loerzer

at San Pietro di Caltagirone
   Jagdgeschwader 27 (Obstlt Eduard Neumann)
      Stab/JG27   ~4x Bfl09F-4
      II./JG27 (Hptm Gustav Rodel)
         StabII./JG27   ~2x Bfl09F-4
         4./JG27   ~12xBfl09F-4
         5./JG27   ~12x Bfl09F-4
         6./JG27   ~12x Bfl09F-4
      III./JG27 (Hptm Erhard Braune)
         StabIII./JG27   ~2x Bfl09F-4
         7./JG27   ~12x Bf109F-4
         8./JG27   ~12x Bfl09F-4
         9./JG27   ~12x Bfl09F-4

---

26. As said above, Luftwaffe strength listed here is the paper (maximum) one.

Unattached[27]
    10.(Jabo)/JG 27   ~12x Bf109F-4/B
    10.(Jabo)/JG 53[28]   ~12x Bf109F-4/B
Sturzkampfgeschwader 3 (Oberst Walter Sieg!)
    Stab/StG3   ~4x Ju87D-1
  From I./StG3
    3./SIG3   ~12x Ju87D-1
  II./StG3 (Hptm Heinrich Heine)
    StabII./StG3   ~2x Ju87D-1
    4./S1G3   ~12x Ju87D-1
    5./StG3   ~12x Ju87D-1
    6./StG3   ~12x Ju87D-1
  III./StG3 (Hptm Kurt Walter)
    StabII./StG3   ~2x Ju87D-1
    7./S1G3   ~12x Ju87D-1
    8./S1G3   ~12x Ju87D-1
    9./SIG3   ~12x. Ju87D-1

at Trapani-Chinisia
  from Auflärungsgruppe (Fern) 122[29]
    1.(F)/122   12x Ju88D-1[30]

  Unattached
    6. Seenotstaffel   ~ 12x Do24T-1[31]

at Grottaglie
  from Kampfgeschwader 54
    IV.(Erg)/KG54 (Hptm Hein Krenkel)
      Stab IV.(Erg)/KG54 ~2x Ju88A-4
      10./KG54   ~12x Ju88A-4
      11./KG54   ~12x Ju88A-4
      12./KG54   ~12x Ju88A-4

at Comiso
  Jagdgeschwader 53 (Obstlt Freiherr von Maltzahn)
    Stab/JG53   ~4x Bf109F-4 (later Bf109G-2)[32]

---

27. As per plan. Historically, during the summer 10.(Jabo)/JG27 and 10.(Jabo)/JG53 were converged into a single Jabo. St. Afrika. According to a different source, at the time Jabo aircraft were Bf109E-7/Bs.
28. Source is unclear about airfield for 10.(Jabo)/JG53 (if San Pietro with the other Jabo or Comiso with the rest of JG53).
29. Stab (F)/I22 and 2.(F)/I22 based on the same airfield (see below) but attached to Luftflotte HQ. Apparently this Staffel covered alone, while the rest of the Gruppe had strategic objectives.
30. The Ju88D-1 listed for most Fern recon units is just indicative, being the most common type. Other aircraft were employed too.
31. Air rescue unit.
32. JG53 and JG77 converted to Bf109G-2s during late summer, exact date unknown. JG27 converted only later, after leaving Africa; it is possible it too would have received the newer type had it been based nearer to home.

I./JG77 (attached)[33] (Maj Heinz Ear)
    Stab I./JG77   ~2x Bf109F-4 (later Bf109G-2)
    1./JG77   ~12x Bf109F-4 (later Bf109G-2)
    2./JG77   ~12x Bf109F-4 (later Bf109G-2)
    3./JG77   ~12x Bf109F-4 (later Bf109G-2)
II./JG53 (Hptm Walter Spies)
    Stab II./JG53   ~2x Bf109F-4 (later Bf109G-2)
    4./JG 53   ~12x Bf109F-4 (later Bf109G-2)
    5./JG 53   ~12x Bf109F-4 (later Bf109G-2)
    6./JG 53   -12x Bf109F-4 (later Bf109G-2)
III./JG53 (Hptm Wolf-Dietrich Wilcke)
    Stab III./JG53   ~2x Bf109F-4 (later Bf109G-2)
    7./JG53   ~12x Bf109F-4 (later Bf109G-2)
    8./JG53   ~12x Bf109F-4 (later Bf109G-2)
    9./.1G53   ~12x Bf109F-4 (later Bf109G-2)

From Zerstorergeschwader 26
    III./ZG26 (Hptm Georg Christl)
        Stab III./ZG26 ~2x Bf110C-4 & D-3
        Stab7./ZG26   ~12x Bf110C-4 & D-3
        Stab 8./ZG26   ~ 12x Bf110C-4 & D-3
        Stab 9./ZG26   ~12x Bf110C-4 & D-3

at Catania[34]
    Kampfgeschwader 54 (Obstlt Walter Marienfeld)
        Stab/KG54   ~4x Ju88A-4
    I./KG54 (Hptm Georg Graf von Platen)
        Stab I./KG54   ~2x Ju88A-4
        1./KG54   ~12x Ju88A-4
        2./KG54   ~12x Ju88A-4
        3./KG54   ~12x Ju88A-4
    KGr606[35] (Hptm Rolf Siedschlag)
        Stab KGr606   ~2x Ju88A-4
        1./KGr606   ~12x Ju88A-4
        2./KGr606   ~12x Ju88A-4
        3./KGr606   ~12x Ju88A-4
    KGr806[36] (Maj Richard Linke)
        Stab KGr806   ~2x Ju88A-4

---

33. Kesselring expected ('hoped for, but not sure') a further Jagdgruppe as reinforcement. The choice of I./JG77 (historically arriving m August) is a guess; he might have had in mind I./JG53 instead (present until April, then sent to Russia).
34. There were two main airfields nearby, Catania-Sigonella and Catania-Fontanarossa. Catania was also the planned base for the many glider units listed below; probably KG54 and I./NJG2 operated from one airfield (it is unclear which one) and the gliders from the other.
35. Subordinate to Stab/KG54 since December 1941. On 10 September renamed I./KG77.
36. Subordinate to Stab/KG54 since December 1941. On 1 September renamed III./KG54.

    1./KGr806   ~12x Ju88A-4
    2./KGr806   ~12x Ju88A-4
    3./KGr806   ~12x Ju88A-4
from Nachtjagdgescwader 2
  I./NJG 2 (Maj Erich Jung)
    StabI./NJG2   ~2x Ju88C-6
    1./NJG2   ~12x Ju88C-6
    2./NJG2   ~12x Ju88C-6
    3./NJG2   ~12x Ju88C-6

at Gerbini
  Kampfgeschwader 77 (Obstlt Hermann Schluter)
    Stab/KG77   ~4x Ju88A-4
  II./KG77 (Maj Heinrich Paepcke)
    StabII./KG77   ~2x Ju88A-4
    4./KG77   ~12x Ju88A-4
    5./KG77   ~12x Ju88A-4
    6./KG77   ~12x Ju88A-4
  III./KG77 (Maj Wilhelm Stemmler)
    Stab III./KG77   ~2x Ju88A-4
    7./KG77   ~12x Ju88A-4
    8./KG77   ~12x Ju88A-4
    9./KG 77   ~12x Ju88A-4
  from Lehrgeschwader 1
    from I./LG1
      3./LG1   ~12x Ju88A-4
    II./LG 1 (Maj Gerhard Kollewe)
      Stab II./LG1   ~2x Ju88A-4
      4./LG1   ~12x Ju88A-4
      5./LG1   ~12x Ju88A-4
      6./LG1   ~12x Ju88A-4

C2) X. Fliegerkorps [135 aircraft] (HQ Athens-Kiphissia) Gen Hans Geisler

At various bases (Kastelli, Skaramanga, Heraklion, Eleusis, Kalamata)

  From Jagdgeschwader 27
    Jagdkommando JG27[37] ~12x Bf109F-4
  Lehrgeschwader (Obstlt Fran: van Benda)
    Stab/LG1 ~4x Ju88A-4
    I./LG1 (part)[38] (Maj Joachim Helbig)
      Stab I./LG1 ~2x Ju88A-4

---

37. Provisional unit. Strength is speculative.
38. The plan listed one unspecified Staffel detached to II. FK.

1./LG1 ~12x Ju88A-4
2./LG1 ~12x Ju88A-4
IV.(Erg)/LG1 (part)[39] (Hptm. Gerhard Richter)
Stab IV.(Erg)/LG1 ~2x Ju88A-4
10./LG1 ~12x Ju88A-4
11./LG1 ~12x Ju88A-4
from Aufklarungsgruppe (Fern) 123
2.(F)/123 4x Ju86P-2,[40] ~8x Ju88D-1
from Aufklarungsgruppe (See) 125
2./SAGr125 ~12x Arl96A-3
Aufklarungsgruppe (See) 126[41] (Obstlt Hermann Kaiser)
Stab/SAGr126 ~2x Ar196A-3 & He60D
1./SAGr26 ~12x Ar196A-3 & He60D
2./SAGr26 ~12x Ar196A-3 & He60D
3./SAGr126 ~12x Ar196A-3 & He60D
Unattached
Luftwaffe-Transport-Staffel 222   5x Bv222V

C3) Fliegerfürher Afrika [150 aircraft] (HQ ?) Gen Otto Hoffmann von Waldau

at Tripoli
from Kampfgeschwader 100
II./KG100[42] (Maj Horst Robling)
Stab II./KG100   ~2x He111H-6
4./KG100   ~12x He111H-6
5./KG100   ~12x He111H-6
6./KG100   ~12x He111H-6

At unknown advanced bases
From Jagdgeschwader 27
I./JG27[43] (Hptm Gerhard Homuth)
Stab I./JG27   ~2x Bf109F-4
1./JG27   ~12x Bf109F-4
2./JG27   ~12x Bf109F-4
3./JG27   ~12x Bf109F-4
From Zerstorergeschwader 26
10./ZG26[44]   ~12x Do177-10

---

39. 12./LG1 based in Africa since January 1942.
40. Stratospheric recon aircraft, immune to any artillery or fighter. Transferring some or all of them to II. FK to shadow Force H makes sense.
41. Aufklarungsgruppe (See) 126 renamed III./KG100 on 20 September. On that day it had nine Ar196As plus nine He111II-6s and was converting to the latter type (conversion never completed, reverting to Ar196 on 18 February 1943). It is unclear if it had already received some He111H-6s at this stage.
42. Based in Africa but to be employed for night bombing against Malta. During C3 it would have dropped mannequins as decoys.
43. The plan listed one unspecified Gruppe of JG27 left in Africa; choice of 1. is mine.
44. Usually attached to III./ZG26 and not listed separately in the plan. However, since it was usually stationed in Libya for convoy escort duty (and with ineffective 'fighters' to begin with) it seems logical to leave it there. It is included in C3 air cover operations.

Axis Air Order of Battle   267

From Sturzkampfgeschwader 3
    1./StG3 (part)[45] (Hptm Heinrich Eppen)
        StabI./StG3   ~2x Ju87D-1
        1./StG3   ~12x Ju87D-1
        2./SlG3   ~12x Ju87D-1
From Lehrgeschwader (Obstlt Franz von Benda)
    from IV(Erg)./LG1
        12./LG1   ~12x Ju88A-4
from Aujklarungsgruppe (Heer) 12
    4.(H)/12   ~12x Bf109F-4 & Bf110C-4
from Aufklarungsgruppe (Fern) 121
    1.(F)/121   ~12x Ju88D-1

    6./KG26[46]   ~ 12x He111H-6/LT

F5) **Transport Units** (XI. Fliegerkorps ??) [371-plus aircraft][47]

at Gerbini
    Kampfgruppe zur besonderen Verwendung 102 (?)
        Unclear structure[48] 53x Ju52/3m (from Grottaglie)
    Kampfgruppe zur besonderen Venvendung 300 (?)
        Unclear structure 53x Ju52/3m (from Bari)
    Kampfgruppe zur besonderen Verwendung 400 (?)
        Unclear structure 53x Ju52/3m (from Vibo Valentia)

at Comiso
    Kampfgruppe zur besonderen Verwendung 600 (?)
        Unclear structure 53x Ju52/3m (from San Pancrazio)
    Kampfgruppe zur besonderen Venvendung 800 (?)
        Unclear structure 53x Ju52/3m (from Lecce)

at Reggio Calabria
    Kampfgeschwader zur besonderen Verwendung 1 (?)
        III./KGzbV1 (?)
            Unclear structure 53x Ju52/3m (from Foggia)

at Catania
    Glider units[49] (see below) (from Brindisi)

---

45. The plan listed an unspecified Gruppe less one unspecified Staffel left in Africa; choice of 1. and 2. is mine.
46. KG26 based elsewhere (I. at Bardufoss and III. at Banak in Norway, II. at Saki on the Black Sea) but undergoing torpedo training at Grosseto (one of the very few things Italians could teach them) during summer, one Staffel at a time. In August it was the turn for 6./KG26, which took part in the Pedestal battle. For some reason Kesselring did not list this unit.
47. The transport units would probably be subordinated to Student's XI. Fliegerkorps. The identification of the transport units is tentative; listed are the seven Ju52/3m Gruppen employed in the Mediterranean at some time during summer 1942.
48. Kesselring was explicit about these units being built up to a strength of fifty-three aircraft each.
49. The identification of the glider units (and their strength) is even more conjectural. See below.

From Kampfgeschwader zur besonderen Verwendung 323[50] (Ob Gustav Damm)
1./KGzbV323 (Major Gunther Mams)
    Stab 1./KGzbV323   3x Me323C-0 & D-0
    1./KGzbV323   6x Me323C-0 & D-0
    2./KGzbV323   6x Me323C-0 & D-0
    3./KGzbV323   6x Me323C-0 & D-0
    4./KGzbV323   6x Me323C-0 & D-0

Available Glider Units[51]

Luftlandegeschwader 1[52] (Genmaj Rudiger van Heyking) Stab LLG1 ~4x tug[53]
    I./LLG1
        Stab I./LLG1 ~2x tug
        1./LLG1 ~12x tug, ~15x DFS230[54]
        2./LLG1 ~12x tug, ~15x DFS230
        3./LLG1 ~12x tug, ~15x DFS230
    II./LLG 1
        Stab II./LLG1 ~2x tug
        4./LLG1 ~12x tug, ~15x DFS230
        5./LLG1 ~12xtug, ~15x DFS230
        6./LLG1 ~12x tug, ~15x DFS230
    III./LLG 1
        Stab III./LLG1 ~2x tug
        9./LLG1   ~12x tug, ~15x DFS230

Luftlandegeschwader 2[55] (Obstlt Richard Kupschus)
    Stab LLG2 ~4x He111H
    I./LLG 2
        Stab I./LLG2 ~2x He111H
        1./LLG2 ~12x He111H, ~15x Go242

---

50. Formed in August 1942 (and so not listed by Kesselring in his 31 May plan). Strength is paper TOE. The exact number of aircraft in existence at the time is somewhat unclear (different authors providing different values); averaging sources, it seems there were (including prototypes) seven Me323C-0s (four engines) plus fifteen Me323D-0s (six engines). This more or less translates into a single Staffel of C-0s plus two Staffeln of D-0s. Most of both were converted gliders, originally born as Me321C-0 and Me321 D-0 respectively. The C-0 variant required a (large) towing aircraft to take off with a full payload, but once in flight did not require further assistance, and after being emptied could return home on its own.
51. There were other DFS230 and Go242 units in existence at the time, but they were employed on the Russian Front.
52. During summer 1942, I./LLG1 based at Athens-Tatoi, rest of LLG1 kept as reserve in Germany, 7./LLG1 and 8./LLG1 not in existence.
53. Towing aircraft for DFS230s could be either the Do17, Ju87, Hs126, He46 or Avia 534.
54. Staffel strength (for both DFS230 and Go242 units) is only indicative. At the time there was no scarcity of gliders, and the numbers listed are probably underestimated; on the other hand, towing aircraft were not abundant, and the numbers listed are probably overestimated.
55. During summer 1942 kept as reserve in Germany, 4./LLG2 not in existence, 3./LLG2 only formed in August 1942.

Axis Air Order of Battle

    2./LLG2 ~12x He111H, ~15x Go242
    3./LLG2 ~12x He111H, ~15x Go242
II./LLG2
    Stab 11./LLG2 ~2x He111H
    5./LLG2 ~12x He111H, ~15x Go242
    6./LLG2 ~12x He111H, ~15x Go242
    7./LLG2 ~12x He111H, ~15x Go242
    8./LLG2 ~12x He111H, ~15x Go242
Verbindungskommando (S) 2[56] (Hptm Fromert)
    StabVK.(S)2 ~2x He111H
    1.(DFS)/VK(S)2 ~12x tug, ~15x DFS230
    2.(DFS)/VK(S)2 ~12x tug, ~15x DFS230
    1.(Go)/VK(S)2 ~12x He111H, ~I5x Go242
    2.(Go)/VK(S)2 ~12x He111H, ~15x Go242
Kampfgeschwader zur besonderen Verwendung 2[57] (Ob Ulrich Buchhoh)
    Stab KGzbV2
    1.(GS)/KGzbV2 ~5–6x Me321
    2.(GS)/KGzbV2 ~5–6x Me321
    3.(GS)/KGzbV2 ~5–6x Me321
    4.(GS)/KGzbV2 ~5–6x Me321

---

56. Organized to support 2. Luftflotte supply missions. During summer 1942 based mostly at Lecce. I suppose the (S) means Schlepper (tractor).
57. This was the only Me321 unit in existence at the time. During summer 1942 it was employed on the Eastern Front, but I suppose it would have been redeployed in the Mediterranean had C3 gone ahead. According to some sources, by this time 1. and 2. Staffeln had already been disbanded. Different sources places Staffel paper TOE at either five or six gliders each. Strength is only indicative; at the time there were many more gliders still available (some to be eventually converted into Me323s). The real problem was the towing: there were only four aircraft able to handle them with a minimum of safety. They were the last two Ju90 prototypes (Ju90V7 and Ju90V8 only ones with BMW 801 engines) and the two He111Z prototypes (code unknown). Ten more He111Zs were built during 1942. The exact date is unknown but it seems it was late in the year. Otherwise, the only towing method was the hair-rising 'troika' of three Bf110s that was dangerously prone to accidents. Employing it over open sea, where the smallest problem means disaster, seems unlikely.

Appendix D

British/Maltese Land Order of Battle

Allied OoB, Malta (Compiled by Vance von Borries, 2007)
13 August 1942

Malta Governor General and Commander-in-Chief:
General, The Viscount Gort, VC
Lt Governor: Edward Jackson

Malta HQ
HQ located at 'Auberge de Castile et de Leon', Valletta;
GOC Malta: Maj. General Ronald Scobie after July 1942

1 Infantry Brigade
Cmdr: Brig. K.P. Smith, OBE
Bde HQ near Marsa Sirrocco Bay at Bubakra

2 The Devonshires
Cmdr: Lt Col A.W. Valentine, MBE
2nd in Cmd: Maj. G.R. Young
Adj.: Capt. I.F.A. Edgar
Coys: HQ coy, at Tarxien and Ashiak
A–E

1 The Dorsetshires
Cmdr: Lt Col W.H.B. Ray
2nd in Cmd: Maj. R.M. Nicol
Adj.: Capt. N.H. Golding
Coys: HQ coy, at Zeitun
A–E

1 The Hampshires
Cmdr: Lt Col J.L. Spencer, MC
2nd in Cmd: Maj. H.D. Nelson Smith

Adj.: Capt. I. Methven
Coys: HQ coy, at Sheleili (near Gudja)
A–D

3 King's Own Malta Regiment
Cmdr: Lt Col Mario Apap Bologna
Coys: HQ coy, at Qrendi
A–D

2 Infantry Brigade
Cmdr: Brig. F.A.J.E. Marshall
HQ (formerly at Ta'Qali Airfield) in Victoria Lines between Tarja Bty and Falka Gap

1 Kings's Own Malta Regiment
Cmdr: Lt Col Newell
Coys: HQ coy near Mosta
A–E
Coy D has mostly Gozo personnel
Coy E, could have as many as 250 men; generally intended for providing replacements personnel but it did man a defended locality.

2 King's Own Malta Regiment
Cmdr: Lt Col A.V. Mallia
Coys: HQ coy – Casa Torregiani (Wardija Ridge)
A–E
Coy E, could have as many as 250 men; generally, intended for providing replacements personnel but it did man a defended locality.

2 Royal Irish Fusiliers (Princess Victoria's); The 'Faughs'
Cmdr: Lt Col A.A.J. Allen
HQ coy at Tas-Salib crossroads on Wardija Ridge
A–D

8 (Ardwick) The Manchester Regt
Cmdr: Lt Col G.A. French
HQ coy at San Pawl tat-Targa,
A–D

3 Infantry Brigade
Cmdr: Brig. I. de la Bere
HQ (formerly at Valletta) at Birkirkara

11 Lancashire Fusiliers
Cmdr: Lt Col G.F. Page
Coys: HQ coy – Birkirkara
A–E

2 Queen's Own Royal West Kents
Cmdr: Lt Col R.O. Pulverman
Coys: HQ coy – civil abbatoir near Luqa airfield
A–E

10 King's Own Malta Regiment
Bn formed 4 May 42 at Paceville. Bn still considered as a 'static' unit since it was built from the former 'Static Defence Group' using the best personnel in that group of older men; main role was to guard vulnerable points (harbour installations, supply depots, ammo dumps, power station, wireless station, etc). Bn units were split and deployed as platoons and sections between Valletta (docks), Luqa and beach posts and helped garrison coastal forts; Bn divided administratively into two company commands (A and B).

1 Cheshire Machine-gun Battalion
Cmdr: Lt Col D.E.F. Waight
Coys: HQ coy, at bastion at Floriana
A–D

4 Infantry Brigade
Cmdr: Brig. F.G.R. Brittorious, DSO, MC
HQ at Castello Tas Sultan (near Dingli)

4 The Buffs (Royal East Kents)
Cmdr: Lt Col David P. Iggulden
Coys: HQ coy – Nadur Tower
A–E

8 King's Own Royal Regiment (Lancaster)
Cmdr: Lt Col L.H. Westropp
Coys: HQ coy – Palace at Girganti
A–D

1 Durham Light Infantry
Cmdr: Lt Col E.A. Arderne
Coys: HQ coy – Boschetto Gardens
A–D

Miscellaneous Army units
1 Independent Troop Royal Tank Regiment
First tanks arrived 10 November 1940; eventually numbered about 154 men under Maj. R.E.H. Drury; personnel drawn from 3 Hussars and 7 RTR.
Tanks on Malta:
    4x Matilda Mk. III. All four arrived Nov 40 as
        No.1 Independent Troop, RTR with three officers, sixty-five men.
    6x Mk VIB light tanks; two arrived in Nov 40, arrival of other four not known.
    4x A9 cruiser – arrived 16–19 Jan 42
    4x A13 cruiser – arrived 16–19 Jan 42

The cruisers were from 6RTR with eighty-five men under Maj. S.D.G. Longworth. These (less a few detached) were massed with Western Bde in vicinity of Verdala Palace to provide strength to a brigade-level counter-attack.

The Malta Pioneer Group, Royal Engineers (later: 201 Pioneer Group, RE), formed 1942.

The RE manned searchlights ('Defence Electric Lights') until October 1940 at which time searchlights were turned over to the RMA; Maltese personnel in RE left along with the searchlights. At all times the Group furnished personnel for airfield repair and other special duties.

> 16 Sqn RE, established September 1938; all Maltese; had three officers and 151 men in January 1941.
> 24 Sqn, RE; established September 1938
> (?) 2601 Sqn, RE; all Maltese
> 173 Tunneling Coy; arrived 24 July 1941
> 127 Bomb Disposal Section
> 128 Bomb Disposal Section
> RE Stores
> RE Workshops

Malta Volunteer Defence Force (Home Guard)

They numbered some 3,000–4,000 men, ages 17 to 70, at the height of the siege but were very lightly armed (personally owned weapons only) and likely would not be very steady. In the UK the Home Guard was widely regarded as a joke. Since they certainly knew the terrain it is more likely that a few personnel would be attached to every regular army unit, thereby giving that unit more mobility and defensive adeptness; for instance, twenty-two Maltese were attached to every AA battery (for duty relief so that regular personnel might get rest). They might also be included in many other duties, such groups as the Air Observer Corps, Civil Protection or Air Raid Precaution Corps. Their general duty was internal security to protect the villagers and keep the roads clear.

Conscription was introduced on Malta on 3 March 1941.

HQ Royal Artillery Malta
Cmdr: Maj. Gen. C.T. 'Joe' Beckett; arrived 6 May 41
HQ was at Auberge de Castile until too much bomb damage. HQ moved to a convent at Rabat in April 1942.
Gun Room Cmdr: Maj. G.J. Bell

12 Field Artillery Rgt, RA
Cmdr: Lt Col W.E. Vaudrey

Troop	Position (all except G Troop are four guns)
A	Behind Victoria Lines (in January 42 at Iz-Zebbieh)
B	Musta
C	Ta'Dekotzu
D	Gebel Ciantar
E	Addoloratta (a Cemetery)

Troop	Position (all except G Troop are four guns)
F	Tal Handaq
G	In Imseriah area (in January 42 at Ta Buleben); two guns

26 Defence Rgt, RA
Cmdr: Lt Col J.S. Symons

Bty	Troop	Guns	Position
15/40	A	4x 6in How	North of Ghaxaq; mobile, used as field artillery
15/40	B	4x 6in How	Gebel Ghawzara; mobile, used as field artillery
15/40	C	4x 3.7in How	On road between Dingli and Rabat;
48/71	D	4x 18-pdr	Ta Buleben
48/71	E/1	2x 18-pdr	Gebel Ghawzara
48/71	E/2	2x 18-pdr	Ta'Qali airfield
48/71	F/1	2x 18-pdr	Dragonara Bty
48/71	F/2	2x 18-pdr	Marku Bty
48/71	F/3	2x 18-pdr	Balbane Bty (near Kalafrana)
48/71		8x 18-pdr	deployed as single guns at many locations

Index

Abyssinia *see* Ethiopia
Allen. LtCol. A. A. J. 86, 160, 182, 184, 187
Arderne, LtCol. E. A. 89, 137, 148
Auchinleck, Gen. Claude 56, 65, 72–3, 201
Aumier, Capt. 140, 162

Badoglio, Gen. Pietro 10, 14, 17
Bambilla, Lt. Carlo 192
Barrington, Major Ben 160–1, 189
Barthet, Maj. F. E. T. 140
Barlow, Lt. Thomas E. 167
Bastico, Gen. Ettore 69
Beak, Gen. Danial, M. W. 54, 72, 98
Becker, Haupt. Karl–Heinz 145, 148, 157, 161–3, 171
Beckett, Gen. C. T. 102–103, 149, 152, 165, 167, 185, 192
Benbow, Maj. 193
Bere, Bgen. Ivan de la 84, 86
Bergamini, Adm. Carlo 114, 146, 148, 170, 180–1, 184
Bethke, Haupt. Hans–Günther 120
Biancheri, Adm Luigi 117, 145, 192
Bologna, LtCol. Mario A. 85
British Army
   and infantry organization 82–84, 103–104
   Eighth Army 52, 56, 65, 72, 202
   4th Indian Division 29
   6th Australian Division 35
   7th Armoured Division 29
   New Zealand Division 29
   6th Royal Tank Regiment 89
   7th Royal Tank Regiment 89
   12th Royal Artillery Regiment 90–91, 138, 188
   26th Defense Regiment 90, 155, 165, 171, 188
   Southern (1) Brigade 54, 84–85, 92, 98, 103, 141–2, 158, 185, 187
   Northern (2) Brigade 85–6, 92, 98, 143, 158, 162
   Central (3) Brigade 86–7, 92
   Western (4) Brigade 86, 88–9, 98, 135–7, 158–9
   1st Bn, Cheshire 38, 59, 83, 86–7, 149, 164, 182, 192
   1st Bn Dorsetshire 15, 85, 149, 156, 158–9, 162–3, 192–3, 195
   1st Bn Hampshire 38, 55, 85, 87, 98, 141, 159, 163, 171, 182
   1st Bn Kings Own Malta 15, 86, 149, 159–160, 184–5, 191–3
   1st Bn Durham Light Infantry 54. 65, 88–9, 136–7, 145, 148, 159, 162–4, 172, 182, 187, 192, 194
   2nd Bn Kings Own Malta 15, 86, 149, 159–160
   2nd Bn, Devonshire 15, 84, 142, 147, 156–8, 162, 164, 167, 172, 182, 185, 192–3, 195–6
   2nd Bn, Queen's Own Royal West Kent 15, 87, 138–9, 143, 147, 159, 182
   2nd Bn Royal Irish Fusiliers 15, 57, 86, 98, 143, 149, 158, 160–1, 164, 167, 173, 182, 184–6, 189–192, 194
   3rd Bn Kings Own Malta 85, 103, 138, 140–1, 146, 162, 192–3
   4th Bn, Buffs 32, 65, 88, 137, 145, 149, 159, 161–4, 167, 169, 172, 182, 187, 192, 194

8th Bn, Kings Own Royal 46, 65, 88, 103, 136–7, 145, 148, 159, 163, 173, 185–6, 191, 194
8th Bn Manchesters 22, 45, 85–6, 88, 139, 149, 159–60, 184, 192–3
10th Bn Kings Own Malta 147
11th Bn Lancashire Fusiliers 46, 86–87, 139, 149, 159–60, 185–90, 192
Brittorous, Col. Francis G. R. 86, 88, 137, 148–9
Brookman, Lt. C. E. 152–3
Bulteel, Capt. T. O. 176
Burges, Lt. George 35
Burrough, R.Adm Harold M. 77–78, 183–4
Büttner, ObL 143

Cagnolo, Lt. Antonio 152
Calabria, battle of 28–29
Caldwell, L.Sgt John 160
Camossa, Col. Luigi 138, 158
Campioni, Adm. Imigo 28, 33, 116
Cape Bougaroun, battle of 173–6
Cape Matapan, battle of 39–40
Carboni, Gen. Giacomo 125, 133, 171, 188, 190, 197, 203
Casey, Robert 62
Casero, Col. Giuseppe 133
Cavagnari, Adm. Domenico 8, 17–18, 26–7, 33
Cavallero, Gen. Ugo 51, 55, 66, 69, 71, 144
Chamberlain, Neville 9, 11
Chaplin, Maj. H. D. 140
Churchill, Winston ix, 33, 37, 40, 58, 69, 150, 199, 202
  and Malta 25, 62–63, 74, 78
  aggressive demands of 33, 41, 47–8, 53, 56, 61, 65, 75, 80, 183, 195–6
  policies of 18–20, 32
Ciano, Galeazzo 14, 16, 49. 133
Code Breaking 16, 100–101
  Enigma 45, 100
  C35 45, 100
  C38M 45, 100–101
  ULTRA 36, 48–9, 55–6, 63, 66, 72–3, 81, 97, 100–101

Convoys
  Beta (Duisberg) 49, 51, 101
  Coat 32, 88
  Collar 33
  Excess 36
  Halberd 47
  Harpoon 61, 67–8, 80, 87
  Hats 30
  M41 52
  M42 52
  M43 55
  MF3 31
  MW8 53
  MW9 55
  MW10 57, 89
  Substance 46, 88
  T18 55
  Tiger 42
  Vigorous 61, 67, 74, 87, 114
Courten, Adm. Raffaele De 114, 178, 180
Crete, battle of 43–44
Cunningham, Adm Andrew B. 20–1, 25, 28–9, 37–9, 44, 47–9, 55, 58–9, 75

Davidson, Maj. 148
de'Flamini, Capt. Luca G. 166
Dobbie, William G. S. 20–1, 25–6, 30, 44, 54, 56, 59, 61–5, 92
Doran, Cmdr. A. E. 155
Duke, Capt. H. 162, 173
Dyke, Major 162

Ethiopia 7

First Sirte, battle of 52–3
Ferrini, Lt. R. 184
Fleet Air Arm
  830 Squadron 25, 45, 50
Folgore Parachute Division
Ford, Adm. Wilbraham 20, 48, 54
Fougier, Gen. Rino 133
Fraser, Capt. C. E. 137
Frattini, Gen. Enrico 111, 158 164, 171, 190
French, LtCol. G. A. 86, 185, 193

Gandin, Gen. Antonio 55
Garabaldi, Gen. Italo 40
Garrone, Lt. Giovanni B. 153
Geisler, Gen. Hans F. 34, 36, 122
George Cross 60–1
Germany
   and Greece 40
   and Italy 10,
   and North Africa 34–5, 40, 55
   and Soviet Union 13, 43, 45
   foreign policy of 6–7,
   planning vrs Malta 38
German Fallschirmjaeger 43, 66, 73, 118–20, 122, 130–1, 137, 173, 182, 185, 199
   1FJR 135, 157, 160, 171, 188, 192, 194, 199
   3FJR 135, 140–1, 164, 182, 190
   Ramcke Bde 135, 140
   I/FJR1 135–6, 145, 148, 171
   II/FJR1 135–6, 144–5, 148, 182
   III/FJR1 145, 148, 163, 171
   I/FJR3 146
   II/FJR3 140
   III/FJR3 142, 190
   I/RAM 143, 172, 182
   II/RAM 146, 162, 172, 192
   III/RAM 141, 163
   Fallschirmkorps–Pioneer 146, 158, 162
Giaretto, SgtMaj Mario 189
Gort, Vicount *see* Prendergast, John S. S.
Granato, Capt. Savatore 166
Gray, Lt. Gordon 80–1, 154, 157
Graziani, Marshall Rodolfo 29, 33–35, 40
Great Britain
   and Italy 11,
   and Germany 15
   and Greece 32, 38, 40
   and Malta 13, 15,
   and North Africa 29,
   battle doctrine 82
   politics of 9,
   strategy of 30
Greece, invasion of 31–2
Grimley, Lt. Col A. 84, 193
Gröschke, Maj. Kurt 144, 148, 162–4
Guglielmo, SubLt, Giuseppe 65

Hamilton, Capt. G.W. 192
Harrison, Lt. Peter R. H. 167
Harwood, Adm. Henry 61, 67–8, 73–4, 78, 150, 170, 180–1, 195
Heilmann, Oberst Ludwig 140–1, 158, 160, 164, 182
Heyte, Maj. Freidrich von der 119, 141, 162, 192–193, 195
Hicks, Maj. Garnet 188
Hitler, Adolf
   and Malta 43, 55, 131, 187, 200, 202
   and Mediterranean 46, 48, 51, 70–1
   and Mussolini 31–2, 63
   foreign policy of 6–7, 11–13, 27–8
Horton, Adm. Max 79–80
Howard, Capt. Mike 156, 162, 173, 182
Hübner, Maj. Friedrich 119

Iachino, Adm. Angelo 33, 39, 52–3, 57–8, 114, 169, 183
Iggulden, Col. David P. 88, 162
Italy
   and France 27
   and Great Britain 8, 11
   and Greece 31–32
   and North Africa 29–30, 33–5, 45
   economics of 4–5,
   history of 2–3,
   plans against Malta 8, 11, 26–7, 43, 72
   politics of 3–4,
Italian Folgore Division 56, 66, 71, 111, 122, 130–1, 160–1, 182, 188, 191, 193, 199
   1st Brigade 138, 164, 173, 194
   2nd Brigade 161, 164, 190
   II/1/FOL 138–9, 160, 173, 190
   III/1/FOL 138, 147, 159
   IV/1/FOL 188–190
   VII/2/FOL 190
   VIII/ Guastatori 195

Jackson, Edward St J. 21, 68, 134, 192, 196
James, Lt. Jimmy 138
Jodl, GenOberst. Alfred 187, 202
Johnson, Lt. Ted 160–1, 189–91, 197

Kesselring, FM. Albert ix, 51, 55–7, 64, 66, 70–3, 119, 144, 146, 187, 202
King, Capt. R. 163, 182
Krazert, Major 142, 190–1
Kriegsmarine
   3rd Schnellbootflotille 121
   Deutsches MarineKommando Italien (DMI) 121
   KM Operations Staff 48
   submarines 46, 48
   Hermes (DD) 154–5, 157
   U–73 169
   U–331 50
Kroh, Major Hans 182

Laffredo, Capt. Felice 195
Langridge, Lt. L. W. 135
Leatham, Adm. Ralph 54, 59, 79–80, 151, 159
Lloyd, Air Marshall Hugh P. 45, 59, 62–3, 72, 102, 203
Loerzer, Gen. Bruno 52, 56, 81, 121
Lombardo, Lt. Antonio 152
Longworth, Maj. S. D. G 89, 185–6, 188
Lorenzelli, Gen. Dante 128
Lucerna, Lt. Col Alberto 158
Luftwaffe 70, 72, 131, 144, 147, 158, 163, 169, 182, 188, 193–194
   7/26 Jagdgeschwader 37
   7th Flieger Division 38
   Fallschirmjaegers *see* German Fallschirmjager
   Fliegerfuhrer Afrika 122
   Fliegerkorps II 51–2, 56, 63, 81, 101, 121
   Fliegerkorps X 34, 41, 44, 122
   Fliegerkorps XI 122, 143
   22nd Air Landing Division 38

Mack, Capt. Philip J. 41
Main, Lt. J. W. 154
Mallia, LtCol. A. V. 86
Malta
   bombing of 24–5, 36, 41–3, 59–60, 73
   conditions on 41, 47, 50, 53, 56, 58, 60–1, 68, 102
   defense of 9, 13, 15, 25, 34, 47, 205
   defense plan, 1942 97–100
   history of ix–x
   loss of 204
   politics of 1, 12–3,
   terrain of 100, 132–3
Malta Garrison
   Armor 89–90, 98, 137
   Artillery 90–5
   Infantry 82–9
Malta Invasion, C3 51, 55–6, 63, 66–7, 69
   Famagosta 124–6, 151, 170
   Larnaca 126–7
   Cipro 127–8
Marenco, Capt. 160, 190
Mars, Lt Alastair C. G. 166
Marshall, Bgen. Frederic A. J. E. 85, 88
Mason, Capt. C. 190
Mautino, Capt. Carlo 190
May 10th, aerial battle of 64
Maynard, Air Cmdr. Forster H. M. 21, 32
Molotov–Ribbentrop Non–Aggression Pact 13,
Muncheberg, ObL Joachim 37
Munich Agreement, 1938 11
Mussolini, Benito ix, 203
   and Hitler 31–2, 63, 71, 200
   decision for war 14, 16–8
   politics of 3–4,
   foreign policy of 3, 7, 29

Newell, LtCol. E. J. 86, 185, 193
Nicasro, GuardM Franco 166
Norman, Lt. C. P. 134

O'Connor, Gen. Richard 34–5
Operations
   Brevity 88
   C3 *see* Malta Invasion C3
   Calandar 62
   Crusader 49, 72
   Dunlop 41
   Guado 39
   Hats 30
   Hurry 29
   Husky 202
   Judgment 32
   Lustre 38
   Magic carpet 46

Malta 74
Mercur 43
Mittelmeer 34
Pedestal 74, 96, 201
Perpetual 49
Picket 57
Pinpoint 73
Sonneblume 35
Spotter 56
Spotter II 57
Stab 75
Style 88
Theseus 65–6, 200
Torch 202
White 33
Winch 41

Padella, Maj. Vincenzo 188
Peal, Lt. J. 153
Pearse, Lt. C.E. 154
Page, LtCol. G. F. 87, 185, 187–91
Parani, Gen. Alberto 105
Park, Air Vmarshall Keith 72–73, 75, 80–1, 134
Parona, Adm. Angelo 114, 178, 180
Petris, Lt. Mario de 167
Pecori, Lt. Renato 169
Pisani, Carmelo B. 65
Pizzolato, Gen. Gavino 112
Prendergast, John S. S. (Gort) 63, 68, 80, 134, 149, 151, 159, 168, 184–7, 191–2, 194, 196–9
Pound, Adm Dudley 25, 47–8, 59, 74, 195
Prasca, Sebastiano 31
Pricolo, Gen. Francesco 17, 29, 133
Puccini, Lt. S. 184
Pulverman, Col. R. O. 87, 143, 182

Raeder, Gadm Erich 38, 46, 48–9, 67
Raffaelli, Gen. Ferdinando 176
Ramcke, Gen. Bernhard 56, 71, 119, 140–1, 144, 158, 160–1, 164, 171–2, 188, 190, 192, 197–9
Rau, Major 163
Regia Aeronautica 21, 27–30, 44, 117–8, 130–1, 143, 164, 169
  1st Reparto Paracadutisti 113, 122, 145

Battaglione Riattatori "Loreto" 113, 122, 145, 160, 187
Regio Esercito
  and infantry organization 105–110
  1st Assault Division – Superga 110, 127, 145, 156, 192
  1st Parachute Division *see* Italian Folgore division
  4th Assault Division – Livorno 110, 122, 126, 129, 131, 144, 151, 156, 167, 170, 187, 192
  10 Raggruppamento Corazzato 113, 170
  20th Division – Friuli 107, 122, 124–5, 128–31, 133, 144, 151, 164–5, 170, 183, 187–8, 190, 192, 199
  26th Division – Assietta 107, 129, 131, 171
  54th Division – Napoli 108, 129, 131
  80th airtransportable Division – Spezia 112, 130
  Ariete Armored Division 65
  Battaglione Speciale Arditi 112, 154
  Battaglione Nuotatori–Guastatori 112
  Gruppo Battaglioni da Sbarco 113, 126
  Milizia Volontaria Sicurezza Nazionale (MVSN) 108–109
  P Battalion 1132
  Tenth Army 30, 35
  Trieste Armored Division 65
Regia Marina 22–3, 39, 71, 156, 201
  and fleet doctrine 116–7
  Forza Navale Speciale 117, 144, 157
  First Squadra 114
  Second Squadra 114, 126, 144, 146, 170
  3rd Division (CA) 114, 170, 178
  5th Division (BB) 114
  7th Division (CL) 114, 169
  8th Division (CL) 114, 170, 178
  9th Division (BB) 114
  Abruzzi (CL) 50, 180
  Alagi (SS) 184
  Alberico da Barbiano (CL) 52
  Alberto da Giussano (CL) 52
  Andrea Doria (BB) 22, 114, 146, 151, 170
  Antares (TP) 153
  Aquila (CV) 40

Axum (SS) 184
Bande Nere (CL) 57–8
Bolzano (CA) 28, 180
Caio Dulio (BB) 22, 32–3, 114, 146, 170, 178, 180
Cascino (TP) 153
Conte di Cavour (BB) 22, 33, 114
D'Aosta (CL) 180
Dagabur (SS) 169
Diana (SLP) 46
Eso (ML) 153
Fiume (CA) 39
Gorizia (CA) 52, 57, 177, 180
Guilio Cesare (BB) 22, 28, 66, 114, 169
Lanciere (DD) 58
Littorio (BB) 22, 32, 52, 57, 68, 114, 169, 179
Orione (TP) 145, 192
Pegaso (DE) 156, 167
Pola (CA) 39–40, 183
Procione (TP) 144, 151
Roma (BB) 114
Scirocco (DD) 58
Sebenico (DD) 156, 166–7
Trento (CA) 49, 52, 57, 68
Trieste (CA) 49–50, 179–180
Turbine (DD) 156, 166–7
Uarsciek (SS) 169
VAS 201 (AS) 152
VAS 211 (AS) 166
Vittorio Veneto (BB) 22, 32–3, 39, 52, 114, 169, 183
Zara (CA) 39
X Flottiglia MAS 46, 53
San Marcos Marines 112, 122, 144, 151, 171, 173, 191, 193
Bafile Bn, San Marcos 112, 127
Grado Bn, San Marcos 112, 124, 171
Riccardi, Adm. Arturo 33, 38–9, 55
Ricci, Pvt. Drago 160
Ricciarini, Capt. G 176
Ritchie, Gen. Neil 65, 72
Rommel, Gen. Erwin 35, 40–1, 49, 52, 55, 63, 65–6, 69–73, 200–201, 203–204
Roatta, Gen. Mario 51
Rosenbaum, Capt. Helmut 169

Royal Air Force 37, 62, 95, 204
  38 Squadron 47
  104 Squadron 47, 66
  105 Squadron 47
  107 Squadron 47
  126 Squadron 47
  148 Squadron 32
  185 Squadron 47
  249 Squadron 47
  261 Squadron 29
  Faith, Hope, Charity 25
  Hal Far Fighter Flight 21, 35
Royal Navy 44, 73, 96, 159, 168
  and Malta plans 76–8
  Mediterranean Fleet 20, 36, 53, 75
  3rd Motor Launch Flotilla 80, 121, 151–2
  4th Destroyer Flotilla 52
  10th Submarine Flotilla 47, 61, 79–80, 159
  14th Destroyer Flotilla 41, 57
  15th Cruiser Squadron 52, 57
  22nd Destroyer Flotilla 57
  Force B 50
  Force H 79
  Force K 48, 50, 53
  Force X 75, 77–9, 183–4
  Force Z 78–79, 183
  HMS Ajax (CL) 38, 50, 87
  HMS Argus (CV) 20, 29, 33
  HMS Ark Royal (CV) 33, 41, 49
  HMS Arethusa (CL) 76, 88, 166, 177–8
  HMS Aurora (CL) 48, 52–53
  HMS Badsworth (DE) 80–81, 154–5, 157
  HMS Barham (BB) 40, 44, 50, 88, 91
  HMS Berwick (CA) 33, 88, 91
  HMS Birmingham (CL) 76, 166, 177–8, 180–1
  HMS Cairo (CLAA) 68, 96, 183
  HMS Charybdis (CLAA) 96
  HMS Cleopatra (CL) 57, 76, 178
  HMS Dido (CL) 44, 57, 76, 179–180
  HMS Eagle (CV) 20, 63, 73, 96, 169, 201
  HMS Edinburgh (CL) 86
  HMS Euryalus (CL) 52, 57, 76, 178–180
  HMS Fiji (CL) 44
  HMS Formidable (CV) 39, 42, 44
  HMS Furious (CV) 75, 79, 176

Index   281

HMS Glasgow (CL) 88, 91
HMS Glorious (CVL) 21
HMS Gloucester (CL) 38, 44, 87
HMS Grampus (SS) 26
HMS Hebe (MS) 80
HMS Hermoine (CL) 68, 74, 88
HMS Hythe (MS) 80, 154–5
HMS Illustrious (CV) 30, 32, 36–7
HMS Indomitable (CV) 96
HMS Janus(DD) 41
HMS Jersey (DD) 43
HMS Jervis (DD) 41, 166
HMS Kandahar (DD) 53
HMS Kimberley (DD) 50
HMS Kingston (DD) 50, 57
HMS Kent (CA) 31
HMS Kenya (CL) 96
HMS Laforey (DD) 184
HMS Lance (DD) 48
HMS Legion (DD) 52, 57
HMS Lightning (DD) 184
HMS Lively (DD) 48
HMS Lookout (DD) 184
HMS Malaya (BB) 20, 68
HMS Manchester (CL) 88, 96
HMS Matchless (DD) 80
HMS Maori (DD) 52
HMS Mohawk (DD) 41–42
HMS Naiad (CL) 52
HMAS Napier (DD) 76
HMS Nelson (BB) 96
HMS Neptune (CL) 50, 53
HMS Nigeria (CL) 96
HMAS Nizam (DD) 76
HMAS Norman (DD) 76
HMS Nubian (DD) 41
HMS Odin (SS) 26
HMS Olympus (SS) 26
HMS Orion (CL) 38, 44, 87
HMS Orpheus (SS) 26
HMS Otis (SS) 26
P222 (SS) 80
HMS Penelope (CL) 48, 52–3, 57
HMS Phoebe (CLAA) 96, 175
HMS Queen Elizabeth (BB) 53
HMS Ramilles (BB) 20, 33

HMS Renown (BC) 33, 75
HMS Resolution (BB) 20,
HMS Rodney (BB) 96, 175
HMS Roqual (SS) 26
HMS Royal Sovereign (BB) 20,
HMS Rye (MS) 80, 154–5
HMS Sirius (CLAA) 96
HMS Speedy (MS) 80, 154–5
HMS Sikh (DD) 52
HMS Southampton (CL) 36
Ultimatum (P34–SS) 80, 159, 166–7
Umbra(P35–SS) 80, 159
Una (N87–SS) 80, 135, 151, 159
Unbroken (P42–SS) 80, 159, 166–7
Undaunted (N55–SS) 42
Unique (N95–SS) 35
Unison (P43–SS) 80–1
United (P44–SS) 80, 159, 166–7
Unruffled (P46–SS) 80, 135, 144, 159
Upholder (P37–SS) 35, 42, 47, 61
Upright (N89–SS) 35, 52
Uproar (P31–SS) 80, 159
Urge (N17–SS) 52, 58
Usk (N65–SS) 42
Utmost (N19–SS) 35, 50, 80, 144, 159
HMS Valiant (BB) 30, 36, 40, 53, 135
HMS Victorious (CV) 96
HMS Warspite (BB) 20, 36, 40, 44
HMS Wolverine (DE) 169

Ruck–Keene, Capt(S1) Philip 79
Ruspoli, LtCol. Carlo 190–1
Ruspoli, Capt. Constantino 189

Salton, Capt. J. 173
Schultz, Obert Karl–Luthor 136
Scobell, Gen. Sanford, J. P. 20, 45, 54
Scobie, Gen. Ronald M. 72, 81, 134, 143, 149, 159, 171, 185, 187, 192, 194, 196, 198
Second Sirte, battle of 57–8
Shaw, Maj. G. V. 143
Shepard, Maj. W. 190
Simmons, Lt. R. N. 137
Simoni, Capt. 188
Simpson, Capt. George 35, 42, 61–2, 79–81, 159

Sired, Ronald 178
Smith, Capt H. D. 171
Smith, BGen. Pearce 54, 84, 162, 185, 197
Spencer, LtCol. J. J. 85, 171, 182
Stevens, Lt. J. S. 135, 144
Straehler–Pohl, Haupt Günther 193, 195, 198
Strategy meetings
   Catania 56
   Castle Klessheim 63
   Merano 38, 42
   Monichkirchen 43
   Siggiewi 185-7
Stead, Lt. G. W. 80, 152–154
Strickland, Mabel 62–3, 199
Strowlger, LtCmdr. E. J. 80
Student, Gen. Kurt 66, 100–101, 144, 146, 160, 187–8, 199
Syfret, Adm. Edward, N. 149, 169, 174, 183

Tandillo, Col. 190
Targia, Lt Gaetano 169
Tedder, AOC Arthur 67, 78, 81
Third Sirte, battle of 177–82
Tiesenhausen, Obl Hans–Dietrict von 50
Tur, Adm. Vittorio 117, 144, 148, 152, 155–6, 162, 164–5, 170, 182, 184, 192

United States
   bombers 79, 170, 204
   declares war 52
   USS Wasp 62–3, 203

Valentine, Col. A. W. 84, 142, 173, 182
Vaudrey, LtCol. W. E. 91
Vella, Capt. Charles 141
Vian, Radm. Philip 52–3, 57, 67–8, 77–9, 150, 159, 166, 170, 177, 180–1, 183, 195

Waight, LtCol D. E. F. 87
Walker, Capt. E. 188, 190
Wanklyn, LtCmdr. Malcolm 42, 42, 61
Waters, Cmdr. H. G. 184
Wavell, Gen. Archibald 33, 40
Wehrmacht
   Second Army 40
   5th Light Motorized Division 35
   Twelfth Army 40
   15th Panzer Division 65
   21st Panzer Division 65
   90th Light Division 65
   66 abV 120–1, 126
Weichold, Vadm. Eberhard 121, 154, 157, 204
Westropp, LtCol. L. H. 88, 185
Witzig, Maj. Rudolf 146

Young, Major Guy 164, 192–3, 195, 198

Zara, Adm. Alberto da 68, 114, 169, 183
Zanninovich, Maj. Mario 139, 162, 173, 190, 193